.

SAGE was founded in 1965 by Sara Miller McCune to support the dissemination of usable knowledge by publishing innovative and high-quality research and teaching content. Today, we publish more than 750 journals, including those of more than 300 learned societies, more than 800 new books per year, and a growing range of library products including archives, data, case studies, reports, conference highlights, and video. SAGE remains majority-owned by our founder, and after Sara's lifetime will become owned by a charitable trust that secures our continued independence.

Los Angeles | London | Washington DC | New Delhi | Singapore | Boston

Approach of ICT in Education for Rural Development

Thank you for choosing a SAGE product!
If you have any comment, observation or feedback,
I would like to personally hear from you.
Please write to me at **contactceo@sagepub.in**

Vivek Mehra, Managing Director and CEO,
SAGE Publications India Pvt Ltd, New Delhi

Bulk Sales

SAGE India offers special discounts
for purchase of books in bulk.
We also make available special imprints
and excerpts from our books on demand.

For orders and enquiries, write to us at

Marketing Department
SAGE Publications India Pvt Ltd
B1/I-1, Mohan Cooperative Industrial Area
Mathura Road, Post Bag 7
New Delhi 110044, India

E-mail us at **marketing@sagepub.in**

Get to know more about SAGE

Be invited to SAGE events, get on our mailing list.
Write today to **marketing@sagepub.in**

This book is also available as an e-book.

Approach of ICT in Education for Rural Development

Good Practices from Developing Countries

Edited by

Zeng Haijun
Xia Weifeng
Wang Jinghua
Wang Rong

 www.sagepublications.com
 Los Angeles • London • New Delhi • Singapore • Washington DC • Boston

First published in 2015 by

 SAGE Publications India Pvt Ltd
B1/I-1 Mohan Cooperative Industrial Area
Mathura Road, New Delhi 110 044, India
www.sagepub.in

SAGE Publications Inc
2455 Teller Road
Thousand Oaks, California 91320, USA

SAGE Publications Ltd
1 Oliver's Yard, 55 City Road
London EC1Y 1SP, United Kingdom

SAGE Publications Asia-Pacific Pte Ltd
3 Church Street
#10-04 Samsung Hub
Singapore 049483

UNESCO International Research and Training Centre for Rural Education (INRULED), located at Beijing Normal University
No. 19 Xinjiekouwai Street
Beijing 100875, China

Published by Vivek Mehra for SAGE Publications India Pvt Ltd, typeset in 10/13 Berkeley by RECTO Graphics, Delhi, and printed at Saurabh Printers Pvt Ltd, New Delhi.

Library of Congress Cataloging-in-Publication Data

Approach of ICT in education for rural development : good practices from developing countries / edited by Zeng Haijun, Xia Weifeng, Wang Jinghua, Wang Rong.
   pages cm
 Includes bibliographical references and index.
  1. Educational technology—Developing countries. 2. Economic development—Effect of education on—Developing countries. 3. Rural development—Developing countries. I. Zeng, Haijun, editor of compilation.
  LB1028.3.A68   371.3309172'4—dc23   2015   2015010746

ISBN: 978-93-515-0189-3 (HB)

The SAGE Team: Rudra Narayan, Sandhya Gola, Nand Kumar Jha, and Rajinder Kaur

Contents

List of Tables

List of Figures

List of Abbreviations

ABC	Alphabetization a Base Cellulaire
ARMM	Autonomous Region of Muslim Mindanao
ASPROED	Association of Professional for Quality Education
ATACH	Association of Active Chilean Telecenters
BBS	bulletin board system
BIAV	Bosomtwe Integrated Aqua Life Village
BNU-KSEI	Beijing Normal University-R&D Centre for Knowledge Engineering
CAPAM	Commonwealth Association of Public Administration and Management
CDI	Committee for Democratization of Information Technologies
CERADEL	Centre de Ressources et d'Appui au Developpement Local (Centre for Resources and Action for Local Development)
CERNET	China Education and Research Network
CIDR	Centre International de Developpement et Recherche (International Centre for Research and Development)
CIPP	Context-Input-Process-Product
CLP	Cocoa Livelihoods Program
COCOBOD	Ghana Cocoa Board
CSR	Corporate Social Responsibility
CTA	Centre for Agricultural and Rural Cooperation
DC	dominant force-center
DepEd	department of education
DRDF	Demographic Research and Development Foundation
ECHOES	Empowering Cocoa Households with Opportunities and Educational Solutions

ECIP	Espaces Communautaires d'Informationet de Promotion
ECLAC	Economic comisión for Latin America and the Carribean
EDUSAT	education based on television programs transmitted via satellite
EFA	Education for All
ELSA	Education and Livelihood Skills Alliance
EWB	Engineers Without Borders
FAI	Foundation for Agricultural Innovation
FAI	Foundation for Agricultural Innovation
FGM	female genital mutilation
FHL	Filipinas Heritage Library
GDP	gross domestic product
GGS	Govi Gnana Seva
ICT	information and communication technology
ICTRD	Indian Council for Technical Research and Development
IDICN	Informatization Development Index in China
IDRC	International Development Research Center
iERD	ICT in education for rural development
IFAD	The International Fund for Agricultural Development
IICBA	International Institute for Capacity Building in Africa
IIITM-K	Indian Institute of Information Technology and Management, Kerala
INRULED	International Research and Training Centre for Rural Education
ITN	Innovative Teachers Networks
KISSAN	Karshaka Information System Services and Networking
KNUST	Kwame Nkrumah University of Science and Technology
KSWAN	Kerala State Wide Area Network
KWs	knowledge workers
LAN	local area network
LGDA	Lower Guruve Development Association
LGOP	Leading Group Office of Poverty Alleviation and Development
LGU	local government units
LKR	Sri Lankan Rupee

MDEP	Modern Distance Education Project
MEDA	Mercado Electrónico Del Agua
MOA	Ministry of Agriculture
MoE	Ministry of Education
MOFCOM	Ministry of Commerce
MOST	Ministry of Science and Technology
MOTECH	maternal health mobile phone program
MSSRF	M.S. Swaminathan Research Center
NABARD	National Bank for Agriculture and Rural Development
NAT	National Achievement Test
NDG	Nokia Data Gathering
NED	Nokia Education Delivery
NGOs	nongovernment organizations
NISG	National Institute for Smart Government
NISMED	National Institute for Science and Mathematics Educational Development
ODL	open distance learning
OUC	Open University of China
PAR	Participatory Action Research
PiL	Partners in Learning
PPP	Productive Pedagogical Projects
QEISRD	quality education for inclusive and sustainable rural development
RBM	result-based management
RMAF	Ramon Magsaysay Award Foundation
RSITC	Rural Schools of Information Technologies and Citizenship
S&T	science and technology
SAEPA	Student Association of Educational Poverty Alleviation
SCNU	South China Normal University
SERIFED	Sericulture Cooperative Federation
SITC	Schools for Information Technologies and Citizenship
TBGIRI	Tropical Botanical Garden and Research Institute
TOT	training of trainers
UAST	Union of Universities for Agricultural Science & Technology and Education
UNDP	United Nations Development Programme
UNESCO-PAD	UNESCO Sector Policy Advice

UNESCO	United Nations Educational, Scientific and Cultural Organization
UNIMAS	University Malaysia Sarawak
USD	US Dollar
USSD	Unstructured Supplementary Service Data
VCT	virtual classroom tour
VFPCK	Vegetable and Fruit Promotion Council Kerala
VOD	video on demand
VSAT	very small aperture terminals
WAP	Wireless Application Protocol
WCF	World Cocoa Foundation
WorldEd	World Education
WWWF	World Wide Web Foundation

Foreword

Education for All (EFA) is a global movement led by the United Nations Educational, Scientific and Cultural Organization (UNESCO), which aims to meet the learning needs of all children, youth, and adults by 2015. Significant measurable progress has been made in several aspects. Most of the developing countries, nevertheless, have hardly reached the target for the decade set in 1990. Rural population in developing countries comprises more than half of the world's population. Therefore, it is a big challenge to provide quality education to rural people in developing countries. There is a need to give priority to education for all rural population by identifying and addressing the specific needs of this target group.

As a Category 2 Centre engaged in research and training for rural education within UNESCO, International Research and Training Centre for Rural Education (INRULED) initiates and facilitates exchange and dissemination of experience in international rural education within the EFA framework. INRULED undertakes human resource development programs for international rural education for UNESCO member states, especially in developing countries.

In developing countries, the development of quality education for all in rural areas is the most challenging task. Addressing this challenge is the concern for UNESCO, China, and other developing countries, and it is also INRULED's specific mission. INRULED works to bring about positive changes in the thinking and behavior of the rural population and to achieve inclusive and sustainable development in rural areas through education, research, and training. In particular, INRULED actively establishes and expands partnerships with Africa-oriented institutions which consist of international exchange and cooperation programs, academic seminars, information exchange, joint research, and training workshops. Our current program covers four main areas: skills development for rural transformation, quality teachers for rural schools, gender equality and women's leadership, and information and communication technology (ICT) in education for rural development.

ICT in education is a major driver and key component of educational development and reform. It can promote modernization and accelerated development of education, which is critical for socioeconomic development. Because it is a major challenge for developing countries to ensure rural people's access to quality education, ICT can be an important lever to improve rural education and sustainable rural development. INRULED is continuing the program "ICT in Education for Rural Development (iERD)—Good and Best Practices" with UNESCO, International Institute for Capacity Building in Africa (IICBA), and Beijing Normal University-R&D Centre for Knowledge Engineering (BNU-KSEI). The aim is to share experiences of ICT in education for rural development among UNESCO member states, to propose suggestive iERD policy framework based on case studies and pilot centers of digital learning and poverty reduction, and to provide special training workshops for policymakers, researchers, and project managers. As an outcome of the iERD program, the report titled *Approach of ICT in Education for Rural Development* includes 21 cases from some developing countries. The purpose of collecting cases across the globe is to share experiences among developing countries on ICT in education for rural development.

In the years ahead, we will continue our work of research, capacity building, networking, and information dissemination for developing countries. As education in Africa is a top priority for UNESCO and INRULED, we intend to play an increasingly important role in China–Africa cooperation in terms of education and rural development.

As always, we look forward to working with our partners and stakeholders in the years ahead.

Dong Qi
Director, UNESCO-INRULED

Preface

There are presently nearly 3.1 billion people or 55% of the total population of the developing world living in rural areas, and at least 70% of the world's poorest people are from those areas. For the next two decades, it is estimated that the majority of the population living in developing countries will continue to be rural (IFAD, 2010), and it will be a major challenge to ensure their access to quality education for inclusive and sustainable rural development (QEISRD).

The iERD program was initiated in 2012 by UNESCO's INRULED, along with three other partners, that is, UNESCO Sector Policy Advice (UNESCO-PAD) and ICT in education, IICBA, and BNU-KSEI.

In light of UNESCO's framework, iERD is aiming at sharing good practices, analyzing challenges and constraints in the implementation of ICT in education, and exploring innovative approach to strengthen policymakers' capacity in designing projects and policies of iERD. The program focuses on three key questions:

- What are policies and projects related to iERD and what is the role of ICT in QEISRD?
- What are the common challenges and constraints faced by developing countries in this field?
- How to promote iERD in an innovative way?

The program starts by collecting good and best practices from China, Africa, Asia-Pacific, and Latin America. On the basis of experience and lessons learned from these cases, the program will work out an approach for informationization of rural education in China and the policy framework of iERD and organize training for policymakers, education managers, and policy researchers in developing countries. The collected cases focus on the combination of ICT and rural issues. Cases are diversified:

- In view of regions, cases can be collected in whole China or specific areas, in different countries or regions, or in different experimental sites or demonstration spots.
- In view of types, cases can be split into the categories of engineering project, scheming project, experimental project, demonstration project, policy project, research project, training project, and comprehensive project, and the size, project period, and starting time are flexible (these statements apply to the projects that have been completed, or are being implemented at the moment, or will be conducted in the future).
- In view of beneficiaries, cases are directed at rural residents (inclusive of those in the mining regions), such as students, teachers, farmers, migrant workers, women, children, the elderly, doctors, officials, technical workers, and certain communities, whose size is not strictly defined.
- In view of contents, cases can be focused on ICT infrastructure in rural schools, construction of digital learning center in rural areas, ICT skills training, ICT courses in rural schools, ICT integrated into courses, open and distance learning and blended learning, digital learning resource sharing and support services, and application of e-administration and diversified issues.
- In view of implementing institutions, cases can be carried out either jointly or separately by international organizations, government departments and agencies, higher education institutions, research institutes, corporations, and associations and foundations.
- In view of technical methods, however advanced or backward they might be, as long as they are suitable to a particular case, one can make use of either jointly or separately the Internet, radio, television, mobile phone, CD and VCDs, multimedia classroom, and electronic teaching materials.

By the end of 2012, in collaboration with UNESCO-PAD, IICBA, BNU-KSEI, and other institutions, 21 cases on iERD were collected from some developing countries in the world. Nine of them are from China, which are included in the first part of the book, while four cases are from Africa, five are from Asia, and three are from Latin America which make up the second part of the book.

Cases from China

- ICT integration in rural classrooms: Modern Distance Education Project in primary and middle schools in rural China
- Educational Technology Promotes the Quality of In-class Teaching in Rural Primary and Middle Schools: BNU pilot program on leap-frog development of basic education
- Open Distance Education Training "Capable to Work, Willing to Stay" Talents for Rural Areas: "One Village, One College Student" Program by The Open University of China
- Spreading Knowledge, Eradicating Poverty: Tsinghua University poverty alleviation project through distance education
- Agriculture-related educational training and S&T promotion service system: Internet-based Union of Universities for Agricultural Science & Technology and Education
- The application of extensive distance training to professional development of rural teachers: The Training Program for Rural Elite Teachers in Central and West China
- Distance education for teachers in less developed areas: Case of School of Distance Education, Shaanxi Normal University
- Online training for substitute teachers in underdeveloped areas of economically developed cities: Experience from Guangdong province in China
- Innovative teachers achieve better IT integration in teaching: Ministry of Education—Microsoft (China) "Partners in Learning" project

Cases from Asia, Africa, and Latin America

- ICT for rural education and development: Success factors and lessons learned
- Summary tables of the cases on iERD from Asia, Africa, and Latin America
- e-Bario: Telecenters for remote and rural communities (Malaysia)
- e-Krishi: The online platform for small farmers (India)
- Mahiti Manthana—ICT for empowerment of rural women (India)

- Text2Teach: Mobile-based video lessons for Philippine schools (Philippines)
- Tradenet: The mobile trade platform for small farmers (Sri Lanka)
- MEDA: An online platform for water trade and information (Chile)
- Rural Schools of Information Technologies and Citizenship (Chile)
- Telesecundaria: An educational model for rural secondary schools (Colombia)
- Sharing Content in Local Language and Voices: Podcasting Pilot Project in Zimbabwe's Mbire district (Zimbabwe)
- CocoaLink (Ghana)
- Farmerline (Ghana)
- Womens' Action Network (Burkina Faso)

There are many challenges faced in effective implementation of ICT for rural development; therefore, policy recommendations are made to help drive and stimulate innovation and creativity through ICT use and reduce the digital divide and social exclusion in rural areas. The cases included in this book typically represent the ICT educational applications in China and examine how current policies can support the overall development progress. It is expected to share good practices and to focus on spreading them among three targeted groups of people: young people in rural areas, teachers at rural primary and high schools, and "left-behind" rural women.

Many experts from international society pay attention to Chinese experience on e-learning. Michael Trucan, Senior ICT and Education Policy Specialist of World Bank, thought this book, which provided a helpful list of some of the largest and most interesting ICT/education initiatives that have taken place in rural China over the past decade, may also provide a useful starting point for international researchers and policymakers looking to learn more about related Chinese experience (http://blogs.worldbank.org/edutech/ict-and-rural-education-in-china).

ICT, which breaks limits of time and space, can contribute to universal access to education, equity in education, promotion of quality teaching and learning, teachers' professional development and efficient education management. These can be important levers to improve rural education in less developed and developing countries. The good practices of ICT development in education will help improve people's capacity on ICT, advance education informatization, and promote social and economic development in the global community, especially in the rural areas of the developing countries.

What we have collected is just a drop in the ocean of iERD practices. The book is imperfect in many respects as limited by our time and energy. Anyway, we will go on looking for good practices of iERD and share them with those who are interested. Meanwhile, it is appreciated much that if you contact INRULED with wonderful iERD cases (www. inruled.org/iERD).

Zeng Haijun
UNESCO-INRULED
Beijing, China

Acknowledgments

We would like to extend our sincere thanks to all those who have helped us make this book possible and better. As part of the iERD program, the book has gained strong support of INRULED, especially Professor Dong Qi, the director of INRULED and president of Beijing Normal University.

We express our deep appreciation to partners of iERD project, Dr Miao Fengchun, program specialist of UNESCO-PAD, Dr Engida Temechegn, program officer of IICBA, and Professor Huang Ronghuai, the director of BNU-KSEI.

Special appreciation is also extended to kind-hearted domestic and international experts of e-learning who shared with us precious opinions and suggestion for the book, in particular, Stephen Harggard, Shafika Isaacs, Eilean von Lautz-Cauzanet, Michael Trucano, Yang Zongkai, Li Daoliang, Wu Di, Wang Li, and Sun Qiurui.

We would like to offer our gratitude to Chinese team members as well who have devoted impressive efforts to the book, especially Wang Ying, Zhao Yuchi, Ge Yi, Jia Zhuxin, Zhang Hong, Chen Peng, Wang Yunwu, and Zhang Jinbao.

We are also grateful to the institutions which provided case materials and the authors who have made these cases known to the public including Wang Zhuzhu, Yu Shengquan, Zhang Zhijun, Diao Qingjun, Wei Tao, Hao Yingping, Jiao Yiju, Liang Shuhua, Liu Weibin, Wang Hai, Long Youhua, Li Dan, Zhang Jufan, Xu Xiaoyi, Wang Yanchang, Zheng Lanqin, Fan Xinmin, Ma Guogang, Liu Yansheng, Zhang Yan, Li Wei, Liao Qiong, Niu Xuesong, Pan Hewei, as well as Alvin W. Yeo, Ambili Menonand Noufal, K.P. Noufal, Maria Sergia Rosario Catangay, Mary-Ann Santiago, Ireneo Demecais, Sriganesh Lokanathan, Sameera Wijerathna, Oscar CristiMarfil, John Zoltner, Joel Selanikio, Esteban Taha, Clara Helena Agudelo, Mary Luz Isaza Ramos, and others.

The book would not have been possible without the hard work of other two editors who have contributed their time, thoughts, and resources to the book.

Our sincere thanks also goes to the SAGE team, including Rudra Narayan, Sandhya Gola, Clare Sun, and others.

Last but not the least, we would like to express our thanks to our families and friends for their valuable encouragement and strong spiritual support.

Zeng Haijun
UNESCO-INRULED
Beijing, China

Liu Jing
UNESCO-INRULED
Beijing, China

1

Approach for Informatization of Rural Education in China*

Zeng Haijun, Huang Ronghuai,
Zhao Yuchi, Zhang Jinbao,
Wang Rong, and Ge Yi

An Overview of Socioeconomic Development in Rural China

The population of mainland China reached 1,347,350,000 in 2011, of which 51.3% (690,790,000) was urban and the remaining 48.7% (656,560,000) was rural. The urban population, for the first time, was more than half of the total population in mainland China.[1] The average

* Education informatization is a concept in the Chinese language and cultural context equivalent to the universal concept of information and communication technology (ICT) in education.

[1] Urban and rural population refers to population living in urban or rural areas within the territory of China. The population of China was 1,370,536,875 in 2010, of which 50.32% (674,149,546) lived in rural areas.

per capita annual income of the rural population was CNY (Chinese Yuan) 6,977 (approximately USD 1,100) with a median of CNY 6,194, which was about one-third of the median figure for urban population. Food expenditure accounted for 40.4% of the total expenditure of rural population. The latest rural poverty alleviation standard sets the average per capita income of CNY 2,300 or USD 365 as the poverty threshold. According to the standard, 122,380,000 people in rural China qualified for poverty alleviation assistance. A total of 764,200,000 people were employed in mainland China, out of which 359,140,000 were in urban areas. There were a total of 252,780,000 peasant workers in mainland China, out of which 158,630,000 were migrant workers and 94,150,000 were local. Local peasant workers accounted for 37.2% of the total population in mainland China.[2]

The administrative and policy context is also important to appreciate. There are mainly four levels of administrative divisions in China: province, prefecture, county, and township. Less common is the three-level division that excludes the prefecture level. Informatization has to work through that structure. There is also a geographical dimension: the western part of China occupies 71.5% of land but has 27.0% of the national population. It is economically less developed with a larger number of people living below the poverty line and has a large population of minority groups. The government promotes urbanization with a Chinese flavor. This places the emphasis on development of large, medium-sized, and small cities and townships, following the principles of balancing urban and rural development, rational planning, land saving, comprehensive function, and driving the development of small cities and townships alongside that of medium-sized and large ones. These urbanization policies aim to generate a sustainable mechanism by which industry supports agriculture and urban areas support rural areas. The overall goal is progress in integrating economic and social development in urban and rural areas.

---

[2] National Bureau of Statistics of China. "2011 China National Economic and Social Development Statistics Bulletin." Retrieved Feb 22, 2012 from http://www.stats.gov.cn/tjgb/ndtjgb/qgndtjgb/t20120222_402786440.htm. All the national data in the bulletin do not include Hong Kong, Macao, and Taiwan except administrative divisions, land and resources, and forestry.

An Overview of Informatization in Rural China

China underwent rapid informatization between 2000 and 2010, especially in rural areas, as part of a widespread process of economic and industrial expansion. In 2010, the proportion of the villages and towns with access to the Internet in China had reached 100%, of which 98% had the access to the broadband Internet. At the same time, the number of the Internet users in China's rural areas had reached 125 million, accounting for 27.3% of the total netizens. The sample survey shows that the number of computer ownership for rural residents in China had risen to 10 computers per 100 households. Moreover, 100% of the national administrative villages and 94% natural villages had over 20 households with access to telephone. The sample survey shows that the number of fixed-telephone ownership per 100 households in China's rural areas was 65, whereas that of the mobile phone ownership was 120. The comprehensive coverage rates of radio and TV were 96.78% and 97.62%, respectively (Li, 2011).

However, China still lags behind other countries and regions with the highest level of informatization. Informatization Development Index in China (IDICN) reached 3.55 in 2010, ranking China at 80th position in the world with a low level of informatization (see Table 1.1).

Within the overall picture of rapid informatization, the level of progress has been variable in different parts of China. Economically more developed regions are rapidly catching up with the advanced level internationally, whereas less well-off regions are experiencing slower progress.

During the "Twelfth Five-year Plan" period (2010–2015), the Chinese government set the goal of comprehensively improving the level of informatization to build the next generation of information infrastructure, accelerate economic and social informatization, and strengthen network and information security.

Rural informatization is the specific focus of this book, and in China the process of major application and promotion of information and communication technology (ICT) in rural production, life, and social management has enjoyed special conditions. The Chinese government has been focusing on the construction of rural transportation and water

Table 1.1
Comparison of IDICN and the Top Ten Countries, 2008

Country	2000	2002	2004	2005	2006	2007	2008	Rank 2008	2010	Rank 2010
Sweden	0.896	0.966	1.001	1.016	1.025	1.036	1.048	1	8.23	2
Britain	0.832	0.871	0.916	0.943	0.962	1.008	1.009	2	7.60	10
Netherlands	0.851	0.855	0.902	0.925	0.941	0.960	0.967	3	7.61	9
Denmark	0.877	0.910	0.941	0.946	0.952	0.940	0.960	4	7.97	4
Norway	0.828	0.894	0.931	0.937	0.946	0.955	0.960	5	7.60	11
America	0.893	0.905	0.923	0.931	0.934	0.935	0.942	6	7.09	17
Switzerland	0.873	0.895	0.918	0.924	0.924	0.934	0.942	7	7.67	8
Germany	0.822	0.850	0.881	0.894	0.903	0.917	0.925	8	7.27	15
Austria	0.822	0.838	0.872	0.888	0.900	0.910	0.921	9	7.17	16
Iceland	0.864	0.891	0.899	0.904	0.898	0.905	0.913	10	8.06	3
China	0.478	0.534	0.576	0.591	0.612	0.630	0.645	42	3.55	80

Source: Zhou (2011); International Telecommunication Union (2011).

and electricity infrastructure, and these developments have facilitated the application of ICT in rural China. Simultaneously, the government has also made efforts to improve the balanced development and quality of education. The aims of such efforts are to drive the transition of rural production from traditional agriculture that is labor-intensive and semi-closed or closed to modern agriculture that is technology intensive and more open, and ultimately accelerate rural economic and social transition and the development of urbanization.

In terms of information resources, the Ministry of Agriculture has established nearly 40 channels of information collection in the national agricultural system, which covers the main industries and fields from top to bottom, such as plantation, animal husbandry, fisheries, agricultural reclamation, agricultural mechanization, the enterprises in the towns and villages, rural business management, agricultural scientific education, market circulation of agricultural products, and so on. It has deployed over 8,000 points for information collection and has established an indicating and reporting system of information. In 2010, the total number of the agricultural websites had reached 31,108. The Ministry of Agriculture had initially set up the national agricultural portal website with the Chinese agricultural information website as the core along with more than 30 professional websites. The 31 provincial departments of agriculture, over three-fourths of the municipal bureaus of agriculture and nearly half of the county-level sections of agriculture have established local area network (LAN) and service websites for agricultural information.

In addition, regarding service system, the Ministry of Agriculture has set up 19 provincial, 78 municipal, and 344 county-level service platforms of integrated information for the issues of peasants, rural areas, and agriculture. The three main telecom operators have built their own service platforms for rural information, such as "Access to Agricultural Information," "Information Field," "New Horizon of Agriculture," and so on. At the same time, more and more enterprises involved in agribusiness set up their own service platforms of information to advertise their products and carry out online services, e-commerce, and other business activities. Moreover, 100% of the provincial departments of agriculture in China have set up the organizations with the function of carrying out the informatization work. Almost 97% of the municipal bureaus of agriculture and over 80% of the county-level agricultural sections have set up the organizations for information management and services. More than 70% of the villages and towns have set up more than one million rural stations for information service with over 700,000 rural information messengers.

Rural Chinese (48.7% of the population) have achieved a modest participation in informatization, at roughly half the level of urban users. The number of Internet users in China reached 513 million by the end of 2011, of which some 136 million are residents of areas classified as rural, accounting for 26.5% of the national total. The number of mobile phone Internet users reached 356 million, out of which 27.3% are rural residents. Rural residents using the Internet from fixed devices or mobile devices are mostly young males who typically engage for long periods of time and mainly for entertainment purposes. The lack of IT skills among rural residents is a major obstacle to the development of Internet use in rural China. The 57.8% of rural residents who are not Internet users say that they "don't know how to use computers/the Internet." A policy has identified the need to improve the skills and awareness of Internet use among rural residents, in addition to improving Internet-related infrastructure, in order to reduce the urban–rural gap in Internet use (China Internet Network Information Center, 2012).

Recent Trends in Development of Education in Rural China

Overview of the Development of Education in China: All Sectors

This section describes the institutional background to informatization in China in terms of scale, numbers, and trends. China has the largest education system in the world in terms of the number of schools, students, and teachers. There were a total of 531,000 schools in China in 2010 (see Figure 1.1), with 260 million degree students, 56,248,000 nondegree students, and 141,390,000 full-time teachers. Education informatization, therefore, affects an exceptionally large number of individuals

Figure 1.1
Types of Schools in China, 2010

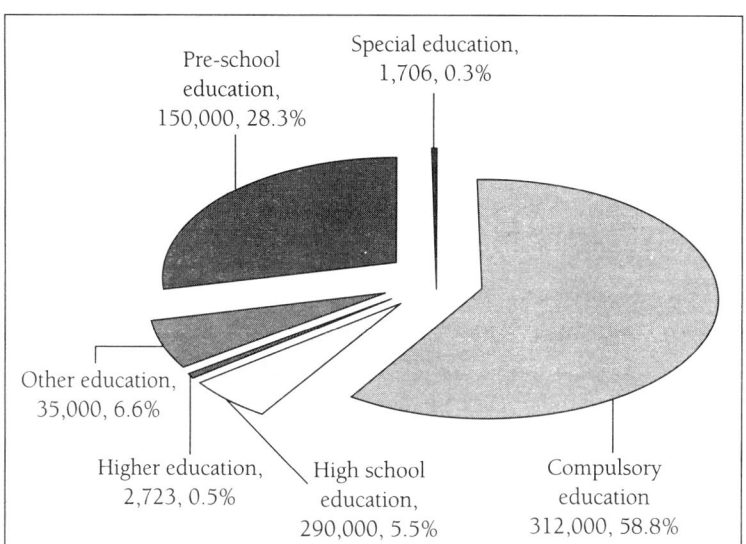

Source: MoE (2011).

and institutions. Its impact on progress and reform in teaching, schools, and education is potentially extremely large.[3]

Within this system, some areas are expanding, while others are shrinking. In terms of numbers enrolled, the gross number of students in senior high schools and higher education, which are at the peak of the pyramid, has been on the increase with the rapid development of the scale and prevalence of education. The number of students in primary and junior high schools, which are at the bottom of the pyramid, is declining with the decrease in school-age population. In 2010, the number of students receiving compulsory[4], senior high school, higher, preschool, special, and other types of education, respectively, accounted

---

[3] If not otherwise specified, the source of all data in the graphs includes: the Department of Development and Planning, the Ministry of Education (MoE, 2011), Brief Statistical Analysis of Educational Development in China in 2010.

[4] Compulsory education in China includes 6-year primary education and 3-year junior high school education.

Table 1.2

Scale of Degree Education in China, 2005–2010

Unit: 1,000s

Year	Higher Education	Senior High School Education	Junior High School Education	Primary School Education	Preschool Education
2005	23,000	40,309	62,149	108,641	21,790
2006	25,000	43,419	59,579	107,115	22,639
2007	27,000	45,288	57,362	105,640	23,488
2008	29,070	45,761	55,850	103,315	24,750
2009	29,790	46,409	54,409	100,715	26,578
2010	31,050 (11.4%)	46,706 (17.8%)	52,793 (20.6%)	99,407 (38.9%)	29,767 (10.2%)

Source: MoE (2011).

for 59.5%, 17.8%, 11.4%, 10.2%, 0.2%, and 1.0% of the total number of students in China (see Table 1.2).

In terms of participation in education, expressed by the gross enrollment ratio, the UN measure of the number enrolled compared to the number entitled by age to enroll, there have been increases in every sector, but the growth the gross enrollment ratio has been strongest in senior high school level. This is also the sector with the highest growth in provision. The most dramatic story of the years 2005–2010, therefore, is the huge increase in provision and uptake of senior high school education (see Figure 1.2).

With the increasing prevalence of education generally, and the decline in school-age population, there has been an interesting divergence in the percentage of students receiving noncompulsory versus compulsory education. The percentage (per 100,000) of students receiving noncompulsory education has been on the rise. On the other hand, there has been a decrease in the percentage number of students in the junior areas of compulsory education. In 2010, out of every 100,000 people in China, 2,189 were receiving higher education (577 up over 2005), 3,499 in senior high schools (429 up over 2005), 2,230 receiving preschool education (554 up over 2005), 3,955 in junior high schools (a decrease of 826 from 2005), and 7,448 in primary schools (a decrease of 910 from 2005) (see Table 1.3).

Figure 1.2
Gross Enrollment Ratio for Different Levels of Education in China,
2005–2010

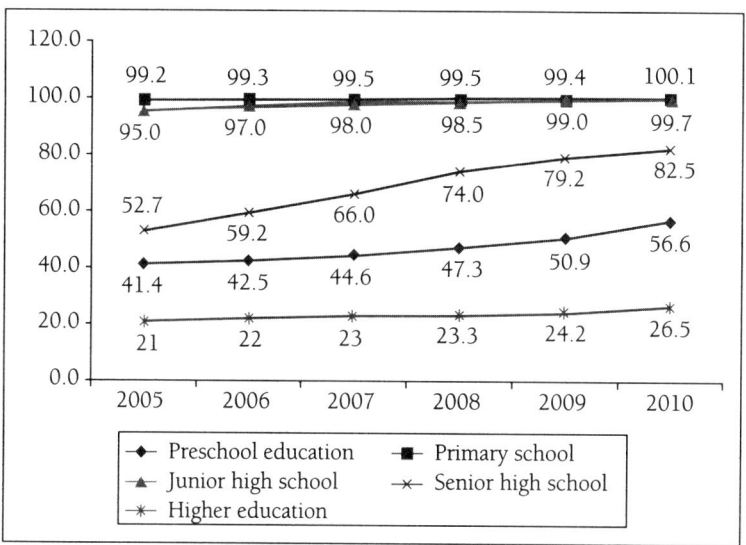

Source: MoE (2011).

Table 1.3
Average Number of Students per 100,000 People in China,
2005–2010

Year	Higher Education	Senior High School Education	Junior High School Education	Primary School Education	Preschool Education
2005	1,612	3,070	4,781	8,358	1,676
2006	1,816	3,321	4,557	8,192	1,731
2007	1,924	3,409	4,364	8,037	1,787
2008	2,042	3,440	4,227	7,819	1,873
2009	2,128	3,482	4,097	7,584	2,001
2010	2,189	3,499	3,955	7,448	2,230

Source: MoE (2011).

The numerical goals of educational planning between 2005 and 2010 were met, according the collected data. The basis for the execution of "National Framework for Medium and Long-term Educational Reform and Development Plan (2010–2020)" (hereafter referred to as "Framework for Educational Plan") (see Table 1.4) therefore looks secure.

Table 1.4
Main Goals for National Educational Development in China

	Achieve-ment of 2005	Achieve-ment of 2010	Goal for 2010	Goal for 2015	Goal for 2020
Preschool Education					
Numbers of children in preschools (1,000s)				34,000	40,000
Gross enrollment ratios of one year preschool education				85%	95%
Gross enrollment ratios of two years preschool education				70%	80%
Gross enrollment ratios of three years preschool education	41.4%	56.6%	55%	60%	70%
Compulsory Education					
Numbers of students in schools (1,000s)		15,220		161,000	165,000
Gross enrollment ratios of junior high school education	95%	100.1%	98%		
Retention rate of junior high school education	92.8%	93.8%	95%		
Consolidation rate				93%	95%

Table 1.4 continued

Table 1.4 continued

	Achieve-ment of 2005	Achieve-ment of 2010	Goal for 2010	Goal for 2015	Goal for 2020
Literacy					
Young adults illiteracy rate	3%		2%		
Senior High School Education					
Gross enrollment ratios	52.7%	82.5%	80%	87%	90%
Numbers of students in schools (1,000s)	40,310	46,706	45,100	45,000	47,000
For: Ordinary senior high school	24,090	24,388	24,100		
For: Vocational school	16,000	22,318	21,000		
Vocational Education					
Full-time students of secondary vocational schools				22,500	23,500
Full-time students of tertiary vocational schools				13,900	14,800
Higher Education					
Gross enrollment ratio	21%	26.5%	25%	36%	40%
Total students (1,000s)	23,000	31,050	30,000	33,500	35,500
For: Postgraduate	980	1,538	1,300	1,700	2,000
For: Ordinary undergraduate	15,620	22,318	20,000		
For: Undergraduate of adult education	4,360	5,360	6,000		
Continuing Education					
Continuing education for in-service employees				290,000	350,000

Source: MoE (2011).

Development of Rural Education in China: Sector by Sector

Preschool Education

Overall, in 2010, there were 150,400 independent kindergartens and 98,000 primary school-affiliated kindergartens and preschools in China, with 29,766,700 students, 1.3 million principals and teachers, and a gross enrollment ratio of 56.6% for preschool education. In rural China, there were 96,000 primary school-affiliated preschools and 115,000 kindergartens with 222,410,000 students accounting for three-fourths of the national total. In addition, 90.8% of students enrolled in primary schools in rural China received preschool education. The percentage in western China was 81.7%, 14.9% lower than that of the urban areas (see Table 1.5).

Compulsory Education

In 2010, there were 257,400 primary schools in China with 16,917,000 enrolled students, 99,407,000 admitted students, and 17,396,400 graduates. Primary schools in rural China enrolled 13,777,000 students, accounting for 81.4% of the national total.

Regarding junior high schools, there were 54,900 junior high schools (including 100 vocational junior high schools) in China with 17,165,800

Table 1.5
Number of Students in Kindergartens in China in 2010 and the Percentage of Students That Ever Received Preschool Education

Areas	Preschool Pupils (1,000s)			Ratio of Pupils Admitted to Primary School Who Have Accepted Preschool Education (%)		
	Total	*Urban*	*Rural*	*Total*	*Urban*	*Rural*
Nationwide	29,767	7,526	22,241	91.9	96.6	90.8
Eastern China	13,612	4,157	9,455	96.3	95.9	96.4
Central China	8,292	1,756	6,537	94.1	98.0	93.4
Western China	7,863	1,613	6,250	83.7	96.6	81.7

Source: MoE (2011).

prospective students, 52,793,300 enrolled students, and 17,503,500 graduates. In rural China, junior high schools enrolled 13,684,000 students, accounting for 79.7% of the national total. With the decrease in the number of school-age population, the number of enrolled students receiving compulsory education in rural China was also decreasing year by year (see Table 1.6).

Gap in compulsory education prevalence is narrowing. The differences in net elementary school enrollment rates in different regions of China have been narrowing (see Figure 1.3). The Compulsory Education Funding Guarantee Mechanism is improving. In the past few years, the government has exempted all the expenses at the compulsory education stage, the provision of free textbook has been expanded from rural school to urban school, and the government has been improving the standards and quantity of the financial aid to poor students. In 2010, China had 130 million rural students under compulsory education who enjoyed complete exemption of tuition fees and textbook expenses. In central China and western China, about 12.28 million poor rural students attending boarding schools under compulsory education stage are receiving financial aid to their living expenses, and more than 29 million urban students at compulsory education stage are exempted from tuition fees. The plan to improve less-developed rural schools under the compulsory education program has been implemented, and efforts have been made to liquidate the debts related to rural compulsory education.

Table 1.6

Number of Enrolled Students in Compulsory Education in China, 2010

Areas	Primary School Education (1,000 person)			Junior High School Education (1,000 person)		
	Total	*Urban*	*Rural*	*Total*	*Urban*	*Rural*
Nationwide	99,407	18,205	81,202	52,793	10,591	42,203
Eastern China	34,428	8,996	25,432	18,678	5,013	13,665
Central China	34,252	5,047	29,205	17,647	3,121	14,526
Western China	30,728	4,162	26,566	16,468	2,456	14,012

Source: MoE (2011).

Figure 1.3
Net Enrollment Rate for Elementary School Education by Regions in China, 2001–2010

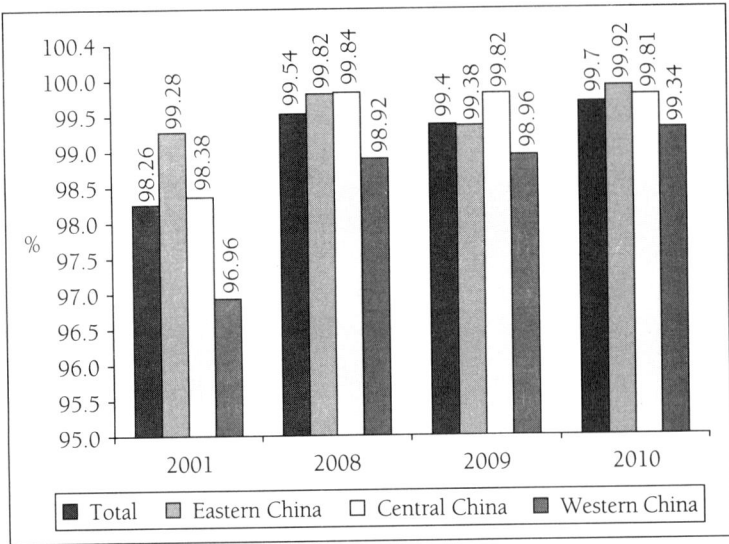

Source: Chinese National Commission for UNESCO & Nation Center for Education Development Research (2011).

Student–teacher ratio in compulsory education in rural China has been improving generally, but there are national disparities. In 2010, the student–teacher ratio in primary schools in rural China reached 17.4:1, as compared to 15.6:1 in primary school in urban areas. The student–teacher ratio in primary schools in western China amounted to 17.5:1 in 2010, as compared to 21.0:1 in 2005. Student–teacher ratio in junior high schools in rural China was 15.0:1, similar to the level in junior high schools in urban areas (see Table 1.7).

During the process of urbanization, the Chinese government has paid special attention to compulsory education for three groups of recipients: boarders, children of migrant workers, and left-behind children.[5] The three groups are all disadvantaged groups in compulsory education stage.

---

[5] Left-behind children refers to children who are left in villages and towns by their parents working in cities.

Table 1.7

Student–Teacher Ratio in Compulsory Education in China, 2010

Areas	Primary School Education			Junior High School Education		
	Total	*Urban*	*Rural*	*Total*	*Urban*	*Rural*
Nationwide	17.7	19.2	17.4	15.0	15.0	15.0
Eastern China	16.8	18.5	16.3	14.1	14.2	14.0
Central China	18.5	19.5	18.3	15.0	15.4	14.9
Western China	17.9	20.6	17.5	16.1	16.5	16.1

Source: MoE (2011).

Table 1.8

Percentage of Boarding Students in Compulsory Education in China, 2010

Areas	Primary School Education (%)			Junior High School Education (%)		
	Total	*Urban*	*Rural*	*Total*	*Urban*	*Rural*
Nationwide	10.4	3.2	12.1	43.7	14.5	51.0
Eastern China	4.7	2.7	5.4	30.4	12.9	36.8
Central China	11.9	4.2	13.2	48.1	15.1	55.2
Western China	15.3	3.0	17.2	54.0	16.8	60.5

Source: MoE (2011).

In 2010, there were 33,435,200 boarding students receiving compulsory education in China. About 10.4% and 43.7% students, respectively, in primary and junior high schools were boarding students. The percentage was 17.2% and 60.5% in rural areas in western China, far exceeding the numbers in urban areas in eastern China (see Table 1.8).

Out of all enrolled students receiving national compulsory education in China, 11,671,700 were children of migrant workers, 8,643,000 and 3,028,800 in primary and junior high schools, respectively. Close to 60% were in urban areas in eastern China and around one-fourth in western China (see Figure 1.4).

There were 22,715,100 left-behind children, 14,617,900 and 8,097,200 in primary and junior high schools, respectively, which took

Figure 1.4
Number of Children of Migrant Workers Receiving Compulsory Education in China, 2007 and 2010

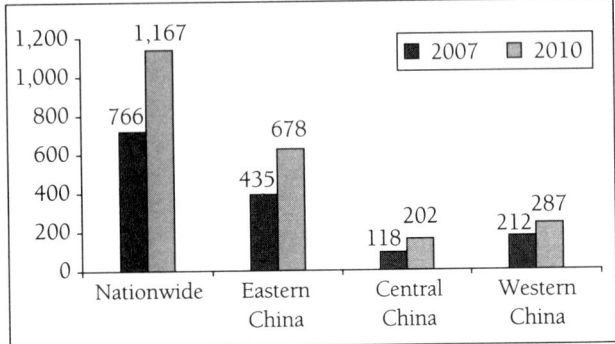

Source: MoE (2011).

Table 1.9
Number of Left-behind Children in Compulsory Education in China, 2010

Areas	Left-behind Children in Rural Areas (1,000s)			Ratio to Full-time Students in Rural Areas (%)		
	Total	Primary School Education	Junior High School Education	Primary School Education	Junior High School Education	
Nationwide	22,715	14,618	8,097	18.0	19.1	
Eastern China	3,565	2,133	1,432	8.4	10.1	
Central China	10,774	7,109	3,665	24.3	25.2	
Western China	8,376	5,376	3,000	20.2	21.3	

Source: MoE (2011).

up 22.9% of the total children in compulsory education (see Table 1.9). Education for these children is one of the more serious problems in rural education, dragging the process of education modernization. It is also spread disparately across the regions and sectors. One of the major challenges for education informatization is to address this problem to some extent.

Senior High School Education

There were 28,584 senior high schools (including regular senior high schools, adult senior high schools, and secondary vocational schools) in China, with 17,066,600 prospective students, 46,773,400 enrolled students, and a gross enrollment rate of 82.5%. Senior High Schools in western China enrolled a total of 49,960,000 prospective students and had 13,033,000 enrolled students, accounting for 28% of the national total.

There were 14,058 regular senior high schools in China, out of which 60.9% were in rural areas. Regular senior high schools had 8,362,400 prospective students, 7,944,300 graduates, and 24,273,400 enrolled students, which accounted for two-thirds of the national total. The regular senior high schools in urban areas also enrolled students from rural China. There were 1,518,200 full-time teachers in regular senior high schools in China. The student–teacher ratio was 15.99:1 nationwide and 17.2:1 in western China (see Table 1.10).

Within the high school data, there are further trends worth highlighting. Vocational high schools have increased the number of prospective students that go on to graduate from junior high schools, including previous junior high school graduates, junior high school graduates that are not going to regular senior high schools, young people that have returned to rural areas, and military retirees. The percentage of enrolled students aged 18 and above has been on the increase. Agricultural and rural vocational education has been developing rapidly. In 2010, a total of 2,209,000 students were enrolled in agriculture-related majors, an increase of 47.4% over the previous year. Out of all students enrolled

Table 1.10

Number of Regular Senior High Schools, Students, and Full-time Teachers in China, 2010

	Schools	Graduates	Students Admitted	Enrolment	Full-time Teachers
Total	14,058	7,944,335	83,623,59	2,427,3351	5,041,576
Urban	5,494	2,773,848	2,930,927	8,582,032	1,272,483
Rural	8,564	5,170,487	5,431,432	1,569,1319	3,611,291

Source: MoE (2011).

in vocational high schools, the percentage of students in agriculture-related majors has been on the rise year by year, a 10% increase in 2010 over 2009 and a 23.3% increase over 2005. The number of prospective students in majors related to rural economic management, agricultural technology, animal husbandry, and veterinary medicine has also been increasing rapidly. For the 2010 data, see Figure 1.5.

The government has increased investment in vocational education:

- *Establish the Student Aid System for Secondary Vocational Education.* In 2006, China implemented student financial aid program for secondary vocational education. The financial aid covers all rural students and poor urban students. Every year, the first- and second-year students receive financial aid of CNY 1,500 per person. Over 16 million people benefit from this aid. In 2007, the central and local government budgets for financial aid were over CNY 10 billion

Figure 1.5
Students Enrolled in Agriculture-related Majors in Vocational High Schools in China, 2010

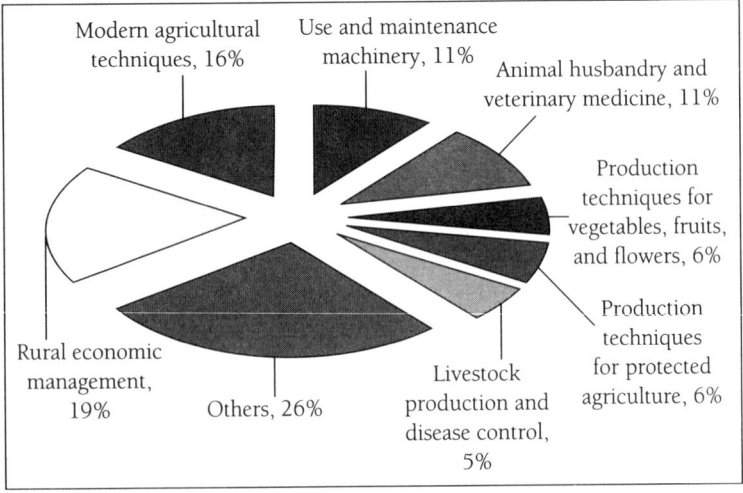

Source: MoE (2011).

- *Gradually Improve the Free Secondary Vocational Education Program.* Since the autumn semester of 2009, the State has begun to exempt tuition fees of poor rural students and students majored in agriculture in vocational schools.
- *Implement the Sunshine Program for Rural Labor Training which Aims to Improve the Quality and Employability of Rural Labors.* The training expenses are shared between governments and farmers. The government subsidy is from the poverty reduction fund of both central and local governments. The subsidy takes the form of training coupons which are given to the trainees directly. From 2004 to 2007, the accumulated central fiscal input was CNY 2.15 billion, and the local government input was over CNY 3 billion.

Higher Education

There were 2,358 higher education institutions (including 323 independent colleges) in China in 2010, of which 1,112 were universities and colleges offering undergraduate courses, 1,246 advanced vocational (professional) schools, 265 adult universities, and 69 pilot e-learning colleges. 538,000 students were enrolled in master's programs; 6,618,000 in bachelor's programs (2% in agriculture-related majors); 2,084,000 in adult universities, and 1,664,000 in e-learning programs (see Table 1.11 and Figure 1.6).

Table 1.11

Number of Enrolled Students in Higher Education in China, 2005–2010

						Unit: 1,000s
Student Types	*2005*	*2006*	*2007*	*2008*	*2009*	*2010*
Postgraduate	365	398	419	446	511	538
Ordinary Undergraduates	5,045	5,461	5,659	6,077	6,395	6,618
Undergraduates in Adult Education	1,930	1,844	1,911	2,026	2,015	2,084
Undergraduates in Distance Education	891	1,133	1,234	1,472	1,626	1,664

Source: MoE (2011).

Figure 1.6
Enrollment Increase in Higher Education, 2005–2010

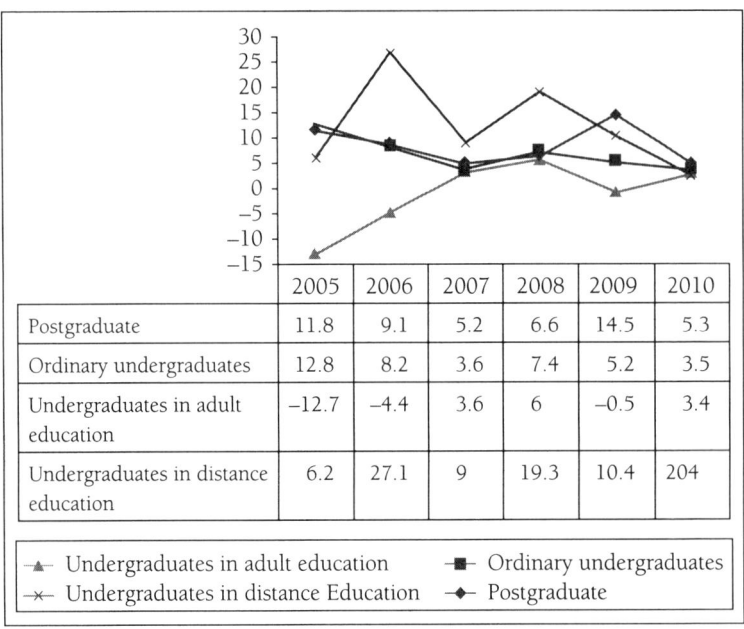

	2005	2006	2007	2008	2009	2010
Postgraduate	11.8	9.1	5.2	6.6	14.5	5.3
Ordinary undergraduates	12.8	8.2	3.6	7.4	5.2	3.5
Undergraduates in adult education	−12.7	−4.4	3.6	6	−0.5	3.4
Undergraduates in distance education	6.2	27.1	9	19.3	10.4	204

— ▲ — Undergraduates in adult education   — ■ — Ordinary undergraduates
— ✕ — Undergraduates in distance Education   — ◆ — Postgraduate

Source: MoE (2011).

By the end of 2010, there were 3,910 national excellent-rated courses, consisted of 2,516 undergraduate courses, 1,000 higher vocational college and junior college courses, and 394 other courses. In 2008, the MoE approved the establishment of the resource center and the recourse network for national excellent-rated courses, so as to optimize the resources of national excellent-rated courses, build up China's largest resource library and promote the disseminating and sharing of higher education quality resources. The recourse network for national excellent-rated courses has uploaded over 20,000 courses of all kinds and at all levels. It is equipped with various functions, such as information posting, course demonstrating, course searching and course evaluating, to help teachers and students enjoy the online educational service network.

The distribution of growth between regions has been a point of emphasis in central government policy, which aims at a balanced development of higher education in different regions and specially emphasizes the rapid development of higher education in central and western China. In 2010, enrollment of undergraduates in western China increased at the fastest rate with enrolment of total 1,534,000 students, an increase in 6.8% over the previous year and 40.7% over 2005. The proportion of teachers with master's degrees in universities in western China has been increasing rapidly, narrowing the regional gaps.

Other Education[6]

- *Special Education for Disabled Students.* There were 1,706 special education schools in China in 2010, 56% of which were in rural areas. Special education schools had 39,700 full-time teachers, 64,900 prospective students, 425,600 enrolled students, and 58,900 graduates, with two-thirds of them from rural areas (see Table 1.12).

Special students attending regular primary schools, regular classes in junior high schools, and special education classes of regular school total 39,700 prospective students and 259,600 enrolled students, respectively, accounting for 61.26% and 60.99% of the total number of students in special education.

- *Education for Minorities.* This is a topic to which the Chinese government pays significant attention in different ways including offering free compulsory education in minority areas and providing various favorable policies and subsidies to minority groups

Table 1.12
Number of Schools, Classes, and Students in Special Education in China, 2010

	School	Class	Graduate	Entrant	Enrolment
Total	1,706	16,263	58,941	64,869	425,613
Urban	750	8,974	18,139	19,329	130,981
Rural	956	7,289	40,802	45,540	294,632

Source: MoE (2011).

[6] Special education for disabled students and education for minorities are included in the above education system and not regarded as a type of education.

and minority areas (see Table 1.13). Fifty-two percent of students enrolled in compulsory education in minority areas were from minority groups, with almost equal enrollment rate of male (98.9%) and female (99.0%) students. There were, respectively, 2,267,000 and 2,280,000 prospective students in rural primary and junior high schools in minority areas.

- *Private Education.* Education run by nongovernment sectors has been driving the diversification of rural education. There were 676 private colleges and universities with 4,767,000 admitted students in China in 2010, out of which 145 were in western China enrolling 20.3% of all students. The number of enrolled students in private vocational high schools accounted for 16.9% of the students enrolled in private colleges and universities and 19.3% were in western China. There were 5,351 private primary schools in China with 72.6% in rural areas; 4,259 private junior high schools with 66.1% in rural areas; and 1,020,000 private kindergartens with 74.3% in rural areas.

- *Training.* In the past 10 years, China has put great efforts in developing vocational and training, and increasing the aid to vocational

Table 1.13

Number of Enrolled Minority Students in Different Levels of Education in China, 2005–2010

Educational Stages	2005	2006	2007	2008	2009	2010
No. of Full-time Students (1,000s)						
Preschool Education	1,342	1,411	1,580	1,697	1,894	2,127
Primary School Education	10,781	10,813	10,742	10,708	10,591	10,482
Junior High School Education	5,338	5,234	5,134	5,055	5,028	4,982
Ordinary Senior High School Education	1,595	1,695	1,751	1,769	1,787	1,833
Vocational School Education	617	732	857	961	1,072	1,200
Higher Education	1,288	1,460	1,520	1,647	1,793	1,916

Source: MoE (2011).

training and education for poor population in order to improve the skills of those people, helping the unemployed and rural surplus labor with the opportunity of reemployment or transfer employment, and improve their income. Such efforts have helped to lift tens of millions of rural population out of poverty. In 2010, there were 2,637,000 students registered in higher education training and 6,882,000 graduated; 52,919,000 students registered in secondary education training and 59,864,000 graduated; 4,936,000 students registered in professional certificate training and 7,108,000 graduated; 5,614,000 registered in job certificate training and 7,862,000 graduated. The number of training students in rural areas in central and western China is lower than that in urban areas in eastern China.

In recent years, the education system is actively developing rural technical training and rural worker transfer training rural adults. From 2005 to 2007, 140 million people received practical rural skill training. Practical rural skill training activities are offered to over 45 million people on average every year, and the annual average training rate is about 9%. From 2005 to 2007, 106 million people were receiving rural labor transfer training. Rural labor transfer training activities were offered to over 30 million people in average every year, and annual average training rate was about 7% (See Table 1.14).

Table 1.14
Data on Farmers' Education and Training in China, 2005–2007

Year	Rural Labor Population	Rural Practical Skill Training	Annual Rate of Practical Skill Training	Rural Labor Transfer Training	Annual Transfer Training Rate
2005	50,387	4,793.18	9.51%	3,270	6.49%
2006	50,387	4,520.58	8.94%	3,506	6.96%
2007	50,387	4,670.35	9.27%	3,815	7.18%
Total	1,51,161	13,984.11	9.25%	10,591	7.01%

Source: Research Report on Rural Adult Continuing Education (2008).

An Overview of the Development of Education Informatization in China

Education informatization in China can be categorized by the internal division of labor in education administrative departments and by the different levels of education concerned. Based on this approach, the operative categorization is as follows:

- *Informatization of Basic Education.* Mainly focusing on the development of education informatization in primary, middle, and regular senior high schools, initiated and invested by the government and designed for schools, students, and teachers.
- *Informatization of Vocational Education.* Including the development of education informatization in secondary and advanced vocational schools with a focus on secondary vocational schools and initiated and invested by the government. Note that higher vocational schools are often included in the higher education system and therefore its education informatization is included in education informatization of higher education.
- *Informatization of Higher Education.* Mainly referring to education informatization of universities and colleges, including regular and professional schools as well as graduate educational institutions, thereby covering education informatization for higher professional education, regular undergraduate education, and graduate education. Colleges and universities are the main targets of education informatization.
- *Informatization of Continuing Education.* Mainly referring to degree education by e-learning and distance training in demonstration universities and open universities, with the use of ICT to conduct systematic and interactive teaching that effectively connects teachers and students in different places.
- *Informatization of Teacher Education.* Mainly referring to the use of ICT to conduct e-learning and training to primary and junior high school teachers, including training of ICT skills and teaching techniques. It is initiated and invested by the government and often included in the informatization of basic education.

Education informatization covers information infrastructure, information resources, information technology application, information professionals, information policies and standards, and industrial environment (see Figure 1.7).

The development of education informatization in China has gone through four stages whose dates can be roughly given as: the initial development of computer-based education (1980s), rapid development of computer-based education (1990s), rapid development of infrastructure buildup (2000–2007), and the development of application capability (2007–). These dates are approximate and slightly different timescales have been followed in different parts of the system.

Figure 1.7
Six-factor Model of Education Informatization

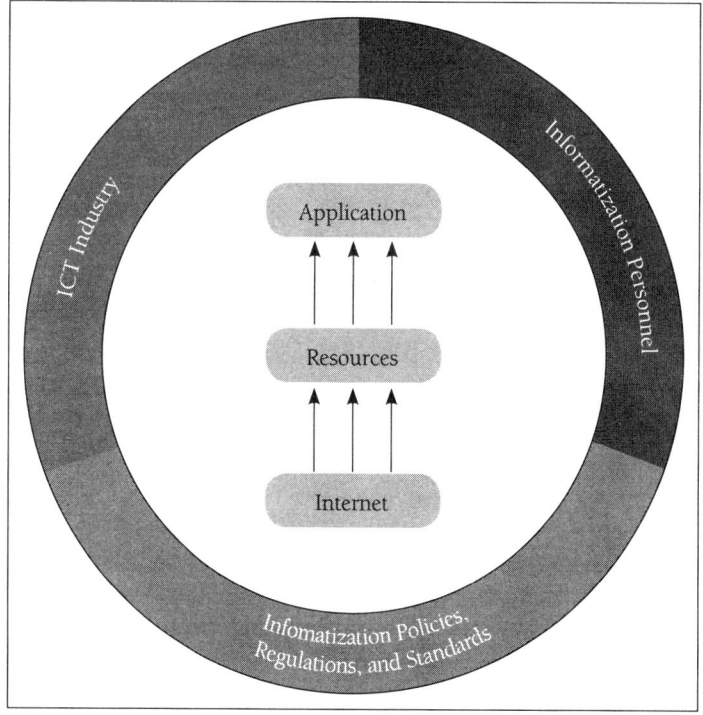

Source: Huang et al. (2007).

Projects have defined progress as much as dates. From the launch of China Education and Research Network (CERNET) in 1994, which may be considered as the first highly significant project in informatization, there has been a series of further important projects including the 211 Project, 985 Project, Action Plan for Educational Development toward the 21st Century, "School-to-School Project," Distance Education Project for Rural Primary and Junior High Schools, Campus Network in Universities in Western China and E-learning Pilot Projects in Universities and Colleges, and so on.

Overall, the development of Education informatization in China has been characterized by rapidity, and this aspect may be hailed as a major success. The principles and approaches that have achieved this may be outlined as follows:

- Infrastructure buildup is the precondition of education informatization and has received proper attention: CERNET and CERNET2 have one network center and 38 core nodes. The transmission rate of the national backbone network is 2.5–10 Gbps and that of local backbone network is N*155 Mbps–2.5 Gbps. CEBS at sites have covered all provinces and cities in China, especially rural and remote areas in western China, with more than 650,000 registered terminals. CERNET and CEBS at are interconnected and form a modern distance education transmission network. In the meantime, education MAN, computers, and multimedia systems have also been widely installed.

- The construction of information resources is the core of successful education informatization. In general, the resources system and basic education resources centers have been primarily built to meet the needs of rural primary and junior high school education. China Academic Library and Information System, China Academic Social Sciences and Humanities Library, digital museums, and China Equipment and Education Resource System have also been established. More than 10,000 online and video courses are now in the public domain.

- The application of information technology and information resources is the goal of education informatization. A wide range of different types of application platforms and digital learning resources have been used to deliver various modern distance education and training courses. The administration of digital education has also been developing in parallel, and IT-based services around information publication, online admission, career services, degree certification, statistics, and online cooperative research have had significant impact in the public education service.

- Information professionals are the key to education informatization and their quantity standard has been increasing: in basic education, 100% of senior high schools, more than 90% of junior high schools, and around 20% of primary schools offer information technology courses to education staff. Around 10 million teachers attended the first round of information technology training from 2003 to 2010 and the second round that started in 2010. The training has gradually improved teachers' teaching ability. The number of information professionals in higher education has been increasing rapidly.

- Policies and standards as well as industrial environment are the basis for education informatization. MoE has set up a leadership team in charge of the decision making, coordination, and promotion of education informatization. Major national planning frameworks have provided support for the education informatization. Research into the standards of educational information technology has also enabled connection between different systems, the coordination and sharing of resources, and has successfully solved several key problems in hybrid network, interconnection, resources sharing, and e-learning. Commercial companies play the most active role in producing the technologies, products, and services related to education informatization.

Data and research (MoE, 2011) confirm that the progress in education informatization in China has been significant, especially in the execution of modern distance education projects in primary and junior high schools in rural China that have benefited more than 100 million rural students in central and western China.

Nevertheless, despite these achievements, or perhaps because of them, problems in rural education informatization, such as "high input and poor output," "low efficiency," "digital gap," and "isolated island" are acknowledged by all participants in the system. The list of unsolved challenges looks like the following:

- *Unsustainable Inputs.* The inputs into education informatization in China are insufficient considering the scale of its education system. Different levels of education have different focuses concerning education informatization, and therefore the maintenance and upgrade of facilities, sufficiency and variety of resources, quality of construction teams, sustained capital input, and the application of research findings cannot be guaranteed and an effective long-term mechanism is yet to be established.
- *Imbalanced Infrastructure Buildup.* The central and local government has increased the amount of input into education informatization, especially in the construction of infrastructure in western China and rural areas. However, there are huge gaps in terms of the development of education informatization among regions, urban and rural areas, and different schools. Infrastructure including network, terminal and multimedia classroom and so on still needs to be upgraded and expanded.
- *Structural Insufficiency of Information Resources.* There are structural imbalances leading to specific problems and defects in certain categories of specialized education resources, such as training for adaptable technical talents, and digital learning resources needed for rural and farmer technical training. Scattered resources, repetitive construction, low level of standardization, outdated mindset, and systematic defects are all obstacles to resources sharing.
- *Insufficient Application of Information Technology in Education.* The integration of information technology into teaching is often insufficient, and there is often poor combination of information resources, application systems, and IT-based teaching. Modern distance education still needs to be improved in application innovation, efficiency and effectiveness of the application of facilities and resources, and technical support services.
- *Greater Progress Needs to be Made in Teacher Training.* The scale of training needs to be increased as a great number of primary and junior high school teachers in rural China do not have basic

computer skills; teachers lack the ability to transform traditional teaching with information technology; the current education technical support team that serves education informatization application projects cannot meet the demand for technical support, and it is one of the reasons for the idling or wasting of the technology infrastructure.

- *The Formulation and Promotion of Technology Standards Need to be Strengthened.* The draft, approval, promulgation, and promotion of technology standards are lagging behind the actual practices, resulting in the phenomenon of "isolated island" in the construction of resources and information systems. The standards in effect cannot be effectively executed in the design and execution of informatization projects.

Informatization in Rural Basic Education

Higher Prevalence of Computers and Digital Campus

Two projects in particular, the "School-to-School Project" and "Distance Education Project for Rural Primary and Junior High Schools," have together led to significant breakthroughs in infrastructure construction for rural basic education informatization. More than 100 million primary and junior high school students in rural areas in central and western China have benefitted under these programs. In 2010, the number of computers per 100 students in regular primary and junior high schools in China was, respectively, 4.1 and 6.4, and 3.5 and 6.0 for rural areas. The percentage of primary and junior high schools in all areas with "Digital Campus"[7] was 15.9% and 46.4%, respectively, an increase of 8% and 19.7% over 2005. The figures for primary and junior high schools in rural areas were 12.6% and 42.6%, respectively, 52.1% and 28.9% lower than the level in urban areas (see Table 1.15).

The number of seats in multimedia classrooms per 100 students in regular primary and junior high schools in China were 7.7 and 12.5, respectively, and 5.5 in rural primary schools, less than one-third of that in urban primary schools. The figure for rural areas in western China was

---

[7] "Digital Campus" refers to schools which have local area network in campus and Internet access.

Table 1.15
Number of Computers per 100 Students and the Percentage of Digital Campus in Compulsory Education in China, 2010

	Computers per 100 Students			Digital Campus (%)		
School	*Total*	*Urban*	*Rural*	*Total*	*Urban*	*Rural*
Primary School	4.1	7.2	3.5	15.9	64.7	12.6
Junior High School	6.4	7.8	6.0	46.4	71.5	42.6

Source: MoE (2011).

Figure 1.8
Number of Seats in Multimedia Classrooms per 100 Students in Compulsory Education in China, 2010

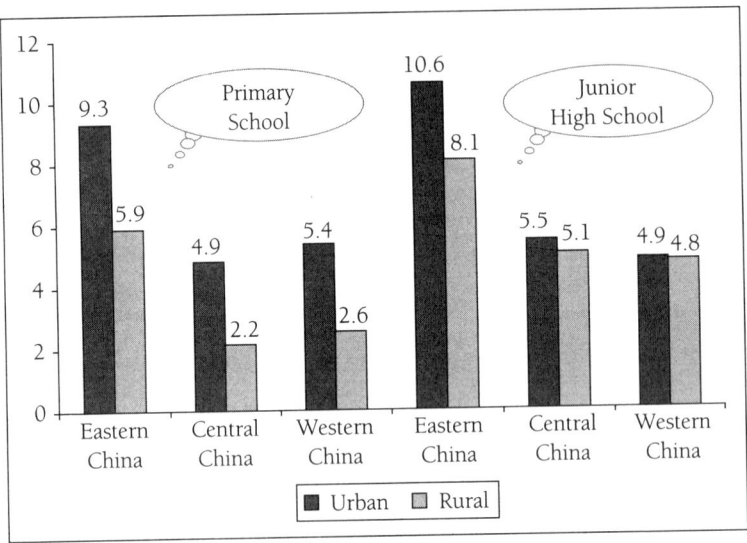

Source: MoE (2011).

below 3. The figure for junior high schools in rural areas was 10.8, half of that for junior high schools in urban areas (see Figure 1.8).

The number of computers and seats in multimedia classrooms per 100 students in regular senior high schools in China were 10.9 and 30.3. The average number of ICT teachers was 2.7 per school (see Table 1.16).

Table 1.16

Changes of Informatization Facilities in Regular Senior High Schools in China, 2009–2010

Region	Computers per 100 Students		Multimedia Seats per 100 Students		No. of ICT Teachers per School	
	2009	2010	2009	2010	2009	2010
Nationwide	10.4	10.9	28.9	30.3	2.6	2.7
Eastern China	14.0	14.6	42.7	43.1	3.0	3.2
Central China	7.8	8.2	19.2	21.0	2.3	2.4
Western China	8.8	9.2	22.0	24.0	2.4	2.5

Source: MoE (2011).

Figure 1.9

Number of Computers per 100 Students in Compulsory Education in Minority Areas in China, 2005–2010

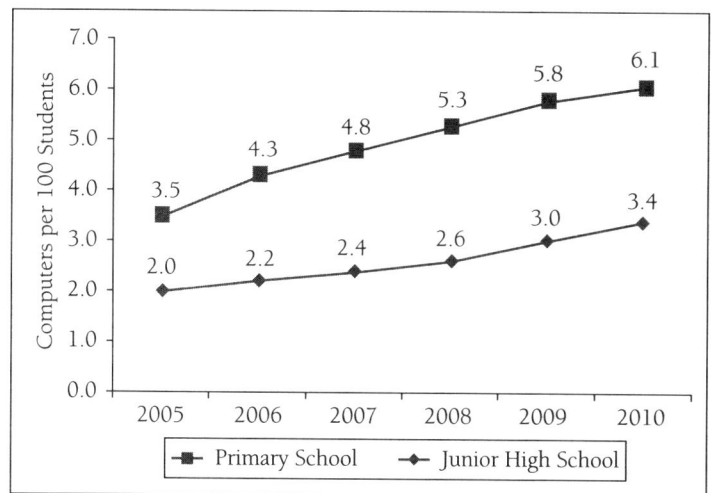

Source: MoE (2011).

The number of computers per 100 students in primary and junior high schools in minority areas were 3.4 and 6.1, respectively, 1.7 less than the national level; the percentage of primary and junior high schools in minority areas with digital campus were 5.6% and 24.9%, respectively, 10.3% and 21.5% lower than the national average (see Figure 1.9).

Insufficient Number and Training Opportunities for Rural ICT Teachers

In 2010, the average number of ICT teachers in primary schools in rural China was 0.4, less than one-third of the number for primary schools in urban China. The average number of ICT teachers in junior high schools in rural China was 1.5, 1.1 less than the number for junior high schools in urban China (see Table 1.17).

The method of training rural ICT teachers shows an interesting variation between levels. In primary schools, the proportion of ICT teachers versus those that received training in urban and rural China was, respectively, 2.0:1 and 2.9:1, a difference of 45%. There were apparently more training opportunities for teachers in urban areas. In junior high schools, the proportion in urban and rural China was, respectively, 2.5:1 and 2.2:1, a difference of only 12%. Junior high school teachers in rural China had more training opportunities (see Table 1.18). The number of ICT teachers versus those that received training in regular senior high schools in China was 1.6:1, with equal opportunities for teachers in eastern and western China.

There are six stages in the ability of information technology application (knowing, learning, understanding, familiarizing, adjustment, and innovation). Sample studies show that most teachers are still at the stage of "learning" (52%) and "knowing" (24%). As for ways of learning, 35% of teachers rely on "self-study," 29% on "school-organized training," 26% on "township/county-level computer training," and

Table 1.17

Average Number of ICT Teachers in Compulsory Education in China, 2010

Areas	Primary School (per person)			Junior High School (per person)		
	Total	*Urban*	*Rural*	*Total*	*Urban*	*Rural*
Nationwide	0.4	1.5	0.4	1.6	2.6	1.5
Eastern China	0.7	1.4	0.5	2.0	2.7	1.9
Central China	0.3	1.5	0.3	1.3	2.3	1.2
Western China	0.4	1.6	0.3	1.6	2.7	1.4

Source: MoE (2011).

Table 1.18

Number of ICT Teachers and Those Who Ever Attended Training in Compulsory Education in China, 2010

	Primary School			Junior High School		
Areas	*Total*	*Urban*	*Rural*	*Total*	*Urban*	*Rural*
Nationwide	2.7	2.0	2.9	2.2	2.5	2.2
Eastern China	2.3	1.6	2.7	2.0	1.9	2.1
Central China	3.1	2.8	3.1	2.4	3.1	2.3
Western China	3.0	2.5	3.0	2.3	3.9	2.1

Source: MoE (2011).

Table 1.19

Average per Capita Input for Informatization of Compulsory Education in China, 2010

	Primary School		Junior High School	
Areas	*Urban*	*Rural*	*Urban*	*Rural*
Nationwide	1,063	771	1,714	599
Eastern China	1,275	1,516	2,653	998
Central China	130	362	475	485
Western China	1,816	468	1,188	342

Source: MoE (2011).

9% on "national standard training for ICT teachers in primary and junior high schools."

Urban–Rural Gaps in Terms of Average per Capita Input for Informatization

In 2010, the average per capita input for informatization targeted at primary school students was CNY 803. The figure was CNY 599 for primary school students in rural China, only 35% of the level for primary school students in urban areas. The figure for junior high school students was CNY 829, CNY 771 for junior high school students in rural China, which was 73% of the level for urban areas (see Table 1.19).

Improvement of ICT Application and Consolidation of Information Resources

The challenge of improving the informatization of rural basic education has been addressed in several ways. In terms of technology infrastructure, education policy has stressed three areas, as follows:

1. Increased prevalence and promotion of information technology education in primary and junior high schools.
2. Increased prevalence and application of the Internet to enable students to take full advantage of online resources.
3. Developed modern distance education to bring affordable quality resources to rural areas.

In terms of skills and knowledge development, mandatory information technology courses operate as the main channel of training for primary and junior high school students. Almost 100% senior high schools, around 90% junior high schools in rural China, and 20% primary schools in rural China offer information technology courses. IT-based education has become the new norm. Schools that can afford it have commonly applied information technology and resources to course preparation and classroom activities. It is common for teachers to use online resources for course preparation.

Digital learning resources are a key component of information technology application. The Chinese government has employed different methods to create resources, such as inviting bids and investment to encourage companies to publish digital learning materials. A national basic education resources center has been built to meet the needs of primary and junior high schools in rural China. The resources center has seven categories of resources covering 36 majors, 4,129 hours of education resources, 2,869 hours of learning assistance, featured education, and video training resources, 12,507,000 entries of multimedia education resources (the figure updates on a daily basis), and different kinds of teaching materials for grade 1 to 9 students. Rural modern distance education projects have brought such resources to classrooms and this has had a significant effect on the improvement of teaching quality.

Informatization of Vocational Education in Rural China

Vocational Education[8] represents one of the least informatized areas of schooling in rural China. According to data of 2010, every 100 students in secondary vocational schools had 13.2 computers, 7.8 Internet access points, and 19 multimedia classroom seats (see Table 1.20).

In 2010, informatization input per student in secondary vocational schools in China was CNY 164.9, lower than the levels for primary and junior high schools. Total input of information technology training was CNY 18,164.1 (see Table 1.21). Informatization of vocational education in China lacks funding and a sound supporting environment for resource sharing and public service system, all of which impair the effectiveness of digital resources in vocational education.

Despite the difference in inputs, the prevalence of student computers, teacher computers, and multimedia facilities is high in secondary vocational schools. One-third of secondary vocational schools use multimedia facilities for more than 80% of the time. Most schools have digital teaching resources, out of which around 15% are provided by the government for free. Four types of resources are commonly used

Table 1.20

Changes in Informatization Facilities in Secondary Vocational Schools in China, 2009–2010

	Computers per 100 Students		No. of Network of Information Point per 100 Students		Multimedia Seats per 100 Students	
Areas	*2009*	*2010*	*2009*	*2010*	*2009*	*2010*
Nationwide	12.8	13.2	7.8	7.8	17.2	19.0
Eastern China	15.3	15.5	10.1	9.0	24.3	26.1
Central China	11.4	12.1	5.6	6.5	13.1	15.2
Western China	10.9	11.3	7.5	7.7	12.8	13.7

Source: MoE (2011).

[8] Vocational Education in Chinese context refers to education in secondary vocational schools and junior colleges.

Table 1.21

Average per Student Input of Informatization and Total Input of Information Technology Training in Secondary Vocational Schools in China, 2010

Areas	Expenditure per Student on Informatization (CNY)	Expenditure on Information Technology Training (1,000 CNY)
Nationwide	164.9	181,641
Eastern China	181.0	67,265
Central China	148.3	72,004
Western China	162.3	42,372

Source: MoE (2011).

by teachers at secondary vocational schools: digital teaching plans (34%), teaching design documents (22%), teaching resources (22%), and non-PPT teaching materials (15%). Moreover, 10% of secondary vocational schools have online teaching or assisted teaching platforms.

Informatization in Colleges and Universities in Western China

Western China represents the frontline of informatization progress in Chinese education. This is the area with the greatest economic, cultural, and physical challenges. In general, there are variations in the level of assets across China, for example, between local and centrally funded colleges and universities.

In 2010, the total assets of informatization facilities in colleges and universities in China reached CNY 62.49 billion, an increase of 19.4% year on year. Average assets per student reached CNY 2,383, an increase of 14.4% year on year. Average assets per student of colleges and universities under MoE reached CNY 5,567, an increase of 18.8% year on year. Average assets per student of local colleges and universities were only CNY 1,915, one-third of those under MoE (see Figure 1.10).

Geographical variations also exist. For every 100 students, regular colleges and universities in China owned 21.8 computers for teaching purposes. The figure for western China was 18.3 for colleges and

Figure 1.10

Average Informatization Assets per Student of Regular Colleges and Universities in China, 2009–2010

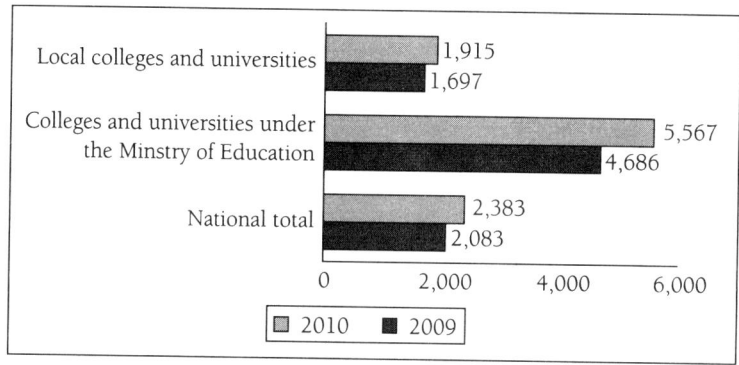

Source: MoE (2011).

Table 1.22

Number of Computers per 100 Students in Regular Colleges and Universities in China, 2005–2010

Higher Education Institutions/Areas	2005	2006	2007	2008	2009	2010
Nationwide	19.1	18.6	19.9	20.4	20.9	21.8
Directed under MoE	21.7	23.0	24.3	25.0	25.8	25.8
Regional	18.6	17.8	19.2	19.7	20.1	21.2
Eastern China	20.5	19.8	21.3	22.0	23.0	24.4
Central China	16.9	15.9	17.2	27.9	28.2	29.0
Western China	17.5	16.8	18.0	17.9	17.7	18.3

Source: MoE (2011).

universities. This compares to a national average of 21.2 for local colleges and universities (see Table 1.22). More than 95% of colleges and universities in China have reported the establishment campus networks, increased prevalence of computer and multimedia systems in their teaching activities, and improved application of information technology in teaching, scientific research, and management. In 2007, the "Campus Computer Network Construction Project for Universities in Western

China" had established advanced and stable campus network with access to CERNET in 143 colleges and universities.

From 2003 to 2010, MoE established "Online Course Construction Project of the New Century," "University High-quality Curriculum Construction Project," and "University Teaching Quality and Reform Project," and developed a series of basic and demonstration online courses, video open courses, case databases, test databases, curriculum platform, digital libraries, and digital museums to evaluate and support the more than 4,000 national-level top-quality courses.

In 2010, the average number of online courses taught in each college or university in China was 67.9. The figure was highest at 111.2 for undergraduate colleges and universities and lowest at 29.3 for professional collages. The average number of online courses taught in each college or university under MoE exceeded 400, whereas the figure was only 50.9 for local colleges and universities (see Figure 1.11). The discrepancy highlights the significant increases in output of informatization in establishments under direct MoE control.

Figure 1.11
Average Number of Online Courses per College or University in China, 2005–2010

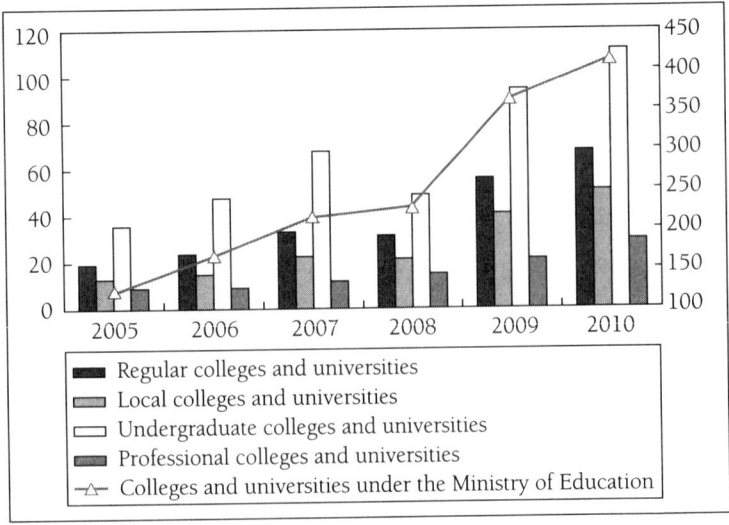

Source: MoE (2011).

According to data from 2007, 598 schools had computer science and technology courses and 11,280 information technology-related majors, with more than 2.78 million students. There were 37 national demonstration software colleges in China, 20 integrated circuit talent training centers, 40 LINUX training and promotion centers, and 49 colleges and universities with the department of information security.

E-learning in Colleges and Universities for Rural China

Continuing education, in the Chinese context, refers to educational activities, especially adult education, for all members of the society following regular school education. It is an important part of the lifelong learning system. In the current higher continuing education system in China, correspondence education fails to provide high-quality off-campus learning support owing to cost and technical issues. It is widely expected that, with the increasing use of the Internet, there will be change and reform for continuing education by distance methods.

Open universities are undergoing a program of reform to provide digital learning support and bolster mixed format of education with partial or full delivery by the Internet. Full-time learning for adult is no longer recommended and it is expected that its practice will eventually disappear. The main goal of current reforms of the open universities is to explore the format of an open university and to establish a distance open-learning mechanism and public service platform. Qualifications achieved by self-study are now regularly delivered through an online education resource sharing system and a digital public learning support service system. E-learning in colleges and universities has become a mainstream and distance continuing education, as well as public service platforms, has been constructed with the assistance of satellite, TV, and Internet access.

Since 1999, MoE has approved 68 colleges and universities together with the Open University of China to conduct pilot projects of modern distance education, including both degree and nondegree education by e-learning, to explore online teaching and management mechanisms and to build online resources. E-learning in these colleges and universities has been through several stages in its development, and has achieved notable improvement in terms of quality and teaching standards. Mechanisms have been established for teaching, management, service, and technology. Significant quantities now exist of digital learning resources, platforms, as well as thousands of subsidiary learning centers for the open colleges and universities. The stimulus has attracted an estimated more than 100,000 entrepreneurs in e-learning colleges and centers and hundreds of e-learning companies, creating an e-learning system, service, technology, policy, supervision, and industry chain with Chinese characteristics. As an example of the role of corporate supply, MoE specially approved Open Education Management System, Learning Management System DEE—Distant Education Environment, and China Cyber Learning to conduct pilot projects concerning off-campus learning support service systems. At the end of 2010, the 68 e-learning colleges and universities, as well as the Open University of China, had enrolled 11.15 million students and had 6.04 million graduates.

The development of the open colleges and universities takes place against a background of growing e-learning offer from all categories of Chinese institutions. In 2010, across all of China in all educational establishments there were 4.53 million students enrolled in e-learning with 1.74 million prospective students and 1.11 million graduates (see Figure 1.12).

The impact of these developments is potentially significant, to the extent that the open universities, colleges and associated learning centers serve rural population. The Chinese government certainly has encouraged colleges and universities to take full advantage of e-learning to promote the transfer of quality education resources to rural areas in western China and to provide talents for the construction of the new countryside. There are 13 regular colleges and universities, 14 provincial-level open universities, and more than 2,500 off-campus learning centers in western China that provide e-learning programs to a total of more than 1.5 million students.

Education Informatization for Teachers in Rural Primary and High School

The supply of teachers in all parts of China is a major issue, and the extent to which informatization can address problems is an important

Figure 1.12
Number of Students in Online Advanced Degree Education in China, 2000–2010

Unit: 1,000s

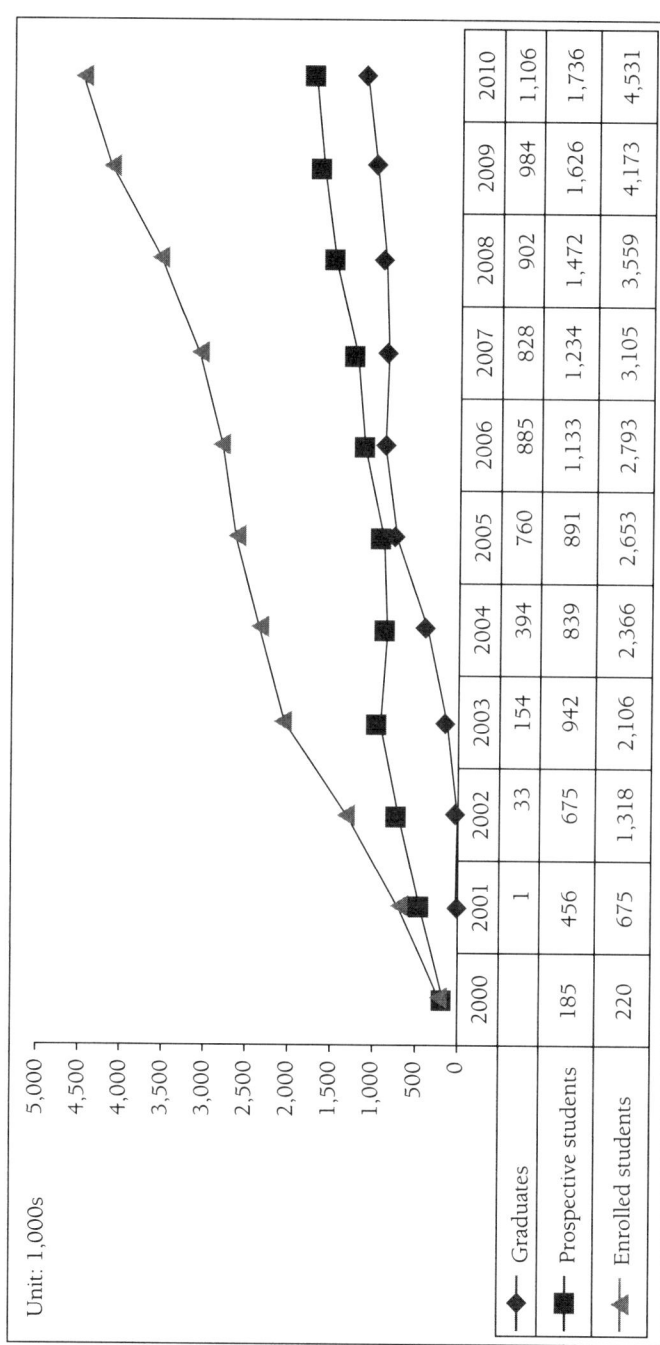

	2000	2001	2002	2003	2004	2005	2006	2007	2008	2009	2010
Graduates	185	1	33	154	394	760	885	828	902	984	1,106
Prospective students	220	456	675	942	839	891	1,133	1,234	1,472	1,626	1,736
Enrolled students		675	1,318	2,106	2,366	2,653	2,793	3,105	3,559	4,173	4,531

Source: MoE (2011).

Figure 1.13
Number of Full-time Teachers in China, 2009–2010

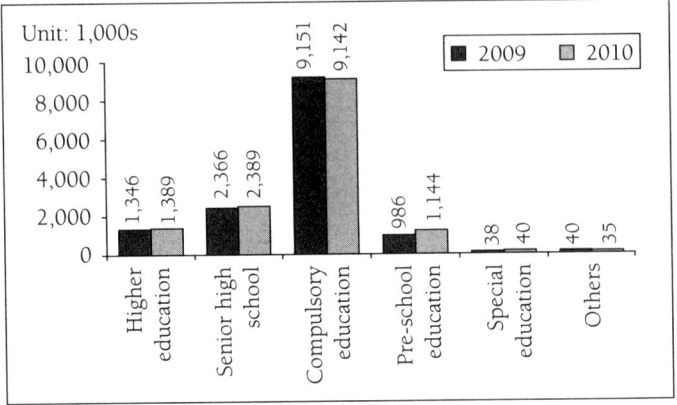

Source: MoE (2011).

question. In 2010, there were 14,139,000 full-time teachers in China (see Figure 1.13). The student–teacher ratio in regular universities was 17.3:1 in 2010; 15.5:1 for junior high schools in 2009 and 15.0:1 in 2010; 17.9:1 for primary schools in 2009 and 17.7:1 in 2010. The student-teacher ratio in secondary vocational schools was 26.1:1 in 2009 and 26.7:1 in 2010, reflecting a serious teacher shortage. The student–teacher ratio in kindergarten was 20.4:1 in 2009 and 20.6:1 in 2010, also showing an aggravated shortage of teachers (see Table 1.23).

In 2010, there were 9 million full-time teachers in compulsory education, out of which 5.6 million were in primary schools and 3.5 million in junior high schools. In terms of level of qualification, 75.4% of teachers in rural primary schools had junior college diplomas, an increase of 23.2% over 2005. The rural–urban gap in proportion of primary school teachers having junior college diplomas decreased from 25.8% in 2005 to 17.0% in 2010. In rural junior high schools, 59.4% of teachers had bachelor's degrees, an increase of 30.5% over 2005. The rural–urban gap in proportion of junior high school teachers having university diplomas decreased from 33.5% in 2005 to 23.2% in 2010 (see Table 1.24).

In November 2004, MoE released "Technology Competence Standards for Primary and Junior High School Teachers (Trial)," the first

Table 1.23
Student–Teacher Ratio in Schools in China, 2005, 2009, and 2010

Types of Educational Institutions	2005	2009	2010	Increase from 2005 to 2010 (%)
Ordinary Higher Education Institution	16.7	17.3	17.3	0.6
Ordinary Senior High School	18.5	16.3	16.0	–2.5
Vocational School	22.5	26.1	26.7	4.2
Junior High School	17.8	15.5	15.0	–2.8
Ordinary Primary School	19.4	17.9	17.7	–1.7
Preschool	19.9	20.4	20.6	0.7

Source: MoE (2011).

of its kind in China. The ministry also launched "National Primary and Junior High School Teacher Technology Ability Improvement Plan," and established a training, test, and certification system for school teachers. Alongside this, MoE has organized education technology training that focuses on the integration of information technology into the teaching process. More than 10 million teachers were trained, and their capacity of technology application was greatly improved.

Basic Experience of Rural Education Informatization in China

In summary, and looking at all the developments and case studies reviewed here, we may say that the Chinese government has launched a series of important projects and policy mechanisms to provide a solid basis for the development of rural education informatization. Education informatization infrastructure system in rural areas has been established everywhere, even if on a preliminary and pilot base in some locations. Most rural schools have campus network, access to the Internet through different channels, and information terminals. Digital learning resources have been transferred to rural areas through a range of different

Table 1.24
Levels of Education of Teachers in Compulsory Education in China, 2010

| Areas | Primary School Education (above junior college diplomas, %) | | | | Junior High School Education (above university diplomas, %) | | | |
	Total	Urban	Rural	Rural–Urban Division (%)	Total	Urban	Rural	Rural–Urban Division (%)
Nationwide	78.3	92.4	75.4	17.0	64.0	82.7	59.4	23.3
Eastern China	81.7	93.3	78.0	15.3	71.5	86.6	66.0	20.6
Central China	75.3	91.6	72.7	19.0	57.1	77.5	52.8	24.7
Western China	77.5	91.4	75.6	15.8	62.5	80.4	59.4	21.0

Source: MoE (2011).

arrangements. Application of rural informatization education has been extended and strengthened. Online education targeted specifically to western China and rural areas has been developing steadily. Education informatization has been an important element in delivering education equality in rural areas, improvement of education quality, and innovation of education formats. The development of rural education informatization in China for the past decade can be said to have demonstrated the following basic experiences:

First, participation of central government and all public services is a condition for rural education informatization in china. The Chinese government made the policy decision to drive the development of education modernization through education informatization, and made great investment in construction of campus networks for universities in the west, the school-to-school project, and the modern distance education project for rural primary and junior high schools. These projects have been significant not only as demonstrators but also as ways of reducing the risks and costs of adopting technology in rural schools. The initiatives of the central government have led local governments, schools, and enterprises to invest in the development, promotion, and application of education informatization. The education industry has become an important field for the sales of ICT products and services. National software, hardware, and integration service providers have played a key role in technology support for the national projects.

Second, it is an effective strategy to rapidly popularize rural education informatization through large-scale implementation that focuses on key problems and regional gaps. Based on the current situation in China, the Internet and satellite TV network were combined for rural schools. This provided rural schools with a digital and interactive education environment as well as Internet access within a short period of time and quickly brought digital infrastructure to rural teachers and students. The Chinese government did not force uniformity in the implementation of the projects but provided special support to western and rural schools based on regions and school conditions. For instance, the modern distance education project for rural primary and junior high schools adopted three formats based on different school categories in its implementation.

Third, integration and application are the internal drive for the development of rural education informatization. At the initial stage, rural education informatization faced the difficult tasks of establishing the network, setting up resource centers, and recruiting staff. The Chinese government has always regarded application as the key to promoting education informatization. Infrastructure and resources construction, as well as information technology education and education technology training, were all developed with a view to serving the reform and development of education, scientific research, and education management. Information technology education was incorporated into the curriculum to facilitate the reform of teaching and learning. E-learning was vigorously developed, the scale of education enlarged, and the quality of education improved. E-government was developed and a service-oriented government established. The importance of information technology in promoting effective and quality teaching has been widely acknowledged in the education community as well as among the general public, though such its significance is to be explored further.

Fourth, incentives for innovation and competition are an important way to promote the development of rural education informatization hand in hand with the IT industry. The broad application of information technology in education serves as an excellent driving force and a perfect test ground for innovations of the IT industry. The development of the new-generation IPV6 (Internet Protocol Version 6) network infrastructure, education technology standards, "Z+Z mathematics teaching platform," online cooperative learning platform, and other tools is suitable for rural education informatization in China. In the era of globalization and informatization, rural education informatization should not only borrow the advanced technologies from abroad, but also help enhance domestic innovations to increase the competitiveness internationally.

Needs Analysis of Rural Education Informatization in China

Although the development of rural education informatization in China has made a great progress, some difficulties and challenges still remain. These can be identified as follows: lack of effective long-term mechanism to ensure sustained input with a large population covered by the rural education system; poor coverage of informatization infrastructure leading to great regional gaps; insufficiency of high-quality digital learning resources in rural schools and low effectiveness of resources sharing and application; lack of an effective mechanism for the construction of high-quality education resources and poor involvement of market forces; insufficient integration of information technology and low level of application; lack of basic computer skills among some rural teachers who still could not use information technology in teaching; constraints for the training of rural teachers such as large population, rapid update of technologies, and limited training resources; insufficient integration and consolidation of the rural education management informatization system to enable effective resources consolidation, exchange, and sharing and to resolve the problem of "information isolated island." It still requires major efforts to promote rural education informatization.

Despite these yet unfinished challenges, China's experience has proven that rural education informatization is an effective way of changing the methods, solving related problems, and promoting the rapid and sustainable development of rural education. It provides strong support for the consolidation and sharing of education resources to promote education equality and narrow regional gaps. Moreover, it is an effective way to improve the quality and efficiency of rural education and to enhance the role of education services in the social development of rural areas.

One constructive way of analyzing the problems and achievements is to look at the range of diverse needs in the development of education informatization. These needs are not always aligned, and may even conflict at times.

- The need to promote digital learning is very widely dispersed. Education informatization needs to be improved in the basic education, vocational and adult education, higher education, and teacher education in rural areas. The objectives are similarly broad: to enable digital teaching and learning, advance the construction of the digital learning platform and resources, reform the traditional way of teaching, and make innovations in skills training.
- The need to develop distance education. It is important for further development of distance education, build distance education

platform, and construct supporting digital teaching resources to improve rural education resources and ensure education opportunities for people in rural areas.

- The need to build a lifelong learning system. A lifelong learning system facilitates the construction of a learning-oriented society. Efforts should be made to take full advantage of education institutions and on-campus and distance digital learning platform and resources to promote the development of learning-oriented rural communities.

- The need to provide teacher training. Teachers need to learn information technology for self-improvement and the improvement of their teaching quality. Therefore, it is important to build the capacity of rural teachers to use information technology through training, especially distance education and other innovative training mechanisms for primary and junior high school teachers.

- The need to improve education administrative management and service ability. It is important to promote digital administration to improve the quality, services, and efficiency of education administrative management.

- The need to construct digital campuses. Schools are the focus of education informatization. Digital campus is an important channel for schools to improve their teaching and administration, as well as the quality of services provided for teachers, students, and the society.

- The need to realize consolidation and sharing of education resources. There are many education institutions scattered all around China, with many overlapping projects. The regional gap of education resources is a great concern in the achievement of education equality and the harmonious development of the society. Education informatization could help consolidate education resources and build a platform and centers for resource sharing to facilitate the transfer of high-quality education resources to rural, central and western, less-developed, border, and minority areas so as to narrow regional gaps, reduce input, and promote the harmonious development of public education.

Trends Analysis of Rural Education Informatization in China

In my opinion, China's experience has shown that the development of rural education informatization involves building of solid education and information infrastructure and network environment, development and implementation of application projects, promotion of digital learning resources centers and public service systems, training information professionals, and construction of a socialized, multifaceted, and open security system. Based on China's experience, an ideal prescription for rural education informatization would feature the following principles:

- First, a support environment for typical application and public services should be constructed, most importantly the network environment and low-cost terminals. Access to different networks such as the Internet, telecommunication network, broadcast network, cable TV, and power grid, should be provided to users, and these networks should be interconnected. Priority should be given to rural and remote areas (central and western China) to bring digital learning resources and support services to all regions and to meet the learning needs of different groups at low costs.
- Public service, typical application, and shared resources are the purpose and core of education informatization. These play a role in the construction of digital learning resources centers and learning centers, the development and improvement of various application systems and tools, and the integration of information technology into education administration. In addition, it is important to build a service portal open to the general public, improve open administration and social supervision, and enhance the quality of digital education and learning support services.
- Mechanisms, policies, standards, and technologies are the "soft" factors that support the development of education informatization. Creating an adequate soft environment requires the establishment of safety mechanisms that integrate government regulation and market adjustment, improvement of relevant policies and

regulations, enhancement of the construction and application of standard systems, and technical breakthroughs.

- The development of information technology and information science is the precondition for the further development of education informatization. Information professionals are one of the keys of informatization. Therefore, it is important to improve training for informatization professionals. To this end, it is critical to stick to education innovation, promote the integration of information technology with different disciplines, improve the talent training system, and train informatization professionals that meet the needs of the society.

Rural education informatization in China has three main challenges in the future:

- narrowing of the digital gap between different regions to achieve education equality;
- sustained improvement of application and increase of investment return;
- the new curriculum reform.

Innovation and reform have become the core value and focus of the current development of education informatization. This means efforts in the future will need to focus on extending and accelerating the reform of the education system. Education informatization will spread and become more service oriented. Indeed, the national plan for education aims at "accelerating the process of education informatization," and the specific measures include:

- acceleration of infrastructure construction by increasing the computer ownership per 100 students in primary and junior high schools;
- provision of facilities for multimedia distance education to rural primary and junior high schools;
- promotion of the development and application of top-quality education resources;

- establishment of national digital education resources databases and public service platforms for effective sharing with a view to better distance degree education;
- construction of the national education management information system and public service platforms;
- completion of the national and provincial education information databases and a monitoring and analysis system for education quality, student mobility, resources allocation, and student employment status.

In March 2012, MoE released the Ten-year Development Plan for Education Informatization (2011–2020). The plan aims at the universal extension of education informatization infrastructure and application of education information resources by 2015. The plan also calls for major improvements in education management informatization, the preliminary establishment of security mechanisms for education informatization, in-depth application of information technology in education, and partial integration of information technology into education. In the longer term the plan also aims at further integration of information technology into education, and innovation, reform, and breakthroughs in several areas (see Table 1.25).

Tasks specifically for rural education informatization include:

- To give special support to the informatization in rural, remote, less-developed, and minority areas and the construction of public service systems to narrow the digital gaps among regions, urban and rural areas, and schools; to achieve 85% of Internet access in rural primary schools with a speed higher than 2Mbps by 2015; to achieve student–computer ratio of 10:1 for primary schools, 8:1 for junior high schools, 5:1 for senior high schools, and teacher–computer ratio of 3:1 for primary and junior high schools; to build multimedia classrooms in all rural primary and junior high schools and kindergartens; to achieve full coverage of digital teaching resources across the curriculum for all majors in rural primary and junior high schools; to ensure that 80% of rural primary schools have common course tools and individualized digital education resources.

Table 1.25
China's 10-year Development Plan for Education Informatization (2011–2020)

2015 *(stage of application of integration)*	2020 *(stage of integration and innovation)*
Broadband access, standardized facilities, preliminary integration of hybrid satellite-terrestrial network and establishment of basic environment	Full coverage of satellite-terrestrial network, seamless broadband Internet connection, prevalence of learning terminals, and improvement of basic environment
Increase the number and improve the quality of digital learning resources; higher integration of resources and curriculum; preliminary integration of information technology and teaching	Greatly improve the scale and coverage of resources; further integration of information technology into teaching; reform teaching format and methods
Consolidation of current education management and development of new systems to realize "data exchange"	Comprehensive application, development, and improvement of education information management and decision making platform to realize "process repeatability"
Preliminary establishment of support team for technology research and development, operation and maintenance service, management decision making, as well as funding input, and talent training mechanism	Reform of talent training and scale-up of service team; further application of standards; establishment of sustainable development mechanism
All students receive information technology education and all teachers pass the basic level of education technology competency standards	All students have basic information technology skills and teachers pass the medium level education technology competency standards
Preliminary integration of information technology and education to change education environment; full integration to enable partial reform; strong influence of information technology on education system	Establishment of open education informatization support environment and an education informatization support system for learning-oriented society

Source: MoE (2012).

- To improve informatization by building digital campuses for vocational schools, especially in rural areas; to realize universal coverage of distance vocational education in rural and remote areas; to ensure sharing of vocational education resources with schools in rural areas.
- To further improve the construction of university informatization infrastructure in central and western China; to enhance resource building and application capacity building, as well as education management and service informatization; to promote balanced development of informatization in universities; to create suitable forms of support for informatization in universities in western China and encourage sharing of teaching and scientific research resources.
- To increase the input on education informatization to facilitate its development, especially by providing funds to rural and remote areas.

Appendix: Summary Tables of the Cases on iERD from China

Table A1.1
Characteristics of Context-specific ICT within Successful iERD Projects

Project	Adaptation of ICT to the Rural Context
ICT Integration in Rural Classrooms: Modern Distance Education Project in Primary and Middle Schools in Rural China	The project trains primary and secondary school teachers in Central and West China through online material and satellite-based content that is available even in those areas with poor Internet connection. Students can follow via Internet classes which are hold in other schools.

Table A1.1 continued

Table A1.1 continued

Project	Adaptation of ICT to the Rural Context
Educational Technology Promotes the Quality of In-class Teaching in Rural Primary and Middle Schools: BNU Pilot Program on Leapfrog Development of Basic Education	Teachers are trained both with print and digital material. Furthermore, each school receives a package with digital and print material that complements the information provided in the traditional workbooks of the curriculum.
Open Distance Education Training "Capable to work, willing to stay" Talents for Rural Areas: "One Village, One College Student" Program by The Open University of China	Participants are trained through a combination of paper-version textbooks, DVD-based self-study, TV teaching, online teaching, face-to-face group instructions, one-on-one tutoring, and learning groups.
Spreading Knowledge, Eradicating Poverty: Tsinghua University Poverty Alleviation Project through Distance Education	The project equips selected training schools for teachers, middle and primary schools, vocational schools and other training institutions with satellite signal receiving devices and educational resources free of charge. Learners can download courseware and flexibly arrange time for study. It enhances the flexibility for teaching centers to adjust training contents and schedule, and enables courses of multiple training classes to be integrated and played on demand.
Agriculture-related Educational Training and S&T Promotion Service System: Internet-based Union of Universities for Agricultural Science & Technology and Education	The delivered training to rural students studying agriculture and forestry is tailored to the interests of rural students, and focuses for example on practical skills, information knowledge and skills, entrepreneurial knowledge and practice, village management, small town building, rural sanitation and epidemic prevention, and transfer of rural labor, and academic education for related people. The used ICT are, e.g., databases with agricultural information, videos on agricultural practices and print material distributed to the locally launched "demonstration

Table A1.1 continued

Table A1.1 continued

Project	Adaptation of ICT to the Rural Context
	centers." In order to allow working students to enroll in these courses, distance teaching, face-to-face tutoring, video-on-demand systems, social practice and field visits are organized. Some students (farmers) receive learning packages that allow them to learn without Internet from home.
The Application of Extensive Distance Training to Professional Development of Rural Teachers: The Training Program for Rural Elite Teachers in Central and West China	Rural schools are equipped with computers, DVD and satellite devices that allow teachers to access easily quality education material and to prepare efficiently their lessons. The teaching material is also available in minority languages.
Distance Education for Teachers in Less Developed Areas: Case of School of Distance Education, Shaanxi Normal University	The project offers teachers the possibility to enroll in distance education bases training sessions that combine real-time teaching and non-real-time teaching. They learn from home or in one of the 12 county learning centers where the material and Internet connection is available. The training is adapted to their schedule and IT environment. As the Internet bandwidth is very low in the target area, the courseware is also composed of CDs as well as video and audio programs.
Online Training for Substitute Teachers in Underdeveloped Areas of Economically Developed Cities: Experience from Guangdong Province in China	The project provide the computer rooms and multimedia classrooms in local teacher training colleges and central primary schools in a planned way to the substitute teachers who did not have access to the Internet and couldn't play DVDs at home. The project also dedicatedly organized eight remote video Q&A activities to specifically help trainees solve a variety of typical problems they encountered in their learning and teaching practices.

Table A1.1 continued

Table A1.1 continued

Project	Adaptation of ICT to the Rural Context
Innovative Teachers Achieve Better IT Integration in Teaching: Ministry of Education – Microsoft (China) "Partners in Learning" Project	Teachers are trained by Microsoft with a specific curriculum for training of middle and primary school IT teachers and through online resources and print material (manuals).

Source: Author.

Table A1.2
Role Distribution within Partnerships of Successful iERD Projects

Project and Target Area	Main Partners and Role
ICT Integration in Rural Classrooms: Modern Distance Education Project in Primary and Middle Schools in Rural China	• Ministry of Education: *Conceptualization, funding, training* • Local governments: *Monitoring, funding* • Educational Technology Association: *IT expertise, content development* • People's Education Press: *Content development* • Chinese Education Satellite Broadband Network: *Provision of satellite network*
Educational Technology Promotes the Quality of In-class Teaching in Rural Primary and Middle Schools: BNU Pilot Program on Leapfrog Development of Basic Education	• Modern Educational Technology Research Institute of Beijing Normal University: *Conceptualization, monitoring* • Ford Foundation, Beijing Western Sunshine Rural Development Foundation, Give2Asia Foundation and Chen Yet-Sen Family Foundation: *Funding*
Open Distance Education Training "Capable to Work, Willing to Stay" Talents for Rural Areas: "One Village, One College Student" Program by The Open University of China	• The Open University of China: *funding, conceptualization, content development* • 42 provincial-level radio and TV universities and 1,171 affiliated teaching stations: *Monitoring, IT expertise*
Spreading Knowledge, Eradicating Poverty: Tsinghua University Poverty Alleviation Project through Distance Education	• Tsinghua University: *Conceptualization, design, funding, monitoring, content development* • Local education centers: *Monitoring, training, support*

Table A1.2 continued

Table A1.2 continued

Project and Target Area	Main Partners and Role
Agriculture-Related Educational Training and S&T Promotion Service System: Internet-based Union of Universities for Agricultural Science & Technology and Education	• Ministry of Education, Ministry of Science and Technology, and Ministry of Agriculture: *Funding* • Union of Universities for Agricultural Science & Technology and Education: *Conceptualization, monitoring, content development* • Various agricultural experts, e.g., China Association of Senior Scientists and Technicians: *Content development*
The Application of Extensive Distance Training to Professional Development of Rural Teachers: The Training Program for Rural Elite Teachers in Central and West China	• National Training Program Office/Ministry of Education: *Monitoring, funding* • Teachers.com.cn: *Content development, conceptualization, support* • National expert teams: *Content development*
Distance Education for Teachers in Less Developed Areas: Case of School of Distance Education, Shaanxi Normal University	• School of Distance Education, Shaanxi Normal University: *Conceptualization, design, funding, monitoring* • 12 local off-campuses/learning centers: *Local monitoring, support*
Online Training for Substitute Teachers in Underdeveloped Areas of Economically Developed Cities: Experience from Guangdong Province in China	• The Department of Education of Guangdong Province: *Coordination and planning, organizational leadership, and quality supervision* • South China Normal University: *IT expertise* • Competent education authorities of prefecture-level cities: *Training, support* • Teacher training colleges in counties (districts): *Training*
Innovative Teachers Achieve Better IT Integration in Teaching: Ministry of Education - Microsoft (China) "Partners in Learning" Project	• Ministry of Education: *Conceptualization, funding* • Microsoft China: *IT expertise, funding, field monitoring, content development, training* • Beijing Normal University/Yizihyou University/East China Normal University: *Content development*

Source: Author.

Table A1.3

Participatory Approaches during the Preparation and Implementation of Successful iERD Projects

Project	Preparation Phase	Implementation Phase
ICT Integration in Rural Classrooms: Modern Distance Education Project in Primary and Middle Schools in Rural China	• Needs assessments in the provinces contribute to the design of the project modules.	• The provinces set up their own project leading groups headed by the government leaders with respective management systems and were responsible for the planning in their own regions, the theoretical approval of the plan, the tendering and procurement, the organization and management, as well as the inspection and acceptance. The municipal and county-level governments also established the leading groups and working organizations headed by the government leader that were responsible for the detailed implementation of the project.
Educational Technology Promotes the Quality of In-class Teaching in Rural Primary and Middle Schools: BNU Pilot Program on Leapfrog Development of Basic Education		• Teachers regularly report back to the principal teacher team in order to reflect on issues and improve the functioning and content of the program.

Open Distance Education Training "Capable to work, willing to stay" Talents for Rural Areas: "One Village, One College Student" Program by The Open University of China	• Provincial-level radios deliver courses and are field partners of the centrally located Open University. • The local teachings stations manage autonomously the program in their area.
Spreading Knowledge, Eradicating Poverty: Tsinghua University Poverty Alleviation Project through Distance Education	• Distance training centers are created in selected educational institutions in rural areas and are in charge of the local implementation of the project.
Agriculture-Related Educational Training and S&T Promotion Service System: Internet-based Union of Universities for Agricultural Science & Technology and Education	• 10 local centers, called demonstration bases, are set up in the field and managed by local groups: The Information Service Leadership Group and Office, an expert team and a IT Team. These local groups are the bridge between the universities and the rural areas.
The Application of Extensive Distance Training to Professional Development of Rural Teachers: The Training Program for Rural Elite Teachers in Central and West China	• Organization of needs assessments: The results of these assessments influenced the project design. • Organization of meetings with administrators and tutors in order to explain them the purpose of the distance teaching program. • The education administrations at the municipal and county levels are responsible at the outset for defining needs and providing funding. During the implementation, they were responsible for participant evaluation by questionnaires which they also analyzed. The administrations summarized all local work and submitted reports to the Provincial Program Office after the completion of the training.

Table A1.3 continued

Table A1.3 continued

Project	Preparation Phase	Implementation Phase
Distance Education for Teachers in Less Developed Areas: Case of School of Distance Education, Shaanxi Normal University	• Surveys and needs assessments were conducted in the 12 counties of the implementation area.	• Local learning centers are established in the rural areas and employ rural inhabitants.
Online Training for Substitute Teachers in Underdeveloped Areas of Economically Developed Cities: Experience from Guangdong Province in China	• Demand survey in two counties which contribute the design and implementation plans.	• Strengthen hardware and software construction of training platforms and organize experts to prepare training handouts and record training courses.
Innovative Teachers Achieve Better IT Integration in Teaching: Ministry of Education–Microsoft (China) "Partners in Learning" Project		• Interviews with local teachers played an important role during the evaluation phase.

Source: Author.

Table A1.4
Training and Support Activities

Project	Training Characteristics	Informal Support and Assistance
ICT Integration in Rural Classrooms: Modern Distance Education Project in Primary and Middle Schools in Rural China	• Training is imparted on the national, provincial, municipal and school level in order to explain how to integrate efficiently the DVDs, satellite based material and computers in the lessons. Teachers were trained to be tutors and train other teachers.	• A technical support service systems of national, provincial, municipal and county levels is available.
Educational Technology Promotes the Quality of In-class Teaching in Rural Primary and Middle Schools: BNU Pilot Program on Leapfrog Development of Basic Education	• Teachers engaged in the pilot research are enrolled in training sessions on theories, modes, methods and technology. Basic training is done collectively for all teachers involved, while enhancement training is implemented by issuing training materials and one-on-one tutorial as well as e-learning modules.	• The research team regularly visits pilot schools to organize activities such as watching and learning, comment on outstanding classes, class attending, class evaluation, seminars, and guidance on teaching designs.
Open Distance Education Training "Capable to work, willing to stay" Talents for Rural Areas: "One Village, One College Student" Program by The Open University of China	• Open University of China has set up the Program teaching center team, a group of the best teachers from the provincial radio and TV universities. The team members use seminars and peer exchange to explore problems and develop with solutions, including sharing of teaching resources, and teacher training.	• The local teaching stations provide support for the local implementation, including teaching management, guidance, coordination and policy support.

Table A1.4 continued

Table A1.4 continued

Project	Training Characteristics	Informal Support and Assistance
Spreading Knowledge, Eradicating Poverty: Tsinghua University Poverty Alleviation Project through Distance Education	• Training is imparted on a face to face and distance basis and adapted to teachers and students.	• The distance education centers are composed of information specialists and technical and act as local help desk.
Agriculture-Related Educational Training and S&T Promotion Service System: Internet-based Union of Universities for Agricultural Science & Technology and Education	• Farmers can enroll either in distance courses via the demonstration centers (local field centers) or benefit from the "Learn to Farm" digital resource package that trains them with digital, but offline material.	• Participants can obtain support and advice in the local demonstration centers.
The Application of Extensive Distance Training to Professional Development of Rural Teachers: The Training Program for Rural Elite Teachers in Central and West China	• Administrators and tutors receive training. • Teachers participate in online courses and seminars and are supported by dedicated tutors. Online group discussions per are organized.	• Teacher.com.cn provides support via email and a call center. • Teaching administration personnel provides all-round follow-up services. Teacher.com.cn has a policy of "dedicated management" for each program in each province, assigned dedicated teaching administration personnel to each province to follow up duties in online and offline program management.

Distance Education for Teachers in Less Developed Areas: Case of School of Distance Education, Shaanxi Normal University	• Training is imparted in the 12 county learning centers.	• The project developed the following material in order to provide support and to specify requirements: Student Manual, Training Manual for Teachers, Management Manual for Learning Centers and Staff Manual.
Online Training for Substitute Teachers in Underdeveloped Areas of Economically Developed Cities: Experience from Guangdong Province in China	• Training is imparted on a face to face and distance basis.	• The project opened computer rooms and multimedia classrooms in local teacher training colleges and central primary schools, organized eight remote video Q & As and face-to-face instruction.
Innovative Teachers Achieve Better IT Integration in Teaching: Ministry of Education—Microsoft (China) "Partners in Learning" Project	• Training for IT teachers is imparted and includes basic training, intermediate and advanced training, adapted to the skills level of teachers.	

Source: Author.

Table A1.5

Development and Enhancement Strategies of Successful iERD Projects

Project	Development Strategy
ICT Integration in Rural Classrooms: Modern Distance Education Project in Primary and Middle Schools in Rural China	• Progressive expansion of the project to an increasing number of provinces. • Conduction of evaluations and needs assessments. • Improvement of used technology/replacement process.
Educational Technology Promotes the Quality of In-class Teaching in Rural Primary and Middle Schools: BNU Pilot Program on Leapfrog Development of Basic Education	• Regularly organization of tests in pilot schools and classes and conduction of comparative tests in order to evaluate the impact of the program. Feedback from education authorities, teachers and parents is sought in time to improve the program design. • The pilot program has evolved through four phases by the end of 2012, namely preliminary establishment of theoretical approach, improvement of theoretical approach, deepening of pilot exploration and expansion of pilot areas.
Open Distance Education Training "Capable to work, willing to stay" Talents for Rural Areas: "One Village, One College Student" Program by The Open University of China	• Conduction of surveys among participants in order to evaluate efficiency and impacts of the program. • Conduction of data reports. • Continuous expansion of the program to other rural universities.
Spreading Knowledge, Eradicating Poverty: Tsinghua University Poverty Alleviation Project through Distance Education	• Conduction of impact evaluation. • Progressive expansion of the project to more schools. • Development of courses and management procedures.

Table A1.5 continued

Table A1.5 continued

Project	Development Strategy
Agriculture-Related Educational Training and S&T Promotion Service System: Internet-based Union of Universities for Agricultural Science & Technology and Education	• Continuous content development. • It is planned to extent the distribution of "Learn to Farm" packages to more villages.
The Application of Extensive Distance Training to Professional Development of Rural Teachers: The Training Program for Rural Elite Teachers in Central and West China	• Continuous evaluation and needs assessment (questionnaires, surveys) in order to evaluate the amount of participants, challenges they face and assess the quality of courses. • Continuous content development and extension of offered courses.
Distance Education for Teachers in Less Developed Areas: Case of School of Distance Education, Shaanxi Normal University	• Overall evaluation of the project after three years of implementation. • Progressive expansion in form of multiple off-campus centers and learning centers.
Online Training for Substitute Teachers in Underdeveloped Areas of Economically Developed Cities: Experience from Guangdong Province in China	• Demand survey. • Content development. • Formative assessment for each trainee. • Investigation on the effects of the training.
Innovative Teachers Achieve Better IT Integration in Teaching: Ministry of Education—Microsoft (China) "Partners in Learning" Project	• Conduction of reports, questionnaires, field interviews and on-site surveys by a dedicated panel of investigation in order to evaluate the attitudes of local teachers towards the training and their IT skills. Analysis of progress and results.

Source: Author.

Bibliography

Brief Statistical Analysis of Educational Development in China in 2010. Retrieved from http://www.moe.edu.cn/publicfiles/business/htmlfiles/moe/s6200/list.html (accessed February 27, 2012).

China Internet Network Information Center. (2012). 29th Statistical Report on Internet Development in China. Retrieved from http://www.cnnic.cn/research/bgxz/tjbg/201201/t20120116_23668.html (accessed January 16, 2012).

Huang, R., Jiang, X., & Zhang, J. (2007). *Innovation and Reform: The Core Value of Education Informatization.* Beijing: Science Press.

International Telecommunication Union. (2011). The Information Society 2011. Retrieved from http://www.itu.int/net/pressoffice/backgrounders/general/pdf/5.pdf (accessed March 1, 2014).

Li, Daoliang. (2011). *Report on Rural Informatization Development in China.* Beijing: Publishing House of Electronics Industry.

Lv, X., & Qin, J. (2011). National Report on Education for All in China 2010. Chinese National Commission for UNESCO, UNESCO International Research and Training Center for Rural Education & Nation Center for Education Development Research.

MoE (Ministry of Education). (2011). *Construction and Application of Education Informatization in China Special Research Report.* Beijing: Higher Education Press. Retrieved from www.moe.edu.cn

———. (2012). Ten-year Development Plan for Education Informatization (2011–2020). Retrieved from http://www.moe.edu.cn/publicfiles/business/htmlfiles/moe/s3342/201203/xxgk_133322.html (accessed March 12, 2013).

Zeng, H. (2012). *Study on Public Support Service System of E-learning.* Beijing: Higher Education Press.

Zeng, H., & Fan, X. (2007). Reflections on the New Framework of Education Informatization Development: Guided by Public Service, Typical Application, and Shared Resources. *Distance Education in China,* 3:11–16.

Zeng, H., & Ma, G. (2009). *About Online Education.* Beijing: Higher Education Press.

Zhou, H. (2011). *Analysis and Prediction of Informatization in China.* Beijing: Social Sciences Academic Press.

2

ICT Integration in Rural Classrooms*

Wang Zhuzhu, Zeng Haijun, and Wang Ying

Overview

The Modern Distance Education Project (MDEP) targeted at rural primary and middle schools (hereafter referred to as "the Project") is a large-scale distance education construction project focused on the

* This case report is mainly based on Building the Bridge to the Future: Modern Distance Education Project for China's Rural Primary and Middle Schools written by the Project Office and published by People's Education Press in February. This report summarizes and analyzes the implementation background, contents and effects of the modern distance education project for rural primary and middle schools in China during 2003–2007. Before, during, and after this, the Chinese government also implements other relevant basic education informatization projects, which also involve information infrastructure construction, resource development, teacher training, application, management, support services, standards, key technology, industrial development and other aspects in rural primary and middle schools so as to jointly promote educational informatization in rural China. For instance, in 2010, 100 students in

integration of modern information and communication technologies (ICT). The intended beneficiaries were learners and teachers in rural primary and middle schools in 23 provinces (autonomous regions and municipalities). The MDEP was established in partnership with the Xinjiang Production and Construction Corps. The Project is a commitment by the Chinese government to address the concerns of quality basic education resources in rural areas by focusing on improving the quality of rural education through informatization and promoting balanced development of urban and rural education as part of attempts to realize educational equity.

The Project started in 2003 and ended in 2007. The central and local governments invested a total of RMB 11.1 billion to equip 360,000 rural primary and middle schools and teaching stations in the central and western China. The Project involved the distribution and use of 440,142 sets of CD players for teaching, 264,905 sets of satellite teaching receiving devices and 40,858 sets of computer classrooms.

The central government also provided 10% of the grant funds for five provinces in eastern China to support undeveloped areas and promote modern distance education in local rural primary and middle schools. Together, these devices formed a basic digitized teaching and learning environment within the broader campus network. Its purpose was to deliver excellent resources to rural schools through the above three technical modes. It creates the conditions for rural primary and middle schools to deliver IT courses and utilize multimedia teaching in different disciplines to improve the quality of education. The aim was to enable millions of Chinese rural students to share quality educational resources with urban students, to narrow the "digital divide" between urban and rural education in China, and to promote the balanced development of

---

rural primary and junior middle schools had 3.5 and 6.0 computers for teaching separately, the proportions of campus network building in rural primary and junior middle schools were 12.6% and 42.6%, which had distinguish changes compared to that when the project completed in 2007. Chinese government has formulated Educational Informatization Development Plan 2011–2020, which continues focusing on supporting the informatization in primary and middle schools and the construction of public service system in rural areas, remote and poor areas and minority areas with the efforts to narrow down the gaps among regions, cities and schools.

compulsory education. This project has been hailed as "the bridge to the future" and "the most welcomed project."

Owing to unfavorable conditions for education informatization[1] in Chinese rural communities, the Project experienced many implementation challenges. These include limited human resource capacity and follow-up funding, inadequacy of devices, low levels of use and integration of ICT in teaching, and lack of resource infrastructure. In an attempt to consolidate the gains made through the Project, the Chinese government continued to invest in modern distance education in rural primary and middle schools through the implementation of other relevant projects. The 2011–2020 Plan prioritizes the educational informatization in rural primary and middle schools and the construction of the public service system in an attempt to explore low-cost and high-efficiency solutions for the delivery of basic education in rural China.

Implementation Background

In 2002, China's rural population was 780 million, comprising 60.91% of the total population of 1,285 billion. At the time there were 421,427 rural primary and middle schools which equaled 81% of the total number of rural primary and middle schools. The number of students was 112,505,063, accounting for 60% of the total number of rural students, while full-time teachers in rural primary and middle schools totaled 5,364,728, accounting for 53% of the total number of teachers in China (National Bureau of Statistics of China, 2003).[2] Under the influence of

---

[1] Educational informatization is the concept in the cultural context of Chinese language, which refers to "ICT in Education" in the common concept internationally. It refers to the process of using ICT to promote educational reform and development in the field of education.

[2] The national statistics in this report do not include Hong Kong and Macao Special Administrative Regions or Taiwan Province, except for the administrative divisions, the territory areas and forest resources. In the educational statistics of China, they are categorized by regions into three types, which are urban, county or town, and rural, while in the population statistics, they are only urban and rural categories. In the report, rural areas especially refer to the rural areas below county or town; but in other reports released by Ministry of Education,

a number of factors including an undeveloped local economy, financial difficulties and serious shortages of investment in education, rural education has historically had a weak foundation, resulting in compulsory education[3] being far behind the national average. By 2002, 410 county-level administrative units in western China were still not realizing China's "two basics" programs.[4] As a result, the Chinese government prioritized the development of rural education that involved significant effort to promote the balanced development of education, which is not just the strong aspiration of millions of rural citizens.

Facing the opportunities and challenges brought by the rapid development of ICT, the Chinese government issued the *Education Revitalization Action Plan in 21st Century* in 1999, which proposed the implementation of the MDEP to form an open education network and build a lifelong learning system. Ministry of Education (MoE) held a National Conference of Information Technology Education in Primary and Middle Schools in October 2000, which proposed to use educational informatization to drive the modernization of education and to promote the leap-forward development of basic education. At the conference, it was decided to establish IT courses in 90% of primary and middle schools in China within 5–10 years, and to implement a campus access to ICT project[5] in the primary and middle schools in China. The latter enabled about 90%

---

sometimes it combines county or town with rural areas in the concept of "an extensive rural area."

[3] China implements nine-year compulsory education system, which generally means six years of primary school and three years of junior middle school. Compulsory education is totally free of charge, with the fund guaranteed by the State Council and local governments at all levels in accordance with the *Law on Compulsory Education*.

[4] The "two basics" refers to the basic implementation of the nine-year compulsory education and basic elimination of illiteracy among young and middle-aged people.

[5] Campus Access to ICT Project is the construction and application projects of educational informatization for all primary and middle schools across the country. Modern distance education project for rural primary and middle schools focus on rural primary and middle schools in the central and western regions, which is the top priority of the constructive contents of Campus Access to ICT Project.

of independent primary and middle schools all over China, to access the Internet or connect to Chinese education satellite broadband network[6] so that teachers and students in primary and middle schools can share online educational resources.

In order to overcome the "digital divide" and extend quality educational resources to every rural school, the Chinese government implemented a series of educational projects since 1999, such as the Training Project for Tomorrow Female Teachers, Campus Access to ICT in Primary and Middle Schools, MoE—Li Ka-shing Foundation "Modern Distance Education Project for Western Primary and Middle Schools," Poverty Reduction Demonstration Project of Modern Distance Education, Demonstration Project of the Establishment of Campus Network Classrooms in Primary and Middle Schools and Rural Computer Network Information Stations in the Central and Western China, China—UNDP Distance Education Projects and China—UNICEF Love Students Distance Education Project (Yang, 2008).

These projects and sample pilots greatly promoted the educational development in the western region and rural areas in China and brought hope to underdeveloped areas. They have not only provided these areas with a large number of information technology equipments and educational resources, but also trained several discipline backbone and IT teachers (Wei, 2010).

On the basis of implementation of the above projects, in order to further strengthen rural primary and middle school education, in May 2003, approved by the State Council, MoE,[7] National Development and Reform Commission[8] and Ministry of Finance[9] (hereafter referred to as

[6] Chinese education satellite broadband network was opened in October 2000, which provides services of all kinds of educational TV programs, audio broadcast and IP data broadcast to China.

[7] Ministry of Education is the ministry under the State Council in charge of national education academics and language and characters.

[8] National Development and Reform Commission, as the functional institution of the State Council, is a macro-control department in charge of comprehensive study of the economic and social development policies to keep the overall balance and guide the overall economic system reform.

[9] Ministry of Finance is the ministry under the State Council in charge of the nation's financial affairs.

the three ministries), jointly issued a document about the implementation of modern distance education pilot demonstration project for rural primary and middle schools in the central and western China. At the National Rural Education Conference held in September 2003, it further proposed "to basically equip middle schools with computer classrooms, primary schools with satellite teaching receiving devices, teaching CD player devices and teaching CDs, and primary teaching stations with teaching CD player devices and teaching CDs in rural areas of China within five years. Together these served to drive informatization in the development of rural education." Thus, modern distance education project for rural primary and middle schools has become the "five-year plan" for China's basic education since 2003.

Implementation Plan

According to the requirements of "overall plan, first pilot, experience summarization and key breakthroughs," the three ministries studied and formulated the framework for pilot projects in November 2003. This pilot experience informed the overall implementation plan of the project in November 2004.[10]

Project Objectives and Main Tasks

The Project covered all rural primary and middle schools, regardless of their basic conditions, regional situations, school sizes, and teaching levels. The beneficiaries of the Project included all teachers and students in rural primary and middle schools, as well as rural cadres who are the local villagers. The Project was led through implementation. It is a comprehensive systematic project integrated with the construction of educational information infrastructure, the establishment of educational resources, teacher training, and management assurance as shown in Figure 2.1.

---

[10] Ministry of Education, National Development and Reform Commission and Ministry of Finance. Overall Implementation Plan of Modern Distance Education Project for Rural Primary and Middle Schools. Retrieved from http://www.sdpc.gov.cn/fzgh/ghwb/115zxgh/P020070924559936413170.pdf (accessed November 22, 2004).

Figure 2.1
The Overall Framework of the Project

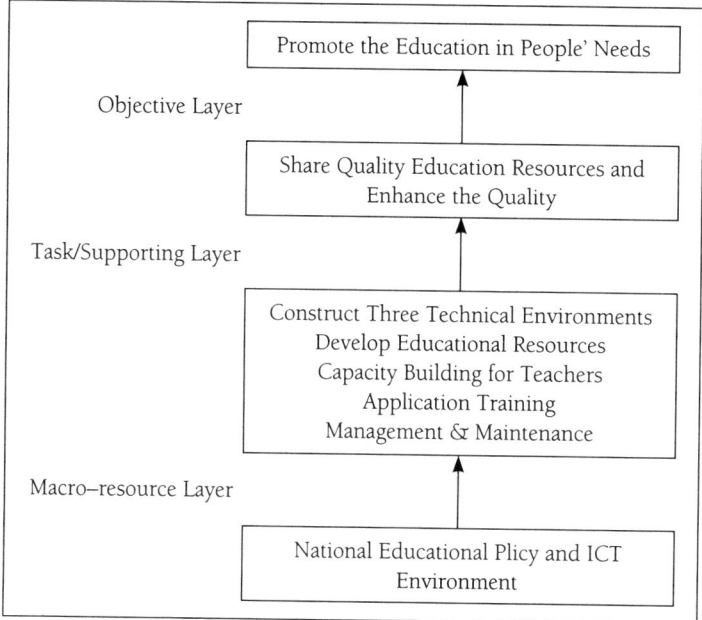

Source: Office of Modern Distance Education Project for China's Rural Primary and Middle Schools (2009).

Objectives: By 2007, the foundation for the gradual popularization of information technology education in rural schools was established. Quality educational resources were provided to rural primary and middle schools continuously, so were teacher training, in order to improve the quality of education in rural primary and middle schools. Rural schools played an important role in promoting local cultural and information exchange, which served the delivery of rural vocational and technical education, adult education, rural cadre education, and rural economic and social development and transformation.

Main tasks: To equip 37,500 rural junior middle schools across the country with computer classrooms, 384,000 rural primary schools across the country with satellite teaching receiving stations, and about 11 rural primary teaching points with teaching CD player devices and sets of teaching CDs;[11] to strengthen the construction of teaching resources with more than 4,000 hours of CD teaching resources, more than 11,000 hours of satellite teaching resources and more than 6,000 hours of computer network teaching resources; to strengthen teacher trainings such as to train 1–2 faculties who are familiar with teaching and technical management for each rural primary and middle schools to actively promote the application of the three modes in the teaching in rural primary and middle schools.

Project Modes

The Project mainly adopted three teaching modes, which include teaching CD player station, satellite teaching receiving station and computer classrooms. Based on the completion of the basic equipment, different schools could enhance the standards according to local situations.[12]

Mode 1: Teaching CD Player Stations

The teaching CD player stations were equipped with televisions, DVD players and sets of teaching CDs (shown in Figure 2.2). The average budget of each station is RMB 3,000. Teaching CDs are played to teach and help students, help teachers prepare lessons, as well as to carry out training activities for peasants. The mode is easy to operate, with low cost and easy to maintain and use, which is very suitable for rural primary schools, especially for rural primary school teaching points in remote and poor areas in the central and western China.

Mode 2: Satellite Teaching Receiving Stations

Except for the equipment demonstrated in Mode 1, satellite teaching receiving stations are provided with outdoor satellite receiving

[11] This was the data at the project design in 2003. After that, due to the investigation of rural school distribution, the number of rural schools and teaching points decreased year by year. By 2007, there had been 271,584 primary schools, 83,118 rural primary teaching points and 32,865 rural middle schools in the rural areas below the county or town level in China.

[12] Ministry of Education. Technical Plan for the Terminal Receiving Points of Modern Distance Education Project for Rural Primary and Middle Schools. Retrieved from http://www.moe.gov.cn/publicfiles/business/htmlfiles/moe/s3333/201001/xxgk_82045.html (accessed March 23, 2006).

Figure 2.2
System Structure of Teaching CD Player Station (Mode 1)

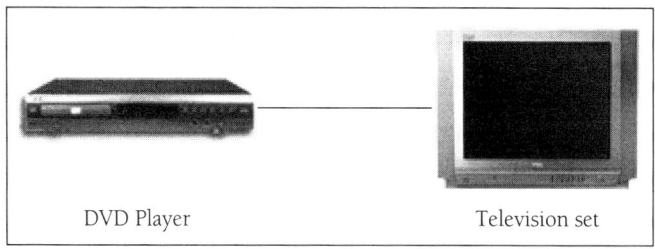

| DVD Player | Television set |

Source: Office of Modern Distance Education Project for China's Rural Primary and Middle Schools (2009).

equipment (antennas, LNB, etc.), satellite TV equipment (satellite TV receiver, TV set, etc.), satellite data reception equipment (<built-in> satellite data reception card, <built-in> modem, <built-in> CD writer, computer, etc.), Internet access devices, printers, UPS power supply, and other equipment (shown in Figure 2.3). The average budget for each station is RMB 16,000. The equipment can receive a great number of quality educational resources quickly via Chinese education satellite broadband transmission network. It can not only adopt the applying functions in Mode 1, but also realize the live and taped "classroom in air"[13] for synchronous and asynchronous teaching and learning, study tutoring both in and out of the class, help teachers to prepare lessons and carry out teacher trainings, and implement community education in rural areas.

Mode 3: Computer Classrooms

On the basis of Mode 2, the computer classrooms were upgraded as multimedia classrooms and included a projector, central control system, DVD player, TV set, computer network, which included a server, switch, teacher's computer and student's computer, and network printer (shown in Figure 2.4). The average budget for each classroom is RMB 150,000.

---

[13] "Classroom in air" is a metaphor in Chinese language context. It refers to a type of classroom forms that use ICT to move the teaching process on the Internet via live or taped broadcasting the videos, audios, courseware, blackboard writing, etc. for the interaction between teachers and students.

Figure 2.3

The System Structure of Satellite Teaching Receiving Station (Mode 2)

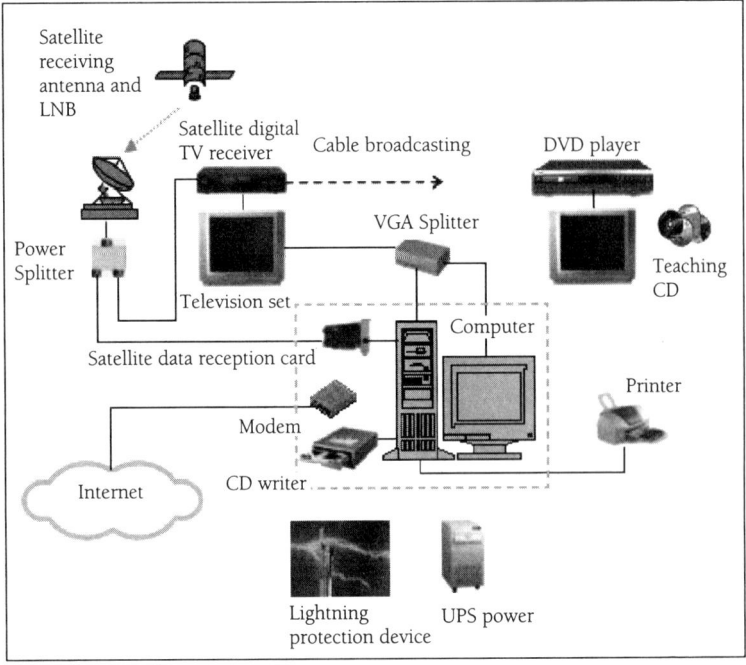

Source: Office of Modern Distance Education Project for China's Rural Primary and Middle Schools (2009).

The equipped targets are rural junior middle school. In addition to all functions of Mode 1 and Mode 2, the computer classroom could also provide online learning environment for students to participate in distance education. It is used to start IT courses, to carry out lesson planning, activities of teaching and research and teacher trainings in the network environment, and also implement peasant training, access to and publish information online to provide service for trade for peasants.

Why were these three technical modes chosen? At that time, there was "digital divide" between China's urban and rural areas. The transportation is challenging in rural areas, where many primary and middle

Figure 2.4
The System Structure of Computer Classrooms

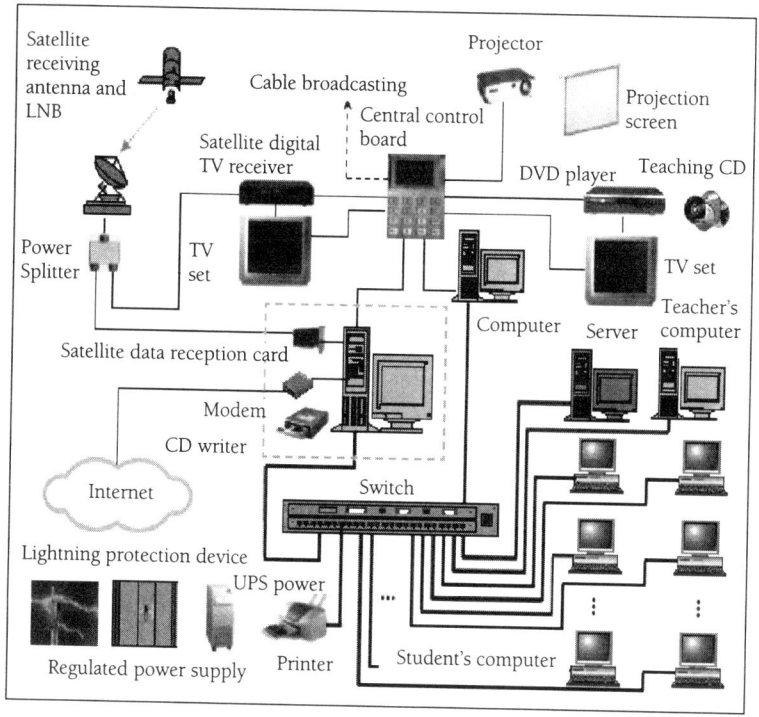

Source: Office of Modern Distance Education Project for China's Rural Primary and Middle Schools (2009).

schools are widely dispersed. In order to solve the "last-kilometer" problem of the ICT in rural schools,[14] it was impossible to introduce Internet access in urban households in the short term. Consideration had to be given to rural information infrastructure environment and their shortage of technicians and funds, as well as the cost related to infrastructure development. It was a realistic choice to use CDs, satellite receiving equipment, and computer classrooms as carriers of low-cost

[14] The "last-kilometer" refers to the connection between the switch of network service providers and the terminal devices such as user's computers.

and high-efficiency content without the space constraints. Indeed, this technical route was integrated only at primary school level. It could not solve the two-way transmission of data or realize interactive learning in the network environment. It needed to be improved by gradually adopting new technical solutions that combine new and conventional technologies in the future development.

Project Funding

The budget of the project is RMB 10 billion, but the actual investment is RMB 11.1 billion. Of this, the central special fund invested RMB 5 billion, accounting for 45.1%, while local governments invested RMB 6.1 billion, accounting for 54.9%, thereby exceeding the budget of RMB 1.1 billion. It was mainly used in the allocation of equipment, the construction of teaching resources and corresponding teacher trainings.[15]

Project Schedule

See Table 2.1 for the project schedule.

Construction Contents and Effects

During 2002–2003, the feasibility of the Project was studied and a panel of experts was organized to study and formulate the implementation plan and the three mode design. Pilot demonstration projects were initiated during 2003–2004, when central government invested RMB 364 million to complete the construction of 20,977 teaching CD player stations,

[15] The common problems of Chinese educational informatization projects are "hardware over software" and "construction over application." The proper proportion of investment among hardware, software and other resources and human resources should be 4:3:3. However, according to the budget of the equipment in each station in three modes, the investment in hardware accounts for 85%, leaving very limited budget for resource construction and teacher training. For instance, the total amount of the expense of the project in Shaanxi Province is RMB 551,377,000, among which hardware costs RMB 471,830,000 (86%), software RMB 23,554,000, resources RMB 23,000,000, and teacher training RMB 32,973,000.

Table 2.1
Project Schedule

Years	Project Coverage Areas
2003 (Pilot)	Choose 2–3 municipal administrative regions of moderate population, with required working basis and corresponding conditions as key breakthrough for pilot project in the 12 provinces (autonomous regions and municipalities) in the western China, the Xinjiang Production and Construction Corps and the six provinces in the central China.
2004	Mainly cover eight provinces (autonomous regions and municipalities) in western China, parts of eight provinces in central China and some poverty-stricken areas of two provinces in eastern China.
2005	Give support to six provinces (autonomous regions and municipalities) where the coverage of the Project has been greatly enhanced, while other places in the central and western regions are also addressed.
2006–2007	Complete the construction of the Project in remaining areas so as to cover all rural primary and middle schools.

Source: Office of Modern Distance Education Project for China's Rural Primary and Middle Schools (2009).

48,605 satellite teaching receiving stations and 7094 computer classrooms in 20 provincial pilot units. Since the end of 2004, the Project had entered the stage of universal application, where the development of content was added to the hardware environment, the development and delivery of quality teaching resources, teacher training, and the exploration of application modes.

Construction of the Hardware Environment

By the end of 2007, 23 provinces in the central and western China as well as the Xinjiang Production and Construction Corps have been equipped with 440,142 sets of teaching CD players, 264,905 sets of satellite teaching receiving devices and 40,858 sets of computer classrooms, covering over 95% of the rural primary and middle schools in China (shown in Table 2.2).

Table 2.2
The Equipment Allocation of Three Modes of the Project

Regions	Provinces	CD Player Devices (Set)	Satellite Receiving Devices (Set)	Computer Classrooms (Set)
Total		440,142	264,905	40,858
Western China	Inner Mongolia	9,790	5,181	1,087
	Guangxi	28,542	11,851	1,621
	Chongqing	15,309	9,361	1,187
	Sichuan	38,461	13,342	4,416
	Guizhou	21,177	14,588	1,572
	Yunnan	41,510	14,442	1,932
	Tibet	2,048	435	52
	Shaanxi	34,265	20,151	1,974
	Gansu	22,064	13,150	1,552
	Qinghai	3,313	1,660	395
	Ningxia	3,998	2,135	279
	Xinjiang	8,387	4,600	1,107
	The Xinjiang Production and Construction Corps	3,765	450	246
Central China	Hebei	19,381	14,041	3,729
	Shanxi	37,059	24,218	2,326
	Liaoning	10,248	9,018	1,350
	Jilin	7,841	3,931	1,103
	Heilongjiang	10,914	9,180	1,620
	Anhui	23,083	14,419	2,869
	Jiangxi	14,421	8,007	1,642
	Henan	38,964	33,746	3,642
	Hubei	17,322	14,414	1,814
	Hunan	24,949	19,829	3,019
	Hainan	3,331	2,756	324

Source: Office of Modern Distance Education Project for China's Rural Primary and Middle Schools (2009).

The Project has improved the hardware technical environment in rural primary and middle schools. It achieved access to at least one computer in all six-year primary schools in rural areas. In this way, these schools could receive weekly updated educational resources broadcasted via the satellite by the MoE. It enriches the content of the teachers' lesson preparation and presentation and students' learning and extracurricular activities so that children in the extensive rural and remote areas could experience the value of digitization. For example, after the implementation of the Project, the number of computers in the rural schools in Chongqing municipality had grown by 62% and the number of computer teachers by 81%, and the rate of students and computers in the rural schools in Gansu province has increased by more than three times. At the same time, the rural schools have given full play to the comprehensive functions of the Project, which have resulted in an integrated platform for rural economic and social development, as they have strived to establish the schools as the cultural centers, the cadre education centers, practical technical training centers for peasants and the promotion of centers for agricultural science and technology in rural areas.

Resource Construction and Transmission

Owing to the geographical, historical, economic, and social development factors, rural primary and middle schools in China were challenged with access to books, audio-visual, and multimedia resources on teaching and learning. The information age widened the existing gap of educational resources between urban and rural schools in China. For this reason, the Project emphasized the "integration" of resource construction. It used the methods of collection, commissioned development, and integrated generation to construct targeted, high-quality, systematic and applicable educational resources (shown in Table 2.3). These were to be delivered to rural schools via CDs, satellite broadband network, and free Internet access to support teaching and learning.

MoE, local educational administrative departments, schools, and corporations made respective contributions to the resource management, construction, and application (shown in Figure 2.5).

Table 2.3
The Category of Main Resources in the Project

Types of Resources	Main Forms	Targeted Objects and Methods	Targeted Requirements
Teaching resources	Teaching resources of small class	Mainly used in the teaching of different subjects for primary schools, which teachers can use directly in teaching or assisting teaching	To help teachers give lessons
	Resources of knowledge points Tutoring of the important and difficult points	Mainly used in the teaching of different subjects for different grades in primary schools and junior middle schools in order to assist teachers' teaching	
Learning resources	Inquiry learning resources	Mainly used to support the subject teaching in primary and junior middle schools and students' inquiry learning in comprehensive practical activities	To help students with learning
	Self-study resources	Used for the individualized learning of students and reviewing lessons.	
Thematic educational resources	Educational resources of core value Ideological and moral education resources Legal education resources	Used in thematic educational activities in relevant grades of primary and junior middle schools or to enrich extra-curricular activities	To help schools to implement quality education

Table 2.3 continued

Table 2.3 continued

Types of Resources	Main Forms	Targeted Objects and Methods	Targeted Requirements
	Health and safety education resources Science education resources Activity resources of the Young Pioneers, etc.		
Teacher training resources	Teacher ethics and self-cultivation resources The new curriculum reform training resources New technical training resources Training resources of the three modes Excellent case resources, etc.	Used for professional development of teachers	To help teachers with learning
School management resources	Principal training resources Fund management training resources Principal leadership training resources, etc.	Used to help principals to improve by daily learning	To help the principals to improve
Minority language resources	Resources of the minorities to learn Chinese	Used in the teaching of the minorities to learn Chinese	To help minority teachers and students to equally access to quality educational resources
	Compilation and translation of national distance education resources	Used for the teachers and students who use the minority language in teaching	
	Thematic resources of the minorities	Used in assisting the minority teachers to organize various activities	

Source: Office of Modern Distance Education Project for China's Rural Primary and Middle Schools (2009).

Figure 2.5
The System of the Management, Construction, and Application Plan of Project Resources

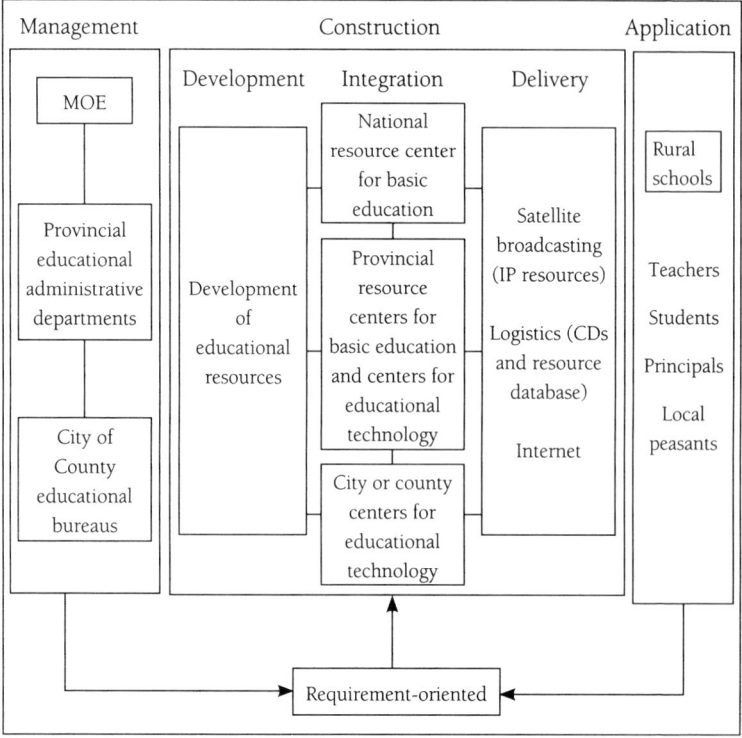

Source: Office of Modern Distance Education Project for China's Rural Primary and Middle Schools (2009).

Collect Commission and Integrate the Development of Free Educational Resources

MoE encouraged the whole society to participate in the construction of quality education resources for rural primary and middle schools. It also collected and selected resources from provincial education departments, colleges and universities, publishing houses, and corporations. Dozens of units won the bid to develop excellent resources.

MoE allocated special funds to commission units that had design capabilities, experience with developing good educational resources and an established social reputation to develop specific educational resources. For example, the People's Education Press was commissioned to develop teaching CDs for small classes,[16] which enabled rural primary schools and teaching units to use the teaching CD players to provide lessons in English, music, art, and other courses that could not be provided due to the limited conditions in the past. The Project also allocated special funds of RMB 10 million for the development of the resources for the minorities to learn Chinese, and another RMB 22 million for the resource construction of minority languages, such as Tibet, Uighur, Kazakhstan, Mongolia, Korea, Yi, and other minorities (Zeng, 2011).[17]

The educational resources purchased by MoE and the systematic resources presented in the form of web pages through integration are delivered through the channels of primary schools and middle schools of the project IP data package, respectively. The National Resource Center for Basic Education of MoE systematized, supplemented, and improved various purchased resources during the process of integration.

In addition, the Project also received a variety of resources donated by the enterprises, publishing units, and science and technology institutions.

Develop the Educational Resources That Are of Local Characteristics and Suitable for Local Needs

The Project mobilized the power of local governments, encouraged the enthusiasm and creativity of schools, teachers and students, and through bid procurement, developed locally relevant resources. For example, some provinces had established resource centers for basic education that used the co-operative ways to introduce excellent national or

[16] Teaching CD for small class especially refers to the video of imitating teaching process in the scenario of small class consisting of one excellent subject teacher and several students. Generally, it lasts only 15–20 minutes, which is different from the video of real classroom teaching. It highlights the interpretation of teachers and the interaction of students in the teaching and shortens the repeated exercises and consolidating activities, so it is convenient for rural teachers to display or use as teaching assisting resources.

[17] The amount of budget is great compared with the total investment of the project, but the budget used for resource construction is not much. For example, in 2007, the project only invested RMB 60 million to bid for commissioned development of new resources.

international resources for basic education and equip rural primary and middle schools with sets of teaching CDs and teaching resource databases. All levels of centers for educational technology and departments of teaching and research in Shaanxi province had formed the mechanism of promoting resource construction by training, applying, contesting, and researching through the annual contest of selecting excellent lessons and courseware (Lv, 2007). Hubei province adopted the parallel mechanism of self-development, collection and purchase, integrated and developed the resources such as English class on the air, rural practical technical education, and so on. Xinjiang developed "a resource supermarket" of modern distance education in primary and middle schools in local minority languages and in Chinese (Project Office, 2009).

Use the Integrated Way of Satellite, CD and Network to Deliver the Resources to Rural Schools and Classrooms

The Project used integrated the use of satellite broadcast, CD, and network to deliver the resources. For instance, it applied good logistics to send sets of teaching CDs to rural teaching points. It broadcasted teaching resources via the Chinese Education Satellite Broadband Network, and enabled accesses to digital learning resources via the Internet (Zeng, 2011). Some central rural primary schools that have the capacity of receiving satellite resources also used their computers to write the resources in CDs required by rural teaching points and provided them to the schools in the neighborhood.

The Project had initially formed the resource system that could satisfy the needs of distance education in rural primary and middle schools, which was welcomed by rural teachers, students, and peasants. It distributed over 65 million teaching CDs to rural schools at the average of 225 CDs for each school. More than 200,000 rural primary and middle schools registered in the National Resource Center for Basic Education of Ministry of Education, so that they could receive 10G satellite teaching resources every week (Project Office, 2009).

The resources for students and classroom teaching constituted 70% of the total available resources. For instance, the teaching CDs for small classes covered all grades and all disciplines in the primary schools. Multimedia teaching resources covered 9 disciplines in junior middle schools and 8 disciplines in primary schools. Video resources covered 11 disciplines in junior middle schools and 7 disciplines in primary schools and the multimedia resources sent by the IP channel covered 10 versions of textbooks, 12 disciplines in junior middle schools and 7 disciplines in primary schools (Project Office, 2009). These resources became important media for hundreds of millions of rural children who could make contact with the outside world and broaden their knowledge. It empowered millions of teachers with tools to implement the new curriculum reform and make students enjoy learning and overcome the problem that they were "unable to teach or teach well." Importantly, it also helped to address the serious shortage of English, art, and music teachers.

Teacher Training

Teacher training confronted quantitative and qualitative challenges. First, the training covered a wide range and a large number of teachers. MoE had to train provincial, municipal, and county-level backbone teachers who were responsible for training millions of rural teachers (shown in Figure 2.6). Second, rural teachers with relatively weak

Figure 2.6
Training Plan of the Project

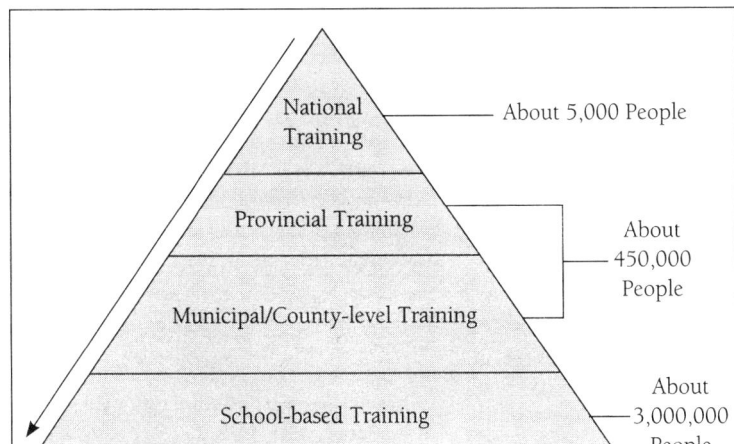

Source: Office of Modern Distance Education Project for China's Rural Primary and Middle Schools (2009).

competencies were trained to "understand well, learn well and implement effectively in the class."

National Modular Training Courses and Participatory Training Methods

The Project developed the training curriculum and textbooks consisting of three modules (shown in Figure 2.7), and composed of application guidebooks for teachers (shown in Table 2.4). National training mainly adopted the training methods of "learning by doing," case-based teaching, and participatory collaborative learning. During 2005–2006, MoE commissioned the Central Centre for Educational Technology to carry out tour trainings in the application of three modes of teaching in

Figure 2.7
Three Modes of the Project Training

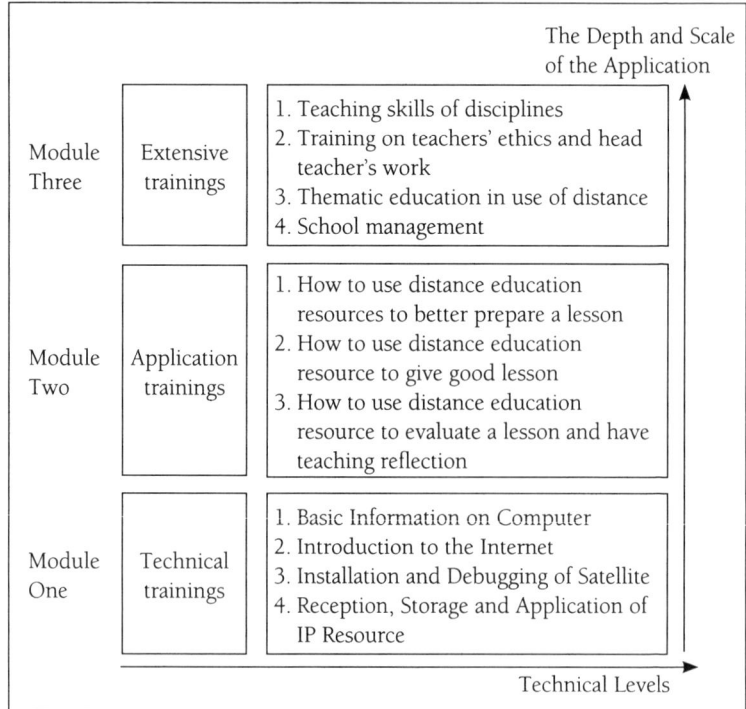

Source: Shanghai Academy of Educational Sciences.

Table 2.4
Study Guidance for Teachers' Application Guidebooks

	Mode 1: CD Play	*Mode 2: Satellite TV*	*Mode 3: Computer Classroom*
What to use	Devices, resources, participants	Devices, resources, participants	Devices, resources, participants
How to use	Prepare lessons Give lessons Evaluation Case study	Receive resources on time Prepare lessons Give lessons Evaluation Case study	Maintain the normal operation of the network Receive resources on time Prepare lessons Give lessons Evaluation Case study
Help	Teaching problems Technical problems	Device supporting services Learning and exchanging among the practitioners Make use of supporting service system established on different levels	Device supporting services Learning and exchanging among the practitioners Ask the experts for help Search for the answers on the Internet
Review and summary	Write reviews	Write blogs School-based examination	Teaching reflection Write essays
Case study	Mathematics for primary school	Chinese for primary school English for primary school	Physics for middle school Geography for middle school

Source: Shanghai Academy of Educational Sciences.

selected counties of each provincial project unit. There were over 15,000 frontline teachers and more than 100 backbone teachers directly participating in the training by lectures, discussion, observation, learning by doing, training reflections, and other activities. The backbone teachers also participated in training how to tutor. The teaching plans, teaching methods, teaching cases, and media resources used and modified in the training became important materials of the network curriculum package of the training of teaching application (shown in Figure 2.8). Rural teachers reflected that they could use the content directly after the training, which they could also use at home. Xinjiang organized provincial trainings for backbone teachers in this way: 3,000 discipline teachers have been trained within one year, among whom minority teachers account for more than 80% (Project office, 2009).

MoE also used the network information platform to carry out large-scale distance teacher training. In August 2007, over 130,000 rural teachers of primary and middle schools in 100 counties in the western China participated in the national distance training program, which not only reduced the costs but also prevented them from travelling to the city for training. The teachers believed that the training reflects the word "close," which meant being close to teaching, close to the textbooks, and close to the students.

Local Governments and Project Schools Jointly Carry Out Teacher Trainings

Led by the national teacher training program, local and school-based training expanded the beneficiaries of the project trainings. For example, the rural schools in some areas combine thematic research of distance education, daily teaching, and research activities to help teachers solve the problems in teaching and learning in the units divided by learning administrative districts. The Department of Education of Shaanxi Province proposed standards and requirements from the aspects of management system, training methods, curriculum integration, discipline application, evaluation and examination required for project schools to realize the "four combinations" in practice, which are the combination of application skills and training on curriculum reform, centralized trainings, thematic training, classroom teaching, competitions, and teaching application and services for the rural areas (Lv, 2007).

Figure 2.8
Example of Teaching Plan for Expert Tour-trainings

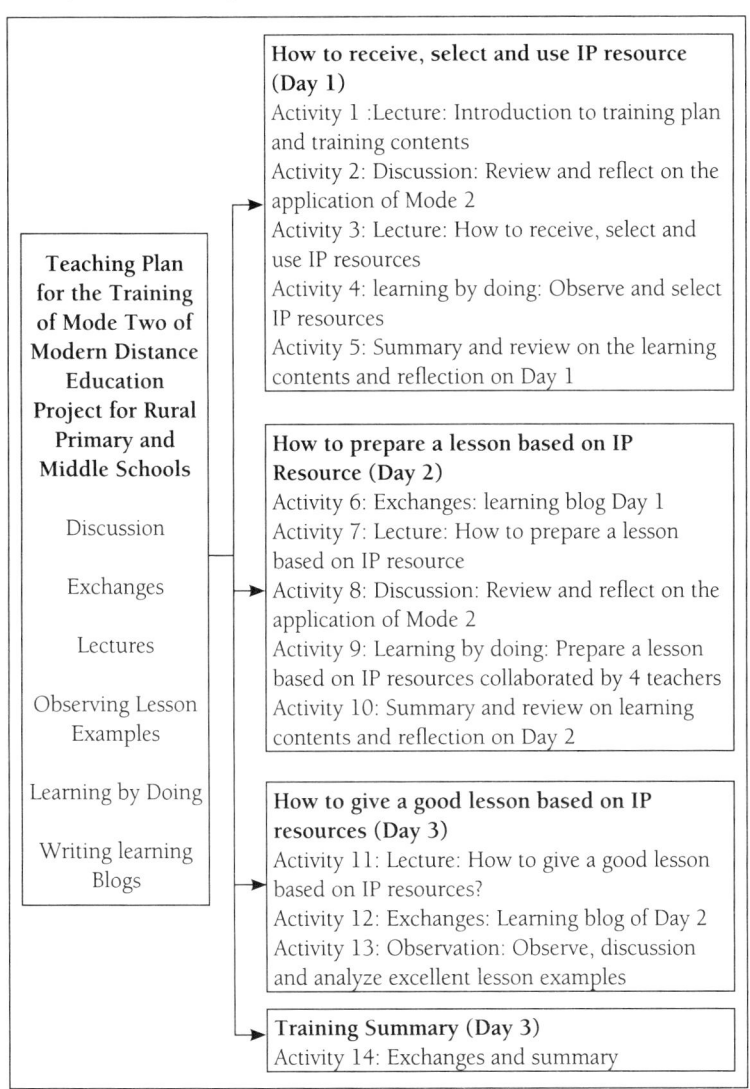

How to receive, select and use IP resource (Day 1)
Activity 1 :Lecture: Introduction to training plan and training contents
Activity 2: Discussion: Review and reflect on the application of Mode 2
Activity 3: Lecture: How to receive, select and use IP resources
Activity 4: learning by doing: Observe and select IP resources
Activity 5: Summary and review on the learning contents and reflection on Day 1

Teaching Plan for the Training of Mode Two of Modern Distance Education Project for Rural Primary and Middle Schools

Discussion

Exchanges

Lectures

Observing Lesson Examples

Learning by Doing

Writing learning Blogs

How to prepare a lesson based on IP Resource (Day 2)
Activity 6: Exchanges: learning blog Day 1
Activity 7: Lecture: How to prepare a lesson based on IP resource
Activity 8: Discussion: Review and reflect on the application of Mode 2
Activity 9: Learning by doing: Prepare a lesson based on IP resources collaborated by 4 teachers
Activity 10: Summary and review on learning contents and reflection on Day 2

How to give a good lesson based on IP resources (Day 3)
Activity 11: Lecture: How to give a good lesson based on IP resources?
Activity 12: Exchanges: Learning blog of Day 2
Activity 13: Observation: Observe, discussion and analyze excellent lesson examples

Training Summary (Day 3)
Activity 14: Exchanges and summary

Source: Shanghai Academy of Educational Sciences.

Teachers in Eastern and Western China and Urban and Rural Areas Acquire Professional Development Hand in Hand through Distance Education

Because of the impact of the Project, the assistance and support of the developed eastern region to rural education in the western region extended to online collaborative learning. The education administrative departments in some areas actively guided urban schools to prepare and deliver the same lesson with local rural schools via the network, and actively promote and implement online teaching discussions and exchange activities. This resulted in the formation of the web-based learning and the development of a community of urban and rural teachers. Thus, the rural teachers assumed the path of professional development through a "learning— practice–exchange–practice–learning" process.

Over the five years of the Project, the number of rural teachers and technicians participating in the national, provincial, municipal, and county-level training has reached 800,000 (shown in Figure 2.9), accounting for more than 20% of the rural teachers of compulsory education in the central and western China.[18] The training helped rural teachers to learn information technology and educational technology and to master the methods of using modern distance education devices and resources for teaching in a short period of time. The teaching skills and professional levels of the rural teachers participated in the project trainings showed great improvement, in that they could make the classroom teaching form change from "media-centered" to "teacher-centered" and then to "student-centered."[19]

[18] In 2007, full-time teachers in rural primary schools of China are 3,400,420, part-time teachers in rural primary schools are 209,809 and full-time teachers in rural junior middle schools are 1,395,363.

[19] Chinese government has initiated a series of teacher training programs. For instance, MoE promoted network distance training pilots in 2006 and by the end of 2011, the number of trained teachers from kindergartens, primary schools and middle schools had been over 3 million. MoE initiated "National Construction Plan of Educational Technology Capability for Teachers from Primary and Middle Schools" in 2005 and by the end of 2011, the number of trained teachers had been 6 million. In 2003, MoE initiated the implementation of Plan of National Teacher Education Network Association, which focused on innovating teacher training modes and establishing educational resources sharing platform

Figure 2.9
The Numbers of Teacher Trainings at Different Levels of the Project

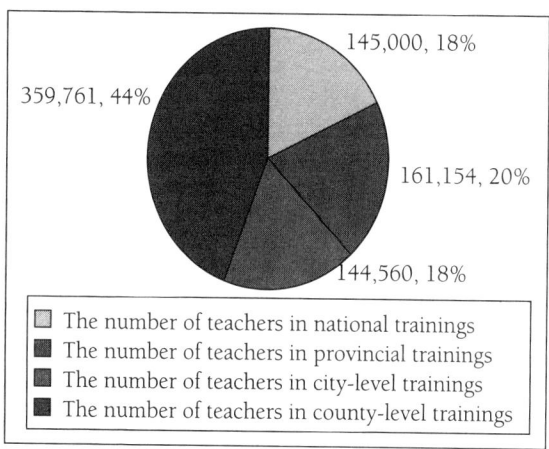

Source: Wang (2008).

Application Modes

MoE issued special guidance on the teaching application of the three modes. Based on the philosophy of a new curriculum, project schools carry out useful exploration and improvement on the teaching application modes in the three technical equipment environment of modern distance education (Chen, 2006).

Teaching Application Mode in the Environment of Teaching CD Player Stations

CD-based Direct Playing Teaching Mode. In this teaching mode, teachers play the CDs in a given order: give instructions before playing, point out the key points during the process, and summarize the content afterwards (shown in Figure 2.10). The teachers become the organizer and player of media, the CDs took the place of the teachers, and teaching

---

for teachers. Intel "Future Education" Project and Microsoft "Partner in learning" Project have trained 1.85 million teachers altogether. "National Training Plan for Teachers of Primary and Middle Schools" implemented in 2010 emphasized distance trainings, which use 20% of the budget to train 80% of the teachers.

Figure 2.10
Direct Playing Teaching Mode in the Environment of Mode 1

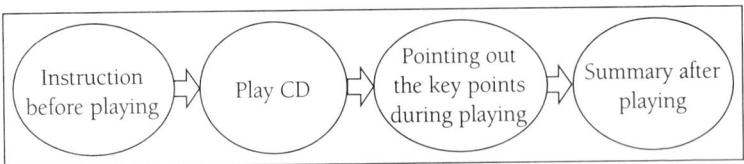

Source: http://www.moe.edu.cn/publicfiles/business/htmlfiles/moe/
moe_2942/200909/51521.html

activities in class utilized media-centered teaching mode. The length of the CD playing is generally 28–40 minutes. They are mainly used in the lectures of ideological and moral education, safety and health education, thematic knowledge, as well as the subject teaching of English, music, and art, because of the lack of professional teachers in rural teaching units (shown in Figure 2.11).

CD-based Dialogue Imitation Teaching Mode. In this teaching mode, teachers imitate the teaching and learning activities of the teachers and students on TV in their classes by playing CDs to learn their teaching ideas, teaching methods, instructional design, and activity design and the methods and techniques of how to control the teaching process and grasp the effects of teaching. The types of CDs used in classroom teaching are mainly interactive teaching, live recording of classroom teaching, and so on. The length of CD playing is normally about 20 minutes. It has formed the special teaching mode of giving classes by the teachers both in classes and on TV (shown in Figure 2.12).

This teaching mode is used in the classes that rural teachers are incapable to teach or have difficulty in teaching. For instance, Mr Li from a rural primary school in Gansu Province does not speak English, so he uses teaching CDs in small classes to teach his students English. His students' English scores assumed the first place of the whole learning administrative district. In the mixed teaching of different grades in rural places, CD resources can be utilized to improve the quality of students' self-learning activities organized by the teachers, which help students to learn better under the guidance of outstanding distance teachers. This provided the opportunity for practicing their capabilities of observation and attention, as well as developing their thinking ability.

Figure 2.11
CD-based Teaching in the Schools in Minority Regions of Western China

Source: http://www.moe.edu.cn/publicfiles/business/htmlfiles/moe/
moe_2942/200909/51521.html

Figure 2.12
CD-based Dialogue Imitation Teaching Mode

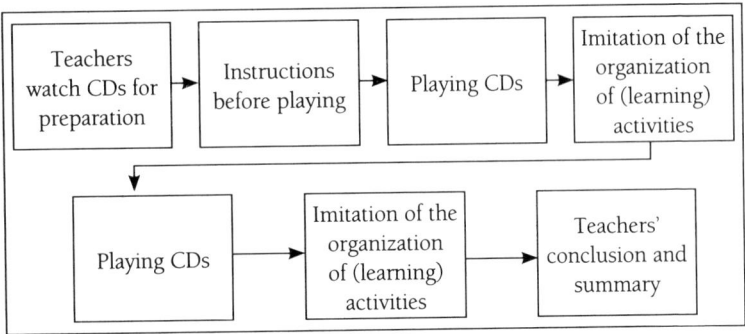

Source: Office of Modern Distance Education Project for China's Rural Primary and Middle Schools (2009).

CD-based Scenario Interactive Teaching Mode. In this teaching mode, the teachers select and modify CD resources according to their own instructional designs. They design scenarios to lead in or present the content, and allow students to participate in interactive activities, such as operation, performance, exercises, and discussions (see Figure 2.13). This enables them to achieve their teaching objectives. There are generally two types of teaching CDs for application: one is published by the press and used in some rural schools with modular designed contents, whereas the other is restructured and modified based on the original teaching CDs that the instructional design required for use by the teachers. This teaching mode required the teachers to demonstrate higher teaching levels and skills, and complement the content of the teaching CDs and their own interpretations in order to enhance the interactions between man and machine, teachers and students, and among the students themselves.

The behavioral changes displayed by rural teachers from resisting the use of CDs in teaching to enjoying their use were influenced by the process of repeated practice, which integrates asking, talking, exercising, and assessment, resulting in better teaching effects. In particular, the teaching CDs for small classes were universally applied (shown in Table 2.5).

Figure 2.13
CD-based Scenario Interactive Teaching Mode

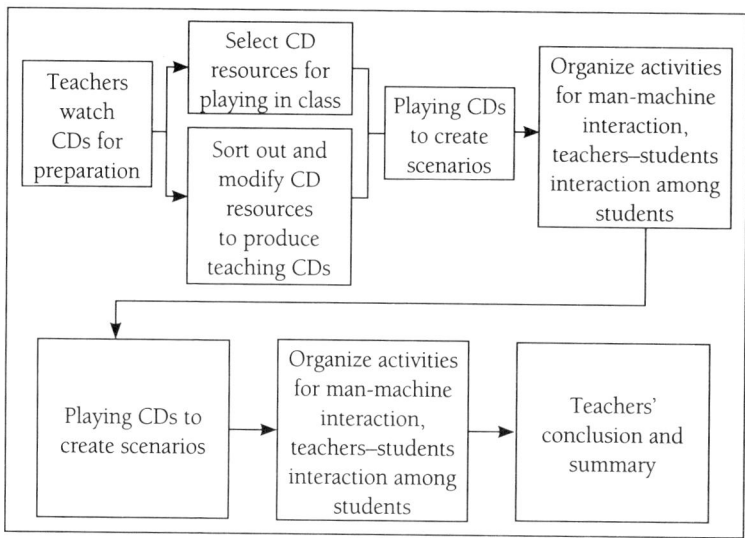

Source: Office of Modern Distance Education Project for China's Rural Primary and Middle Schools (2009).

Table 2.5
The Application Methods of Teaching CDs of Small Class in the Tutoring and Teaching of Primary Chinese

Teaching Objectives	CD Presentation Methods	Effects
Learning Characters	First, ask students to read and look for new characters, and then learn them following the teachers in the CDs.	Conducive to the correct literacy and pronunciation of students.
	Strengthen the inspections in the classroom teaching by timely detecting problems and correcting them individually.	Conducive to correcting the teachers' pronunciation.
	CDs can be played repeatedly when students are unable to learn by heart.	

Table 2.5 continued

Table 2.5 continued

Teaching Objectives	CD Presentation Methods	Effects
Reading aloud	First, listen to the reading audio of the teachers and students in CDs. Then, Read aloud after it or organize the students to do so in different ways. Examine the reading of all students in different ways to avoid the neglecting of any students in collective reading.	Conductive to the correct reading of students and learning Mandarin Chinese. Conductive to correcting the teachers' pronunciation.
Reading quietly	Make use of the scenarios in CDs or teachers' questions to organize teaching. Pause the video when the teacher in CDs asks questions, and ask the students to answer. If students are able to answer the questions or understand the text correctly, it is unnecessary to play the answers of the students in CDs. If play the answers, ask the students to refer to the answers in CDs or encourage them to compete with their fellow learning partners in urban areas. If students are unable to answer the questions correctly, the teacher should not simply play the CD to tell the students the answer, but to propose some easier and more specific questions to help them to think or to help them to analyze why the answer is so.	Guide students to actively think about the questions. Help students to build confidence in learning and to further develop their good thinking habits.

Source: Office of Modern Distance Education Project for China's Rural Primary and Middle Schools (2009).

Integrated Resource Teaching Mode in Teaching CD Player Stations. In this teaching mode, CD resources were not the only teaching resource. Teachers integrated the resources sent by other media or channels in new teaching CDs, such as the resources delivered by satellites or via the Internet. This enabled teachers to develop their personalized teaching styles (shown in Figure 2.14), which also means that the teaching skills and information literacy of the teachers reached a comparatively high level.

Teachers prepared the content used for display in the scenarios in class by searching, downloading, and editing when preparing lessons. The timely display of the content in class make the students feel like they are part of the scenarios so that they can better comprehend the events taking place at a distance, through different senses, which can help them to deepen their perception and understanding. A complete lesson in the CD is played or paused at different times by the teachers. It not only delivers the knowledge and skills just in time, but also cultivates the students' capability of thinking and expression, which makes the rural students feel that they are learning partners with the urban children. For instance, Mr Jiang from a rural primary school in Chongqing Municipality used the CD to give a mathematics lesson "To Learn the Time." The CD was made and used by the mathematics teacher in the central primary school of the town, where the students have positive reflections. This is also a way of serving the primary schools and teaching units in villages by making their own teaching CDs.

Teaching Application Mode in the Environment of Satellite Teaching Receiving Stations

The teaching modes of the applications of satellite educational resources in the classroom teaching are mainly live broadcasting, integrated broadcasting, and multiple combinations (shown in Figures 2.15 and 2.16).

Teaching Mode of Live Broadcasting the Satellite Educational Resources. In this teaching mode, the resources received at the terminals of satellite receivers are directly used in class without the integration or modification. It is easy to operate. It can be divided into synchronous teaching (such as synchronous classrooms, thematic lectures, excellent lesson examples, top-class teacher tutoring, etc.) (shown in Figure 2.17) and asynchronous teaching (shown in Figure 2.18).

Integrated Teaching Mode in Use of Satellite Educational Resources. In this teaching mode, the teachers sort out and modify the received satellite educational resources according to their teaching needs

Figure 2.14
Integrated Resource Teaching Mode in Teaching CD Player Stations

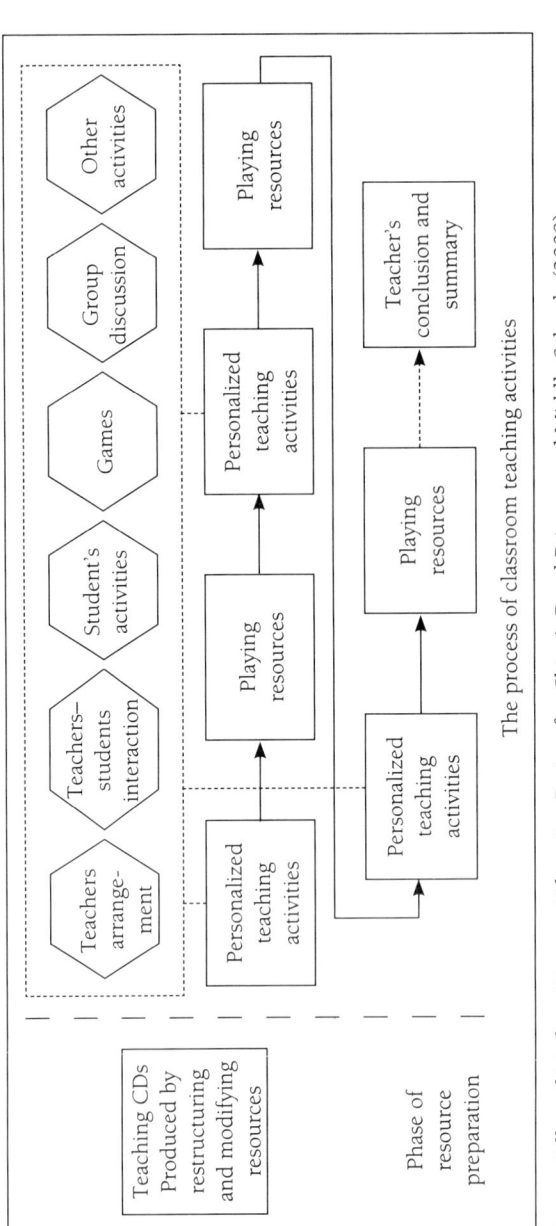

The process of classroom teaching activities

Source: Office of Modern Distance Education Project for China's Rural Primary and Middle Schools (2009).

Figure 2.15
Teaching System Structure of Using Satellite Educational Resources

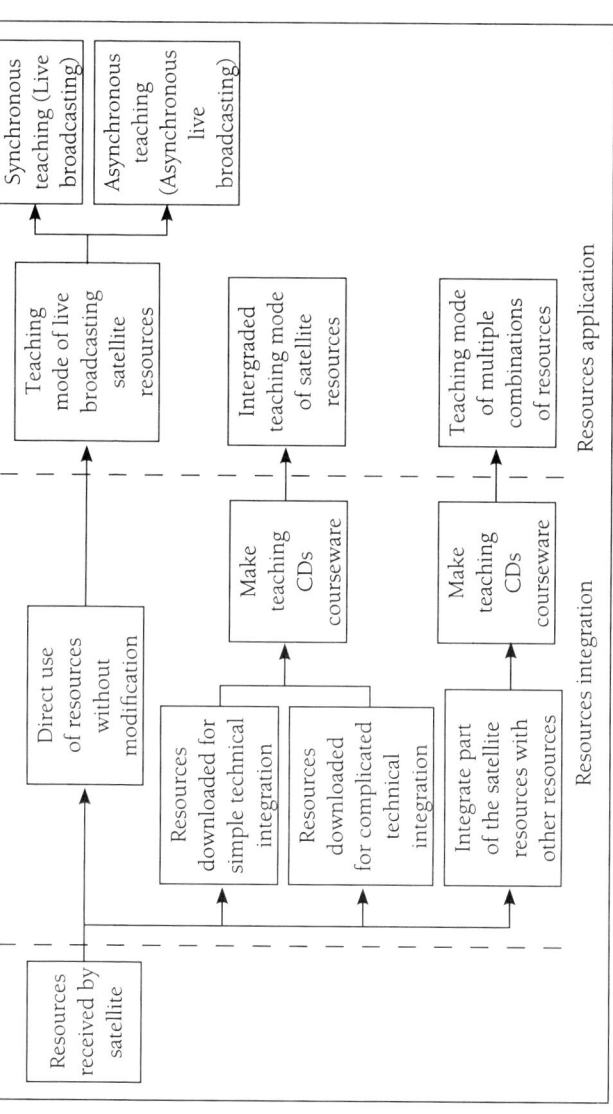

Source: http://www.moe.edu.cn/publicfiles/business/htmlfiles/moe/moe_2942/200909/51521.html (accessed September 14, 2012).

Figure 2.16

Distance Education Based on Satellite Teaching Receiving Stations in Rural Primary Schools of Huining County in Gansu Province

Source: http://www.moe.edu.cn/publicfiles/business/htmlfiles/moe/ moe_2942/200909/51521.html (accessed September 14, 2012).

Figure 2.17

The Teaching Mode of Synchronous Broadcasting in Use of Satellite Educational Resources

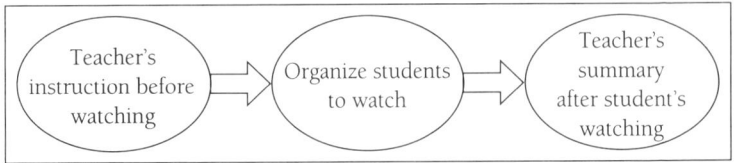

Source: Office of Modern Distance Education Project for China's Rural Primary and Middle Schools (2009).

and instructional design and make their teaching CDs or courseware for use in classroom teaching, which can be classified into the teaching mode of CD-based scenario interaction and that of resource integration (shown in Figure 2.19).

Figure 2.18

The Teaching Mode of Asynchronous Broadcasting in Use of Satellite Educational Resources

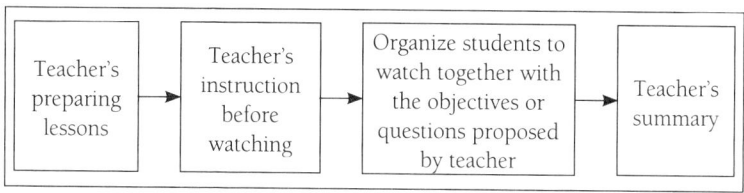

Source: Office of Modern Distance Education Project for China's Rural Primary and Middle Schools (2009).

Figure 2.19

The Integrated Teaching Mode in Use of Satellite Educational Resources

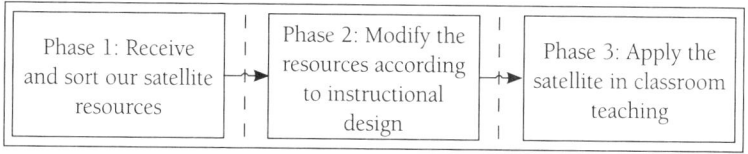

Source: Office of Modern Distance Education Project for China's Rural Primary and Middle Schools (2009).

Teaching Mode of Multiple Combinations in Use of Satellite Educational Resources. In this teaching mode, the teachers select and reorganize the resources for classroom teaching according to their own understanding of the curriculum standards, their grasps of disciplinary teaching contents, and their understanding and mastering of teaching environment and resources. The satellite educational resources are no longer the only resources. More teaching resources can be found on the Internet and from other media. The teaching mode of multiple combinations requires the teachers to have a broad view, better information literacy, and higher capability of disciplinary teaching.

Teaching Application Mode in the Environment of Computer Classrooms

The rural junior middle schools equipped with computer classrooms can allow students to learn information technology and carry out teaching and learning activities in the network environment, including the collective teaching mode, self-inquiry mode, and collaborative learning mode. Many schools also organize the teachers to watch thematic lectures, teaching CDs, and on-air class in computer classrooms for school-based teaching and research activities and the building of teachers' capability of educational technology.

Collective Teaching Mode in the Environment of Computer Classrooms. In a computer classroom environment, the teachers facilitate the learning of the same content at the same time to the whole class, which is mainly used in teaching information technology and listening to the thematic lectures given by the teachers in other schools through distance learning (shown in Figure 2.20). The lessons given by the well-known national teachers are introduced to the classroom via computers

Figure 2.20
The Students in Rural Central Schools of Baokang County in Hubei Province Are Listening to the Lesson Given by the Teacher from Other Areas in the Computer Classroom

Source: The website of Ministry of Education. Retrieved from http://www.moe.edu.cn/publicfiles/business/htmlfiles/moe/moe_2942/200909/51521.html (accessed September 14, 2012).

in the computer classrooms. The rural teachers and well-known national teachers deliver lessons on the same platform via the on-air classroom of distance education, which makes classroom teaching more vivid, livelier, and active.

Self-inquiry Learning Mode in the Environment of Computer Classrooms. In a computer classroom environment, the teachers use the learning resources from the network to propose questions and assign learning tasks for students in the problem-solving or task-driven approaches. The students search for the resources on the Internet with the questions for self-inquiry and self-study. Teachers can have real-time monitoring and individual tutoring to the learning situations of the students by the network system and help those who have difficulty in solving the problems and completing the tasks.

Group Collaborative Learning Mode in the Environment of Computer Classroom. In a computer classroom environment, the teachers organize the students to learn in groups or teams. The students can share their explored or discovered results in their own groups, with the other group members, with their classmates in other collaborative groups, or with their entire class. The teachers can create the atmosphere of collaborative learning by guiding the students to be engaged in collaborative learning activities. Most computer-supported collaborative learning mainly has self-study—collaborative learning mode (shown in Figure 2.21) and inquiry—collaborative learning mode (shown in Figure 2.22) (Huang, 2003).

Improvement of Education and Teaching in Rural Primary and Middle Schools

The effectiveness of the application is an important indicator for evaluating the project. The project focuses on the philosophy of student orientation and effective implementation in classroom teaching with the focus on application and use as well as on producing content construction. It uses training to encourage the application, which further promotes the development. MoE required that the devices utilized in the project would rather be worn out than left in the corner. According to the statistics, about 30% of the project schools could guarantee using the equipment

Figure 2.21
Self-study–Collaborative Learning Mode

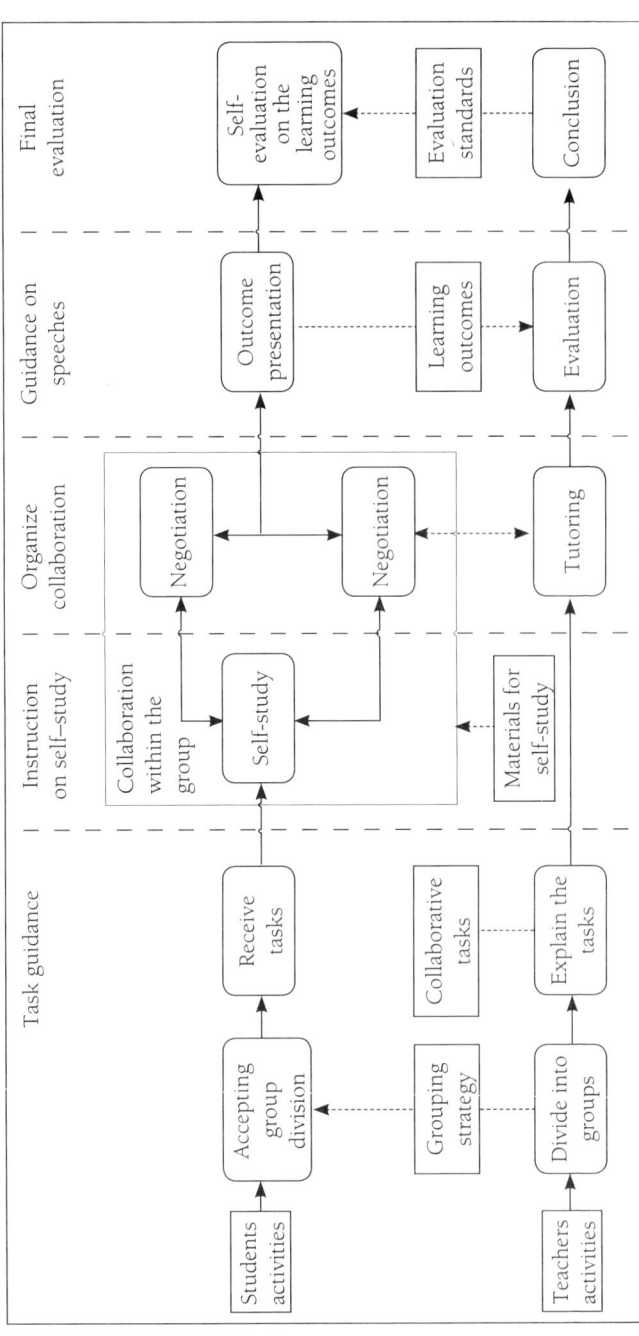

Source: Huang (2003).

Figure 2.22
Inquiry–Collaborative Learning Mode

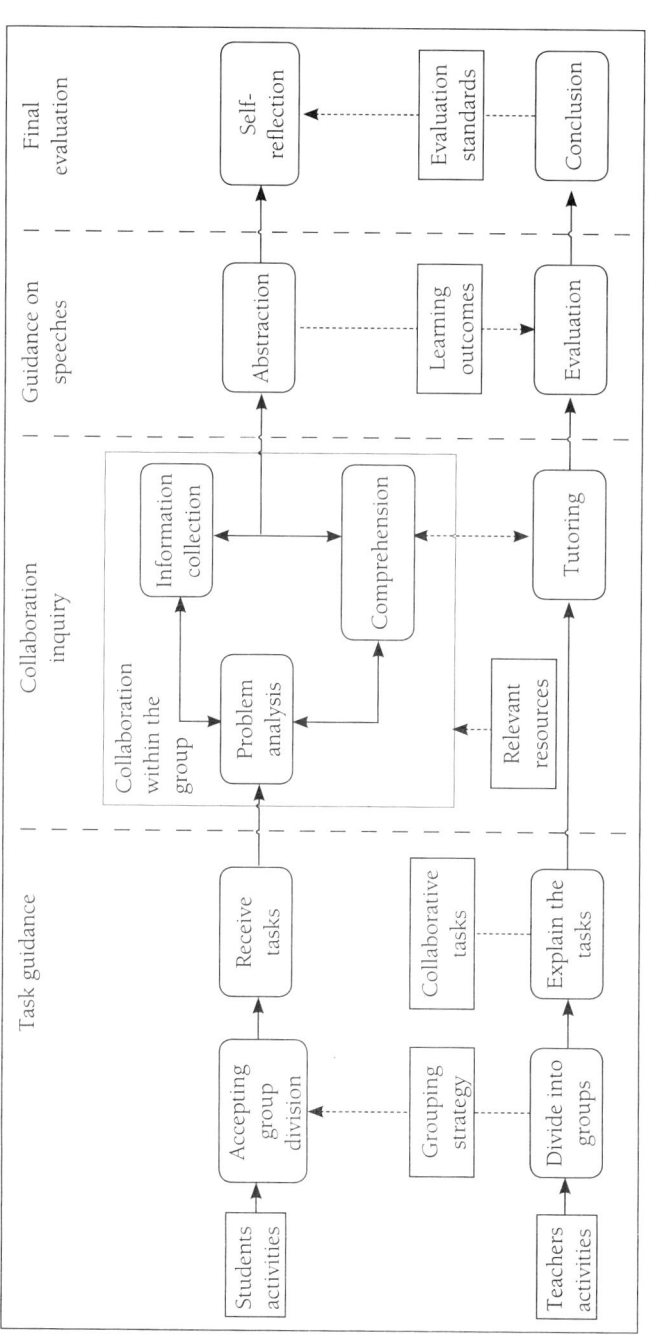

Source: Huang (2003).

20 hours a week, and about 50% about 15 hours a week (shown in Figure 2.23). The requirement of organizing students to watch a movie or entertaining programs on the platform of distance education every week is widely implemented (Project Office, 2009).

In the application of distance education, rural teachers making use of the devices and CDs, IP resources database, and other resource database of the three modes under the guidance of experts, had changed the single mode of "chalk + blackboard" in classroom teaching and carried out new, rich learning activities that the students like very much. In the teaching units of rural primary schools, the teachers could use the CDs to organize the students in mixed-grade teaching to improve their learning quality by self-study and teacher tutoring. In the six-year primary schools, the teachers could increase the frequency and relevance of the

Figure 2.23
The Rate of the Devices Equipped by the Project in Usage

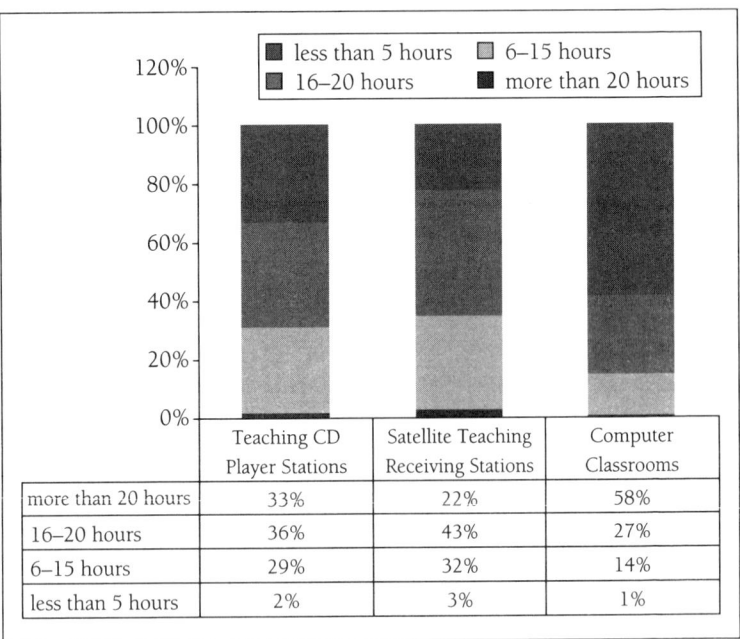

	Teaching CD Player Stations	Satellite Teaching Receiving Stations	Computer Classrooms
more than 20 hours	33%	22%	58%
16–20 hours	36%	43%	27%
6–15 hours	29%	32%	14%
less than 5 hours	2%	3%	1%

Source: Office of Modern Distance Education Project for China's Rural Primary and Middle Schools (2009).

question raised in class so as to promote the interaction of the class and enhance the design level of learning activities by learning and borrowing from the distance education resources. In rural junior middle schools, the teachers could make use of media resources to create learning scenarios for the organization of group collaborative learning and inquiry learning. Rural teachers would no longer just stand on the platform for "chalk and talk."

The Project had not only changed the ways that teachers teach, but also, to some extent, the ways that students learn. The rural primary and middle schools have achieved three changes, such as teaching philosophy of the teachers, teaching methods, and learning habits of the students; three modes, such as more teachers who initially collected teaching information, more teachers who studied teaching voluntarily, and more students who were used to self-study; and three enhancements, such as the efficiency of classroom teaching, students' interest in learning and the level of teaching and research, and the quality of education.

Important Role of Rural Schools in Building New Villages

Schools are the gathering places for talent resources. Rural primary and middle schools have long been the centers for community learning, scientific and technological and cultural as well as knowledge dissemination in rural areas of China. The Project did not only inject the energy in the educational and teaching reform in rural schools, but also provided public service platform of information for modern distance education for rural cadres and the Project promoted cultural and information sharing implemented through local governments. For example, more than half of the stations of modern distance education for Chinese rural cadres relied on the educational system and were built in rural primary and middle schools. Rural primary and middle schools made comprehensive use of the devices of three modes to collect and integrate the IP resources, CD resources, and public television programs according to the needs and development requirements of local industries. This enabled the spread of scientific, technological, and cultural knowledge by broadcasting, TV, and billboard in rural areas. Some schools even provided more specified solutions to plantation and farming technology for local peasants or farmers and the education on sanitation and health and cultivation for women and children under the organization of local government, which made it visible, tangible, operational for the peasants so that they developed the willing to learn, found it easier to learn, and were able to learn.

In the process of serving for the socioeconomic development of rural areas, a set of devices equipped by the Project could be used in three ways: by the students in class, by the teachers after class, and by the farmers when they were on holiday. The approach of using "day and night school" turned one school into two, which effectively reduced the costs, made the relation between the community and schools closer and promoted the service provided by the schools for the social and economic development of the community.

Some schools took full advantage of the distance education equipment to expand the propaganda, which increased the enrollment rates of schools and reduced the burden of some families that have to travel to town for study.[20] And some schools used distance education equipment to strengthen the contact between left-behind children[21] in rural areas and their parents who work in the cities. This not only made up for the lack of emotional care of these students, but also explored a way to strengthen the education for the next generation.

Experience

Attention of Leaders and Sound Institutions Are Prerequisites for the Completion of the Project

The three ministries jointly set up a specialized inter-ministerial coordination group of the Project, in charge of studying and formulating the overall project planning, the implementation plan, unified deployment, organization and implementation, supervision and inspection, and coordination on major issues. The provinces set up their own project leading

[20] In 2011, among the students for compulsory education in China, the number of the children that come with their parents as peasant workers to the cities is 12,609,700.

[21] In 2011, among the students for compulsory education in China, the number of the left-behind children in rural areas is 22,003,200.

groups headed by the government leaders with respective management systems and were responsible for the planning in their own regions, the theoretical approval of the plan, the tendering and procurement, the organization and management, as well as the inspection and acceptance. The municipal and county-level governments also established the leading groups and working organizations headed by the government leader that were responsible for the detailed implementation of the Project. The associations, schools, and enterprises are also the important participating organizations in the implementation of the Project. The Central Center for Educational Technology and the Central Resource Center for Basic Education of Ministry of Education were responsible for the personnel trainings for the Project, the restructuring, integration and delivery of the resources, the support for scientific research and the guidance to application and technical support and service, etc. Rural primary and middle schools are the main objects and beneficiaries of the implementation of the project (shown in Figure 2.24).

Management of Special Funds and the Timely Allocation of Matching Funds Are Important Guarantee for the Project

According to the needs of the Project, the central government had given two-thirds of the grant funds to the western region and one-third to the central region, whereas the eastern region basically relied on the investment of local finance. In addition, local governments were responsible for the funds of project management and the costs of equipment maintenance, which were forbidden to ask the peasants for investments. Most of the regions adopted the ways of investing funds from the provincial, municipal, and county levels. The provincial finance assumed the bulk of the financial responsibility. For instance, Guizhou province allocated matching funds proportionally: 50% of provincial finance, 20% of municipal finance, and 30% of county-level finance. Anhui province allocated the matching funds proportionally: 80% of provincial finance and 20% of county-level finance, Henan province allocated the matching funds half-and-half to the provincial and municipal governments, and the provincial finance of Inner Mongolia autonomous region afforded all matching funds for the project.

Figure 2.24

The Organizational Structure of the Administrative Management and Technical Implementation of the Project

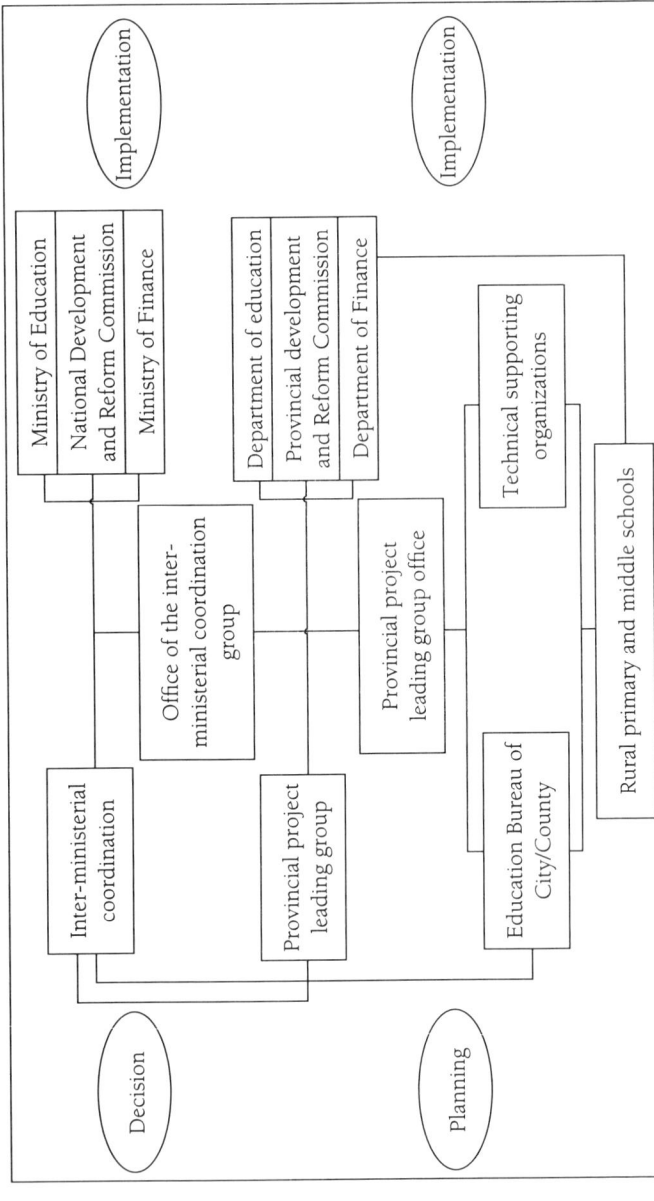

Source: Office of Modern Distance Education Project for China's Rural Primary and Middle Schools (2009).

Public Tendering Is an Effective Way of Ensuring the Quality of Project Equipment

In order to ensure the quality of project equipment, the three ministries specifically issued the equipment tendering, bidding and procurement management solution. The Office of the Inter-ministerial Coordination Group is in charge of the pre-approval of the qualification of equipment suppliers and integrators in order to select the famous domestic enterprises to participate in the construction of the project. Adhering to the principle of "openness, justice and fairness," the local governments formulate the tendering documents and organize public tendering of the Project equipment in accordance to the actual situations and requirements of local rural primary and middle schools.

Overall Coverage of Local Schools Is the Promotion Approach of Realizing the Scale Benefits of the Project

The overall coverage of local schools refers to the rural primary and middle schools in the Project regions, which is reflected in the gradual progress of groups of cities or counties during the same period, resulting in the following scaled benefits.

- First, the three modes could be fully integrated in the school education and teaching in the region so that the technical approaches could achieve the combinations with the daily education, teacher trainings, daily teaching and research, new curriculum reform, and other measures of rural education as well as the that of the local economic and social development of rural areas in the range of the region.
- Second, it formed the working network across the whole region, which was easy for the learning and exchanging among teachers or schools so as to expand good experience and share resources.
- Third, it reduced the cost of the logistics and maintenance of the Project, which made it possible for the localization of the technical support services that was maintained mainly by the counties.
- Fourth, it could gather the forces in the whole province to strengthen the guidance and supervision of the project in the covered regions.

Technical Support Service Systems of Four Levels Are the Guarantee of the Normal Operation of the Project

Relying on the system of centers for educational technology, the Project established the technical support service systems of national, provincial, municipal, and county levels (shown in Figure 2.25). At the national level, the National Resource Center for Basic Education of Ministry of Education integrated and delivered the IP resources of distance education in rural areas. At the same time, it also took the responsibility for the technical guidance of local service centers for technical support at different levels, connects the National Service Call Centre for Distance Education to the local service system as a network by multiple channels, such as telephones, the Internet, and text messages of mobile phones, to solve the queries in the construction and implementation of the Project equipment.

Three Modes Are the Scientific Path of Achieving the Low-cost and High-benefit Project

The Project spent only RMB 10 billion on the arduous task of providing quality educational resources and the training of distance education to hundreds of millions of rural students and peasants, millions of rural teachers, and hundreds of thousands of rural schools in the three modes. It first solved the problem of development from "nothing," which is the wise choice under resource constraints that characterize rural areas.

Problems Facing Sustainable Development

Inadequate Matching of the Level of Human Resources and the Requirements of Distance Education

The Project had organized numerous trainings for management staff, technicians and discipline teachers, but there were still many difficulties with continuous teacher training and their professional development.

Figure 2.25
Service System of Technical Support at the National, Provincial, Municipal, and County Levels

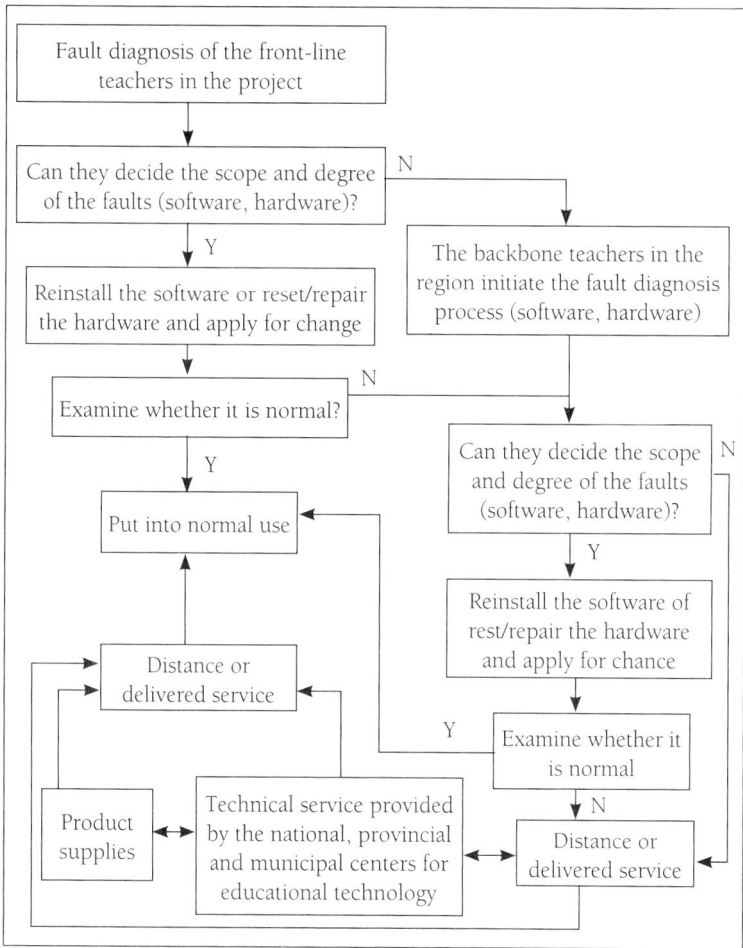

Source: Wang (2009).

- The teachers in some economically undeveloped areas still knew nothing about the Internet or computers. The training at the grass-roots level still only paid attention to the technical issues, which rarely involved the thematic training on the knowledge and skills, such as searching for information with purpose, screening and sorting out information and the integration of technology and curriculum. The effects of some teacher training were not satisfactory, because the teachers' lacked motivation to learn and were even resistant due to their entrapment in the arduous teaching tasks.

- There are problems with the lack of specialized maintenance staff for the equipment that were out of the warranty period in some schools. About 74% of maintenance staff also teach students and have to work extra hours to finish their jobs, let alone they neither have proficient technique nor sufficient fund. If the equipment did not work well, it had to be sent to the provincial after-sale service points for support, which inevitably delayed the classes. The support team of educational technology that provided specialized service for the application project of educational informatization was far from meeting the actual needs. That was one of the reasons why a number of infrastructures were limited or wasted.

- Some schools reflected that the technical training and discipline training were both for teachers. But when they went back to school, the understanding of their principals on distance education could not keep up with them, which prevented them from training the other teachers with the resources.

- School-based trainings had problems with inadequate frequency of training, incomplete content, the lack of accordance and sustainability, so that they could not solve the teaching problems in teaching.

- The funds for teacher training were mainly borne by local governments, who had difficulty allocating funds in time due to their limited financial resources.

Coexistence of Insufficient Equipment and the Low Utilization of Equipment

The investigation showed that 24% of the Project schools have the problems with regard to incomplete and aging hardware equipment and lack of multimedia classrooms, and 29% of the discipline teachers and administrators believe that the problem of "lack of hardware", which results where there are large number of students, is lesser compared to that of the computers, inappropriate equipment, and the lack of multimedia classrooms, computer classrooms, and electronic preparation room (Research Team of the Construction and Application of Educational Informatization, 2010). As the general implementation of the project, the equipment allocated by the project has gradually begun to be operated at full capacity. In the rural schools that have large scales and many classes, the teachers have begun to line up for appointment to give classes using the equipment. There are mainly two reasons as follows:

- First, the allocated equipment was insufficient. When designing the three modes, the objective was to achieve the basic "overall coverage" of distance education in rural primary and middle schools in order to solve the issue of "development from nothing." It was a good strategic selection in the circumstances of insufficient funds and unclear application modes at the time. However, it was apparently not enough for a six-year primary school to have only one computer or a junior middle school with more than 500 students to have one classroom with only 30 computers.
- Second, the maintenance of the equipment was inappropriate. The technicians in part of the schools could not easily clear the fault, nor could the suppliers provide technical services in time. The environment of the computer rooms in some schools was very poor, with unstable supply of electricity and frequent tripping, which resulted in shortening the usage period of the equipment or frequent downtime of the equipment. Part of the software system were expired or damaged due to human errors, which led to the improper use of the equipment. In some schools, the equipment were stolen.

On the other hand, some schools had the problem of low utilization rate of the equipment, which was less than 6 hours a week. The main reasons include:

- First was the issue awareness. Some principals considered distance education a great burden for the rural schools that were already lacking funds. The equipment in some schools was used only when the teachers gave open classes or the superior leaders came for inspection. The computer classrooms in some schools were locked up and the computers were put in the warehouse. The equipment of the Project in few schools had yet been used at the inspection and acceptance of the Project. Some schools shelved the equipment purchased by the government at high prices after using them several times because they were unable to use it or were afraid of damaging it.

- Second was the issue that the resources do not match the textbooks. The versions of the textbooks used in rural schools were published by different publications and in different disciplines, but the free resources sent by the National Resource Center for Basic Education of Ministry of Education only match with textbooks published by the People's Education Press. When the teachers find the resources inconsistent with their textbooks, they are not aware how to use or have the energy to look for the matching resources, therefore they simply do not use them.

Therefore, the development of modern distance education in rural primary and middle schools has to address the lack of equipment and the low utilization rate of equipment, which seem to be a paradox. It emphasizes not only further investment in the equipment, but also the guidance and assistance of the regions and schools with improper utilization.

Lack of Follow-up Guarantee and the Investment of Operation Funds

Modern distance education in rural primary and middle schools cannot be completed with only one-time investment of hardware and software, which also needs the follow-up investments in the updates of the equipment and the resources, the maintenance of the equipment and teacher trainings, etc. Although the government has invested a lot of money in the construction phase of the project, it does not have any clear and rigid policies and regulations on the funding resources for the follow-up work, such as the operation, management, application, and maintenance of the project, which will inevitably lead to the sustainable development of the project without appropriate guarantee (Zeng, 2011).

A survey shows that the funds for the project construction and the purchase of equipment in the Hexi Corridor that are invested by the project are mainly in three ways, among which 77.7% is of the "national project investment and school self-investment," 7.6% is of "the sole investment of the national project" and 14.7% is of "sole investment of the schools themselves." The way of the "national project investment and school self-investment" is the mainstream. The funds for the initial construction of the equipment and resources are mainly borne by the central finance, and teacher trainings are mainly funded by local governments and schools. Once the project is completed, it is largely dependent on the investment of the schools, in particular the teacher trainings, which sometimes are even afforded by the teachers themselves. The national project does not allocate the funds for equipment management, maintenance, and daily operation, which are also raised by the schools, but rural schools do not have the channels or the capacity of raising the funds (Wang, 2009).

Lack of the Structure in the Supporting Educational and Teaching Resources

In the process of resource construction, it lacks the in-depth investigation and analysis on the resource requirements, including the realistic requirements, potential requirements and development requirements of different types of teachers and students in different types of schools in different areas, so there is always a certain gap between the integration, sharing, development and construction of the resources and different types of requirements. Many teachers who have used teaching CDs reflect that the contents of the CDs do not match with the textbooks. Besides, the contents of CDs are designed according to the characteristics of urban teachers and students, therefore, the teaching methods do not apply with the realistic teaching conditions in rural areas, nor are the students find them easy to adapt (Lai, 2009). In addition, the resources provided by the project have a broad coverage with a large amount of data, which are mainly resources of materials, but those that can be directly used in the implementation of self-study, inquiry and collaborative learning are few. The capability of information technology of the discipline teachers in rural primary and middle schools is limited, so it is very difficult for them to find the information as they require to find from several resources or to make major changes to the resources, which will decrease their enthusiasm in using distance education resources for teaching.

The survey found that there are two unavoidable issues of using CDs in rural teaching points in practice. First, the fund provided for each teaching point is only RMB 500–600, which can only be used to purchase 100–200 supporting CDs, so it is difficult to meet the requirements of different disciplines to form a supporting system. Second, the teachers have to prepare lessons, watch CDs, and select teaching methods before applying the teaching CDs in the class, but in a considerable number of teaching units the teachers who are working in mixed-grade classes also have to take care of the students at the school hostels, so they do not have time for preparation. Besides, the constraints of the fund in the teaching units make it difficult for the supplement and update of the CDs (Wang, 2008).

Moreover, the diversion of resources in different construction units causes repeated construction and low degree of standardization, and the left-behind concepts and the defection of the system limit the sharing of resources.

Many Difficulties of the Application of Information Technology in Teaching

The teachers had some difficulties in the application of information technology in teaching. For example, the time-consuming preparation increased the burden of preparing lessons, the teachers lacked adequate IT skills and were bound by traditional teaching concepts; the number of equipment at schools were not enough, and there was a lack of the guidance from the experts and the teaching cases or other reference resources.

Some teachers only used the equipment when there were visitors or they gave open classes, which is a terrible formalism in the tide of educational informatization in rural areas. Most of the teachers did not achieve the real integration of IT in teaching, despite their use of information technology or preparing lessons, giving lessons, and conducting research. The school leaders, discipline teachers as well as students only cared about the scores and the enrollment rate to a higher grade, they paid little attention to the application of information technology in teaching and thought it was enough to simply learn about it in the IT classes. Some leaders even thought that the development of information technology is a sense of school packaging that can produce the effects of attracting more students. However, the comprehensive and in-depth application of information technology in teaching will affect the enrollment rate to a higher grade due to the changes in the teaching modes.

In addition, the implementation of the Project formulated a series of rules and regulations, which were just hung on the wall without implementation. The administrative departments of education made full use of supervision mechanisms, such as the supervisions on the use of funds, equipment, the sorting out of the resources and the application by the teachers. They also adopted the incentive measures to some extent, such as the evaluation and provision of awards, but the evaluation mechanism had not been established. Thus, there was no evaluation on the Project in the perspectives of the application effects of the teachers and students. These were all the problems in the development, so the formation of modern distance education system in rural primary and middle schools in the need of the requirements of the time was a systematic project full of opportunities and challenges, which required the process of repeated cycles.

Expectations and Suggestions

The education informatization in rural areas of China face three major challenges, which are to reduce the digital divide among regions and to realize the balanced development of education, to continuously enhance the application capabilities and investment benefits, and to promote the depth and breadth of the new curriculum reform. Facing the problems in the development, local governments and the teachers and students in rural schools expect to continue the implementation of modern distance education in rural primary and middle schools on the basis of consolidating the existing achievements. Therefore, the suggestions are as follows.

Continuously Increase Investment of the Governments in Modern Distance Education in Rural Primary and Middle Schools

In the face of a huge base of educational development, the overall investment of the construction of Chinese educational informatization is inadequate. The investments at different stages had different focuses. The investment in the future should mainly be used in two aspects:

- First, it focuses on the upgrade and improvement of the infrastructure. It has been proposed to construct the distance education environment and mobile learning environment that have appropriate functions, are easy to use, have rich resources and focus on effectiveness where the students use ordinary computers and the teachers share mobile laptops. According to the local conditions, the local governments and schools can choose the network and mobile learning terminals and technical solutions that are easy to operate and expandable so as to achieve the outcomes of "the access to all classes and the application in all lessons" with the resources into the classroom, into the community and into the peasants' households.
- Second, it focuses on the construction of resources, training funds, and the costs for daily operation and maintenance. It has been suggested that the emphasis should be on the solution to the development of the resources for enquiry-based learning, self-study and collaborative learning that match with the classroom reform for basic education, the construction of the resources for knowledge points as well as the update mechanism of the resources for thematic education and teacher training. In addition, it has been recommended to try to establish the marketing operation system of the construction of school informatization, which means to attract the enterprises to participate in the investment in the construction of modern distance education in rural primary and middle schools under the guidance of the governments.

Focus on Strengthening the Attention and Support of Modern Distance Education to the Disadvantaged Group of People

The development tasks of the educational informatization in rural areas of China in the next decade will focus on the support for the construction of informatization of primary and middle schools and public service system in rural areas, remote and poor areas and minority areas in the efforts to narrow down the digital divide between regions, between urban and rural areas, and between the schools. Modern distance education in rural primary and middle schools should not only pay attention to all rural schools, teachers, and students, but also to those that are still in disadvantaged positions due to various reasons. It is recommended that the students who are studying at the learning points, the students and families left behind in rural areas by their parents who work in cities and the schools, teachers and students of the minorities should be given special attention and support.

The Project will further play the role of rural schools in the training for young peasants and technicians, the education of women and girls, the education of the elders, and the services for the rural areas and the agriculture sector in order to promote the construction of the learning society in rural areas and the socioeconomic development and transformation.

Continuously Strengthen the Capability Construction of Educational Technology of the Teachers in Rural Primary and Middle Schools

The Project will combine the training for teachers on IT and the capacity building of educational technology of the teachers in primary and middle schools, establish the resource centers for teacher training and public learning service centers at local and school levels, organize and promote the teachers in different regions to carry out online inter-school collaborative research and teacher trainings, and build the system of professional development for rural teachers based on the platform of distance education so as to continuously improve the quality of rural teachers.

From Digital to Smart Learning Environment

At the new historical stage of development, the development of educational informatization in rural areas will gradually proceed from the macro to micro construction and from the expansion of scale to the development of connotation with more focuses on the capacity building of the application of educational technology and how technology can promote the changes in learning and teaching methods. The construction of the learning environment is the basis of the changes of learning and teaching methods. It is therefore an important direction of the development of educational informatization in the future, to provide a more convenient, comfortable and effective learning environment for the learners. It is proposed to establish smart classrooms and smart campuses in rural primary and middle schools; to construct a public learning service system and supporting platform based on cloud computing to achieve the changes from digital to smart learning environment (Huang et al., 2012). This means providing appropriate learning resources and convenient interactive tools to automatically record the learning process, evaluating the learning outcomes, and providing the learning support services in accordance with the conditions of learners.

Bibliography

Chen, Q. (2006). Research into the Application Modes of Teaching in the Environment of Modern Distance Education in Rural Primary and Middle Schools. *E-Education Research*, 12: 36–38.

Huang, R. (2003). *Computer-supported Collaborative Learning: Theory and Methods*. Beijing: People's Education Press.

Huang, R., Yang, J., & Hu, Y. (2012). From Digital to Smart: The Evolution and Trends of Learning Environment. *Open Education Research*, 1: 75–84.

Lai, X. (2009). Analysis on the Constraints of Effective Implementation of Modern Distance Education Project for Rural Primary and Middle Schools in Mountainous Regions: Investigation on the Implementation of Distance Education Project for Rural Primary and Middle Schools in Ganzhou City. *Journal of Gannan Normal University*, 6: 92–95.

Lv, M. (2007). The Practice, Problems and Solutions to the Application of "Modern Distance Education Project for Rural Primary and Middle Schools". *China Education Info*, 4: 7–11.

National Bureau of Statistics of China. (2003). *China Statistics Yearbook 2003.* Beijing: China Statistics Press.

Office of Modern Distance Education Project for China's Rural Primary and Middle Schools (Project Office). (2009). *Building the Bridge to the Future: Modern Distance Education Project for China's Rural Primary and Middle Schools.* Beijing: People's Education Press.

Research Team of the Construction and Application of Educational Informatization of Ministry of Education. (2010). *Research Report on the Topic of the Construction and Application of Educational Informatization in China.* Beijing: Higher Education Press.

Wang, Z. (2008). *Research Report on Modern Distance Education Project for Rural Primary and Middle Schools.* Unpublished.

———. (2009). Outstanding Issues in Modern Distance Education Project for Rural Primary and Middle Schools. *Distance Education in China*, 8: 61–65.

Wei, J. (2010). Investigation and Research into the Implementation Performances of Modern Distance Education Project for Rural Primary and Middle Schools: Taking Chang'an District, Xi'an city of Shaanxi Provice as an Example. Master Dissertation of School of Education of Shaanxi Normal University.

Yang, X. (2008). *Cost-benefit Analysis of Modern Distance Education for Rural Primary and Middle Schools.* Beijing: National Defense Industry Press.

Zeng, X. (2011). Review on Modern Distance Education Project for China's Rural Primary and Middle Schools. *China Educational Education*, 1: 31–35.

3

Educational Technology Promotes the Quality of In-class Teaching in Rural Schools

Yu Shengquan, Zeng Haijun, and Wang Ying

Overview

"Educational Technology Promotes the Quality of In-class Teaching in Rural Primary and Middle Schools" is a pilot program led by Modern Educational Technology Research Institute of Beijing Normal University. Against the overall backdrop of accelerated information and communication technology (ICT)-based education development and the ongoing new curriculum reform in China, various methods, such as face-to-face teaching, class attending, teaching evaluation, tutorial, online teaching, online discussion, inspection and evaluation, and cross-school, cross-area and nationwide exchange and seminars, are adopted to integrate ICT into school teaching. The ultimate objective of the pilot program for leapfrog development is to improve teaching quality in rural primary and middle schools to the level of outstanding schools in big cities without prolonged class hours or additional burden on students, and to eliminate significant difference in examination scores and achieve an all-round development of students.

Launched in September 2000, the pilot program has evolved through four phases by the end of 2012, namely preliminary establishment of theoretical approach, improvement of theoretical approach, deepening of pilot exploration and expansion of pilot areas. There are over 390 pilot schools so far, distributed in 27 pilot areas, 16 of which are in rural areas. Targeted at areas and schools equipped with or without the Internet facility, this program has seen a large number of successful cases where ICT-based teaching was implemented using theories, technologies, modes, and methods to improve teaching quality in rural areas. This method could also be widely replicated and popularized.

Background: Enabling Rural Students to Enjoy Education Opportunities Equally

Educational equity includes three aspects: equity in the starting point, the process, and the achievements. It requires considerable human resources, financial resources, and materials to achieve equity in these areas, especially equity in the starting point. However, what truly matters is equity in educational achievements, as long as rural students have access to as good education as urban students, achieve the same examination scores, and meet the same comprehensive quality requirements, inequity in their starting point would not matter much. Conventional theories on educational equity maintain that inequity in the starting point will inevitably result in inequity. However, today the modern e-learning project for rural primary and middle schools is in place, and schools in central and western China are generally equipped with basic ICT-based teaching facilities. If we adopt innovative theories, modes, and methods of ICT-based teaching, will the correlation between starting point inequity and result inequity be changed? The "Educational Technology Promotes the Quality of In-class Teaching in Rural Primary and Middle Schools" program is implemented to practice, explore, and seek the ultimate answer through experiments and research (see Figure 3.1).

Figure 3.1
A 70-Year-Old Professor Educated 60,000 Students in Mountain Areas for 17 Years

Source: Website of the program http://www.etc.edu.cn/

Although in his 70s, Prof. He Kekang is still as dedicated to education as he has always been. Walking on the village paths leading to school, he always tells students: "I don't know what it will look like tomorrow, but I do know what I should do today." He believes that "rural areas are a vast world to be tapped into by educationists. Educational equity and balance are our responsibility. We should strive to provide rural children with fair access to quality education resources."

Objective: Focusing on Both Knowledge and Capability to Achieve All-round Development

Prof. He Kekang, Director of the program, explained the objective of the pilot program for leapfrog development in plain language: "Turning weak schools with poor conditions into good and even reputed schools with high teaching quality; turning ordinary teachers into elite, outstanding and even renowned teachers; turning lagging-behind students with low starting points into students of excellence." Prof. Yu Shengquan, expert of the program team, explained:

> Leapfrogging is not premature development, but a direct tackling of the crucial issues in education development such as improvement of in-class teaching, burden alleviation and education for all-round development. It is intended to push education modernization onto a higher level through innovation and overcoming obstacles.

The objective of the program is to focus on both knowledge and capability to achieve all-round development of students (see Figure 3.2), and

Figure 3.2
Comprehensive Development Targets of the Program

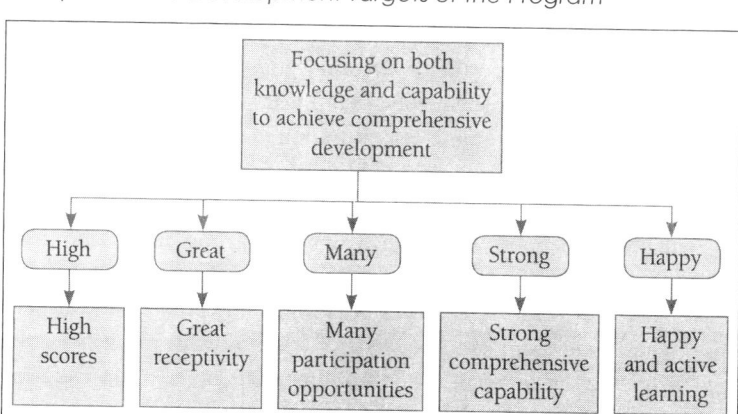

Source: Website of the program http://www.etc.edu.cn/

to achieve better teaching quality without prolonged class hours or burden on students. Specifically:

1. *Chinese.* Enabling students finishing grade-2 schooling to recognize no less than 2,500 Chinese characters, read general newspapers and popular youth materials, and write completely structured logical articles of at least 300 characters using computer (or write articles of at least 150 characters by hand). After finishing each grade, students should reach the same level as students of the same grade in local top-ranked schools in terms of recognizing number of characters, reading and writing ability.
2. *English.* Enabling students to make significant progress in vocabulary, listening, and speaking; enabling primary school students to recognize 2,000 words and to acquire basic listening, speaking, reading and writing abilities. After finishing each grade, students should reach the same level as students of the same grade in local top-ranked schools in terms of vocabulary, reading and writing.
3. *Other subjects.* Achieving considerable improvement in teaching quality and students' all-round development through in-depth integration of ICT and course teaching. Measurement can be made in three aspects: depth reached in meeting the standard teaching targets of the new basic curriculum, improvement of the practical problem-solving ability, and development of the thinking ability.

The reason why this program realized these targets was that the research team developed their own innovative theories on ICT-based teaching, formed a complete set of effective teaching modes and methods, and put them into continuous use in training teachers (see Figures 3.3 and 3.4). On the basis of their study on linguistic psychology and neurophysiology, the team led by Prof. He Kekang put forward the Theory of Semantic Perception in second language learning, laying the theoretical foundation for the leapfrog development experiment in English teaching. On the basis of the laws of children's cognitive development and linguistic development and years of teaching reform practices, the team proposed the New Theory on Children's Development of Thinking as the theoretical foundation of the leapfrog development experiment of Chinese teaching. Combining the two with teaching practices, they

Figure 3.3
*Experiment Model for Leapfrog Development in Basic Education
Established by the Research Team*

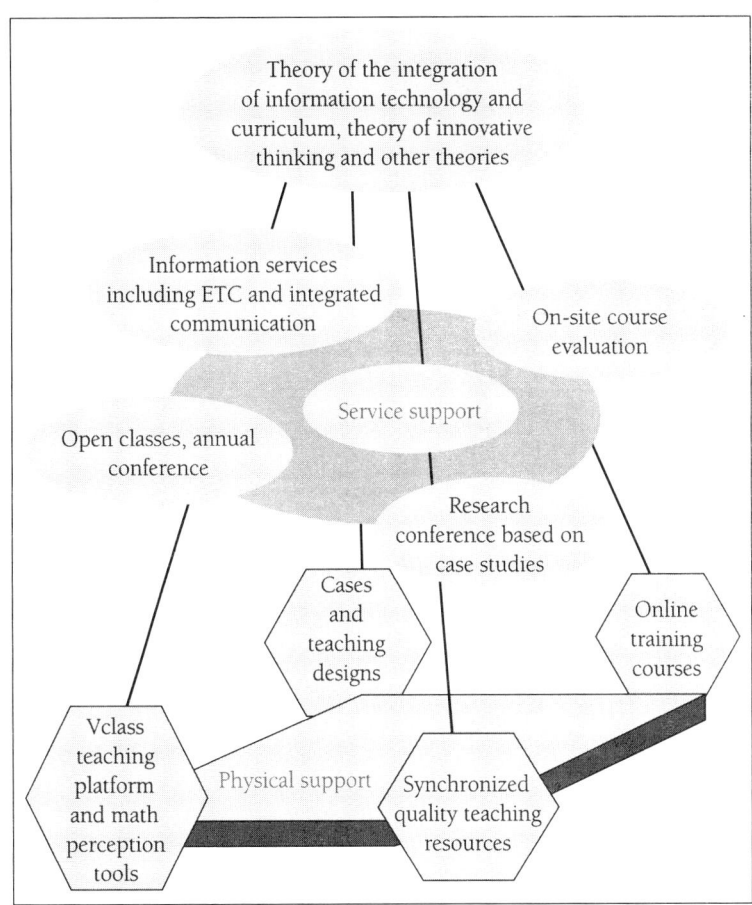

Source: Website of the program http://www.etc.edu.cn/

raised the "dominant force-center" (DC) model, new constructivist theory and innovative thinking theory. Computer- and Internet-based ICT was used as a tool to promote independent learning, facilitate exchange and to create effective motivation. The conventional teacher-centered teaching structure was transformed into the new structure of "teachers as the dominant force and students as the center."

Figure 3.4
Monographs on Basic Theories of the Program

Creative Thinking Theory:
Construction and Demonstration
of the DC Model

New Theory on Children's
Development of Thinking

Theory of Semantic Perception: New
Theory on Children's Linguistic
Development

Integration of ICT and Curriculum:
Teaching Modes and Methods in the
Internet Age

Source: Website of the program http://www.etc.edu.cn/

Implementation

Modern Educational Technology Research Institute of Beijing Normal University, organizer of the program, was founded in 1979, and is the most reputed research and training organization on educational technology in China. Prof. He Kekang, director of the institute, is one of the founders of the discipline of Chinese educational technology, and has been active in teaching for over 50 years. The head research team is set up in the institute to design, implement, manage, coordinate, and monitor the program nationwide. Several research teams are established in program pilot areas, and a subject director is designated by the head research team to design and guide the subject within the areas. Dedicated teams are set up to take charge of teaching guidance, technical service, teacher training, and communication and contact, respectively (see Figure 3.5).

Guidance and Support Service

Regarding teaching guidance, the research team regularly visits pilot schools to organize activities such as watching and learning, comment on outstanding classes, class attending, class evaluation, seminars, and guidance on teaching designs (see Figure 3.6).

The procedure to guide the teaching process is as follows: teachers submit their teaching designs, discuss the designs in groups, teachers implement the designs in class, have group discussions after class, teachers reflect on the teaching, and revise the designs and submit them to the guidance team.

The two key factors during this process are the preparation of teaching designs and reflection on the teaching. Pilot teachers are generally familiar with how to prepare traditional teaching materials, but have little or no idea about teaching design in ICT-based environment. Therefore, pilot teachers are required to have frequent face-to-face or e-mail discussions with the guidance team on their teaching designs.

The guidance team visits pilot schools at least once a month to guide teaching of each pilot teacher by attending and evaluating classes (see Figure 3.7). After the class, team members exchange opinions with school leaders, teaching research staff, and pilot teachers, identifying

Figure 3.5
Organizational Structure of the Research Team and Guiding Areas

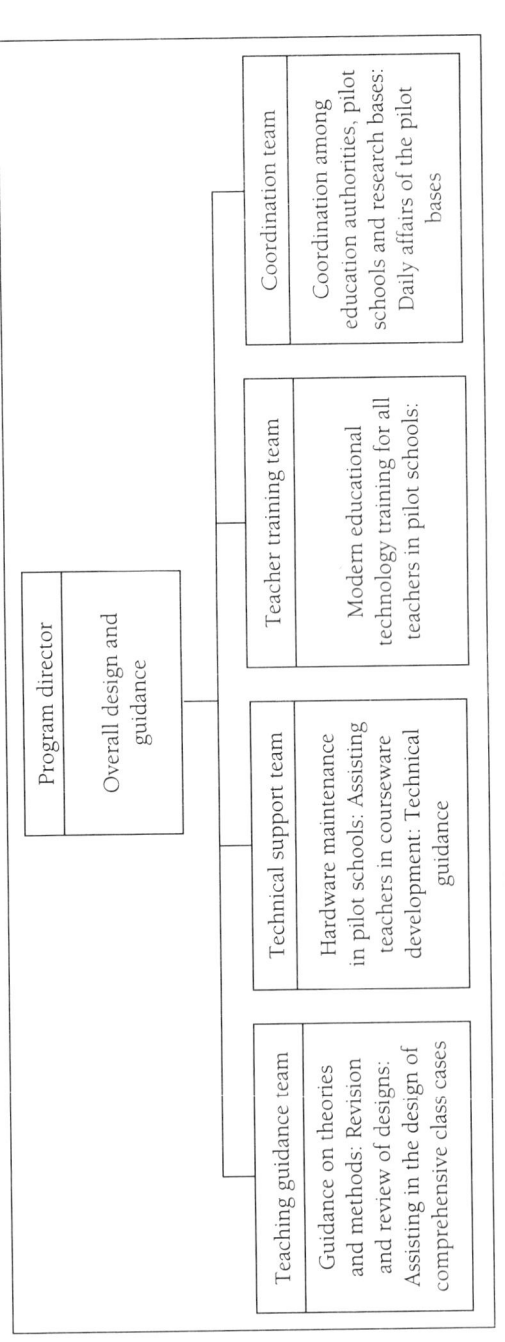

Source: Website of the program http://www.etc.edu.cn/

Figure 3.6
Teaching Guidance in Multiple Forms

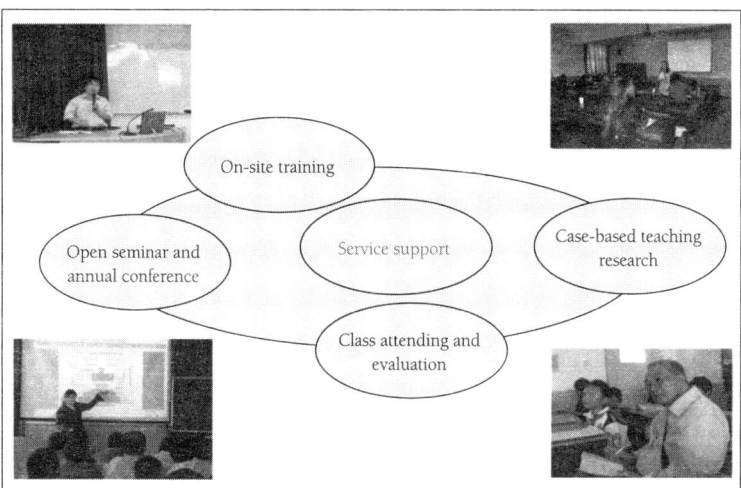

Source: Website of the program http://www.etc.edu.cn/

merits and meanwhile offering advice and feasible methods on how to overcome shortcomings. Activities of each month are publicized and sent via e-mail to related leaders of pilot schools and education authorities to effectively promote the progress of the pilot program.

Pilot teachers are organized to watch and learn from outstanding classes (see Figure 3.8) and listen to comments of experts. In this way, helping pilot teachers to get a vivid perception on innovative teaching concepts before going back to teaching and research makes an effective approach to promote their expertise development.

The leading research team tries to provide officials and teachers in pilot areas with opportunities for cross-region exchange to enhance communication between schools in pilot areas (see Figure 3.9).

Moreover, each research team regularly organizes knowledge tests for students in pilot classes and pilot schools, and conducts comparative tests with major schools in some developed cities to validate the effect of the program. Feedback from education authorities, teachers, and parents is sought in time to improve the program design.

Figure 3.7
Guidance Team Members Attending and Evaluating Classes

A teacher giving a class	A teacher giving a class
Prof. He Kekang attending a class	Prof. Yu Shengquan discussing with a pilot teacher after class
Pilot teachers preparing teaching designs together	Guidance team members discussing with pilot teachers

Source: Website of the program http://www.etc.edu.cn/

Figure 3.8
Model Classes of Chinese and English

Dialogue in English class

Dialogue pairs in English class

Look that!

Bulletin board of a pilot class

Dialogue in a language lab

Character recognition in groups

Source: Website of the program http://www.etc.edu.cn/

Figure 3.9

The 9th National Annual Conference of the Pilot Research on Leapfrog Development of Basic Education

Source: Website of the program http://www.etc.edu.cn/

Training for Pilot Teachers

According to the program progress and specific demand, research teams provide all teachers engaged in the pilot research with training sessions on theories, modes, methods, and technology. Basic training is done collectively for all teachers involved, while enhancement training is implemented by issuing training materials and one-on-one tutorial. All training materials can be uploaded and downloaded on the program website. The program adopts case-based research methods and integrates study, work, and teaching research of teachers to promote their development and meanwhile develop schools into learning organizations.

After communication with pilot teachers, research teams launched an e-learning platform for training to meet the teachers' demand, and introduced the mixed training mode based on experiences from online courses (see Figure 3.10). Online courses are tailored to the scientific research and teaching demand of pilot teachers at various stages, and cover over 30 topics, such concept of the program, program management,

Figure 3.10

Mixed Training Mode Based on Experience-type Online Courses

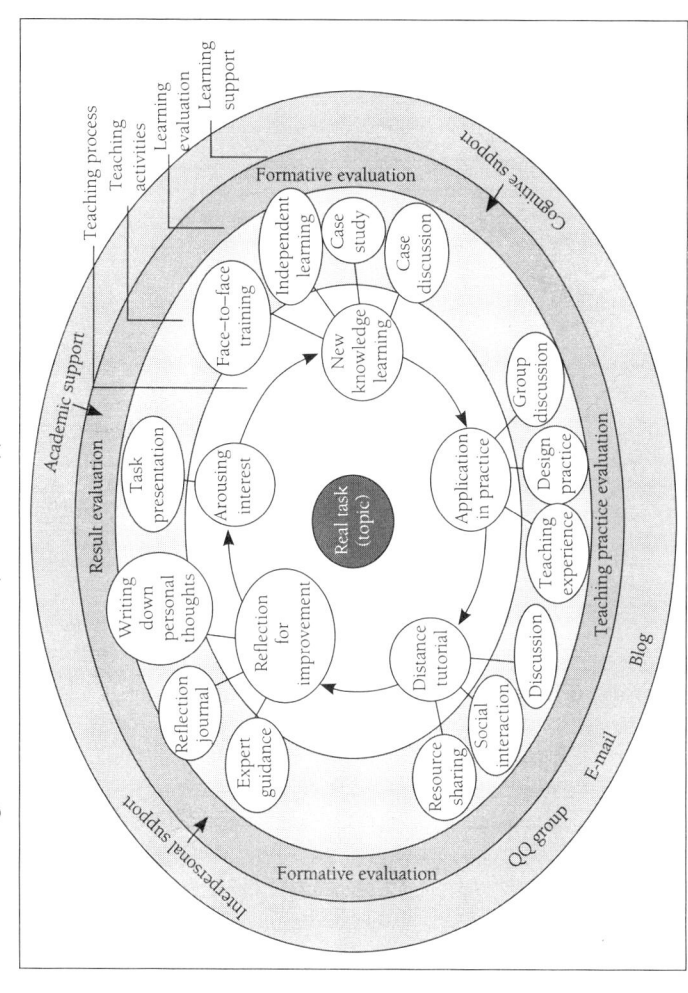

Source: Website of the program http://www.etc.edu.cn/

ICT environment and tools, teaching design, teaching case and common issues (see Table 3.1). The purpose is to help pilot teachers grow from beginners to expert teachers through study of the courses. The training package includes three modules, namely, course introduction, learning manual, and online courses.

Table 3.1
Topic List of Online Teacher Training Courses

Target	Topic
Concept preparation	1. Learning preparation
	2. ICT and curriculum integration
ICT environment and tools	3. Management of online pilot classes
	4. Use of Vclass platform
	5. Application of MS Office in teaching—PPT
	6. Application of MS Office in teaching—Word
	7. Cultivation of students' writing capability
Teaching design	8. ICT-based teaching design
	9. Five-dimensional innovative teaching in primary schools
	10. Five-dimensional innovative teaching in middle schools
	11. Teaching evaluation and reflection
	12. Design of learning resources
Low-grade teaching	13. Case study: *Pinyin* teaching cases
	14. Case study: Chinese character recognition
	15. Case study: text teaching in low grades
	16. Case study: English teaching in low grades
Program management	17. Program management
Addressing common issues in teaching	18. Cultivation of innovative thinking
	19. Transformation of lagging-behind students
Medium/high-grade teaching	20. English of medium/higher grades
	21. Chinese of medium/higher grades

Table 3.1 continued

Table 3.1 continued

Target	Topic
Middle school teaching	22. Case study: ICT integration in liberal arts classes in middle schools
	23. Case study: ICT integration in sciences classes in middle schools
Application of related teaching tools (intermediate and advanced)	24. CAI software
	25. Advanced information search
	26. Multimedia material processing and integration
Actualizing teaching result	27. Topic study and design & teaching design package preparation
	28. Design and preparation of comprehensive class cases
Professional development of teachers	29. Essay writing and research methods
	30. ICT-based Teacher development

Source: Website of the program http://www.etc.edu.cn/

Support Service with Online Platform

The research team has provided an online platform together with technical support. With the platform, the team collets achievements, and communicates with pilot teachers. The online portal offers event announcement, introduction to the program, learning materials, pictures of past events, excellent essays, outstanding cases, teaching resources, common questions and online training, and serves as a window for information exchange between the leading research team and pilot teachers.

The interactive platform for class teaching includes modules such as development evaluation, learning activity design, course resource management, online teaching design, e-profile package, shared reading system, knowledge construction forum, writing and commenting system, class activity bank and journal.

Digital Learning Resource Service

ICT integration in the curriculum is a series of disks containing learning materials. It is issued to each pilot school on a monthly basis to support the conventional class teaching for leapfrog development. The materials cover theoretical learning, practice, teaching forum, training materials, and excellent cases, and are intended to share the latest teaching research achievements with pilot teachers (see Figure 3.11).

The teaching resource website includes supporting resources for textbooks of all versions used in pilot schools, and pilot teachers can easily look up resources according to textbook they use, largely saving the time spent on searching among "the vast sea of information." English resources include 72 online teaching books and 48 nononline resource books in supplement to 10 different versions of textbooks. Chinese resources include 60 online teaching books and 20 offline resource books in supplement to six different versions of textbooks (see Figure 3.12).

Figure 3.11
ICT Integration in Curriculum

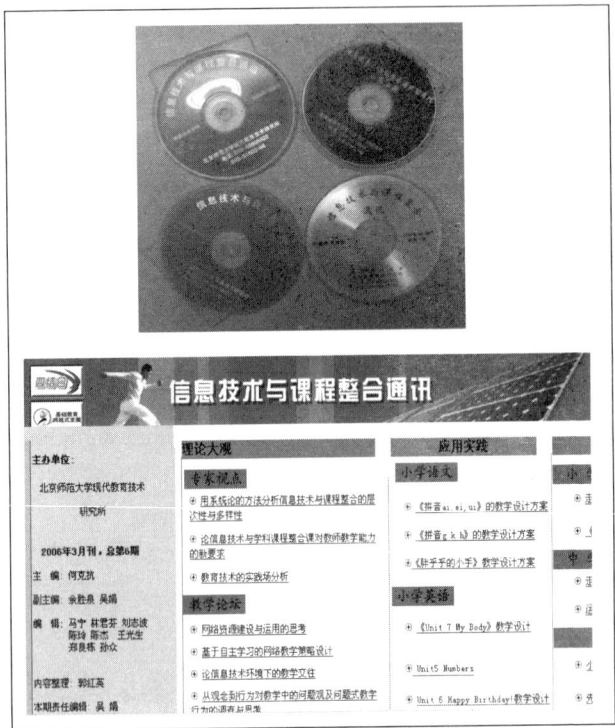

Source: Website of the program http://www.etc.edu.cn/

Figure 3.12
Online and Offline Materials for English and Chinese

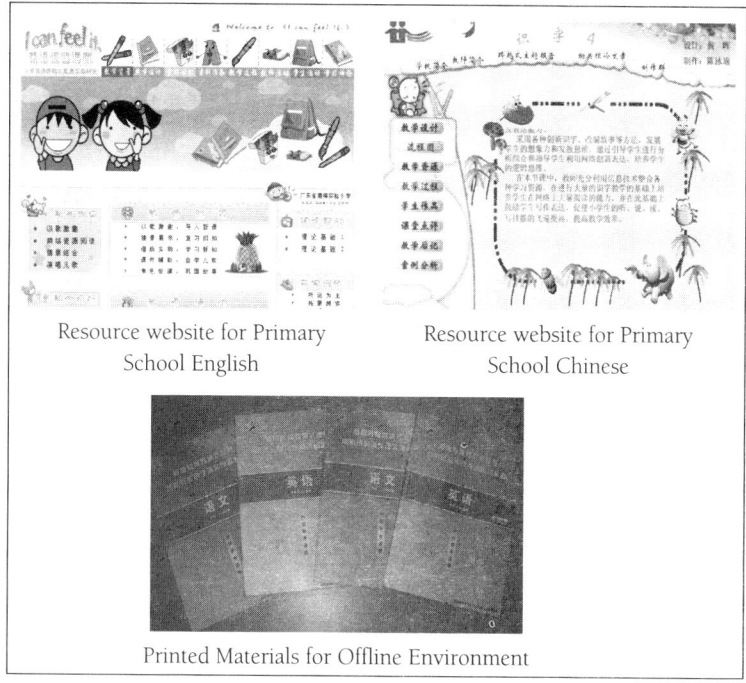

Resource website for Primary
School English

Resource website for Primary
School Chinese

Printed Materials for Offline Environment

Source: Website of the program http://www.etc.edu.cn/

There are now more than 1,000 teaching designs and cases for various knowledge types and class types (see Figure 3.13). Such practical and theoretical achievements are of great value for pilot teachers, especially new teachers, to understand the concepts of the program and to start up their own practice within a short period of time.

Fund

The program is mainly funded by:

1. Program funds earmarked by Beijing Normal University, Ministry of Education, and National Center for Educational Technology as the start-up fund.

Figure 3.13
Collections of Excellent Teaching Designs and Cases

Source: Website of the program http://www.etc.edu.cn/

2. Support of the Ford Foundation, Beijing Western Sunshine Rural Development Foundation, Give2Asia Foundation and Chen Yet-Sen Family Foundation. For instance, Beijing Western Sunshine Rural Development Foundation provided RMB9 million in May 2012 to support launch the program in poverty-stricken areas in southern Gansu over the next six years. Approximately 60,000 middle and primary school students in nearly 400 schools will participate in the program.
3. Fiscal support from education authorities of pilot areas.
4. Donations from individuals or enterprises.

The above-mentioned funds are mainly used for provision of related printed and digital learning resources for students, design and development of teaching resources, teacher training and thematic seminars, and necessary travels, equipment and program management.

Achievements

Objective Evaluation

In June 2007, seven classes from six pilot schools in Yanqing, Beijing and 19 classes from 14 pilot schools in Changping, Beijing were selected for a comparative test; while classes from four reputed schools with high teaching quality in urban Beijing were selected as the control group.

Pilot school got remarkably higher average scores than the control group in terms of English listening, writing, speaking, and total score, got slightly lower average scores in Chinese basics and reading, and got higher average scores in composition and total score.

In June 2006, five pilot primary schools in Fengning County, Hebei province were selected to participate in the comparative test. Grade-2 students in pilot areas of Fengning had a Chinese vocabulary of 2,745.5 characters on average. Four selected schools out of five got better results than the required standard of 2,500, and the remaining one failed to meet the requirement due to replacement of the pilot Chinese teacher and program coordinator at the end of Grade 1.

One rural pilot primary school was selected out of the five for the English test. The excellence rates in speaking, listening, and vocabulary reached 25.45%, 39.29%, and 32.12%, respectively, and the passing rates reached 72.73%, 82.14%, and 66.07%, respectively. In the speaking test, students had acquired 8.91 sentences and 5.69 different structures on average, all reaching up to the basic requirements.

Subjective Evaluation

Some reflections of pilot teachers and comments from pilot schools and parents on the program were quoted as follows:

"Since the engagement in the program, the entire class has made remarkable progress in learning habit, attitude, enthusiasm, comprehensive capability, morale and solidarity." (A pilot teacher from Yanqing, Beijing)

"There is a lagging-behind student in my class. He recognized only a few characters at the beginning, but after one year of learning, teaching and encouragement, he now actively learns new characters in new texts, reads the texts aloud and writes excellent compositions. His parents are quite satisfied." (A pilot teacher from Yanqing, Beijing)

"With practice in the leapfrog research team and with the help of other teachers, I have made progress and some achievements." (A pilot teacher in Changping, Beijing)

"The leapfrog pilot program is one of the most effective programs I've ever seen, and it is closely tied with the practice of teaching. Its achievements in Fengning are inspiring. I hope the research team can keep promoting the valuable experience to more areas and schools, especially the vast rural areas, to benefit more children and teachers." (Director of Education Bureau of Fengning County, Hebei)

"The leapfrog program is conducive to improving the quality of teachers, especially their understanding of modern education concepts and ICT skills." (Vice Principal of a middle school in Foshan, Guangdong)

"The leapfrog pilot program aroused students' interest in learning, and made them more active in participation. In this sense, it not only drove the progress in their daily learning, but also promoted the improvement of the all-round development of students." (Principal of a pilot primary school in Nanshan District, Shenzhen)

"My child used to know nothing, but after one year, he can easily come up with English words, sentences and ballads. I'm really impressed. I cannot tutor my child at all, and I would like to say to the English teacher again: Thank you very much!" (Parent of a pilot school student in Changping, Beijing)

"I don't know much about leapfrog education, but I see progress and better performance of my child. I hope the program can be further promoted to benefit more students." (Parent of a Grade-3 student in Fengning)

Social Feedback

The program was widely and warmly received by the public. It was awarded the first prize of the 4th National Scientific Research Achievement on Education (see Figure 3.14). Mainstream media such as CCTV, CETV, *China Youth Daily*, *Southern People Weekly*, *Wenhui Daily*, *Yangcheng Evening News*, *Guangming Daily*, and *Sina* all covered the program in feature stories.

In November 2008, Chen Xiaoya, then Vice Minister of Education, pointed out after hearing the program achievement report that using ICT to help rural primary and middle schools and teachers improve the teaching quality embodies distinct "Chinese characteristics." ICT-based education in rural areas is about not only the modernization of equipment, but also a drive forward of the modernization of education and focus on class and teaching quality. Quality of education involves not

Figure 3.14
Award Certificate of the Program Achievements

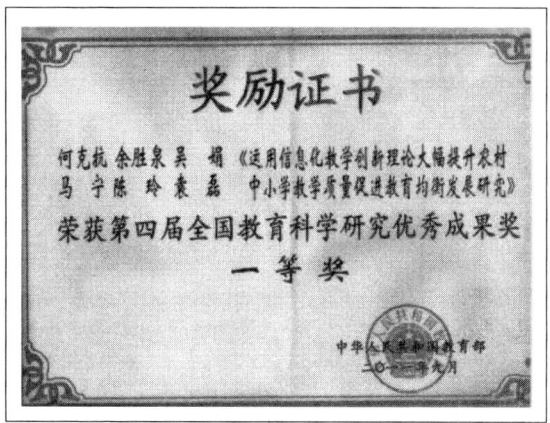

Source: Website of the program http://www.etc.edu.cn/

only conditions and the starting point, but also the process and results, and it is highly rigid in law and cycle. It takes time to explore and summarize and takes great efforts of a large number of research institutes and schools to achieve relative equity in the process and result.

In June 2006, the expert panel of Ministry of Education concluded after inspecting the achievements of the pilot program that this was an outstanding scientific research achievement on education, providing a large number of successful cases of using ICT to considerably promote the teaching quality. Education experts also highly valued the research. Well-known educationist Mr. Tao Xiping, after visiting several pilot schools, commended the program as a down-to-earth innovative research. Educationist Prof. Ye Lan said the program applied and integrated ICT into teaching, explored a path of close combination, and shared development of ICT and educational theories. Famous education expert Mr Wang Benzhong praised the program as "reaching up high and deeply rooted" in a sense that it was an independently innovative theory that bravely challenges international authoritative theories and a down-to-earth program closely linked to primary and middle school teachers and teaching.

Experience: How to Integrate ICT into Teaching?

Guide the Integration with New Constructivism

New constructivism is highlighted here not because it is perfect, but because its learning-oriented teaching concept that students obtain knowledge and meaning through self- construction is a shock to the traditional teacher-centered teaching structure in China. Moreover, constructivism learning theories, teaching theories, and teaching design methods in a constructivism learning environment can provide strong theoretical support for teaching in an ICT-based environment, that is, integration of ICT and curriculum.

Base the Integration on the New DC Teaching Model

We endeavor to create an ICT-based teaching environment and a teaching and learning process featured by "independence, exploration and cooperation" with an aim to transform the traditional teacher-centered teaching structure. Such a transformation should result in a new teaching structure that puts into full play both the dominant role of teachers and the position of students as the center. This requires teachers to pay close attention to the four key factors in their teaching in class, that is, teachers, students, teaching content, and teaching media. Can the position and role of the four factors be changed in some way and to what degree? Which factors are changed and which are not? Why? Only by carefully analyzing and taking corresponding improvement measures can we achieve effective integration.

Conduct Teaching Design by "Focusing on Both Teaching and Learning"

Currently, there are two popular categories of teaching design theories: teaching-centered and learning-centered teaching design. Since each of the category has its own merits and demerits, it is better to combine the two and form a teaching design theory that "focuses on both learning and teaching" (see Figure 3.15). This can exactly meet the requirement of "building a new teaching structure that puts into full play both the dominant role of teachers and the position of students as the center." What is worth mentioning here is that when using information technologies in teaching, teachers should not merely take the technologies as visual teaching tools that aid the teaching, but use more as a cognitive tool to promote independent learning of students, a tool to facilitate communication, and a tool to deepen emotional experience.

Develop Teaching Resources and ICT-based Learning Tools

Concept and understanding are crucial, and changing the concept is the first step to a breakthrough. Technology is not a decisive factor, but proper application of it can solve problems and improve efficiency. Motivation and enthusiasm, even the ability to innovate, of students rely not only on guidance of teachers but also independent and cooperative learning and exploration of learners. This requires an ICT-based learning environment, tools, resources, and support services. ICT-based teaching resources are generally divided into four categories: multimedia materials, multimedia courseware, online courses, and ICT-based learning tools. For the ICT integration in both liberal art and science courses, the first three categories can serve well as tools for cognitive exploration, collaboration, emotional experience, and internalization. The fourth category is mainly used in science courses as tools for cognitive exploration and collaboration.

Explore Different Ways to Integration Based on Subject Features

Based on different teaching stages involved, ICT-integrated teaching modes can be divided into "in-class integration" and "out-of-class integration." Since in-class teaching involves different subjects, teaching strategies, and supporting environments, in-class integration can be further classified. For instance, it can be divided based on subjects such as mathematics, physics, chemistry, Chinese, history, geography, etc.; based on teaching strategy used such as self- exploration, collaborative learning, presentation, lecture, discussion, debate and role-playing; and based on the supporting environments such as the Internet, multimedia,

Figure 3.15
Design of the DC Teaching Model

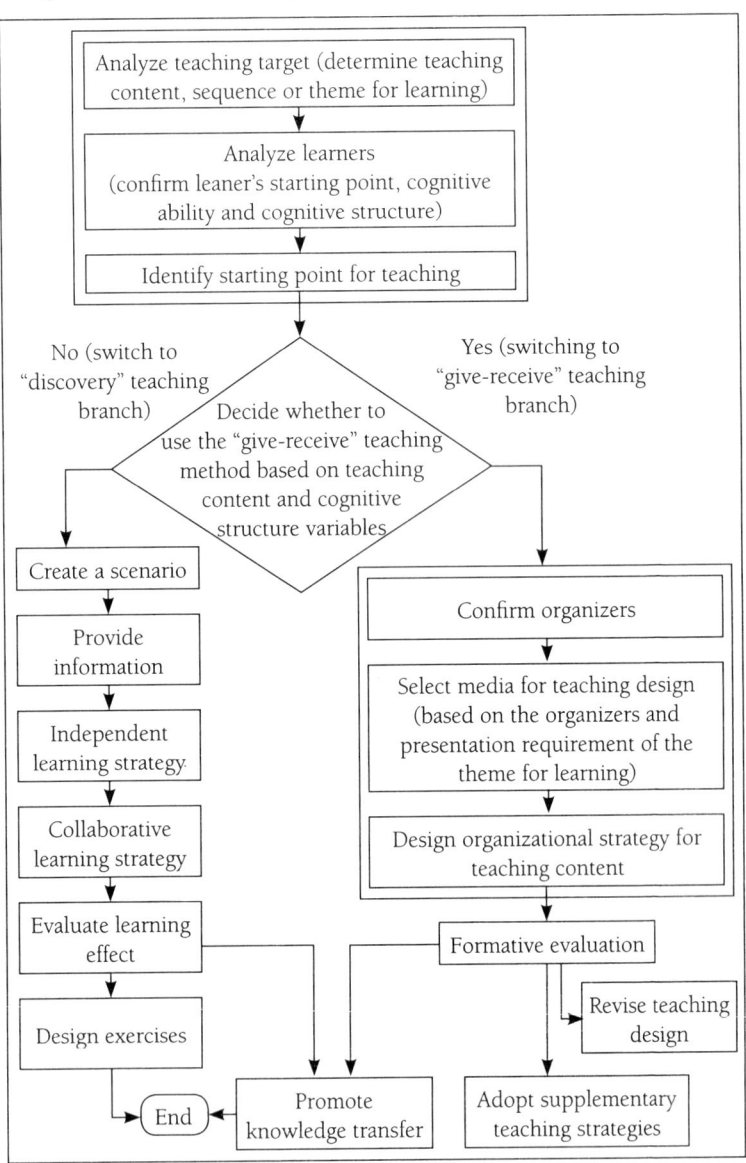

Source: Website of the program http://www.etc.edu.cn/

software, and simulated experiment. All categories have their own implementing steps and methods. The practice of these teaching modes in many pilot schools has proved that if the implementing steps and methods of different teaching modes can be fully understood and flexibly applied, in-depth integration can definitely be achieved.

Bibliography

He, Kekang. (2002). *Teaching System Design*. Beijing: Beijing Normal University Press.

———. (2007). Teaching Structure Theory and the Deepening of Teaching Reform. *Audio-visual Education Research*, 7: 5–10; 8: 22–27.

———. (2008). *Theory on In-depth Integration of ICT and Curriculum*. Beijing: Beijing Normal University Press.

———. (2008). Analysis and Thoughts on ICT Integration in Curriculum in the United States and Construction of a New Integration Theory. *Audio-visual Education Research*. 7: 1–10.

———. (2010). In-depth Thinking on Developing Educational Technology Theory with Chinese Characteristics. *Audio-visual Education Research*, 5: 5–19, 6: 39–54.

———. (2011). New Progress in the Study on ICT-based Education Theories in China. *Audio-visual Education Research*, 1: 1–19.

He, Kekang, Yu, Shengquan, Wu, Juan, Ma, Ning, Zhao, Xinglong, Yuan, Lei, & Qi, Yuan. (2009). Study on Using ICT-based Innovative Teaching Theory to Greatly Improve Teaching Quality in Rural Primary and Middle Schools and Promote Balanced Educational Development. *Audio-visual Education Research*, 2: 5–18.

4

Open Distance Education Training "Capable to Work, Willing to Stay" Talents for Rural Areas*

Zhang Zhijun, Xu Dian, Zeng Haijun, and Wang Ying

Overview

In 2004, Ministry of Education (MoE) launched the "Open Distance Education Training 'Capable to Work, Willing to Stay' Talents for Rural Areas," which is also known as the "One Village, One College Student"

* Open University of China (OUC) has adopted various media formats such as radio, TV, textbooks, audio materials, computer files, and Internet to conduct open distance education nationwide. OUC, provincial-level radio and TV universities and affiliated prefecture-level and county-level branches and work stations have formed an open distance education and teaching system with coordinated planning and multilevel teaching and management. OUC is a higher education

Program (hereinafter the initiative is referred to as "the Program"). This is a significant and important exercise in developing skills and knowledge of rural cadres and farmers at degree level using open distance learning (ODL) approaches. Rural development, entrepreneurship, leadership, and productivity are the stated aims of the Program. The scale and ambition of the Program, and its focus on rural communities, make it an important reference point in China's experience of ICT for Rural Education and Development.

The Program is delivered by the Open University of China (OUC)'s nationwide radio and TV university network to rural young people with high school diplomas. The main recipients are rural cadres and backup cadres, although students are also drawn from other communities, such as veterans, rural science and technology demonstration households, village and township enterprise leaders and entrepreneurs to participate. In the six years since 2004, a total of 280,146 trainees were enrolled, with 73,138 completing the training.

Context: Rural Higher Education Deficit

Higher education uptake in China has been concentrated in urban areas, where the enrollment rate in 2004 was 26.5% to a mere 2.73% in rural China (National Bureau of Statistics of China, 2004). Only 1% of rural workers have a higher education qualification. Higher education is, however, linked with higher income. According to a Jiangsu Provincial Bureau of Statistics (2006) survey, the average per capita income for rural households with a junior college degree was 2.4 times that for illiterate households. Progression for rural students has also been problematic. According to the "Research Report on the Scientific Planning of Education in China" (2010), around 10% of college students in rural

---

institute affiliated with MoE responsible for the planning and guidance of radio and TV universities in China; all levels of local radio and TV universities are led by the same level local government and managed by the same level education administrative departments with guidance and management from upper-level radio and TV universities in teaching.

areas proceeded to higher education institutes and migrated to urban or more developed areas after graduation. The remaining 90% of high school graduates stayed in rural settings and took no further education. The implications on skill level are considerable. Of the 880,000 rural science and technology promoters in China, a crucial role for modernization and development, the majority (60%) have no education beyond secondary. Although rural development demands a large number of medium- and high-level technical talents, the reality is that a lot of talents with higher education choose to work in urban areas or other sectors. The loss of talents in rural areas has to some extent delayed rural development. The challenge addressed by the One Village One College Student Program is: How to further extend higher education to rural areas, how to train more medium- and high-level technical talents for rural areas, and how to enhance the contributions of higher education to rural economic development and rural livelihood.

ODL as a Solution

China's 1998 "Modern Distance Education Program" from OUC and 68 regular distance learning colleges and universities has significantly increased and broadened educational opportunity. By 2010, there were over 4.5 million students enrolled in open distance education, of whom 2.8 million students (61.7%) were at OUC (Zhiyong, 2010). During the same period, the Chinese government also launched a modern distance education project for rural primary and secondary schools and rural cadres, and set up more than 10,000 distance education stations. Such initiatives have helped to redress the urban–rural educational imbalance. More than two-thirds of the open distance education and teaching stations of radio and TV universities are in institutes below the prefecture or city level. Given this serviceable rural-oriented education infrastructure, OUC was the natural partner for a policy of delivering higher education to farmers and developing the talent base for rural economic development and social advancement.

The MoE 2004 document setting out the Program established its key features.

1. The target is to train one college student per year per village at higher education level;[1] this person will then go on to train junior college-level talents in rural areas in support of economic and cultural development and productivity growth. In other words, the Program aims at producing the radiating effects from training one college student who can lead local households, clans and villages.

2. The Program is different from traditional regular higher education formats; the Program uses broadcast, TV, satellite, and Internet to implement open distance education projects.

3. OUC and the national radio and TV university system are to implement the Program under single management of resources and budget.

4. The Program uses existing rural education technical facilities, resources, and teaching stations.

Program Implementation

The lead delivery organization for the Program is OUC. Others In a collaborating role are China's 42 provincial-level radio and TV universities, and 1,171 affiliated teaching stations, whose tasks include providing special institutes for local implementation and promotion of the Program, including teaching management, guidance, coordination, policy support, and creating local management and operational formats. Teaching stations at the county level or lower can take several formats: some radio and TV universities conduct teaching independently, while others coexist as a department of a local school, a teacher training school or a vocational teaching center.

Student Enrollment

The target educational level of Program students is rural graduates of regular high school, vocational high school, technical school, and secondary professional school. Junior middle school graduates can also register for courses. The Program also encourages veterans, agricultural

[1] In 2004, there were 44,067 county and township-level administrative units in China qualifying as "villages"; in 2010, the number increased to 44,906.

science and technology demonstration households, rural cadres, and village and township enterprise leaders and talents to participate in the Program. Special policies have been designed to support enrollment, including planned enrollment, registration, nontransfer of household registration,[2] local enrollment, independent study formats, and credit accumulation. Students those who have fulfilled required credits will be issued a nationally recognized diploma. The fundamental aim of these policies is to ensure a locally based higher education of rural students which will encourage them to remain and to serve in rural areas upon graduation. The wider policy objective is to prevent the loss of talents from rural talent training in regular higher education.

From the fall of 2004 to the fall of 2010, the Program conducted 13 rounds of enrollment with a total of 280,146 students enrolled; a total of 73,138 students have graduated, with a steadily rising trend (see Figure 4.1). The enrollment volumes at the provincial-level radio and TV universities vary from 42,872 at Hunan's Provincial Radio & TV University, to 18 Guangzhou's, while the Open University itself enrolled 1,472. The male–female student ratio is around 2:1, while students in the age groups of 21–30 and 31–40 account for around 70% of the total (see Figure 4.2).

Subjects Studied

The Program has 18 majors organized in three subject areas, that is, plantation, cultivation, and management. Most students (82.6%) are enrolled in management majors, of which three are offered: village and township enterprise management, rural administrative management, and rural economic management (see Figure 4.3). One of the initial program goals, training rural technical talents, appears to be elusive.

Against this imbalance on course subject, it can be argued that the composition of the majors does respond to local economic development needs. For instance, in Jiangsu province where the proportion enrolled in village and township management major is 88% of students (2008 figures), it is also the case that village and township enterprises are developing fast. Similarly, the tea production and processing technology major

---

[2] Students enrolled in regular higher education in China must transfer their household registration to where the schools are upon enrollment.

Figure 4.1
Number of Enrollment per Semester in the Program

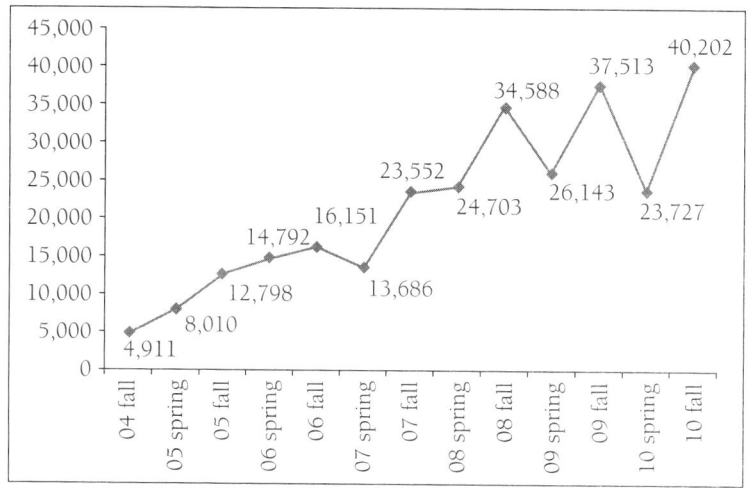

Source: The program website http://ycy.open.edu.cn/

Figure 4.2
Student Age Groups in the Program

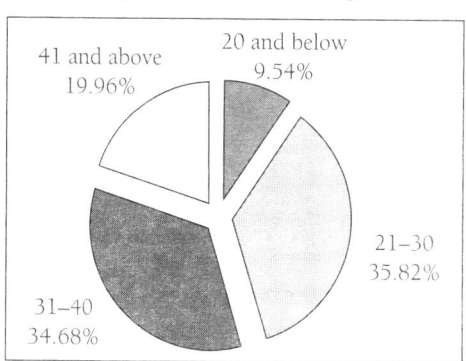

Source: The program website http://ycy.open.edu.cn/

only enrolls students in the tea-producing provinces of Zhejiang, Fujian, and Guizhou.

Given its "training 'capable to work, willing to stay' talents" title, the Program has had to increase its emphasis on practical skills training to

Figure 4.3
Major of Students Enrolled in the Program

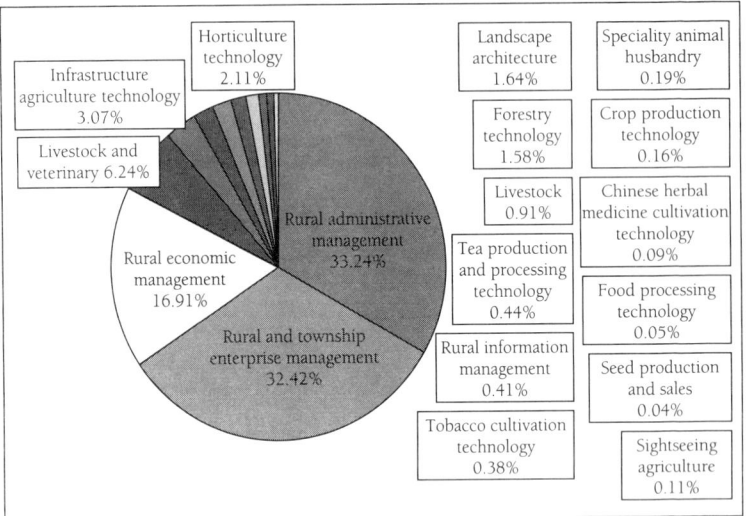

Source: The program website http://ycy.open.edu.cn/

fulfill its mission. Since spring 2012, integrated professional training and certificates have made five courses compulsory for degrees leading to professional positions. These obligatory course elements are based on National Vocation Standards for practical training courses. The four most popular majors (rural administrative management, village and township enterprise management, rural economic management, and rural information management) now handle vocational manager certificates in this way.

Teaching, Resources, and Learner Support

Teaching management and operations in the Program are ultimately the responsibility of OUC. Its remit at national level is the setup of the Program, curriculum design, production of multimedia teaching resources, online support services, teaching inspection, exam design, and exam supervision. The provincial-level radio and TV universities deliver at provincial-level the teaching activities, inspection, and exam services. Their teaching stations provide student services, such as learning support, enrollment, student management, tutoring, learning group activities, and organizing internships and surveys.

Lack of appropriately trained teachers in rural areas has been a challenge for the Program. Some universities do not have full-time teachers for some majors and usually employ local teachers or specialists from research institutes or professional departments for teaching. Both OUC and local radio and TV universities have had to recruit teachers with agricultural expertise to lead the curriculum in each major. To address teacher supply issues, OUC has set up the Program teaching center team, a group of the best teachers from the provincial radio and TV universities. The team members use seminars and peer exchange to explore problems and develop with solutions, including sharing of teaching resources, and teacher training. However, the mechanisms for this are often lacking, and relatively few activities are organized, there is insufficient instruction of teachers, and the sharing of teaching skills across areas is still inadequate.

Teaching methods are based on the characteristics of agricultural production and the learning characteristics of rural students. The method is a combination of paper-version textbooks, DVD-based self-study, TV teaching, online teaching, face-to-face group instructions, one-on-one tutoring, and learning group cooperation (see Figures 4.4 through 4.6). Teaching stations organize students to participate in online teaching activities organized by OUC. Provincial-level radio and TV universities organize face-to-face instruction, video instruction, discussions, Internet

Figure 4.4
Students of the Program Receive Farmland Instruction

Source: The program website http://ycy.open.edu.cn/

Figure 4.5
Veterinary Major in the Program: Practical Lecture

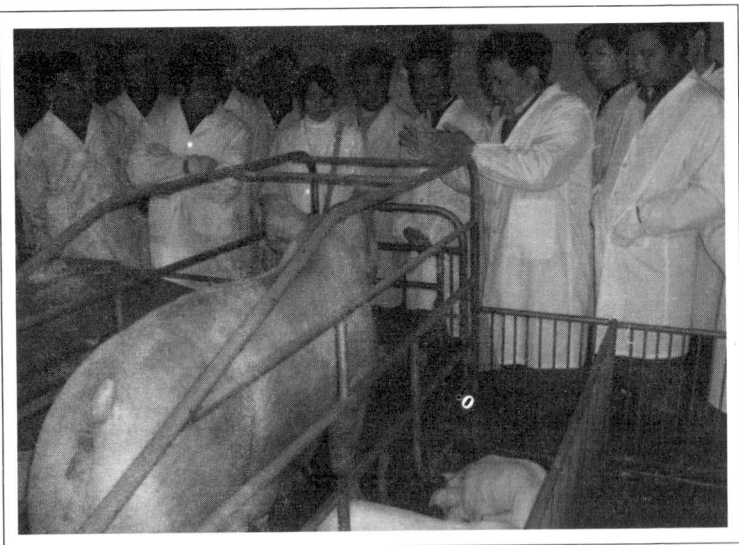

Source: The program website http://ycy.open.edu.cn/

Figure 4.6
Classroom Education Combining Distance Learning Methods and Face-to-Face Instructions

Source: The program website http://ycy.open.edu.cn/

research, or practical activities. The face-to-face sessions are different from traditional formal instruction in that they focus on learning guidance and Q&A to explain the key points, to answer questions raised by students, and to guide students in conducting experiments and internships.

OUC formulates the practical syllabus and decides the contents and requirements of practical teaching. The actual implementation is in the charge of local radio and TV universities who actively connect with the local enterprises of plantation, cultivation and food processing as well as professional households, to provide settings for practical training at off-campus internship practical bases. The Program also conducts practical training or research using enterprises owned by students or other local cultivation sites, and usually employs local professionals who show their techniques to students.

Multimedia resources are a significant element of teaching practice. Curriculum learning packages are specifically devised for the relatively lower pre-enrollment educational levels but richer practical experiences of rural students. The level of difficulty of theoretical learning is reduced, and packages typically feature video materials, learning guidelines, textual materials, formative evaluation manuals, and practical instructions. Students are able to learn anytime and anywhere with the packages.

Online teaching resources from OUC support teaching and learning activities for the Program. The Program website contains 417 video resources and 2,943 other resources (text, HTML, Hyperlink, attachment). From its launch in 2006 at http://ycy.open.edu.cn (see Figure 4.7) to spring 2011, it has registered a total of 4,549 teachers and 297,417 students and has received 7,888,804 visits.

OUC is adapting and hosting other participants' online materials, such as Liaoyuan Radio and TV University's TV teaching Programs for students' self-study and distance learning. Local radio and TV university partners produce resources to reflect localized industries. For example, Hunan Radio and TV University recorded 25 lectures with titles, such as "Pig Farming Technology," "Animal Reproduction Technology," and "Rural Environmental Protection." Beijing Radio and TV University produced an 18-episode series of video lectures series entitled, "Interview of Hot Issues Concerning the 'Agriculture, Farmer, and Countryside' in Suburban Beijing," and others such as "Rural Policy and Regulation Case Study," "Small Township Construction," "Market Research and

Figure 4.7
The Program Website of OUC

Source: The program website http://ycy.open.edu.cn/

Prediction." Zhejiang Radio and TV University compiled text books with titles, such as "Rural Inn Operations and Management,", "Bamboo Cultivation and Utilization," "New Farmer Temperament Training," and more. Altogether, over 100 "agriculture, farmer, countryside" courses are under development by local radio and TV universities led and coordinated by OUC.

Learner support comes in the forms of

- *Online tutoring* using resources on the Program website, such as teaching plans, key point notes, Q&A, and online teaching activities.
- *Face to Face tutoring* at teaching stations by local mid-level technicians in the agricultural or forestry system, hired by the Program

and also compensated by their companies or institutes. Tuition is usually at weekends, with additional lessons before exams.

- *Induction and foundation courses.* OUC requires teaching stations to conduct a 10-day foundation course of "entrance education" to induct students in the methods of open distance education, especially the use of information technology.

- *Information about enrollment, registration, teaching, tutoring, and examinations.* OUC prints out Program enrollment ads, and distributes information on teaching, tutoring, and examinations on the website. Local radio and TV universities additionally use student QQ clubs[3] to distribute information about times of tutoring and final examination instructions.

Costs and Fees

The Program is credit-based and students have eight years from enrollment to obtain the credits required for their diploma. Fees are charged by the course providers, and are usually low.

Examples of different fee arrangements are presented below. There have been several national efforts to reduce fees. OUC has managed to further reduce fees for courses in poorer sectors by 30%, while some provincial radio and TV universities have exempted students from fees. OUC set up the "Hope Farmland" scholarship for enrolled students which in 2009, distributed a bursary of RMB 1,000 to 439 students. Central subsidies to reduce costs include RMB 20,000 financial assistance to the first batch of county-level radio and TV universities to assist with training staff and creating teaching materials. Funding in more remote rural areas in western China is supported by other Program participants: between 2004 and 2006, OUC selected 100 county-level radio and TV universities in Western China and distributed RMB 100,000 in assistance to each. Each corresponding provincial-level radio and TV university and local government gave RMB100,000 as well. The assistance came to a total of RMB 30 million. Similar support reached impoverished

---

[3] QQ is the most widely used Internet instance messaging application in China.

counties in areas outside western China. Levels of assistance vary. In Gansu province, costs are shared on the basis of RMB 2,500 per student for two years from "Yu Lu Plan," 40% exempted by the school, and 10% borne by the individuals. In Zhejiang, tuition of RMB 5,320 per student for 1,000 agricultural students was entirely covered by government, regional and local funds.

To show the range of fee arrangements in the Program, this study selects three cases from the three regions respectively with different levels of economic development. The cases have in common a high level of government support and indeed mandatory recruitment, and support for students geared toward maximum subsidy for those with least financial means.

Costs and Fees Examples

East China: Jiangsu Radio and TV University

Jiangsu province is a developed province in eastern China. Students of the Program in Jiangsu province were 80% from the relatively developed southern areas, with the remainder from economically less developed central and northern areas. In southern Jiangsu province the Program adopted market-based payment model whereby students enrolled voluntarily and paid for the tuition. In central and northern Jiangsu province, the Program required support from the local government. County (city) and village and township governments issued documents that required village and rural cadres to participate in the Program. The tuition fees were paid by the city (county) level, village and township level governments, with some student contribution.

Central China: Hunan Radio and TV University

Hunan province, located to the south of the midstream of the Yangtze River, is an inland province in central China, and Hunan Shaoyang Radio and TV University, a city-level branch of Hunan Radio and TV University, enrolled 917 students in the Program in 2008. Recruitment was supported by a local government decrees requiring counties to arrange around a third of all village or township employees below 45 years old without a junior college degree to participate in degree education every year. Over a third of villages were also required to select at least one student every year to participate in degree education. Students were charged RMB 1,200 for tuition and material fees, with a further RMB 1,500 paid by poverty alleviation institutes, collective income of the villages, or the agriculture assistance funds of counties and villages. The organizational features of the Program at Hunan Shaoyang Radio and TV University therefore included financial and recruitment guarantees.

West China: Yunnan Radio and TV University

Yunnan province is located on the borders of southwestern China. The local government undertook that from 2008 Yunnan province would raise RMB 40,3,181 million to implement the Program in 12,870 administrative villages over five years. For students from the 8,399 administrative villages subject to the poverty alleviation program, the tuitions fees will be shared between the provincial government revenue, Yunnan Radio and TV University, and individuals in the proportion of 55%, 33%, and 12%, respectively. The cost to each student is RMB 684. Students also receive RMB 300 in subsidies for textbooks from the provincial government revenue. For students in the other 4,471 administrative villages, costs are shared in the proportion 45%, 33%, and 22%, respectively, and the fee paid by the student is RMB 1,254.

Program Impacts

Aside from its mere growth, the evidence of the Program's value comes from anecdotal and data reports. The Program has provided education for farmers and disadvantaged groups in rural areas, and students report that they value the learning opportunities. Uptake is broad, with some teaching stations recruiting couples or two generations of family in the same class, and rural women attending classes with their children. The exposure to open learning methods, and the use of computer and Internet to look up information, have provided a basis for entrepreneurship and development. There are encouraging anecdotes of how learning has changed students' destinies. Ma Sunsun, from Shandong province, started working at a local agricultural high-tech production park after graduation. In less than two months, Sunsun got promoted from an entry-level employee to a mid-level manager. According to statistics from Nanjing Radio and TV University, 20% of students have found new jobs with the diplomas obtained through the Program and 10% of students have been promoted by their employers. The verdict of MoE officials from Beijing, after talking to the first batch of graduates of the Program at Beijing Radio and TV University, said that degree education (as opposed to short-term training) and helped students improve their overall competency, broaden their horizons, and increase their development potentials.

Anecdotal evidence suggests that impact often centers on entrepreneurship skills. Among typical stories, Yang Limin, a student of the Program from Yangzhou of Jiangsu province, has transformed the township agricultural resources development company into "Jiangsu Modern Fishing Science and Technology Demonstration Park." Xu Kun, a student from Jiangsu province, set up a goose farming cooperative after graduation, with production value exceeding RMB 10 million. Lin Yuanquan, a student from Shangrao of Jiangxi province, was a seller of flowers, seeds, and plants. Through several years of development, his company has grown into a group covering plantation, horticulture, and real estate development. Luo Mingxiang, a student from Yunxiao county of Fujian province, has set up an energy-saving lighting and electricity company.

The anecdotal evidence for rural areas also suggests impacts on entrepreneurship, although the achievements are more diffuse. More than 30 students of the Program from Yangxin county of Hubei province are reported to have applied their knowledge to promote practical technology and help local people to make money. These students are reputed as "promoters of science and technology, leaders of entrepreneurs, helpers of general public." Hu Fuluo, a student from Xiangtan Radio and TV University in Hunan province, has led the scientific development of his impoverished Taolin village, where annual average income has increased from less than RMB 3,000 to RMB 7,200, giving Taolin village a local reputation for prosperity. Luo Huaizu, a student from the Yanling county teaching station in Hunan province used livestock husbandry knowledge and technology to set up Zhuzhou Tengfei Livestock Company after graduating. The company has five sow farming demonstration villages and supports the development of the hog industry in the county. Jin Qijun from Guizhou province, after learning viticulture, planted improved seeds in 15 mu (1 mu = 1/15 hectare) of village land, reaching annual revenues of RMB 75,000 and inspiring other villagers to make a living from grape growing. Fu Yangzhu, general manager of Fujian Nan'an Jintang Horticulture Company, says that he previously lacked the knowledge and technique to obtain big orders to make significant profit. After participating in the Program, Fu broadened his horizons and learned horticulture and operational techniques, knowledge, and theory. He has developed several new varieties of flowers and plants and is expanding his business.

Rural Cadres: Principal Beneficiaries of the Project

Students of the Program are mainly of the status rural cadres or backup cadres, who are the lowest level of administrators in China's rural areas. The skills they have gained through higher study have developed their ability to support villagers to increase their income, to improve village administration, to mediate disputes over rural land transfer, environmental protection, legal affairs, and so on. The significance of cadres in the Program varies from place to place, as attested by data snapshots from various sources.

- Out of the 2,166 graduates from Beijing Radio and TV University, 38% are rural cadre and 50% are backup cadre. Other 658 graduates of the Program at Beijing Radio and TV University have been selected as new rural cadres.
- Out of the 229 graduates from the county teaching station in Anhui province, 151 were elected in the 2008 election as rural cadres and have become the backbone of new rural construction.
- Out of the 6,085 graduates of the Program in Hunan province, 1% became public servants, 4% became rural cadres, 11% became rural backup cadres, and 81% returned to villages for entrepreneurial ventures or took up job responsibilities in close neighborhoods.
- At a typical "poverty alleviation village" in Wangcheng county, Changsha, Hunan province, four cadres in the village participated in the Program. They used the information technology and entrepreneurship skills from the Program to improve crop planting, and turn the village into a prosperous "new countryside construction demonstration village."

- A village head in Fujian province used the knowledge of township construction to reorganize the layout of the village roads, green space, and development land. Villagers commented that "learning has made a great difference."
- Zhao Yue, a student from Xinmi of Henan province, was elected a village official. He attracted investment and improved the village environment, enabling all households to make a living and lifting per capita income from below RMB 1,000 to RMB 3,800.

Feedback from Program Participants

Feedback from participants of the Program at county-level radio and TV university branches was collected from four school officials from Jinhua County Radio and TV University in Xiaoshan district of Hangzhou, Zhejiang province, and three enrolled students.

School Principals' Feedback

School leadership spoke about the Program at their schools in terms of implementation, achievement of goals, problems, and further development.

School principals are in favor of prioritizing prospective students who can be exemplary representatives of rural living. "Rural cadres can represent the entire village" is the prevailing view. In practice, this has meant preference for crop planting and machine operating skills, and students mainly 25 to 45 years old with a male to female ratio around 7 to 3.

School principals have expanded the meaning of "farmer" from its traditional sense of working in the field a new meaning of someone who participates in corporate management, community services, or sets up their own factories in the farming industries.

Principals had introduced additional forms of adult education, including correspondence education and self-study exams. They also stated a need to improve textbook designs to make them "more suitable to rural college students" and "more specific." Regarding learning formats, principals reported that on-site training was the most popular format, followed by face-to-face instructions. Online learning was not most popular with students, and, according to principals, was also relatively high cost.

Principals identified a gap between outcomes and students' expectations when they join Program, that is, considered a "benefit" but still needs to "better meet the practical needs of the general public and generate economic returns."

Principals finally mentioned the issue of some local entrepreneurs having no interest in receiving degree education. These individuals believe that the knowledge system at degree education is not advanced enough to meet their needs, and they prefer to learn through advanced specialized seminars. These learning needs are, in essence, different from those addressed by the Program.

Principals also pointed out that for rural cadres, government policy drives their appetite for learning, and cadres will be motivated to participate in the Program if "the government requires a junior college degree or higher for rural cadres."

Students' Feedback

Feedback interviews with students focused on socioeconomic background, channels that introduced them to the Program, their learning situation, tuition, and comments on the Program.

Regarding the channels, two students said that they joined the Program through the village and township talent database, which is linked to the Program. Talents from the database who participate in the Program are not charged for the tuition; the students pay only for textbooks and meals. One student joined the Program because he was a rural cadre.

Students stated that only farmers with information sources knew about the Program. Rural cadres are usually the first to know such information and to participate. The cadres will only want to participate if the villagers value the Program, and the Program requirement to use learning tools such as computers is seen to increase its value.

Regarding the learning format of the Program, one student reported: "We're not doing distance learning. We go to the school during the weekend for two full days for study. The format is quite formal. Each class has a class monitor, a commissary in charge of studies, and learning leadership groups." Another stated: "We can directly go to the teachers if we don't understand certain policies or have difficulties during the learning process. We can also talk to teachers over the phone. Teachers will remind students of the next day's class a day ahead. Students need to take a leave if they cannot attend the class." An e-commerce student said that he often viewed online teaching resources. A student dealing with rural tourism projects said that he seldom had time to view online resources due to busy work on the farmland.

Students described their gains from the Program. A student of rural economic management who formerly sold tobacco said that the Program helped reshape his business methods and thinking. For example, he now manages all his projects online. The Program has helped him especially in tax management and information management. The student said that he was able to obtain knowledge and information that farmers did not have. This student reported having had good communications and discussions with fellow students and says that he is willing to introduce the Program to his family members, coworkers, and friends.

Another student of veterinary medicine who used to work on projects in hog and chicken farming said that the Program taught him long-term strategic thinking, and he learned how to scrutinize food safety to avoid losses. He claimed that the use of practical technology helped to break down the conservative mentality in rural areas.

Students those who were interviewed also said that they trusted learning from local educational institutes more than from remote or unfamiliar ones.

Lessons Learned

In analyzing strengths and weakness of the Program, several themes stand out.

Strong and broadly spread policy and capital support have been the foundation of the Program. In 2005 and 2007, the MoE released documents requiring all levels of educational authorities and colleges to promote the development of the Program. These documents received a high level of attention and support from all levels of local governments, who echoed central policy and funding plans at their local levels. Often, local institutions adapted the Program around their existing offer to students. For example, Ganzhou of Jiangxi province conducted the Program in 18 counties and listed it as an important part of the "Farmer Knowledge

Project" and "New Rural Construction" plan. Zhejiang Radio and TV University listed the Program into the provincial "Rural College Student Cultivation Project" in 2007. Hubei province brought up the implementation of the plan of "More than Three College Students in One Village."

The tuition for the Program training lacked thorough policy and funding support at the initial stage, especially in impoverished areas. The MoE did not always have corresponding funding and policy support at all levels of local government. Imbalances in the Program performance were not necessarily linked to the geographical location or the level of economic development. The Program showed that agricultural projects simply cannot be initiated or reach scale without policy support. The process of ongoing government funding and the mechanisms of effective long-term system to ensure the funding of the Program have yet to be put in place.

The Program Management System Has Raised Some Issues

MoE choice of OUC to implement the Program with delivery through the radio and TV university system, rather than other agricultural institutes, brought consequences. Many were positive. These organizations cover all China with a system that has been running for around three decades and is the best distance higher education system in China and reaches local areas, rural areas, and remote and minority areas. Reliance on such a system helps to win policy support while the quasi-government nature of radio and TV universities means functional relationships already exist, and a large network can quickly establish a high level of mobilization nationwide (see Figure 4.8).

However, there are also disadvantages. The multilevel network setup leads to low efficiency. In addition, imbalanced local economic development means that the development of educational projects needs is often shaped by regional characteristics more than national policy.

There Have Been Problems with the Uptake of the Program

Difficult conditions in rural areas and the low economic returns from participating in rural economy have disfavored rural subjects in

Figure 4.8
Radio and TV University Network Structure Overview

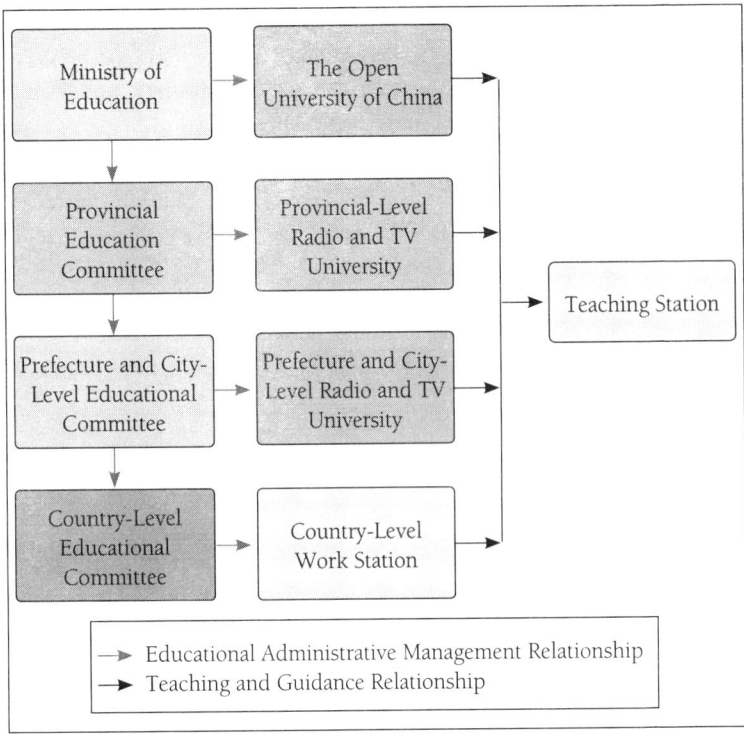

Source: The program website http://ycy.open.edu.cn/

public opinion. More than three decades of radio and TV university education in agricultural science and technology has shown that only a small portion of China's large rural population are willing to learn agricultural science and technology. Regular agricultural institutes are faced with this problem, and the Program has also encountered it. Most radio and TV universities have made efforts to advertise the Program among villages to attract more rural students. But experience has shown that rural education is very difficult and requires special institutes, funding, and personnel to mobilize different parties so that learners, organizers, and local officials can collectively promote the Program.

Teaching Contents Have Not Always Met the Needs of Development

To be sustainable, the Program must closely relate to the local economic development and pillar industries. On one hand, the Program needs to ensure relevance to local conditions. On the other hand, the Program needs to promote economic development down national pathways. This tension means that course content in the Program is routinely evolving and adjusting. For example, "Sightseeing Agriculture" was set up in 2010 respond to the role of tourism in the development of modern agriculture. It is not yet clear whether the future of the Program lie in degree education or advanced practical technology training. The proportion of theoretical education versus practical technology education in curriculum design is disputed. The answers must be based on the goal of increasing the income of rural students and meeting the actual education needs of farmers.

Practical Training in Rural Skills Needs More Emphasis

The initial goal of the Program was to train technical talents, but management has become the dominant skill. There is low demand for plantation or farming-related curricula and teaching resources, but the Program cannot simply cancel majors without many students. In recent two years, the proportions of students in the practical majors has recovered (Yan Bing, 2011) and these developments may point to new ways to emphasize practical farming skills.

Rural Information Infrastructure Has Been Well Used

The Program brings open distance education methods based on information technology to rural areas. This not only stimulates educational projects, but also profoundly alters farmers' profitability and development mechanisms of every kind. Penetration data show the scale of this effect. By 2010, villages and townships in China with Internet access reached 100% and 98% had broadband Internet access. In the meantime, the number of rural Internet users in China reached 125 million, accounting for 27.3% of the total number of Internet users in China. A sample survey shows that the ownership of technology among rural residents has increased to 10 computers, 65 fixed telephones and 120 mobile phones per 100 households. The Program, by making full use of such information infrastructure in rural areas, contributes to developing ICT-based learning and support services.

The Program Can Be Improved

The Program is faced with some difficulties and problems. Regarding policy, some local governments lack strong and sustained policy support to the Program. Regarding concepts, the different levels of radio and TV universities have different understandings of the Program. Some universities understand the Program as a one-off performance project conducted by governments, while others see it as a long-term educational development strategy. Regarding teaching, a severe lack of professional teachers and insufficient teaching resources have hampered progress.

Other specific problems for the Program are:

1. The attendance rate at some face-to-face instruction courses in some teaching stations is low. Data show that attendance is relatively high among new students but falls sharply during the second and third semesters. Causes are thought to include the failure classes to sustain student interest, and work–study conflicts. Poor management at some teaching stations may also be an issue.

2. Poor management of formative evaluations is another concern. Some teachers are known to do a bad job reviewing students' homework. The lack of effective monitoring has led to plagiarism in formative evaluation.

3. The teaching of practical subjects has been weak or nonexistent. Although the contribution of radio and TV universities has meant the Program has access to practical teaching and experiment facilities at some teaching stations, this has meant mainly the signing of a paper agreement and not a lot of practical teaching activities.

Summary and Discussion

The Project has shown that open distance education for rural areas raises fundamental key questions. Are the educational services provided suitable for the demands of rural education? Can the expansion of higher education to rural areas ensure teaching quality? This study suggests that further improvement of the "One Village one College Student" Program depends on the following actions:

- Continuing strong policy and funding support for the Program from the MOE;
- Rapid upgrading of teaching content. This will mean customizing courses with local features, making the curriculum more relevant to learning needs, and establishing new undergraduate majors within the Program;
- Intensive construction of Internet courses and teaching resources, together with strong emphasis on new media and mobile learning terminals;
- Cooperation with sizeable companies in local areas to establish teaching facilities for practical and experimental subjects; general improvement of practical teaching resources;
- More attention to teacher quality. This will mean stronger curriculum teaching teams, funding for teacher training, and support for teachers professional development through domestic and international academic activities;
- Stronger learning support services through curriculum groups and Web2.0 learning platforms; this may involve the Program working alongside national public service systems of modern distance education;
- Conducting graduate follow-up surveys to improve capture of feedback, and understanding of the impact of the Program;
- Increased and improved theoretical and practical research into the Program and exploring hybrid teaching modes suitable to rural learners.

Bibliography

China Education Scientific Planning Leadership Team Office website (2010). "Bulletin of the Theoretical and Practical Achievements of the 'One Village, One College Student' Program Implemented by Higher Agricultural Institutes." *China Education Scientific Research Report* , 1. Retrieved from http://onsgep.moe.edu.cn/ (accessed October 10, 2012).

Compiled by the Department of Population & Employment Statistics (Social, Science and Technology Statistics) of National Bureau of Statistics of China (2004). *China Population Statistical Yearbook*. Beijing: China Statistics Press, 2004.

Compiled by the Rural Social and Economic Survey of National Bureau of Statistics of China (2004). *China Rural Statistical Yearbook*. Beijing: China Statistics Press.

———. (2006). *China Rural Statistical Yearbook*. Beijing: China Statistics Press.

Huaming, Song, & Wang, Rong (2004). "Estimations of Higher Education's Contributions to Agricultural Economic Growth Rate and Policy Guidance." *Issues of Agricultural Economy*, 12: 39–42.

Jiangsu Bureau of Statistics (2006). "Research on the Cultural Qualities of the Population during New Rural Construction in Jiangsu Province." Retrieved from http://www.jssb.gov.cn/jstj/fxxx/tjfx/200611/t20061110_77479.htm (accessed November 6, 2006).

Li, Guiyun (2011). "Calling for the Strong Power from the Bottom of the Heart—Interview with Yan Bing, Vice President of the Open University of China and Director of the Ministry of Education 'One Village, One College Student' Programme." *Distance Education in China*, 6. Retrieved from http://dianda.china.com.cn/zhuanti/2011-08/10/content_4397930.htm (accessed October 10, 2012).

The Open University of China website (2012). "2010 Statistical Bulletin of the Basic Situation of Radio and TV Universities in China." Retrieved from http://www.crtvu.edu.cn (accessed October 10, 2013).

Zhiyong, Ruan (Ed.) (2010). *China Radio and TV University Education Statistical Yearbook 2009*. Beijing: The Open University of China Press.

5

Spreading Knowledge and Eradicating Poverty through Distance Education

Diao Qingjun, Wei Tao, Hao Yingping, Jiao Yiju, Zeng Haijun, and Wang Ying

Overview

At the beginning of 2003, in response to the strategy of western development, Tsinghua University raised funds to launch the poverty alleviation project through education with a view of "Spreading Knowledge, Eradicating Poverty." The project availed of the university's rich education resources and strengths in competent professional cultivation, and fed urgently needed education resources and Tsinghua classes into the remote and poor countryside for free by setting up distance teaching centers enabled by modern information technology. With the support of related government departments and officials taking up provisional posts locally and in cooperation with local villagers, the project attempted to establish a "large-scale, sustainable and effective" poverty alleviation mode through distance education that can be promoted. By the end of 2011, it had set up 1,018 distance teaching centers in 27 provinces, which covered 539 national key counties for poverty relief, and 2,440 "middle and primary schools online for distance education" secondary centers in some village and township schools. Distance and face-to-face training offered free of charge each year exceeded 3,000 class hours, involving over 1.3 million village officials, middle and primary school teachers and students, farmers, technicians, and village doctors. The project has set up a "platform of poverty alleviation with knowledge" for poverty-stricken areas, and will gradually build it into "a platform to integrate social resources" and "a platform to train competent professionals in various fields."

Background

Poverty is one of the most severe challenges to human beings, and China is an active force in the international anti-poverty efforts. In the 21st century, China's poverty alleviation and development work evolves from providing adequate food and clothing to the new stage featured by consolidating previous achievements, accelerating pace to lift people out of poverty, improving ecological environment, enhancing development ability and narrowing development gap, and priority is put on improving self-development ability of the target population. However, work at the new stage still faces grave challenges: First, poverty-stricken population is mainly distributed in remote areas with harsh natural conditions and inconvenient traffic, which makes it difficult to help them have access to adequate food and clothing. Among those already with access to sufficient food and clothing, some still live and work in poor conditions, which makes it arduous to consolidate the previous achievements and prevent reimpoverishment; second, the labor force in poverty-stricken areas on the whole is poorly educated, unable to steadily lift themselves out of poverty through poverty reduction projects.

China proposes to combine special poverty alleviation and society-based poverty reduction, and encourages social forces into the cause.

As a prestigious higher education institution in China, Tsinghua University, boasts rich education resources, and has the ability to provide qualified teachers to help with training in poverty-stricken areas in many fields from basic education to vocational education, from economic growth to environmental protection and from healthcare to cultural development. In addition, with distance education launched back in 1996, the university has accumulated rich experience, built mature technical platforms and competent contingents of professionals for distance teaching. In order to serve the society, the School of Continuing Education took the lead in 2003 to initiate the poverty alleviation project through education, and gradually developed it into a public welfare project involving the university's faculty and students as well as personnel from various sectors of the society.

Implementation

Organizational Structure and Liaison System

Tsinghua University pays great attention to poverty alleviation through education, and sets up a leading group to coordinate and guide related work. The Office of Educational Poverty Alleviation is set up to implement concrete work.

In order to facilitate distance teaching centers to play an effective role and enhance communication between these centers with the Office, Tsinghua University signs a five-year contract with local education institutions selected by those centers such as county-level party schools, training schools for teachers, middle and primary schools, vocational schools, and other training institutions, to provide them with satellite signal receiving devices and educational resources free of charge.

Each distance teaching center is staffed with a director, information specialists and technicians, who take up the job after being verified competent for the posts by tests at the end of free face-to-face training offered by Tsinghua University. The project is also furnished with e-mail addresses, an information management system and a dedicated website. Since 2011, a contact person is designated for each center as the representative of the office, responsible for monitoring the installation, commissioning and performance of satellite receiving devices and work progress at the center by telephone, SMS, e-mails, and QQ.

Building of Distance Teaching Centers

The project is originally intended to cover national poverty counties and gradually expand to provincial poverty counties, previous revolutionary bases, border areas and areas inhabited by ethnic minorities. By the end of 2011, a total of 1,018 distance teaching centers were set up in 27 provinces (see Figure 5.1).

As for the project implementation, some teaching centers have not completed equipment installation because local technical force is insufficient, supporting organizations are replaced, employees are too busy, or leaders do not pay enough attention. So the Office for Educational Poverty Alleviation has dispatched satellite equipment suppliers to assist in installation on site.

In 2011, according to the requirements of teaching centers, an information management system and a courseware downloading system were developed. If unable to receive courses through direct satellite broadcast, learners can download courseware and flexibly arrange time for study. It enhances the flexibility for teaching centers to adjust training contents and schedule, and enables courses of multiple training classes to be integrated and played on demand.

Distance Training and Face-to-Face Training

In order to meet the demand of poverty-stricken areas, the project delivers training in two ways: inviting various groups of people from those areas to Tsinghua University for face-to-face training, and sending out training resources in the following two ways:

First, we directly broadcast live lectures and the recorded ones of Tsinghua University to poverty-stricken areas for free through the satellite equipment and distance teaching centers, so that local people can undergo training without leaving their villages.

Second, we dispatch excellent teachers and students from the university to poverty-stricken areas for tour lectures and voluntary teaching, so that local people can communicate face to face with scholars and experts from various fields.

Figure 5.1
Building of Distance Teaching Centers

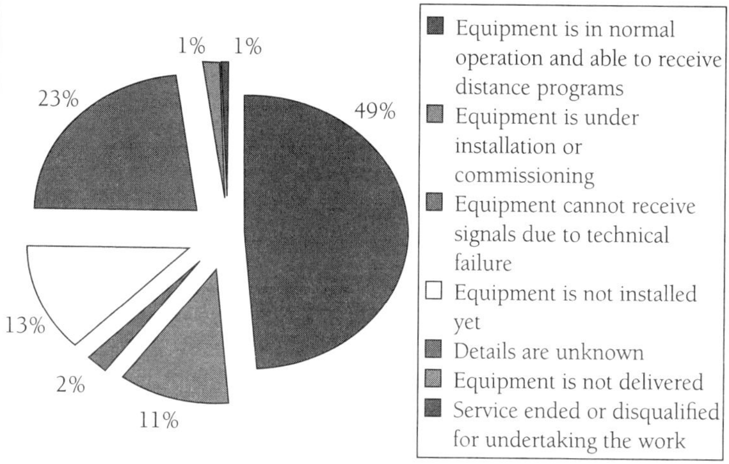

1%
1%
49%
23%
13%
2%
11%
Equipment is in normal operation and able to receive distance programs
Equipment is under installation or commissioning
Equipment cannot receive signals due to technical failure
Equipment is not installed yet
Details are unknown
Equipment is not delivered
Service ended or disqualified for undertaking the work

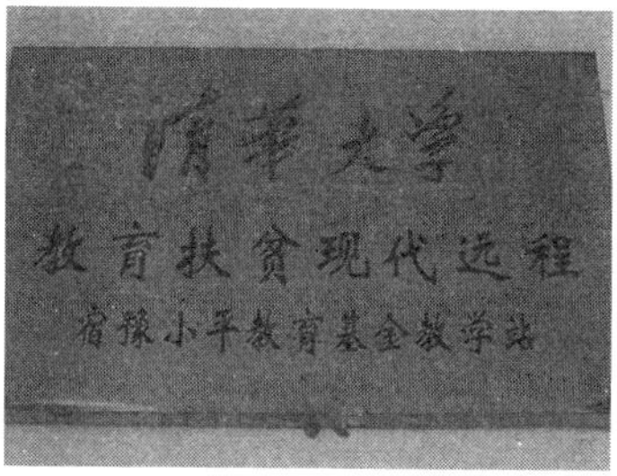

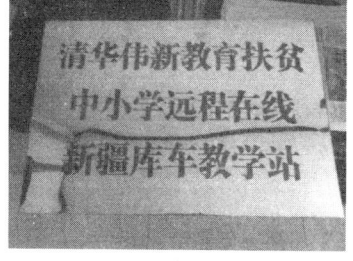

清華大學
教育扶貧现代远程
宿豫小平教育基金教学站
Input of School of Continuing Education, Tsinghua University

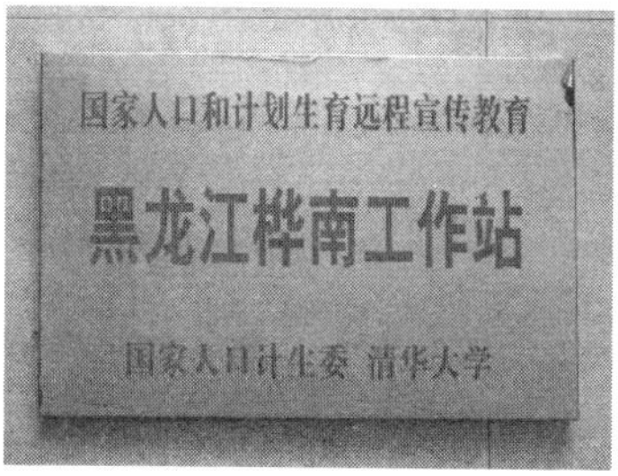

国家人口和计划生育远程宣传教育
黑龙江桦南工作站
国家人口计生委 清华大学
Donations from Hongkong

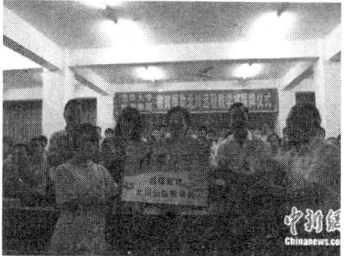

清华伟新教育扶贫
中小学远程在线
新疆库车教学站
Donations from Macao

Donations from the United States

Source: The program website http://www.tsinghuafp.com

Since 2003, the university has offered distance and face-to-face training through distance teaching centers to a total of over 1.3 million people in poverty-stricken areas. Among them, there are 1,103 million middle and primary school teachers and students, 221,000 party and government officials, village medical and healthcare practitioners and birth control officials, and 231 average villagers and technicians (see Figures 5.2 and 5.3).

Take the year of 2011 for instance. Based on the expanded project coverage, the Office for Educational Poverty Alleviation of Tsinghua University launched 35 training programs in total.

- It organized ten training sessions of official ability building with different themes, and broadcasted 82 class hours of national birth control training courses. A total of 755 people participated in the face-to-face training and 30,794 people joined distance training.
- Training for middle and primary school teachers and students, both distance and face-to-face, was offered to 20 classes, mainly

Figure 5.2
Number of Beneficiaries of Distance and Face-to-Face Training

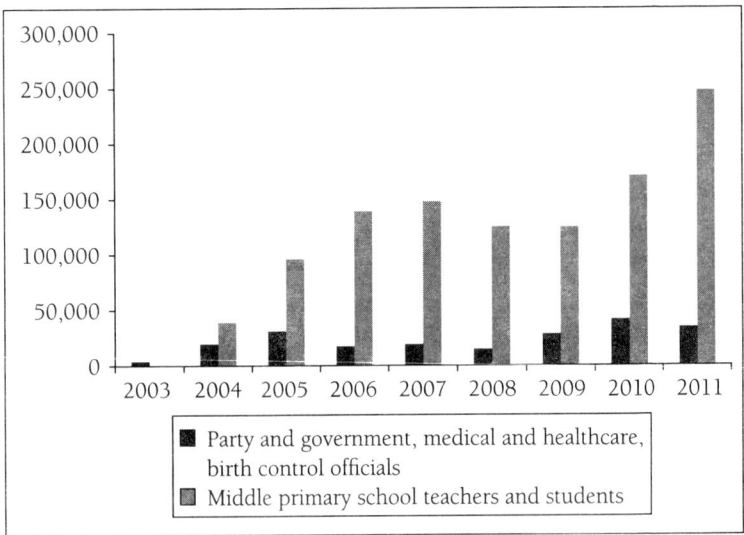

Source: The program website http://www.tsinghuafp.com

Figure 5.3
Scenes of Poverty Alleviation Training

Source: The program website http://www.tsinghuafp.com

including training for elementary English teachers, teachers of major subjects, head teachers and headmasters and training on multimedia application. A total of 149,118 people joined the training, 1,335 of whom received face-to-face training.

- It held Tsinghua University Leadership Forum in nine areas, involving a total of 4,106 trainees.
- With the support of Hongkong Zeng Xianbei Charity Fund, the project organized 161 teachers and students from Tsinghua University and 74 university teachers and students from the United States to offer two-week voluntary teaching in 30 underdeveloped areas that benefited 68,287 people.
- Ten teachers visited 16 counties to give tour lectures, benefiting 3,511 people.
- Student Association of Educational Poverty Alleviation organized 22 voluntary teaching activities at weekend, during which 192 volunteers offered training to 28,577 people.

Platform to Foster Diversified Competent Professionals

The project already transformed the educational poverty alleviation network into a platform for fostering diversified competent professionals that involves middle and primary school teachers and students, party and government officials, urban and rural planning officials, village and township medical and healthcare practitioners, technicians, and average villagers.

Since 2008, depending on "New Countryside Housing Project Office" the CPC Publicity Department set up in School of Architecture, Tsinghua University, the project organized training on new countryside construction in poverty-stricken areas, involving 8,432 officials. The training promoted the national policies and guidelines on new countryside building, and assisted local areas in conducting new countryside housing planning.

Starting from 2008, the project organized a total of nine training sessions for village medical and healthcare management officials, involving over 500 people in face-to-face training and more than 4,000 people in distance training. The university also made use of resources of its affiliated hospitals, integrating medical aid into its poverty alleviation network. Medical knowledge was played on a distance platform for medical and healthcare practitioners, and experts and professors made for poverty-stricken areas to guide local medical work.

National Population and Family Planning Commission started cooperation with Tsinghua University since 2007, and using the university's educational poverty alleviation network set up 466 national population and family planning distance education centers by either cooperating with existing distance teaching centers or setting up new ones. A total of 18,199 community-level family planning officials received the training.

Course Development and Transmission

The key to poverty alleviation through education lies in course development. The project broadcasted nearly 3,000 class hours each year.

- Regarding official training, it developed a series of courses suitable for county-level economic and cultural development such as "county-level economy and opportunities," "urban and rural planning and new countryside construction," "people-first and administration by law," "industrial park building and county-level development," "spokesperson," "investment promotion strategy," and "environmental protection and sustainable development."

- Regarding middle and primary school teachers and students, it developed headmaster management training and teacher training courses.
- As for vocational skills training, it developed such courses as "internship training for junior vocational students," "automobile maintenance training," "young women beauticians training in poverty-stricken areas," and "IT software engineer training."
- In terms of healthcare, it developed courses on "village medical and healthcare management training" and "continuing medical education program," and cooperated with National Population and Family Planning Commission in developing the course of "new household health promotion training" for community-level family planning officials.

Educational poverty alleviation courses must be tailored to development of poverty-stricken areas, instead of blindly replicating theories for developed areas. Therefore, before the project courses were designed, researchers were always sent out for investigation. For instance, Tsinghua University dispatched English teachers to poverty-stricken areas before the English training course for those areas was designed to communicate with local English teachers to learn about their work, find their points of interest and analyze their demand. Course systems established on such basis were then fed back to target trainees for discussion before appropriate course systems were worked out and teaching materials suitable for local areas developed.

Voluntary Teaching of College Students

In December 2006, Student Association of Educational Poverty Alleviation (SAEPA) of Tsinghua University was founded, which organized four activities.

- *Weekend Voluntary Teaching*: SAEPA organized volunteers to give classes in the countryside middle and primary schools every weekend. So far, 57 training sessions have been organized, offering training to over 50,000 local students in 6,000 class hours by 539 volunteers. Tens of thousands of pages of teaching materials were brought to the children.

- *Computer Donation*: The activity was intended to collect computers left unused in the society and by college students, build computer rooms for schools of migrant children and those in poverty-stricken areas, and offer voluntary computer training. A total of 232 computers were donated, and computer rooms were set up in nine primary schools.

- *Making Your Wishes Come True*: Students in poverty-stricken areas wrote their wishes down, and volunteers from Tsinghua University helped these children realize their wishes. In 2011 alone, over 500 students realized their wishes.

- *Dream Class*: The activity was intended to offer training to develop the interest of children of migrant workers in suburban Beijing. Eleven training sessions have been conducted so far, with nearly 100 volunteers offering training to over 400 students.

Since 2006, seven China–US College Student Summer Service activities were held. A total of 1,429 students and 220 young teachers of Tsinghua University along with 432 university teachers and students from the United States, Hong Kong, and Taiwan participated in the activities (see Figure 5.4). Through the practice, the participants had a better understanding about poverty-stricken areas and had a stronger sense of social responsibility.

Figure 5.4
Scenes of China–US College Student Summer Service Activities

Source: The program website http://www.tsinghuafp.com

Funding

From 2003 to May 2012, School of Continuing Education, Tsinghua University invested RMB 15.3725 million, and companies, organizations, and individuals donated RMB 38.6085 million, HKD 1.29 million, and USD 180,000 (see Figure 5.5).

Up to May 2012, the project expenditure totaled RMB 51.0847 million, mainly used for hardware equipment, technical service, training programs, office operations, and site investigation (see Figure 5.6).

As for the operation cost of distance teaching centers, the Office of Educational Poverty Alleviation encourages the centers to properly charge for the platform and resources, but only to maintain its basic operation rather than seek any profit.

Publicity and Supervision

Poverty alleviation through education is a long-term arduous endeavor, which requires great support of all Tsinghua University faculty and students, as well as various sectors of the society. Thus, the project strengthens publicity on related work. Work brief is reported to the university leaders each month, and news release is published via the project website. Meanwhile, distance teaching centers also provide news of various kinds to enrich the website.

Figure 5.5
Tsinghua University Input and Social Donations for the Poverty Alleviation Project through Education

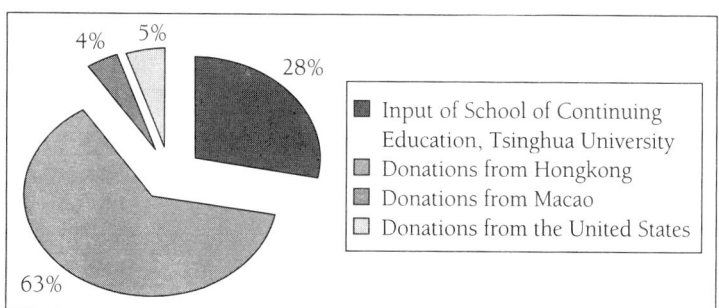

Source: The program website http://www.tsinghuafp.com

Figure 5.6
Expenditure for the Poverty Alleviation Project through Education

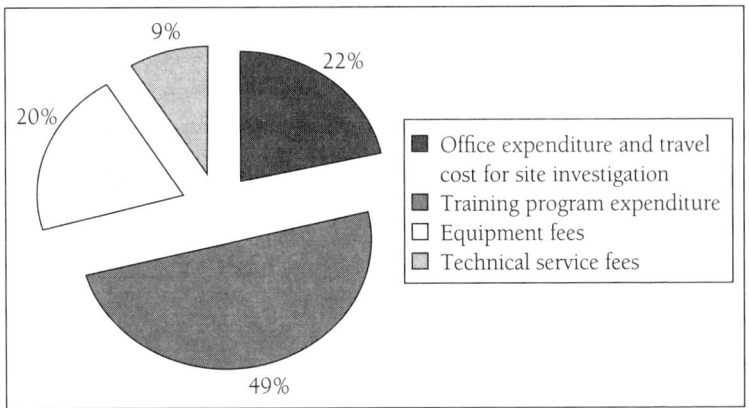

Source: The program website http://www.tsinghuafp.com

Regarding operation supervision of the teaching centers, the Office of Poverty Alleviation through Education requires the centers to submit work progress reports each month. The office representatives pay site visits from time to time.

Achievements

Innovating on Concept of Poverty Reduction and Development

Tsinghua University was the first higher education institution to have raised and practiced the concept of "poverty alleviation through education," and poverty alleviation through distance education, as a new concept in poverty alleviation and development, expanded the participation channels for society-based poverty reduction. Distance teaching centers paved an express way of information to spread knowledge, bringing Tsinghua University classes into the remote and poor countryside and giving a new interpretation for "education serving the society."

Former Vice Minister of Education Wu Qidi said: "The project of poverty alleviation through education of Tsinghua University has not only channeled quality education resources to the population in poverty-stricken areas for whom education is most needed, but also created a good social atmosphere among higher education institutions."

Winning Government Support and Recognition

Since the launch of the project, Tsinghua University won great support of many ministries. Officials serving in provisional posts in poverty-stricken areas from ministries, enterprises, public institutions, and social groups made great efforts to facilitate implementation of the project locally and provided management support. Increasingly, provincial governments cooperated with the university to integrate local official training programs into the educational poverty alleviation, so as to benefit the entire area.

Mr Liu Shuwen, Deputy Division Director of Department of External Cooperation, State Council Leading Group Office of Poverty Alleviation and Development (LGOP), said: "Poverty reduction through education plays a significant role in the strategic system for poverty alleviation and development, and is a fundamental anti-poverty measure. Tsinghua University, a prestigious higher education institution in China and in the world, shows concern for poverty and actively participates in anti-poverty efforts, which reflects its strong sense of political and social responsibility, and embodies its management concept and core competitiveness." In December 2011, LGOP granted the Office of Poverty Alleviation through Education of Tsinghua University the honorary title of "National Exemplary Unit in Poverty Relief and Development" (see Figure 5.7).

Winning Public Attention and Support

The project attracted wide attention and participation of domestic and overseas institutions and individuals (see Figure 5.8). Hongkong-based Weixin Education Foundation has been showing concern for training of middle and primary school teachers in poverty-stricken areas; it has requested Tsinghua University to train middle and primary school teachers and headmasters in target areas and set up distance teaching centers to receive the university's educational resources. Hongkong-based China Fortune Foundation supported the University in offering training

Figure 5.7
Office of Poverty Alleviation through Education of Tsinghua University Was Honored as "National Exemplary Unit in Poverty Relief and Development"

Source: The program website http://www. tsinghuafp.com

to officials in poverty-stricken areas. In order to enhance communication between young Chinese and Americans, Hongkong-based Zeng Xianbei Charity Fund organized a large number of US college students and Qinghua University students each year to visit poverty-stricken areas to offer voluntary teaching, during which mutual exchange between the two sides was greatly strengthened. Tsinghua University and World Bank Institute joined hands in holding 16 training conferences, involving over 11,000 people in training on poverty reduction, quality of ethnic minorities, small city planning, improving investment environment, and developing SMEs, and industrial clusters.

In addition to participating in the University's work, international communities also actively organized discussions on the university's unique mode of poverty alleviation through education. In June 2005, "Knowledge Transmission in the Information Age and Poverty Relief" seminar was held in Tsinghua University, and in November 2007, "Poverty Alleviation through Distance Education and Summer Service Learning" was held.

Mainstream media such as CCTV, BTV, CETV, *Guangming Daily*, *People's Daily*, *China Youth Daily* and *China Education Daily* reported the project in feature stories.

Figure 5.8
Public Attention and Support for the Project

Source: The program website http://www.tsinghuafp.com

Exerting Great Social Influence

The Office of Educational Poverty Alleviation made a survey upon the operation of 100 teaching centers nationwide, and the result is as follows:

What Did Schools in Poverty-stricken Areas Gain?

Around 73% of the interviewees said the training courses for middle and primary school teachers and students improved the comprehensive quality of the participants and drove the entrance rate into higher education institutions to go up year by year.

Yunnan Yanjin No.1 Middle School used to lag behind in teaching quality among local middle schools. Since participation in the project of poverty alleviation through education in 2003, it sees teaching quality improve year by year, and entrance rate into college steadily increase, ranking among the top in local senior middle schools.

What Did Teachers in Poverty-stricken Areas Gain?

Around 80% of the participant teachers believed the courses were excellent and suitable for local teachers. The courses proved effective in helping them update their education concept, improve their attitude towards teaching and learn new teaching methods.

Wang Liqiao, an otherwise introverted teacher in Hua county, Henan province, turned confident after participation in the project, and her teaching methods also became more flexible and interesting. She said: "The Courses of Tsinghua University cleared things up that used to confuse me."

What Did Students in Poverty-stricken Areas Gain?

Around 95% of the interviewees said the project helped local students become more interested in study, get the learning methods suitable for them, improve their attitude toward study, become more confident and have greater aspirations.

A local student said to the China–US College Student Summer Service team at the end of the activity: "Your visit here deeply impressed me, and also made me take a fresh look at my life ahead. I'm more motivated and confident now."

What Did Headmasters in Poverty-stricken Areas Gain?

Up to March 2012, Tsinghua University organized 31 training sessions for a total of 17,910 middle and primary school headmasters nationwide. After the training, they paid more attention to the art of teaching and cognitive development of teachers and students.

After the training, Wang Dexi, a headmaster from Lingshou County, Hebei province said: "Though the training just lasted for a few days, the inspiration and experience I got from it is an enduring treasure."

What Did Officials in Poverty-stricken Areas Gain?

Around 93% of the participant officials believed the training helped them broaden their horizon, acquire new knowledge and skills, transform work mentality, improve their administration ability, and facilitate the daily work.

In 2004, Tsinghua University and Diqing Prefecture Government, Yunnan province signed a cooperation agreement, according to which the former would finance building of two-way interactive distance teaching centers for the latter. According to the training demand of local officials, ten training courses were offered, namely, environment and ecology, urban planning, administration by law, nationality and religion, agriculture and animal husbandry, ecological tourism, reasonable resource development, fiscal management and finance, public administration and party building. Over 400 local county-level officials participated in the one-year study. The official in charge of the project in Diqing said: "For the development of Diqing, we are in urgent need of competent professionals. That Tsinghua University provides training for local party and government officials is the very way to address poverty. Our gross domestic product (GDP) grew by 20% from 2004 to the first half of 2010. Apart from the National Strategy of Western Development, I believe Tsinghua University's intellectual help to accelerate local scientific development also plays an important role. The project works well indeed."

A village leader that participated in the training said: "That Qinghua University contributes to poverty alleviation through distance education affords farmers opportunities to go to college at home. I believe such learning opportunities will help us achieve the goal of leading a moderately well-off life soon."

Promotion Value

First, the project is low in cost and highly operable. Poverty-stricken areas are mostly located in remote regions, where traffic is inconvenient. Face-to-face training at Tsinghua University for all participants would have caused too much expenditure and affected work of local areas. Distance training can save considerable training costs for poverty-stricken areas.

Second, the project is unfolded in a large scale, and has wide coverage. Each session around 80 learners attend the training at Tsinghua University; meanwhile, the university broadcasts the courses through satellite equipment to local teaching centers in a real time manner. In this way, over 1,000 learners are actually studying the related courses through distance learning centers each session.

Third, the project proves to be effective and improves the self-development ability of poverty-stricken areas, so that local people will be able to eventually rely on themselves to lead a better life.

Fourth, higher education institutions join in the social forces to alleviate poverty and put their advantages into play. More universities and colleges are encouraged to join in.

Outlook

At a peasant's home in the underdeveloped area of western China, a young peasant is attending the course "county-level economy and opportunities" and communicating with a Tsinghua University teacher via video broadcasting. His sister is also undergoing the "basic training for English teachers" online ... This is the vision of Tsinghua University's project for poverty alleviation through education which is to afford poverty-stricken people access to the best educational resources and enable them to go to the best university in China without leaving home.

However, some problems still exist, such as insufficient attention from leaders, the unstable employee structure, equipment, and venue needs of the teaching centers.

In order to promote sustainable development of the project, the following measures should be taken:

First, adjust work priority. In the beginning of 2012, Tsinghua University launched the second phase of the project with the focus on course development, fund-raising, building of teaching centers, publicity and promotion, to ensure effective operation of the teaching centers.

Second, enhance management of teaching centers. All teaching centers will be able to participate in the project, and technical support and supervision over the centers will be strengthened.

Third, reinforce building of the interpersonal network. The University will seek wider participation of the international community, so that children in poverty-stricken areas can come in contact with more and better concepts. It will keep strengthening ties with charity organizations and benevolent individuals to raise more funds to enrich the project and improve training quality.

Fourth, improve distance training and support service. More efforts will be made to develop training based on the satellite radio and TV network, Internet and mobile network, so as to enable flexible transmission and play of training courses. Efforts will also be made to expand mobile study and service.

6

Agriculture-related Educational Training and S&T Promotion Service System

Liang Shuhua, Liu Weibin, Wang Hai, Zeng Haijun, and Wang Ying

Overview

The Internet-based Union of Universities for Agricultural Science & Technology and Education (UAST), created in November 2003, is mainly composed of higher education institutions. It is designed to use modern information technology to integrate the rich science and technology (S&T) and education resources of the universities and build a platform for sharing agricultural information and technologies with the support of agricultural S&T parks, agricultural research institutes, rural S&T promotion organizations, and under the leadership of the Chinese Ministry of Education (MoE), Ministry of Science and Technology (MOST), and Ministry of Agriculture (MOA). The aim is to turn UAST into a comprehensive service system of educational training and S&T promotion for agriculture, farmers, and rural areas.

UAST operates like a business. It has launched its official website and the sub-websites of its partner universities and demonstration bases, developed a number of S&T platforms including expert database, databases of S&T achievements by category, library of cases of the industrial application of S&T, agricultural information bank and multimedia courseware library, and trained over 500,000 farmers, rural officials, and party members.

Background

In March 2003, agricultural and forestry universities had a seminar on invigorating agriculture through science and education in Xiangling county, Shaanxi province. Attendees at the seminar discussed how to integrate resources for an IT-based agriculture. During that period, China's agricultural technologies were obsolete, there was a lack of conditions and information for agricultural production, extensive management and operation caused low land efficiency, resources were scattered, and it was rather hard for the rural China to increase the overall economic benefits and shake off poverty. In such a context, the top priority of China's efforts to promote IT application in agriculture to build an efficient agricultural information service system and provide agriculture-related educational training, S&T promotion, and comprehensive information services. It was after the seminar that the design of UAST started.

China's higher education institutions have rich resources in terms of talent and S&T information, advantages in multiple disciplines, and great research strength, and thus are the most important resource bank for agricultural S&T and farmer education (promotion and training). Higher agriculture education combines teaching, scientific research and promotion, aims to promote education across all sectors, and takes S&T promotion and talent cultivation in rural China as its major task. CETV and some local education TV stations disseminate agricultural technologies in rural China through satellite. The nationwide distance education network for rural primary and secondary schools covers every village and township throughout the country and turns all rural schools into a base for the government to serve "agriculture, farmers, and rural areas." All these have laid a solid foundation for the creation of UAST.

Implementation Plan

Mainly composed of higher education institutions, UAST is designed to use modern information technology to integrate the rich S&T and education resources of universities and build a platform for sharing agricultural information and technologies with the support of agricultural S&T parks, agricultural research institutes, and rural S&T promotion centers. The aim is to turn UAST into a service system of educational training and S&T promotion for agriculture, farmers, and rural areas.

UAST focuses its efforts mainly on the following:

- Training on rural development and transfer of rural labor transfer and academic education, specifically including the training on practical skills, information knowledge and skills, entrepreneurial knowledge and practice, village management, small town building, rural sanitation and epidemic prevention, and transfer of rural labor, and academic education for related people.
- Delivery of services for the translation of S&T achievements into agricultural productivity, including S&T achievement promotion, expert consultation and distance disease and pest diagnosis.
- Talent exchanges, enterprise and product shows, agricultural e-commerce, and S&T trade to improve agricultural S&T service.
- Creation of channels for international exchanges, including the platforms for introducing the S&T achievements of other countries, international online trading platforms and international online education platforms, with the reliability of trading systems and smooth market development ensured.

The structure of the UAST service system is as follows:

- One information center, that is, UAST Information Center.
- Two focuses of service, that is, educational training and S&T promotion.

- Three types of supporting organizations, that is, higher education institutions with a large number of agriculture and forestry majors under MoE, agricultural S&T parks under MOST, and agricultural research institutes and S&T promotion centers under MOA.
- Four-level management structure, that is, national (Information Center in Beijing), provincial/municipal (sub-centers), prefecture/ county-level (bases), and village-level (service stations).

The management of UAST can be carried out at three levels. Coordination and Leadership Group consisting of relevant ministry leaders make plans for and lay down requirements on UAST; higher education institutions, agricultural S&T parks, research institutes, and enterprises jointly set up the governing board of UAST; specific services are delivered by the newly founded company under the guidance of the governing board.

The service of UAST is targeted at agricultural S&T parks, agriculture-related enterprises, major growers and breeders, local agricultural S&T educational institutions, trade associations and average farmers. Attaching importance to both priorities and the general public, UAST strives to develop seven types of people for rural areas, that is, managers (rural officials), information specialists (people engaged in information service delivery), dealers (people buying and selling rural commodities), technicians (technical personnel for agriculture), entrepreneurs (people leading others to get rich), health workers (rural health personnel), and people engaged in industry (migrant workers in cities).

Implementation Progress

Introducing Innovative Service Approaches and Creating Suitable S&T Education and Information Service Platforms

UAST has set up over 10 demonstration bases with distinctive features, four two-way satellite stations and 24 one-way satellite stations (see Figures 6.1 and 6.2). Two-way video interactive system, courseware video player system, and related expert systems have been installed on

Figure 6.1
UAST and County Government Work Together to Build Demonstration Base No.1

Source: The program website http://www.uast.com.cn

Figure 6.2
UAST and County Government Work Together to Build Demonstration Base No.2

Source: The program website http://www.uast.com.cn

the basis of the modern distance education network for rural primary and secondary schools. At each demonstration base, Information Service Leadership Group and Office have been set up, a localized expert team and an IT team have been established to serve as a bridge between universities and rural areas.

Integrating Rural Information Resources and Building a Digital S&T Resource Platform

UAST member universities have built over 30 large databases, such as expert information bank, multimedia database, S&T achievement database, practical technique database, and the database on crop disease prevention and pest control. They have also developed 180 multimedia courseware integrating text, images, animation, audio and video, compiled and printed over 20,000 copies of agricultural S&T materials, and filmed over 100 hours of TV programs on practical agricultural techniques. To meet the needs of rural learning and leisure centers, they have especially developed the "Learn to Farm" digital resource package that integrates over 2,600 video clips, including movies, dramas, comic dialogues, practical techniques, stories about how to get rich, laws, health and fitness, and the total capacity reaches 1,000 GB.

Developing Distance Academic Education and Launching an Education Program Targeting New Countryside Officials

UAST has created an educational platform for rural officials to study without leaving their workplaces, delivered higher education to rural areas in the form of distance education, and launched an education program targeting new countryside officials. The program is targeted at rural community officials, back-up officials, backbone farmers, staff of specialized rural cooperatives, and other officials working for rural communities. The aim is to cultivate managerial and technology talents with the passion for the countryside, the sense of social responsibility and sound S&T knowledge.

The program combines academic education and training, offers junior-college-level majors such as rural regional development, and management of agriculture and forestry, and incorporates distance teaching, face-to-face tutoring, video-on-demand systems, discussions, social practice and field visits. Students are recommended by local party and government authorities, and the program is carried out by the Online Education College of China Agricultural University. Local government departments give support with policy and subsidy. Up to now, nearly 1,000 students have been recruited, and a team of highly competent and reliable rural officials familiar with education program has been developed.

Launching "Learn to Farm" Digital Resource Package to Offer Video Service in Rural Areas

Taking rural realities into consideration, China Agricultural University has developed the "Learn to Farm" digital resource package that integrates 2,600 popular video clips in eight categories, such as agricultural technologies, work skills, legal knowledge, stories about how to get rich, popular science, fine arts, and daily-life tips into a 1,000 GB hard disk player of less than 2 kg in weight (see Figure 6.3). After connecting the disk with television and with the help of a remote controller, farmers can repeatedly play any video they need in villagers' committee, farmer schools, and learning and leisure centers (see Figure 6.4). The package offers rich content and a large amount of information. It is cheap and easy to use, and does not need the access to the Internet. As a new tool to disseminate agricultural S&T and rural culture, it meets the general needs of farmers and also provides them with personalized experience.

Figure 6.3
"Learn to Farm" Digital Resource Package

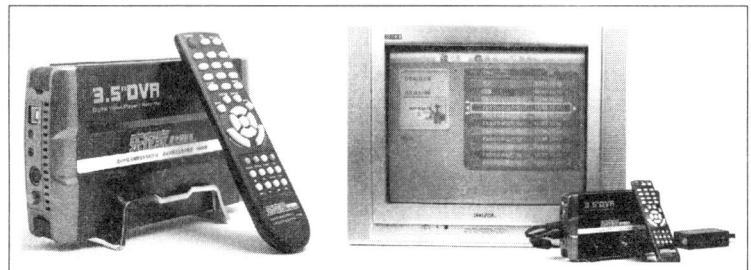

Source: The program website http://www.uast.com.cn

Figure 6.4
Farmers Watching "Learn to Farm" Videos

Source: The program website http://www.uast.com.cn

The package has been introduced to 76 villages of 15 towns, and the videos have been played over 3,000 times for 80,000 people. With its application, villagers have improved their skills, legal awareness, and relations with officials. To quote some villagers, the resource package has helped popularize scientific knowledge, promote agricultural technologies and improve cultural atmosphere, and is indeed the "bond of rural families, among villagers and between officials and villagers, and also a catalyst for promoting cultural progress."

Developing Various Training Activities to Cater to Rural Needs

First, the training session on modern technology for the cattle industry was initiated to explore the way of organizing training and promoting practical technologies (see Figure 6.5). China Agricultural University worked together with China Association of Senior Scientists and Technicians to recruit over 50 experts and professors for setting up an expert team for the cattle industry. The team devised training plans for the cattle industry, and filmed nearly 50 modularized and easy-to-understand multimedia courseware videos both on site and in studio. Audio-video interactive system was used for the 12-hour real-time distance Q&A and consultation. Around 100,000 farmers acquired the information they needed through courseware videos, expert face-to-face training, site tutorship, distance Q&A, seminars, distance discussions

Figure 6.5
Training Session on Modern Technology for the Cattle Industry

Source: The program website http://www.uast.com.cn

and information inquiry. Having solved the practical problems of local cattle raisers, the training session turned out to be very popular.

Second, farmers' competency training was launched to figure out what farmers really need (see Figure 6.6). Thirteen special courses were provided to over 30,000 people through videos, face-to-face tutoring, discussions and online information inquiry, benefiting over 100,000 people.

Offering a Variety of S&T Promotion Services

UAST has organized an expert volunteer team to serve "agriculture, farmers and rural areas." It gathered over 100 experts and professors with expertise, achievements, and experience in different fields to conduct public good activities through the UAST information platform, such as S&T promotion and application, expert consultation, and educational training. The following are some examples.

When over 3,000 mu (1 mu = 1/15 hectare) seed corns in Longhua County, Hebei province suffered rare northern leaf blight, experts from China Agricultural University were organized to conduct real-time distance group diagnosis on the information platform. By instructing local

Figure 6.6

Farmers Engaged in UAST Educational Training, S&T Promotion, and Information Services

Source: The program website http://www.uast.com.cn

technicians and farmer scientists on what to do with the soil and straws, the experts helped to prevent the spread of the infectious disease and save farmers over RMB 4 million of losses.

Aquaculture technology has been popularized in Tianjin. A 24-hour information service system consisting of online diagnosis and decision-making system, distance diagnosis, call center, mobile diagnosis, and STB push system has been put in place, helping to promote S&T popu-larization and improve local scientific aquaculture. The demonstration area in the 10 districts and counties of Tianjin has reached 22,560 mu. With each mu bringing RMB 110.29 on average, the increased revenue stands at RMB 66.8386 million.

The experts worked with Zhujiawan village, Beizhuang town, Miyun county in Beijing and Hurun Food Group to launch e-governance, e-com-merce, information service, and IT-based talent training. Outstanding graduates were selected to serve as part-time assistants to village party branch secretaries and village heads to help with the work of villagers' committees. Over 60 teachers and students were organized to measure land for villages and plan for village development. The experts helped to develop the chestnut website www.banli.net.cn, sponsored the e-display project, provided the live broadcast of meetings to villagers, disseminated information on popular science, and played TV news and entertaining TV programs.

Conclusions

UAST has made some achievements and accumulated some experience during the process of serving agriculture, farmers, and rural areas, mainly including the following:

- Attention and support from leaders are key to the sound operation of UAST and the delivery of better agriculture-related service.

Since its launch in 2003, UAST has gained attention and support from relevant authorities (see Figure 6.7). MoE invested RMB 1.3 million startup funds, and MOST provided RMB 1.8 million for the project "Modern Key Technologies for IT Application in Rural Areas and Demonstration."

Figure 6.7
Ministry of Finance, Ministry of Science and Technology, and Ministry of Education Supporting UAST Work

Source: The program website http://www.uast.com.cn

- Cooperation with universities and sharing of resources are the foundation of UAST's work.
- Working with county governments to launch pilot and demonstration programs is an effective approach to conducting UAST's work.
- Exploring suitable S&T promotion approaches according to local needs and realities is the core role of UAST.

Serving agriculture, farmers, and rural areas through IT application and building new countryside are demanding tasks that will take a long time to accomplish. There are still some problems with UAST in this regard.

- Resource integration and department coordination remain difficult.

Since the foundation of UAST, the absence of a management system and benefiting mechanism has dampened the enthusiasm of member universities. Moreover, due to department segmentation, UAST is progressing slowly on integrating resources of agriculture and S&T systems. More support is yet to be won from related ministries.

- Insufficient funding and project support constrain the development of UAST.

At the initial stage of its development, UAST needs to make a lot of efforts in terms of infrastructure and environment building and data resource development, and the services it provides are mainly experimental and nonprofit. Therefore, insufficient funding is one of the factors that constrain UAST's development and service capacity building.

In addition, given the vast area of rural China, wide gaps between different areas, less-developed rural economy, and low education level of rural population against complex modern information technology and difficulty in connecting rural households to the information network, UAST's system building, service delivery, and S&T achievement demonstration and popularization are all complicated tasks. However, due to various reasons, the support from the Chinese government is far from what UAST needs for development.

In order to achieve the sustainable development of UAST, the following measures are proposed:

1. *Putting in place UAST's management mechanism and gaining more government support.* Research should be targeted at the profiting mechanism for UAST members and their rights and responsibilities should be clearly defined to fire up their enthusiasm. Meanwhile, on the basis of developing the agriculture and forestry universities that are already members, senior vocational schools, agricultural secondary schools, local research institutes, and agricultural S&T parks should also be encouraged to join UAST and become the practice bases for agriculture-related educational training and backbone of S&T service.

2. *Making breakthroughs in project operation and financing.* First, efforts should be made to seek the support of MOST for promoting IT application in rural areas, the support of MoE for educational reform, the support of MOA for the project "Science and Technology into Households" and Sunshine Project, and the support of Ministry of Commerce (MOFCOM) in the Information Service Project for New Countryside. The aim of these projects is to attract the input of higher education institutions and enterprises. Second, support and participation of local governments should be actively sought to combine S&T service of UAST and the work of local governments, promote UAST's development, and extend its influence.

3. *Pooling resources to promote online education for agriculture, farmers and rural areas.* Academic education and nondegree education should be combined, and distance education and face-to-face training integrated to promote online education for agriculture, farmers, and rural areas.

    First, promote the academic education for new countryside officials to cultivate reliable and competent rural officials.

    Second, push forward the continuing education for college graduates as village officials to improve college graduate employment and foster reliable and competent college students for rural areas.

Third, advance the "One Resource Package for One Village" project to offer practical technology training and information service to farmers and improve their skills and cultural life.

4. *Establishing long-term mechanism and improving UAST service through pilot programs.* Demonstration bases should be built in selected representative areas, where depth, breadth, and intensity of S&T service should be stressed. First, related projects should be jointly implemented, including MoE's Modern Distance Education Project for Rural Primary and Secondary Schools and MOA's Agricultural Information Service Pilot Project with "Television, Telephone, and Computer." Second, information specialists should be developed among college graduates as village officials, households selling agricultural materials, and people good at getting rich, so as to facilitate UAST's education service delivery. Third, implementation of projects such as modern technology training for the cattle industry, distance education on business information for 10,000 farmers, and expert pool should be continued. The aim is to promote educational training, S&T popularization and comprehensive information services, and render S&T promotion service mainly through IT application.

7

The Application of Extensive Distance Training to Professional Development of Rural Teachers

Long Youhua, Li Dan, Zeng Haijun, and Wang Ying

Overview

The Training Program for Rural Elite Teachers in Central and West China (hereinafter referred to as "the Program") is a part of the National Training Program for Primary and Secondary School Teachers (hereinafter referred to as the "National Training Program," http://www.ypjh.cn). The Program objective is to provide distance training to over 330,000 teachers engaged in compulsory education in five topics covering 22 subjects in 17 provinces. The bid to implement this was won by teacher.com.cn (http://www.teacher.com.cn), which delivered it with support from Ministry of Education (MoE) and local education administrations. Teacher.com.cn actions included surveys of need, training design, technical setup, resource development, monitoring, administration, and services. Extensive distance training took place from October 2010 to February 2011, delivering professional development content to individual primary and secondary school teachers in central and west China.

As a case in information and communication technology (ICT)-based rural education and development, the Program deserves scrutiny for its speed of execution using existing infrastructure, its focus on rural teachers, and its use of an external delivery partner.

Background

Problems with the Professional Development of Chinese Rural Teachers

Nearly 80% of teachers in China work in townships and rural areas. Training has been a consistent weakness, with problems including scarcity of training opportunities, conflict between work and study, bad transport conditions, shortage of funds and lack of good training materials. The quality of rural teachers is widely acknowledged as too low for the education system to support development and curricular reform. Hence, within China's overall policy to improve teaching competency, the top priority is rural primary and secondary school teachers.

National Training Program as a Solution

The National Training Program, co-launched by the MOE and the Ministry of Finance with a budget of RMB 550 million from 2010 to 2012, addresses the challenge in two parts. There is a demonstrative training program for primary and secondary school teachers, and a training program for rural elite teachers in central and west China. The latter is the focus of this case study.

The training program for rural elite teachers in central and west China had a RMB 500 million budget of central government funds for targeted professional training for rural elite teachers in the compulsory education sector in central and western China. The forms of training were replacement and off-job training,[1] short-term intensive training and extensive distance training. The objective was that the target teachers would take demonstration and exemplary roles in the implementation of curricular reform, education for all-round development and teacher training. At the same time, local governments would be supported to improve their teacher training systems. The Program, implemented by teacher.com. cn, would deploy distance training methods to train over 330,000 elite primary and secondary school teachers in 17 provinces, in five topics, and covering 22 subjects.

Program Design and Conceptual Framework

Professional development of rural teachers by distance training in the Program is practice-oriented, using the principle of action learning. The Program design by teacher.com.cn references the following underlying concepts, and is organized into phases as shown in Table 7.1:

- Learning is not just about acquiring in knowledge, but also the ability to solve problems
- Learning is the summary of and reflection upon previous experience
- Learning is largely a process of social interaction
- Reflection is the key to take more efficient actions in the future based on the ones ability
- Action learning is implemented through the whole training process: course study, thematic seminar, evaluation, and display

---

[1] Senior students at normal colleges/universities and town teachers are organized to teach at rural primary and secondary schools as a temporary substitute for elite teachers, so that the latter could take the three-month off-job training at high-level colleges/universities and at first-rate primary and secondary schools.

Table 7.1
Three Phases of Designing the Training Process

Phase	Task	
Preparation and initiation	Survey and investigation, proposal preparation	Survey the needs of users and design the proposal accordingly
	Training the trainers from different provinces	Gather tutors and administrators from different provinces, explain the training proposal, and allow them to familiarize with the platform
	Trainee registration and program launch	Trainees log on the platform to register before the launch of the training
Implementation	Scheduling	Clarify the specific study arrangement in each phase
	Evaluation	Determine the training result based on the statistical data of trainees exported from the platform
	Selection of outstanding works	Select outstanding works as the fruits of training for purposes of acknowledgement and encouragement
Summarizing	Awarding	Select the outstanding trainee, outstanding tutor, outstanding class teacher, outstanding administrator, and outstanding training institute
	Summarizing	Hold sum-up meeting, and issue certificates of training completion; organize the display of training outcomes and present the awards

Source: The program website http://www. teacher.com.cn

Supervision, Implementation, and Evaluation

The Program involved several different actors in supervision, implementation evaluation and production, with different responsibilities as follows:

1. The National Training Program Office, located in the MOE Department of Teacher Education, coordinated the planning and implementation of the Program.
2. Program Execution Offices in each participating province supervised and evaluated the local distance training activities, the performance of administrators and tutors at all levels, and online platform services, and selected and awarded those with outstanding performance when necessary.
3. The education administrations at the municipal and county levels were also responsible for defining needs and providing funding. During the implementation, they were responsible for participant evaluation by questionnaires, which they also analyzed. The administrations summarized all local work and submitted reports to the Provincial Program Office after the completion of the training.
4. The role of teacher.com.cn was to organize subject experts to prepare content on the various subjects to be covered by the training, to submit their content into the distance training service, to solicit feedback by questionnaire from trainees, administrators, and tutors, to analyze feedback, submit data and materials for overall summary and evaluation.

Teacher.com.cn is a large specialized website dedicated to the diploma and nondiploma training for primary and secondary school teachers and principals across the country. It was founded by Northeast Normal University in alliance with other 18 provincial normal colleges, education departments, and training institutes, and is approved by the MoE Department of Teacher Education. It is also the core website of the Teacher Union of China (www.tuchina.org), which is an online teacher education system covering the rural and urban areas of China.

The website distributes training services and systems for the professional development of primary and secondary school teachers and principals across the country. It also delivers public-facing online support services for the distance training operations run by other training institutes and schools for teachers; in the case of this Program, these inputs were sources from the Northeast Normal University, one of the shareholders of teacher.com.cn.

Implementation Process

- *Initial Survey of Training Needs.* To understand the training needs of each participating province, teacher.com.cn assigned over 130 personnel to set up research stations in these provinces. Information and opinion were gathered from local stakeholders on issues such as program tutoring, management, evaluation, implementation, and planning.
- *Training Modules.* Pre-established courses were the core modules, supplemented by thematic seminars. The principle of "Action Learning" and theory-based practice was embedded in the curriculum and in any expert lectures. Models such as teacher self-study, co-operation problem-solving and loops such as "learning——reflection——practice——reflection again——practice again" aimed to transform the traditional passive learning approach into active learning, and to promote the concept of lifelong learning.

  The training process was divided into two phases: online course study and online seminars (see Figure 7.1). To engage the enthusiasm of rural teachers for learning, these processes focused on final classroom outputs.
- *Technical Platform.* The delivery platform from teacher.com.cn enables the Program to live on a site that has been in operation since 2002, has launched 665 training programs, and served over six million visitors. The teaching management and service platform for distance learning and learning support offers features such as archive, open course sign-up, lesson administration, evaluation, resource sharing, distance seminars, and learning communities. The learning environment supports multiple training modes.

Figure 7.1
Distance Teacher Training Process

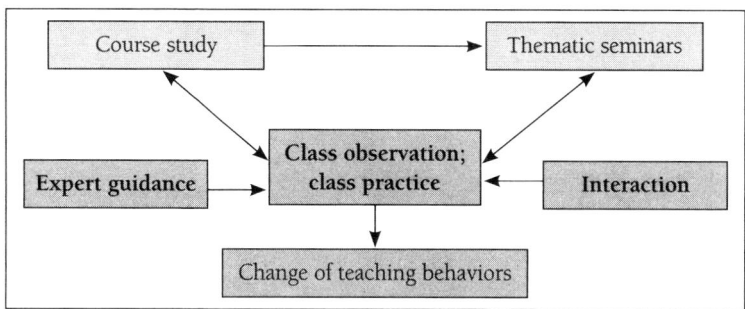

Source: The program website http://www. teacher.com.cn

Its video conference and online test systems are able to support 100,000 simultaneous online users. Student management, site analytics, and progress reporting enable close process monitoring. The system has been used by a range of training agencies.

Training Course

Course developed by teacher.com.cn adopted a seven-factor model of teacher education in action learning formats (see Figure 7.2). The model allows for the value of experience, a problem-focused approach, co-operative learning, combining action with knowledge, the importance of specific circumstances, reflection, and professional guidance.

Courses focused on classroom technique, because the subject-matter knowledge of the target teachers was already assured from their study of the new curriculum reform syllabus at national standard. For classroom technique materials, teacher.com.cn designed over 30 courses for each subject discipline. The courses covered five aspects of classroom technique:

1. Classroom teaching design
2. Classroom teaching strategy
3. Teaching strategy for the core content of the subject
4. Classroom teaching evaluation
5. Research on classroom teaching

Figure 7.2
Seven Factors of Teacher Education

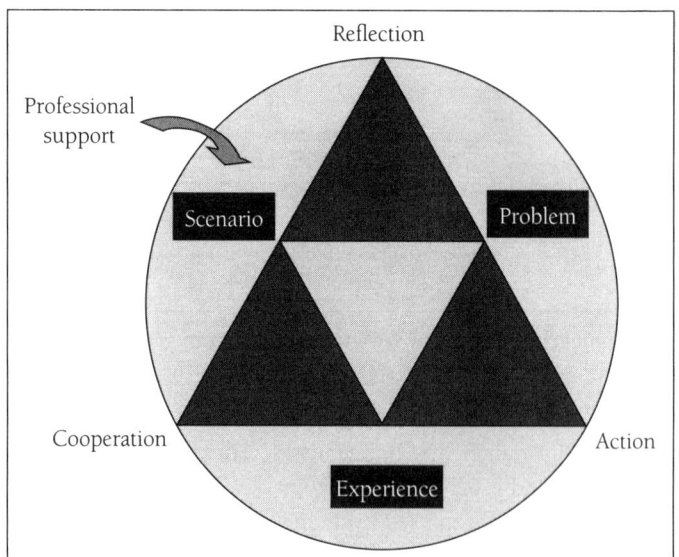

Source: The program website http://www. teacher.com.cn

To realize a coherent course series, the curriculum design blended two approaches: thematic (specific focus on problems associated with each subject) and systematic (common approaches shared across all subjects).

The existing core of pre-established content at teacher.com.cn was boosted with a thread of seminar activity at two levels. One seminar pathway was the "Think and Act" element of thematic courses; the other was a "Thematic Seminar" series taken after the completion of several courses.

Specialist teams comprising educational experts, excellent and specialist teachers, and frontline elite teachers provided guidance to the curriculum R&D teams. Education experts also chaired the development of each subject's series. The chosen course lecturers had senior professional titles, and included a proportion of college teachers, frontline teaching and research personnel, excellent primary and secondary school teachers, and leaders of teaching and research teams who were familiar with teaching practice.

The format of training courses followed a four-session structure (see Figure 7.3).

1. "Thematic Lecture" highlighted professional guidance.
2. "Dialogue" showed the interaction and dialogue between teachers and experts, pointing out solutions to the problems and confusions encountered in practice.
3. "Case Study" guided teachers to learn from more complete cases.
4. "Think and Act" guided teachers to explore teaching knowledge in practice based on their teaching practice in the specific seminar activity.

Learning Support Services

Support, discussion, feedback, and networking services for learners around the Program were considerable. Several learning support forms operated in parallel. They included, national expert teams, video consultations, consulting teams, featured subject channels, hot spot discussions, phone and mail response hotline, and "Classroom in the Air." More details of each are given as follows:

Figure 7.3
Screenshot of a Training Course

Source: The program website http://www. teacher.com.cn

- *National Expert Teams.* These teams consisted of 10 to 20 renowned national experts in the academic branch and discipline concerned, with positions at the forefront of teaching and teaching reform. In addition to serving as the subject leading experts of teacher.com. cn, they participated in and guided the online learning of trainees through answering questions online.
- *Video Consultations.* These were hosted by an expert and were held monthly over three months in each of the 22 subjects on the curriculum. In addition, there were other interactive formats such as lectures, answering common questions, online face-to-face Q&A, online textual Q&A. The process was that teacher.com. cn would collect and sort most common questions in advance, and launch discussions at online forums. Simultaneously, class tutors in each province would organize trainees to participate in video Q&A and other interactive formats on the online platform. Networking was an important aim: grassroots teachers were given the chance to make friends, add to their knowledge, solve problems, and facilitate professional development. Meanwhile, teacher. com.cn launched regular video briefings on the learning situation of trainees.
- *Consulting Teams.* The consulting force of each province was made available to assist experts in providing support. The consulting teams drew on experts from teacher.com.cn, provincial experts, and class tutors. A total of 762 experts were on the provincial expert team, and typically offered professional guidance, hosting of online forums, summaries, comment and other routine supports to the program office in each province.
- *Featured Subject Channels for Resource Sharing.* A total of 22 subject channels were opened for sharing rich teaching materials for each subject. Nearly 10,000 resources and 5 million visits were observed in this support format.
- *"Hot Spot" Discussions.* These take place between trainers and trainees on the platform.
- *Phone and Mail Response Hotline.* Customer service teams at teacher. com.cn call center assigned 12 personnel dedicated to answering the program hotline, and five to answering questions online. A voicemail service was available during the nonmanual handling

section. Group text messaging and group mailing were adopted for major announcements and to assure trainee attendance. The email response desk was staffed 24 hours a day (see Table 7.2). Around 90,000 contacts were handled in these channels.

• *New "Classroom in the Air" Channel.* To package a range of the course resources into an accessible channel for students in areas with poor Internet access, China Education TV Station in collaboration with teacher.com.cn distributed the training courses in its "Classroom in the Air" channel. This is a satellite broadcast of selected course elements, offering solutions to common problems and providing added value through an alternative mode of consumption.

Taken together, these different forms of learner support broke new ground in China for online training. They ended the previous didactic and one-way monotonous form of training. The large uptake of interactive communication was also significant. The scale is in part due to the extension to provincial level of services offered in the main program channels. At provincial level there were over 11 million interactions on subject and class forums and interactive communication between trainees from different provinces. As an example of provincial level interactive channels, Jilin province launched a further four video consultations and

Table 7.2
Statistics about the Inquiries Received by the Consultation Team

Item	Number of Consultants	Number of Inquiries
400 service hotline	12	17,935
Email of the National Training Program	1	3,484
Feedback email	1	1,366
Online customer service	5	3,515
Group text messaging	1	62,735
Service support QQ	11	169
Total	31	89,204

Source: The program website http://www.teacher.com.cn

two forum seminars based on the three video consultations organized at teacher.com.cn.

Teaching Support Services

To address challenges of scale and efficiency, the Program set up features such as One Card One Trainee, dedicated online teacher–supervisors, and regular learning briefings. Further details are given as follows:

- *One Card One Trainee.* The pre-training investigation in participating provinces established that widely varying IT skills would lead to potential problems around logging in, reporting and identity management. Teacher.com.cn adopted the "one card for one trainee" policy, producing 380,000 physical cards with corresponding unique identifier codes for each trainee was entitled to one physical card and one corresponding electronic code. On the back of the physical card, the steps for logging and registration were printed in detail along with the inquiry hotline of teacher. com.cn (see Figure 7.4).

Figure 7.4
Example of the Physical Card

Source: The program website http://www.teacher.com.cn

- *Dedicated Online Teacher-Supervisors.* Teaching administration personnel provided all-round follow-up services. Teacher.com.cn had a policy of "dedicated management" for each program in each province, assigned dedicated teaching administration personnel to each province to follow up duties in online and offline program management. Tasks included, to track each forum section on the main page at various levels, to assess whether trainees had submitted their homework and journals on time, and whether experts and tutors had reviewed and marked the works submitted by trainees as scheduled.

The platform used for 95% of these tasks was a set of up 20 QQ administration clubs and 17 QQ tutoring clubs for each province, used for communication with administrators and tutors at all levels (see Figure 7.5). When a trainee failed to submit homework, the teaching administration personnel would remind him/her using announcement, push-message, top posting on the forum, and group text messaging.

Figure 7.5
Comparison of QQ Club and Telephone Service Channels Used by Teaching Administration Personnel

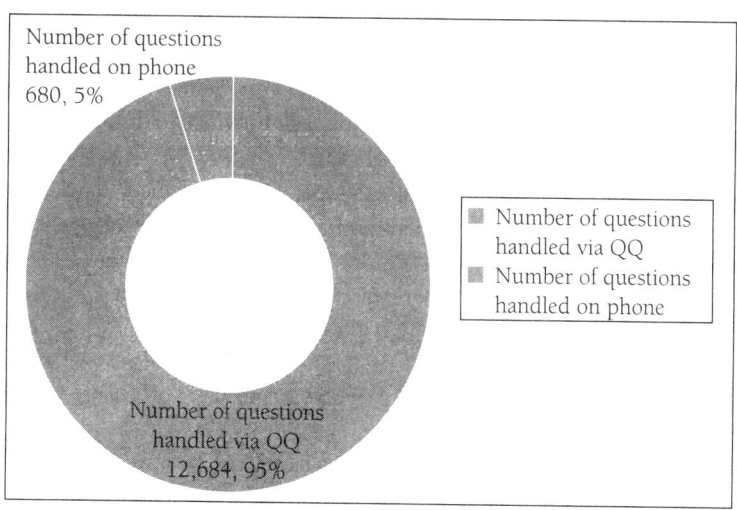

Source: The program website http://www.teacher.com.cn

- *Learning Briefings.* Teaching administration personnel at teacher. com.cn also produced regular learning briefings. These displayed the registration and learning progress of trainees from different classes, counties, municipalities in each participating province, reported expert and tutor consultations, recorded the performance of administrators at all levels and listed the outstanding works of trainees. By February 2011, a total 123 program briefings and 81 learning briefings had been made.
- *Technical Support and Performance.* The Technology Centre consisted of over 40 shift-working engineers offering 24-hour technical support.

During the implementation of the National Training Program, the platform had the overall bandwidth peak of 415.89M and the average bandwidth (24 hours) of 173.25M. Concurrent use peaked at 4000/s, while total visits reached over seven million. Internet traffic on this scale requires a system emergency response mechanism which is shown in Figure 7.6.

Funding

As part of the National Training Program, this program was implemented during a five-year funding window. The National Training Program enjoys a dedicated fund of RMB 500 million every year, about 70% of which is spent on off-job training and short-term intensive training. The MoE stipulates that the fund allocated by each province to distance training shall not exceed 30% of the total funds.

For an indication of marginal costs per teacher trained, if we take the teacher.com.cn 2010 payment of RMB 40 million out of the RMB 500 million funds for delivering around 80 hours of training to about 330,000 teachers, the benchmark marginal cost per hour of additional teacher training in western China is RMB2/trainee/hour. However, this figure does not take account of the sunk costs of the systems or infrastructure costs

The costs of the development and use of courses and the operation and maintenance of the platform accounted for over 50% of RMB 40 million, and the consultation costs of tutors and experts, over 30%. The funds also covered the expenses on plan development, evaluation, organization, and management.

Figure 7.6
Logical Diagram of the Monitoring, Alarm, and Handling Process on teacher.com.cn Platform

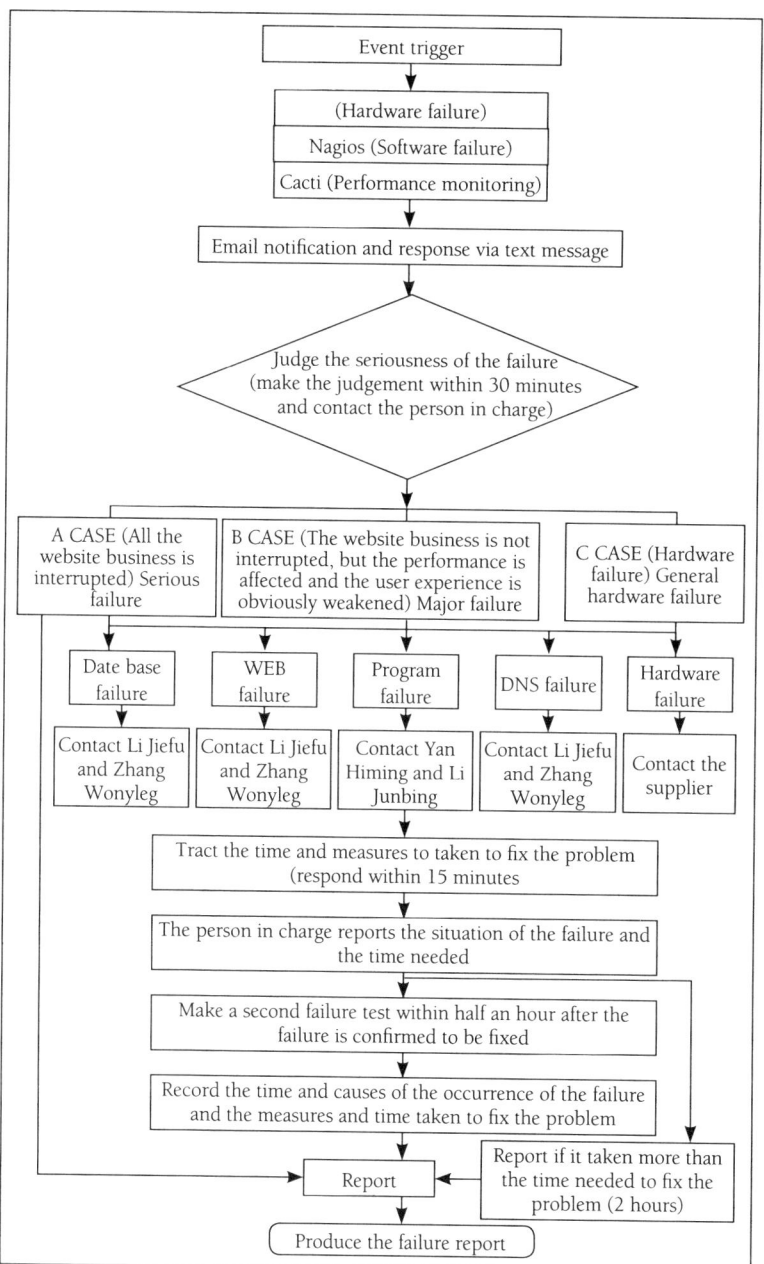

Source: The program website http://www. teacher.com.cn

Process Monitoring and Quality Control

The workflow of program management was a significant element in the program. Teacher.com.cn had a dedicated program work team at the beginning of training to coordinate the training work, and a shared maps of program management workflow (see Figure 7.7), as well as maps of

Figure 7.7
Program Management Standardization Workflow

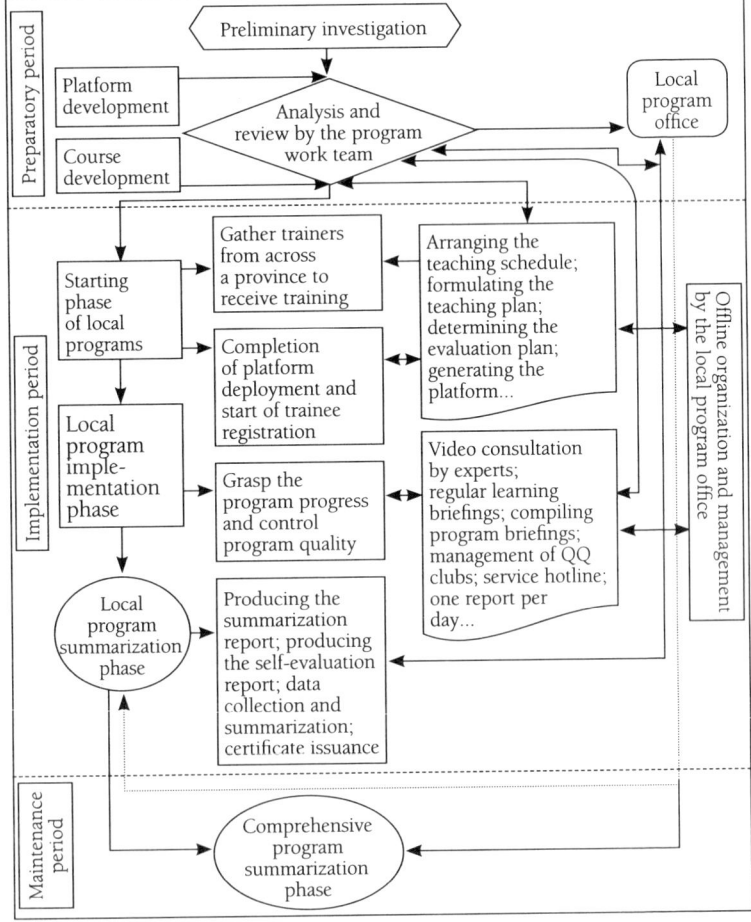

Source: The program website http://www.teacher.com.cn

roles of other partners at provincial and national level (see Figure 7.8). Staff at teacher.com.cn used the slogan of "training means service" to define attitude and service methods.

Teacher.com.cn adopted the supervisory mechanism of "one report per day" to manage progress monitoring across 17 provinces. This meant daily reports of learning, registration, outcomes, briefings, and so on from each province. A daily analysis compared the differences in the progress of the National Training Program in different provinces.

Teacher.com.cn feeds the daily report on the National Training Program to the following recipients:

- MoE Department of Teacher Education
- National Training Program Office
- Department of Education of each participating province

Figure 7.8
Training Organization and Management Workflow

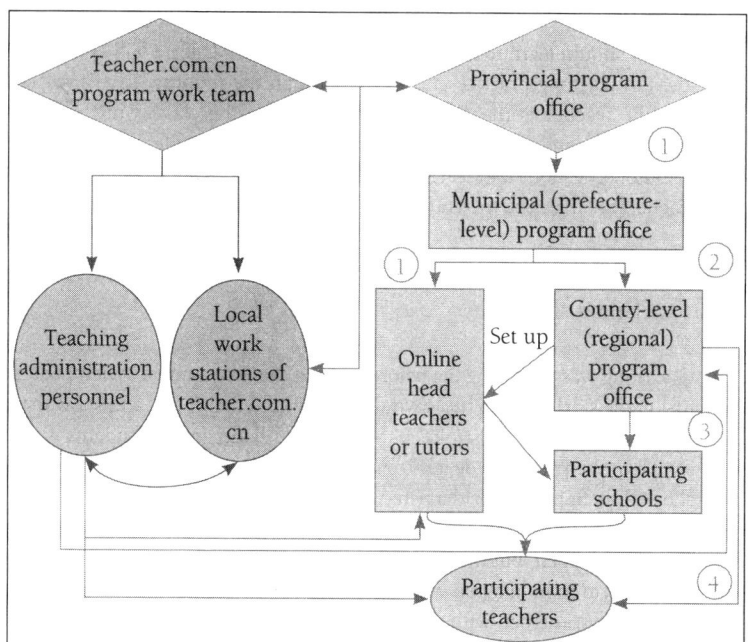

Source: The program website http://www. teacher.com.cn

The Quality Control Department at teacher.com.cn collected and analyzed questions and problems raised by users and fed identified issues back into service improvements.

Online Questionnaire. Teacher.com.cn used voluntary questionnaires to assess the extent to which the program satisfied needs. The questionnaire design focused on trainee's specific needs, platform functions, course requirement, and need for teaching support services. Periodic analysis of questionnaires led to program adjustments. A representative sample of some comments collected in this way is given below.

Teacher Li Bin from Tibet wrote:

> Is there anything I have said and done restricting the development of my students? What kind of changes should I make in order to better cultivate students? ... To clear such doubts, besides receiving training and listening repeatedly to the lectures given by experts, reading has become my first choice. Through training and learning, I have deeply realised that I must stop the practice of cramming classroom education, and instead turn each class and each education cell into a platform for the active participation and development of students. Instead of taking the hand of students and leading them, I should learn to let them walk on their own. Later, I will apply these ideas to teaching practice gradually. Through the training, I have realised that the teacher is the organiser and guider of the class, while students are the doer and explorer of learning. Teachers and students shall discuss common questions and teachers shall propose some core ones. Meanwhile, teachers shall arouse the enthusiasm of students in the teaching process.

Li Taixian, a Chinese teacher in Wentang Primary School, Xiuying District, Haikou stated:

> One thing was bothering me before I joined the Programme. When I taught first grade students to write, I would always hold their hand and show them how to write stroke by stroke. But if I let their hand go, the students would switch to the posture they felt comfortable. I did some demonstrations, and showed them how to hold a pen over and over again, but had little success. Sometimes I wondered whether it was because students' hand bone was too soft to hold a pen. But through the training I found the answer: I could have taught them to hold a pen with both their index finger and thumb first and then support the pen with the middle finger. So I taught them and I found they could hold a pen better than before. I used to ask my students to hold

a pen with the index finger, thumb and middle finger at the same time and it's too confusing for them to grasp the key point.

Teacher Li Xiaoyan, Boye County, Hebei province:

> In last year's open class, I wanted to make a multimedia courseware that allowed students to read the text extensively, with slides automatically switching the pictures and the background music to play nonstop. I sought help from all the teachers known for their courseware skills in the school and studied a lot of materials from the library, but it remained a puzzle because of the backward technology in our remote rural area. In the computer lecture given by Professor Wang Huaiyuan I found the answer to my question. Professor Wang demonstrated and explained to us with great patience and the problem, which seemed so unfathomable to me, became as easy as a piece of cake. Neoimaging, photoshop and audio & visual processing … all the magic that made my courseware splendid could be found here. It was as if I received a wisdom box from the lecture. When I open this box in the future, my lectures will become fresh, vivid and lively.

Ma Lanqiao from Renqiu, Hebei:

> The Programme has put an end to my dull and banal work and learning days. Besides developing teaching plans, reviewing the students' homework, and organising students to prepare for exams—all of which used to bury me—I now have fun producing multimedia courseware and browsing teaching information on the Internet. The Programme has improved my professional competency. I deeply realise my lack of professional knowledge and insufficient utilization of information technology. What I did before was repeat what the book says, which was hackneyed and boring. After receiving the training from the Programme, I will do my best to make each lecture wonderful and classroom education colorful.

Tao Jihong, a history teacher in a junior middle school in Guangxi, remarked on the lecture entitled *The Naval Battle of 1894*:

> "Through training, I came to realise that new teaching concepts and methods have a wider and wider application in the teaching of history. The introduction of subjective evaluation, the development and utilization of classroom education resources, and group study have rejuvenated the once colorless class.

Media Coverage

The program attracted media attention from national-level media and relevant portal websites such as *China Youth Daily*, *Tibet Daily*, sina.com, sohu.com, Tencent, xinhuanet.com, Netease, etc. Articles include interviews and reports with titles such as "Hundreds of Thousands of Rural Teachers Benefit from the Distance Training Program in Central and West China," "Rural Teachers Take the 'Training Program' Express to Receive Training Online," and "Online Teacher Training: Learn at Home."

Summary and Reflection

The program of extensive distance teacher training has had many positive features, which can be summarized as follows:

- State-wide resource sharing using distance learning
- Co-operation and organization among many personnel and levels
- Involvement of national and local experts to enthuse learners
- Active quality control processes
- All-round support services from multiple perspectives and in multiple forms

However, there have been some issues and problems encountered along the way, from which it is possible to draw useful lessons.

- *Information Quality.* Each participating area was doing extensive distance training program for the first time. With no previous experience, some of the initial and ongoing information they submitted was inaccurate or false. As a result, the load of technical adjustments increased and the platform was less stable. A future program should produce specifications regarding the submitting of information in order to reduce the mistakes.
- *Lack of Familiarity with Platform.* Given the tight timescale, tutors, head teachers, trainers and trainees had little time to familiarize themselves with the content and requirements of training. Many were not familiar with the operation of the training platform. As

a result, the learning efficiency was low at the beginning. For a future program, we suggest earlier training of trainers as soon as possible, and the follow-up multilevel training for administrators, tutors, head teachers and trainees.

- *Tutor Quality.* Selection and training of tutors and administrators who are capable, passionate elite teachers, or research personnel could probably have been better. In future exercises, more intensive training will be required to ensure tutors and administrators better understand the process of distance learning, have technical skills, know the courses and are capable at teaching administration and handling feedback.

- *Post-training Support.* The 80 hours of extensive distance learning provided solid support before and during the training period, but not for post-training professional development. This issue deserves more attention in the future. A combination of distance diploma education and nondiploma training may be the way forward.

Look Ahead...

The new reforms of basic education in China are a top–bottom reform that involves the transformation and optimization of teachers' ideas about distance education, as well as reform of materials and curriculum. Through this program, distance teacher training has found its development space and growing point in the reform agenda.

Teachers always need to improve their skills and knowledge through training and education in order to perform their teaching duties. But China's rural areas are significantly inferior to its urban areas in terms of information environment, training activities, and cultural environment. Thus training opportunities are not easily available to rural teachers. Extensive distance training is an important solution for the professional development of rural teachers.

The prospects look good for extensive distance learning approaches playing a role in the future of Chinese educational reform. The Chinese government's increasing input into education and the continuous advance of education informatization have given rural schools better hardware and facilities and more diversified digital learning resources.

There is strong general support for extensive distance teacher training throughout the system. For example, as of December 2011, teacher.com. cn offered 3,321 state-level and local online courses covering every type and level of education, and distance learning assets such as these have a wider impact on teacher quality. Distance education, along with mobile learning and the general support for the professional development of rural teachers, appear to enjoy further development.

8

Distance Education for Teachers in Less Developed Areas

Zhang Jufan, Wang Yanchang, Zeng Haijun, and Wang Ying

Overview

In 2002, School of Distance Education, Shaanxi Normal University, started practice and exploration on distance education for teachers in economically less developed areas. Relying on 12 county-level training schools for teachers in Yulin city, Shaanxi province, the project initiated team building of middle and primary school teachers, building of training bases and building of learning-oriented communities. By the end of 2005, 12% of the teachers in the 12 counties, or nearly 6,000 teachers, had participated in the project. Since 2006, the project has gradually been carried out in more pilot areas and the study results have been promoted to the entire province and other regions. It mainly included constructing a distance education platform integrating satellite and the Internet, developing distance education resources, building a support and service system for teaching, and exploring modes of teaching, management and service.

Background

Since 1999, Ministry of Education (MoE) has approved the program of 68 regular higher education institutions, including Shaanxi Normal University, carrying out pilot programs of distance education. In practice, Shaanxi Normal University noticed that there were only a few learning centers set up by pilot universities in central and western regions and that development between urban areas and rural and remote areas was unbalanced. The problem, if remaining unsolved, would inevitably undermine the overall development of distance education. The pilot programs would not be truly successful without finding a way to provide effective education services to western and remote poverty-stricken areas. To this end, School of Distance Education, Shaanxi Normal University, started practice and exploration on distance education for teachers in economically less developed areas in 2003.

As the practice base of the project, Yulin City is located in the northernmost part of Shaanxi and has 12 counties under jurisdiction. In 2002, there were a total of 34,421 faculty members in the local 6,082 middle and primary schools, and local education was backward with limited resources. Some teachers, especially those in junior and senior middle schools, did not meet requirements on academic credentials. Therefore, it is an actual requirement to develop distance education to drive local basic education development and teachers' team building. As local economy rapidly grew, computer popularization rate was greatly increased, and hardware environment in local training schools for teachers was also improved. For example, multimedia computer rooms have been set up, laying the basic foundation for developing distance education.

Implementation

The project was intended to rely on teachers, disciplinary, and resource advantages of Shaanxi Normal University and use information technologies to construct a distance education platform, develop distance education resources, and build assurance systems for management, service and quality of distance education. By doing so, it tried to explore an educational and teaching mode compliant with the economic level, Internet environment and formal and nonformal educational training demand of teachers in economically less developed counties and villages in western regions, so as to serve the strategy of western development.

Preparation Phase

From November 2002 to January 2003, the School of Distance Education dispatched an investigation team to the 12 counties of Yulin City for field survey twice. Through field visits and symposia, the team better understood local economic status, popularization and application of computer and the Internet, team building of middle and primary school teachers, and market demand for distance education.

On the basis of the investigation, the school developed detailed plans for carrying out distance education among teachers in rural areas, including recruitment plan, major and course plan, cultivation plan for each major and building plan for off-campus learning centers. It also selected a distance education mode that combines real-time teaching and non-real-time teaching and integrates learners' self-study and teaching support services in multiple forms.

Implementation Phase

The project was launched in January 2003, and the following activities were organized:

"Distance Education Website of Shaanxi Normal University" (http://www.sde.snnu.edu.cn) was developed for recruitment, teaching, management and services (see Figure 8.1).

Depending on teachers and resource advantage of the university, and taking the major and course as the basic organizational unit, the school developed distance education resources for over 400 courses of 18 majors, including Chinese language and literature, mathematics and applied mathematics, and computer science and technology. The development process included approval of the project, project team establishment, course planning, course integration, and acceptance. Considering limitations on Internet bandwidth resource in various areas, the courseware included three types: video, audio, and CDs. Except for courseware, teaching resources also included resource bank, bank of most-asked questions and test question bank.

Figure 8.1
Website Structure of School of Distance Education

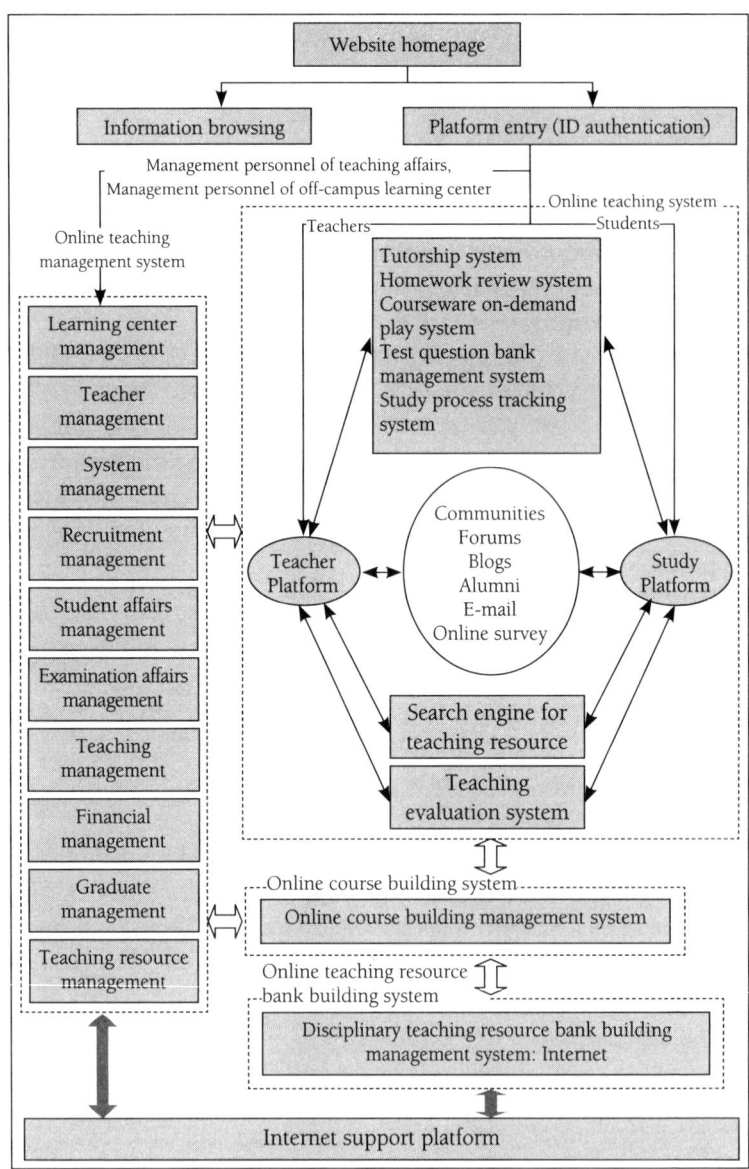

Source: The program website http://sde.snnu.edu.cn/

On the basis of investigation and by referring to related regulations and evaluation index systems of China's MoE and administrative departments of Shaanxi province on building of off-campus learning centers, the school inspected and evaluated the training schools for teachers in Yulin City and counties under its jurisdiction, and set up off-campus learning centers in 12 counties, which greatly facilitated study and training of teachers in counties and townships. After two years of development, the county-level centers made rapid progress in Internet environment, teaching management and teaching support service, and all of them passed evaluation organized by Education Department of Shaanxi Provincial Government.

Compared with large/medium-sized cities and southeastern coastal areas, distance education for teachers in economically less developed areas was restrained by many factors, such as financial affordability of learners, household computer ownership rate, and Internet bandwidth. Moreover, scattered population, inconvenient traffic and shortage of teachers and other educational resources made it more difficult to develop distance education locally. The project selected three basic forms of distance education and study (see Table 8.1).

According to teaching plans, for each course in the credit system, teachers were required by the School of Distance Education to give 15 class hours of lectures, provide 15 class hours of electronic teaching plans and no less than 15,000 words of teaching tutorship materials. Technicians videotaped and processed the entire lectures, and made videos, audios, and text materials as online courseware through a courseware platform. All the courseware was uploaded onto the study platform for learners, so that all learners could select lectures and chapters they needed via Internet for self-study anytime and anywhere.

Presiding teachers lectured on outline of the course, highlighted major and difficult parts, provided corresponding questions for review, made CDs and delivered them to learners, so as to guide and help learners to formulate study plans and work out study methods. Learners could resort to many tools such as FAQs, e-mails, bulletin board system (BBS), and so on to directly communicate with teachers and classmates, to which teachers needed reply. For common questions raised by learners, tutoring teachers sent the questions and answers through group

Table 8.1
Three Basic Forms of Distance Education

	Learning Materials	*Learning Support*	*Targeted Groups*
Study Form 1	Paper materials + online courseware + other online study resources	Courseware play/ online FAQs/online tutorship/discussion/ online tests/expert lectures	Learners unable to have class regularly at off-campus learning centers but with access to Internet
Study Form 2	Paper materials + synchronized teaching content + courseware and other online teaching resources	Real-time teaching/ Courseware play/ online FAQs/online tutorship/discussion/ online tests/expert lectures	Learners able to have class at off-campus learning centers
Study Form 3	Paper materials + "Course Study Manual" CD + other study resources	Teaching materials/ teaching CDs/study tutorship materials/ FAQs by telephone and correspondence	Learners unable to have class regularly at off-campus learning centers and without access to Internet

Source: The program website http://sde.snnu.edu.cn/

messages to related learners, and also could display them in course chatting rooms as reference for other learners.

In principle, homework with no less than 10 open questions and essay questions was assigned twice each semester, and answers should be no less than 5,000 words. Learners were required to finish and submit the homework through the study platform or submit it in paper to off-campus learning centers. The off-campus learning centers organized teachers to correct homework and record scores. Learners can participate in course examination only after their homework scores exceeded the criteria.

Regarding teaching management, apart from daily management over learners of each off-campus learning center, the centers' teaching management function was also enhanced, playing a bigger role in organizing, supervising, inspecting, and guiding study of learners. The management mode of "centralized management and partitioned responsibility" was adopted during the teaching process. The learning centers signed responsibility agreement with managing teachers, agreeing to classify learners into groups by region, so as to track and manage the entire study process of learners from recruitment, enrollment, study, and examinations to graduation.

Study support service could be classified by method into Internet-based online service and telephone-, fax- or correspondence-based offline service targeted at collective FAQs, face-to-face teaching, tutorship, and lectures for all learners at off-campus learning centers and point-to-point individualized teaching support service through emails, BBS, and online video interaction system, and at implementation body into service provided by the School of Distance Education and localized service offered by off-campus learning centers.

By the end of 2005, the number of middle and primary school teachers participating in distance education through seven recruitment sessions in Yulin City already reached over 6,525. In 2005, the school undertook part of the task to help middle and primary school teachers throughout the province meet academic credential requirement, and therefore the number of registered learners noticeably increased (see Figure 8.2).

Evaluation Phase

In September 2005, the project started evaluation for acceptance. The Shaanxi Normal University organized an expert panel to inspect on site and evaluate the off-campus learning centers in 12 counties in hardware building, system building, building of teaching management team, and building of tutorship team.

Figure 8.2
Number of Registered Middle and Primary School Teachers for Distance Education from 2002 to 2005

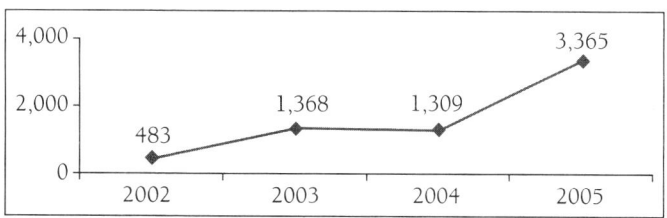

Source: The program website http://sde.snnu.edu.cn/

Responsible persons of the off-campus learning centers were organized to communicate in the form of on-site visits and symposia on project implementation details, experience gained, and existing problems.

Responsible persons of the project from each department and major at the university, teacher representatives, educational technology experts of the university and other institutions, and discipline experts and computer experts were organized to discuss such topics as recruitment of each major, teaching, management, service and building of online education resources, and offer constructive suggestions on further implementation and promotion of the project.

Educational authorities of Yulin City and the 12 counties exchanged opinions with the school on issues such as guideline for the next-step work, measures for improvement and promotion and application of the project achievements.

Promotion Phase

Since the spring of 2006, the School of Distance Education gradually expanded the coverage of the pilot project. By December 2011, 139 off-campus learning centers had been set up in 17 provinces throughout the country. Meanwhile, it actively explored the school-running mechanism by regional cooperation, and founded eight regional teaching service centers, recruiting over 100,000 learners in total.

Among the 139 off-campus learning centers, 87 were located in western regions, accounting for 63% of the total, and the percentage of those relying on training schools for teachers as supporting organizations reached 90%. In Shaanxi province, 100% of the area was covered by off-campus learning centers, and over 80% of the learners were in-service middle and primary school teachers.

The result of the project won the second prize of Excellent Teaching Achievement in Shaanxi province. Moreover, it was praised by *China Education Daily* (May 18, 2006) in the report "Shaanxi Normal University Constructing a New Mode of Continuing Education for Middle and Primary School Teachers" and by *Brief of Ministry of Education* (71st issue in 2006) in the report "Shaanxi Normal University Using Modern Distance Education to Train Western Rural Teachers" (see Figure 8.3).

Figure 8.3

Media Reports on Distance Education of Shaanxi Normal University that Serves Teachers in Western Rural China

Source: The program website http://sde.snnu.edu.cn/

Funds

Start-up funds of the School of Distance Education were mainly raised by Shaanxi Normal University, including:

- *Equipment fees.* Around RMB 1.5 million, including live broadcasting equipment, equipment for students, servers for website building, switchboards, office computers, and servers and computers required by platform and course development.
- *Development fees.* Around RMB 4 million. In particular, RMB 0.5 million was used to develop the teaching support system and RMB 3.5 million to develop courses.
- *Office fees.* Around RMB 0.3 million.
- Recruitment promotion fees: around RMB 0.2 million.

For off-campus learning centers, around RMB 0.2 million was invested in 50-seater computer and multimedia classrooms, and expenditure on recruitment promotion and personnel was decided according to the number of learners.

Fees that learners needed to pay included tuition and teaching material fees. At a standard of RMB 70–80 per credit, the tuition totaled around RMB 5,500 per person for a degree level, much lower than the study cost at regular higher education institutions.

Process Supervision

The School of Distance Education established various standards from the very beginning, including those in course management, teaching material management, major arrangement, teacher management, study process and experiment and training, enrollment status management, course examination management, graduation management, and student support service management.

It also formulated strict operation procedures and management requirements, such as Student Manual, Training Manual for Teachers, Management Manual for Learning Centers and Staff Manual, so as to specify requirements for different roles from different aspects and urge teachers, management, and learners to abide by the standards.

The School of Distance Education tried to study learners' demand and discover defects in the management through questionnaire surveys among learners. After each course examination, it analyzed the examination result and studied the distribution of scores, so as to adjust the difficulty level of the test paper and strategy of test question extraction in a timely manner.

Problems and Countermeasures

Limited by actual conditions and policies, most pilot higher education institutions set up off-campus learning centers at education institutions in prefecture-level cities. Although such centers had better study conditions and teaching resources, learners from remote rural regions paid much fewer visits due to geographic and time limits. When the off-campus learning centers were set up in county-level cities, it was convenient for learners to go there and the centers would be fully used. Therefore, off-campus learning centers of distance education of Shaanxi Normal University took full advantage of existing training schools for teachers in the 12 counties and upgraded hardware and software to meet the demand for modern distance education. Such efforts lowered study cost of learners, increased frequency of learners to study at learning centers, promoted the centers to strengthen infrastructure building, improved school-running conditions, and established a training base for teachers meeting requirements of distance education.

At the beginning of implementation of distance education, the biggest challenge was low public recognition of its teaching quality. By enhancing resource building, strengthening building of off-campus learning centers, establishing quality assurance systems, and reinforcing supervision and feedback for teaching process, the project focused on teaching quality and expanded recruitment scope, gradually improving the public awareness and recognition. Local and provincial education authorities also highly recognized and greatly supported the project.

In practice, due to learners' lack of understanding on online study and shortage of knowledge on computer and Internet operation, online resources were not frequently used and online interactive communication was inactive. Many learners still resorted to teaching materials, CDs, and other traditional methods for study, without tapping into the advantage of online study. Based on the actual conditions for teaching, the School of Distance Education included times of log-in onto the study platform, online communication activity, and other factors into review and evaluation standard to encourage online study and exchange among learners, which helped build up a learner-centered online study environment at the newly developed course platform.

Understanding and attitude of presiding teachers toward online courses determined the quality of online course resources. School of Distance Education and Educational Administration Office of the university jointly initiated the project as a university subject, and the former funded the development. Such a development mode ensured enthusiasm of presiding teachers and quality of online courses to some degree.

Although fee for distance education was relatively low, it was still a burden for teachers in western remote areas. For example, we found that some teachers did not attend the course owing to the tuition fees. Therefore, in 2006, the school started the Action Plan to Support Basic Education in Shaanxi, according to which it would train 100 middle and primary school teachers at academic credential level for free in 50 national-level poverty-stricken counties in Shaanxi each year and encourage the middle and primary school teachers to participate in corresponding in-service continuing education.

9

Online Training for Substitute Teachers in Underdeveloped Areas of Economically Developed Cities

Xu Xiaoyi and Zeng Haijun

Case Overview

During the summer vacation in July and August of 2009, a training program was carried out in the underdeveloped areas of Guangdong province to improve basic competences and teaching skills of primary and secondary school substitute teachers with required education background. Organized and implemented by the School of Distance Learning of South China Normal University (SCNU), the program provided training to 33,205 substitute teachers in the underdeveloped areas of the 15 cities in Guangdong province. Its contents consisted of four aspects, that is, pedagogy, educational psychology, educational laws and regulations, and educational teaching skills. Training for primary school teachers and secondary school teachers was carried out separately in both distance and face-to-face modes.

Program Background

Guangdong, comprising 21 prefecture-level cities, is the most populous province in mainland China. It also boasts an economy featuring the largest scale and the strongest overall competitiveness among all provinces in mainland China. However, regardless how developed a city is, there are still some underdeveloped areas where the relevant authority, due to the financial difficulties, cannot recruit or attract full-time or elite teachers, leaving these vacancies filled by temporary teachers, or substitute teachers. As of 2008, there were altogether 52,185 substitute teachers in Guangdong province, out of which, 42,469 were primary school teachers accounting for 81.4% of the total number and 9,716 were secondary school teachers occupying 18.6%. Moreover, the number of substitute teachers in underdeveloped areas reached 35,075, taking up 67.2% of the total number.[1] Owing to poor welfare benefits and low professional competences, substitute teachers assumed a disadvantaged status among rural teachers. According to a resolution made at a joint conference to "Solve Welfare Benefit Problems for Substitute Teachers and Teachers in Primary and Secondary Schools of Guangdong Province" in April 2009, the SCNU would be specifically in charge of a training program designed to improve basic competences and teaching skills of substitute teachers in all primary and secondary schools of Guangdong province.

Implementation

Implementing Organizations

The Department of Education of Guangdong province was responsible for coordination and planning, organizational leadership, and quality supervision in this program.

The SCNU specifically carried out the program through fully relying on an all-sided distance training system built by its School of Distance

---

[1] Xinhuanet,   http://www.gd.xinhuanet.com/newscenter/ztbd/2008-09/10/content_14362479.htm

Learning and the training bases in different cities and counties of Guangdong province.

Competent education authorities of prefecture-level cities took charge of mobilizing and organizing qualified substitute teachers to receive trainings, registering enrollment and building classes, hiring and managing local training specialists, and supervising and guiding the competent education authorities and teacher training colleges of counties (districts) under their jurisdiction.

Competent education authorities of counties (districts) shouldered many responsibilities, such as cooperating with their superior competent departments to register, organize, and manage their local trainees and assisting the teacher training colleges in arranging training space, facilities and equipment as well as relevant management staff, class advisers, and network technicians.

Teacher training colleges in counties (districts) arranged the specific resources required by trainings, including training rooms, computer rooms, multimedia classrooms, network environment, as well as relevant training personnel.

Demand Survey

In April 2009, led by the Continuing Education Guidance Center of the Department of Education of Guangdong province, a delegation consisting of some members of the substitute teachers training program from the SCNU and Guangdong Institute of Education visited Maoming and Zhanjiang where there were large numbers substitute teachers for a field research. During the trip, they learned in detail about the substitute teachers, training specialists, and IT-applied level in the two places. Moreover, they also listened to the opinions and suggestions from the local education authorities and the leaders of the local teacher training colleges on the implementation of the training program. Based on all the gathered information, the program group worked out an overall training method combing the distance and face-to-face modes. The modified plan of implementation of the training program for primary and secondary school substitute teachers in Guangdong province, issued by the Department of Education of Guangdong province, was a concrete planning for the program, elaborating trainees, training content, time and form, organizational forms, and funds.

The program was designed to give trainings to a total of 33,205 primary and secondary school substitute teachers from the less developed areas of 15 cities in Guangdong province (see Figure 9.1). Its contents consisted of four aspects, that is, "pedagogy," "educational psychology," "educational laws and regulations," and "educational teaching skills." The participants were divided into primary school teachers and secondary school teachers to receive trainings.

In the program, both distance and face-to-face training modes were adopted and the former was the main one. After reading training textbooks and browsing training disks (PC and TV versions), participants were expected to complete the following tasks through the training platform:

- Reading textbooks
- Watching records of lectures (through training disks or network platform)

Figure 9.1
Distribution of Substitute Teachers in Different Cities

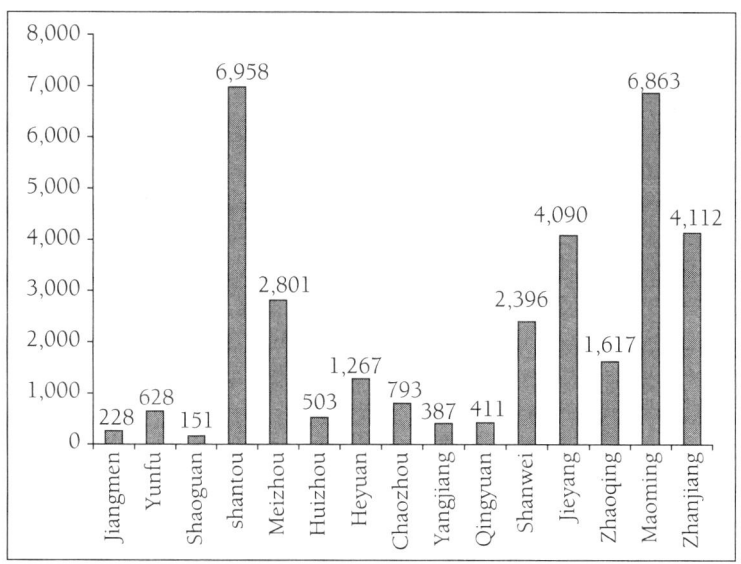

Source: Author.

- Participating in bulletin board system (BBS) discussions
- Completing assignment (and submitting online or in writing)
- Taking part in remote real-time video tutoring and Q&A

While overall planning the centralized face-to-face instruction, the competent education authorities of prefecture-level cities took into consideration many factors, such as transportation, accommodation, and geographical distribution of training specialists and substitute teachers so as to give trainings in local teacher training colleges, primary and secondary schools, and even movie theaters, stadiums and other places flexibly.

Training Environment

In terms of hardware construction, to ensure high-quality online learning for more than 30,000 substitute teachers, the SCNU added to its existing educational network hardware three more servers dedicated for providing the trainees with video on demand (VOD) services and database services.

As for software construction, the training network portal was mainly used to release relevant notices, news, policies and various briefings. The training platforms consisted of online courses, BBS Q&As, remote video Q&As, online self-tests, various extended resources, and so on.

In terms of pooling course resources, the program group selected more than 20 outstanding professional trainers from the whole province to prepare training handouts and record training courses (see Figure 9.2). The handouts (with disks) were distributed to substitute teachers for free before the training and could also be accessed anytime through the online training platforms.

For the construction of training specialists, a total number of 175 local training specialists were given centralized interviews to familiarize them with the training process and methods, duties, highlights, and difficulties. In addition, a working manual was also compiled and issued to class advisors, training specialists, technicians, and remote tutoring experts with a view to helping them clearly understand their responsibilities, operational measures, and requirements for specific work in the training.

Figure 9.2
Covers of Training Courses

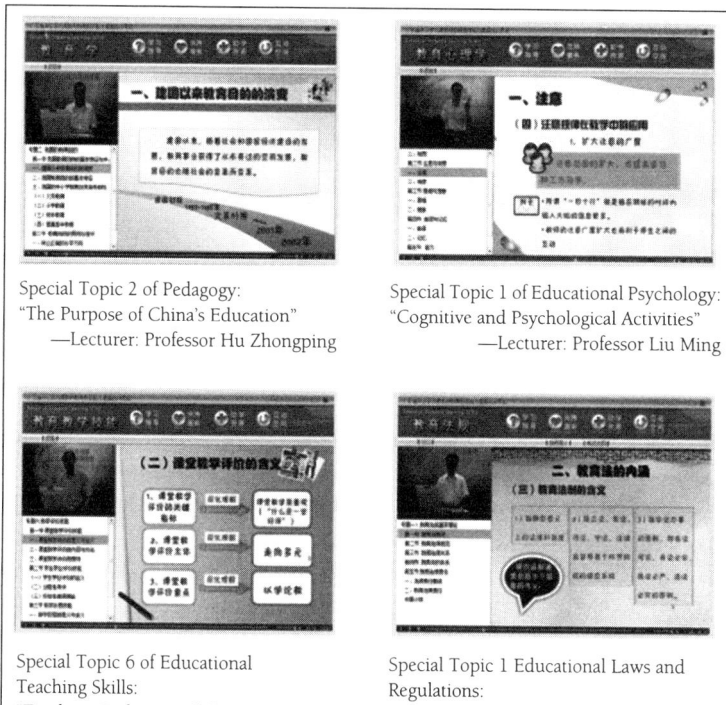

Special Topic 2 of Pedagogy:
"The Purpose of China's Education"
—Lecturer: Professor Hu Zhongping

Special Topic 1 of Educational Psychology:
"Cognitive and Psychological Activities"
—Lecturer: Professor Liu Ming

Special Topic 6 of Educational
Teaching Skills:
"Teaching Evaluation Skills"
—Lecturer: Professor Gao Lingbiao

Special Topic 1 Educational Laws and
Regulations:
"Fundamental Theories of Educational
Laws and Regulations"
—Lecturer: Professor Ge Xinbin

Source: The program website http://dk.gdou.com

Training Process

The registration work followed the procedures where substitute teachers voluntarily applied for, county (district) education bureaus reported, and then municipal education bureaus summarized and submitted the list. After verification, a total number of 32,931 substitute teachers met the entry requirement. They were divided into 344 virtual classes, assigned with 344 class advisors, 175 local training specialists and 12 remote tutoring experts.

After the training started, considering the distribution of local substitute teachers and the conditions of information technology, the computer rooms and multimedia classrooms in local teacher training colleges and central primary schools were opened in a planned way to substitute teachers who did not have access to Internet and could not play DVDs at home.

During distance training, in order to ensure substitute teachers obtain better learning impacts and have opportunities to interact with experts, the program group dedicatedly organized eight remote video Q&As (see Figure 9.3) to specifically help trainees solve a variety of typical problems they encountered during their learning and teaching practices. Accumulatively, 12 experts and about 3,000 substitute teachers participated in the Q&A process and those who did not take part in the live Q&A could watch the interactive on-demand videos through the training platform.

During the training, local training specialists and the expert team organized by the SCNU all fulfilled their responsibilities carefully and logged on the platform to help the trainees solve problems in a timely manner.

In the stage of face-to-face instruction, all substitute teachers managed to overcome difficulties to participate in the centralized trainings. Except for some occasional late cases, the majority of substitute teachers valued the opportunity. They attended classes on time, listened attentively, took notes carefully, and handed in homework as required.

Figure 9.3
Q&A Video Footage

Source: The program website http://dk.gdou.com

Funds

Positioning the program as a free training, Guangdong province distributed training handouts and offered learning resources to trainees free of charge. Accordingly, Department of Finance of Guangdong province allocated RMB 20 million as a special fund for the training.

Funded by some local governments, substitute teachers received free accommodation, chartered bus services (for those living far away from training locations), and even a certain amount of subsidy when participating in the training.

Process Supervision

In July 2009, an inspection team formed by the Continuing Education Guidance Center of the Department of Education of Guangdong province and the SCNU went to Shantou City and Jieyang City to inspect their primary and secondary school substitute teachers training. During the trip, the inspection team listened to the reports on the organization of distance training and the planning of face-to-face instruction by the two municipal education bureaus. Moreover, the team also paid a field inspection to a class where substitute teachers were learning online and held a symposium attended by representatives of substitute teachers to learn how local trainees participated in and evaluated the program.

During the discussions, many substitute teachers expressed their gratitude to the Guangdong provincial government for their care and spoke highly of the training handouts, teaching disks (especially DVDs), training websites and platform that the program group organized experts to design and develop. In their view, these free distributed resources were not only suitable for their actual needs but also user-friendly and effective.

The program paid close attention to formative assessments. Assigned with one task for each course, the trainees were required to submit the homework in writing to the local teacher training colleges or their class advisor before the end of the face-to-face instruction. Then their assignments were marked, registered, attached with an official seal and reported to the program office altogether by the local education bureaus.

Finally, the SCNU issued the training certificate to all concerned substitute teachers.

Results and Effects

The centralized training during a summer vacation achieved good overall outcomes. Most of trainees attached great importance to the program organized by the Guangdong provincial government. They showed high learning enthusiasm and serious attitude, making the pass percentage reach 97.81% (see Figure 9.4).

To learn about how trainees evaluated the training disks, handouts, platforms, and the overall training effects, the program group designed and put the questionnaire on the training platform for substitute teachers to complete voluntarily. A total of 2,067 people filled the questionnaire, accounting for 6.2% of the total number of substitute teachers who received the training. Out of the respondents, 88.6% indicated that they were satisfied with the overall effects of the training (see Figure 9.5).

During the training, visits to the platform increased steadily and the total visits reached 126,863 person-times (see Figure 9.6). Even after the training, many substitute teachers still logged on the training platform for self-study and communication with others. Besides, many trainees raised questions and held discussions actively on the training platform, accumulatively releasing 12,505 postings and 23,341 replies. In addition, the substitute teachers in some areas also took the initiative to build QQ groups for sharing learning experience. Besides, about 15,000 substitute teachers learned mainly through reading the training handouts and browsing DVDs (or CDs).

Figure 9.4
Pass Rate of the Training

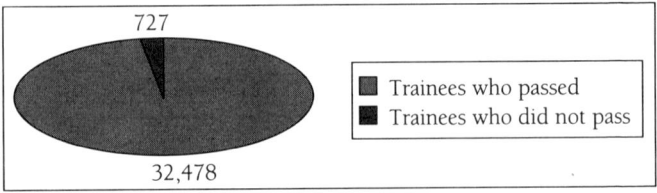

Source: Author.

Figure 9.5
Satisfaction Rate of Substitute Teachers Who Participated in the Training

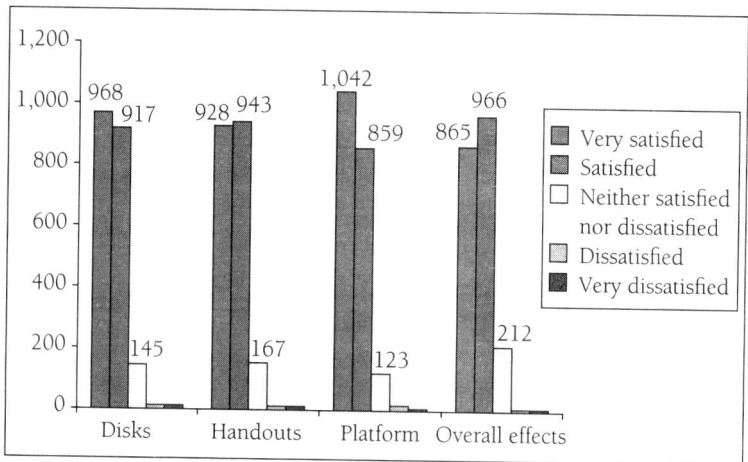

Source: Author.

Figure 9.6
Visits to the Platform during the Training

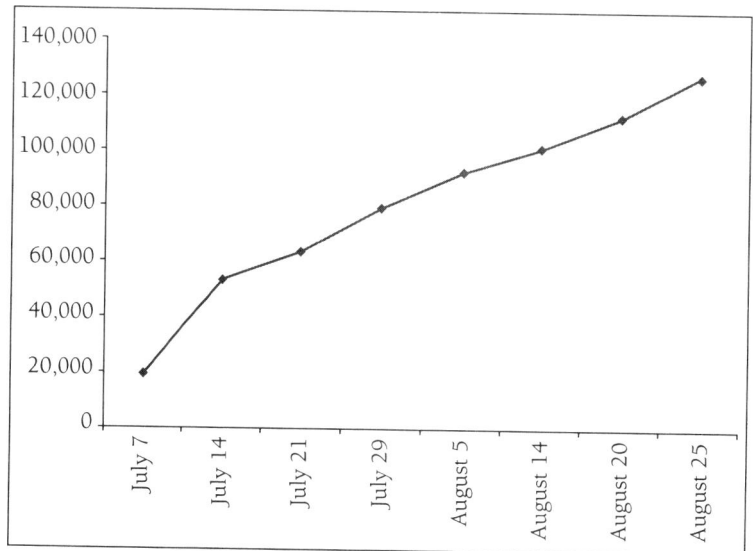

Source: Author.

It is known that most of the substitute teachers could spare two hours per day to study online or read handouts, watch video disks and learning other materials. In order to get access to the Internet and log on the platform for attending the online training, some substitute teachers even took bus to the county, which is tens of kilometers away from their home.

Many substitute teachers left messages and expressed their opinions on the training platform through the "BBS discussion" and the "training survey." They gave high appraisal and recognition to the training, saying that their competence and knowledge had been greatly improved through the training.

Here are some opinions and feedbacks written by some participants in the "training survey":

- I am very grateful that the issues of substitute teachers have been paid great attention, which gives me hope again. I think the training is great: 1. The handouts are content-rich; 2. The disks are attractive; 3. The online platform not only enables us to catch up with instructors' lectures, but also offers us a place to communicate with and learn from each other. I benefit a lot from the learning through diverse methods. Hereby, I would like to express my sincere thanks.

- It is commendable for the program group to get such good handouts, lecture disks, and online teaching support prepared in such a short period of time. I want to give some suggestions here. Without computers, most substitute teachers cannot get an access to some learning methods. Besides, the face-to-face instruction gives us a large amount of tasks within a very short time limit. But most of us have a cell phone which can play MP3 teaching records. If there are MP3 recordings (mainly the contents which need to be memorized), more substitute teachers will benefit. Also, SMS support could also provide us with another alternative.

- I think this training is excellent. First, we can choose learning ways flexibly, such as online distance learning or using a floppy disk at home. Second, the lectures given by experts allow us to learn a lot. Third, during the training, all questions and problems can be answered and solved online so that we can master the key points and difficult parts well.

- The training is very creative and the effects are great. The instructions feature not only clear sounds and natural gestures, but also detailed contents. In one word, thanks for giving us this opportunity.
- I am honored to participate in the training! Through the in-depth study, I get my professional knowledge, teaching skills, and teaching experience improved greatly. I hope that there will be more opportunities like this in future!
- This training shows that the provincial government pays great attention to and concerns about the substitute teachers. We are very touched by the serious and responsible attitude of the teachers from the SCNU. So I would like to express my thanks to all those who concern and cares about us substitute teachers!

Experiences and Inspirations

1. *Network-based distance training was an ideal way to implement large-scale teacher trainings, especially for those in economically underdeveloped areas.*
The program gave trainings to more than 30,000 teachers in 15 economically underdeveloped areas of the Guangdong province. In other words, the training involved a large number of widely distributed substitute teachers who lived in inaccessible areas. Moreover, the time for the training was limited. If traditional training methods were adopted, it would take at least more than a hundred training specialists to conduct lecture tours for several months, which would not only be costly and time-consuming, but also difficult to take unified standards.

Taking into account the actual condition of substitute teachers, the program group adopted both distance and face-to-face modes, which specifically included Internet video on demand, computer and television disks playing, remote video Q&As, centralized face-to-face instructions, online interactions, experts online review, and so on. The distance training featured many advantages, such as sharing resources, considerate support services, and learning process supervision. Therefore, it not only reduced per-capita training costs but also met various needs of substitute teachers with different learning habits and requirements, thus effectively solving the problem that large number of participants had poor access to attending classes due to their wide geographic distribution.

2. *The teachers' lifelong education system based on outstanding normal universities and supported by teacher training colleges in counties (districts), could provide important support for cultivating and training regional teachers and lay an essential foundation for realizing the teachers' lifelong learning.*

This training system, based on the School of Distance Learning of the SCNU and supported by the teacher training colleges on the county level, covered all Guangdong province, especially the poverty-stricken regions like the rural areas. It was a system in which "training institutions move upward and training bases move downward" so that it could effectively and efficiently serve teachers' lifelong education through being a part of the teachers' lifelong education implementation system along with the satellite network and the Internet (see Figure 9.7).

The School of Distance Learning of the SCNU provided substitute teachers with a variety of convenient and flexible preferential policies. The substitute teachers who passed the training could be exempted from

Figure 9.7
Diagram of Teachers' Lifelong Education System

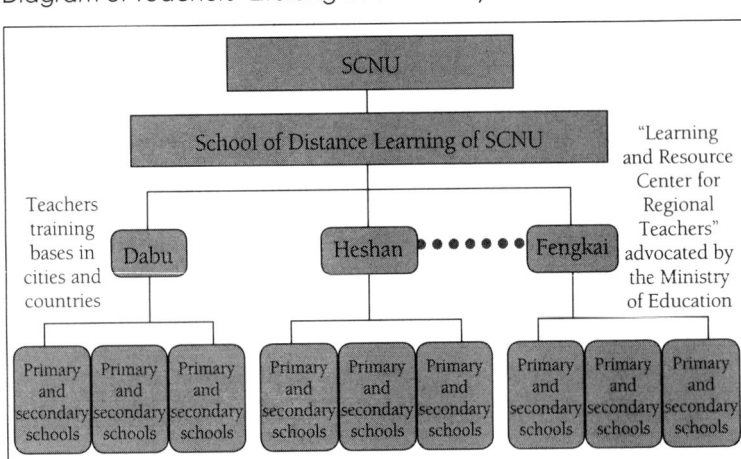

Source: Author.

studying two courses, "Pedagogy" and "Educational Psychology" when they applied for teacher certificates; in case they continued their study for a higher degree, the training courses allowed them to take 16 credits less than others. The integration of nonacademic training and academic education was widely popular among substitute teachers and was highly appraised by the relevant education authorities.

3. *High-quality training curriculum resources (such as printed textbooks, disks, and online courses) were essential and fundamental to deliver a remote teachers' training successfully.*

The excellent completion of the training largely relied on the design and development of high-quality training resources. Repeatedly revised by experts on education and psychology and professionals engaged in compiling remote education textbooks, the training handouts managed to integrate both theories and practices. The handouts not only were closely linked to the examination syllabus designed for substitute teachers' conversion into regular ones but also reflected the new curriculum, ideas, thoughts, and methods of the primary and secondary education reform. What's more, they paid enough attention to the basic education and contained a wealth of high-level case studies which were easy to read and learn. In addition, producing training lectures into online courses and training disks (11 TV DVDs and 1 PC version) could allow substitute teachers to learn at home, at work, or at teacher training colleges as their actual conditions permitted.

4. *Following people-oriented and demand-oriented principle and improving support services continuously were fundamental to guarantee a high quality and fruitful training.*

In the preparation and implementation of the training, the SCNU put itself in substitute teachers' shoes. After a comprehensive investigation, it developed both distance and face-to-face modes and combined online training and disk training to carry out the program. Meanwhile, it also improved the function of the training platform by adding self-tests and auxiliary resources according to substitute teachers' actual needs. In addition, free courses such as "Mandarin Education" were also placed on the platform to help substitute teachers prepare exams for teachers' certificates and improve their own competence. All of these endeavors were highly recognized and praised by the substitute teachers. In the program, each prefecture-level city in Guangdong province offered initiative and active cooperation to help substitute teachers solve problems as much as possible and provide assistance and services for them. For example, substitute teachers who did not have access to the Internet or could not play DVDs were provided with certain learning environment.

10

Innovative Teachers Achieve Better IT Integration in Teaching

Huang Ronghuai, Zhang Jinbao,
Zheng Lanqin, Zeng Haijun,
and Wang Ying

Overview

In November 2003, Ministry of Education (MoE) and Microsoft (China) signed a cooperation framework agreement to support IT-based basic education in China, and launched Phase I of the Partners in Learning (PiL) project. In November 2008, the two parties signed a cooperation agreement for phase II of the project, which focused on innovative teachers, schools and students. By the first half of 2011, 100 rural computer classrooms and 400 innovative multimedia classrooms were built, with 160,000 IT teachers and 50,000 subject teachers trained and over 400,000 students having participated in innovative student activities. Among them, the innovative teacher project explored the mode and organization of online teacher training, and developed teaching materials, online courses and platforms for teacher training.

From 2003 to 2008, Microsoft (China) funded the project with at least USD 10 million in the form of investment, sponsorship, and donation of products and services. By focusing on some rural and remote areas in China, PiL Phase I made the following achievements:

- It equipped 100 rural junior high schools designated by MoE with one computer classroom each to improve the local Internet access, supported the daily operation of the classrooms through a unified platform, and promoted the application of these classrooms by organizing innovative activities and research programs.
- It provided training for IT teachers in central and western provinces, including basic training for 100,000 teachers, intermediate level training for 2,000 teachers and advanced training for 100 teachers. It established representative training modes and procedures, built a PiL curriculum for training of middle and primary school IT teachers, and developed and improved online resources for basic courses, teacher manual for intermediate courses, the advanced courses and the corresponding teacher manual.
- Through joint planning with partners, it developed and put into operation distance education solutions (including Learning Management System [LMS] platform, resource center and Innovative Teachers Networks) together with related resources, and launched "Partners in Learning" portal website.

How to narrow down the digital divide caused by imbalanced regional economic growth? How to make full use of information technology in basic education so as to benefit more people, especially rural teachers and students? PiL Phase II included the following parts:

- Innovative teachers: Expanding IT teacher training, conducting subject teacher training in 100 counties, supporting the development of quality resources, exploring new modes of teacher training, and organizing innovative teacher forums.
- Innovative schools: Assisting MoE in developing and deploying school-oriented public education service platform, offering support to the 1,000 innovative classrooms designated by MoE,

developing multimedia classroom solutions, and facilitating the building of IT-based platform of basic education in China.
- Innovative students: Conducting innovative student activities, building innovative student network and organizing innovative student forums to improve IT education for students, enhance their ability of self-teaching and innovative learning, and strengthen their competence in an all-round manner.

Background

Microsoft undertook to closely cooperate with education professionals, educational institutions, and industrial partners to develop related technologies, tools, projects, and schemes to improve opportunities for teaching and learning, help overcome challenges to education and develop education all over the world. In order to help educational institutions and professionals create a learning environment fit into the 21st century, Microsoft designed the following education roadmap (see Figure 10.1).

PiL was one of the many education projects of Microsoft, and Phase I of the project (2003–2008) was conducted in 101 countries, covering 115,671,260 students and 5,342,982 teachers and school administrators. Phase II (2008–2012) was rolled out in 114 countries, involving the participation of 185,162,660 students and training for 7,786,729 teachers and school administrators. A total of 2,771,696 teachers have registered on the Innovative Teachers Networks. PiL China identified local demand to facilitate project planning and worked with practitioners, researchers and decision makers to construct a sound partnership, so as to create a series of best practices.

PiL China consisted of four parts: the implementation team, partners, the evaluation team and beneficiaries (see Figure 10.2). MoE set up a PiL Coordination Group at National Center for Educational Technology to coordinate project management across the country, make training plans, and supervise project management and execution in each province. Provincial educational authorities designated project leaders and implementation institutions, and organized specific project activities. Microsoft (China) kept close contact with Innovative Teacher Coordination Group for communication and exchange, and provided funds as it promised

Figure 10.1
Microsoft in Education Roadmap

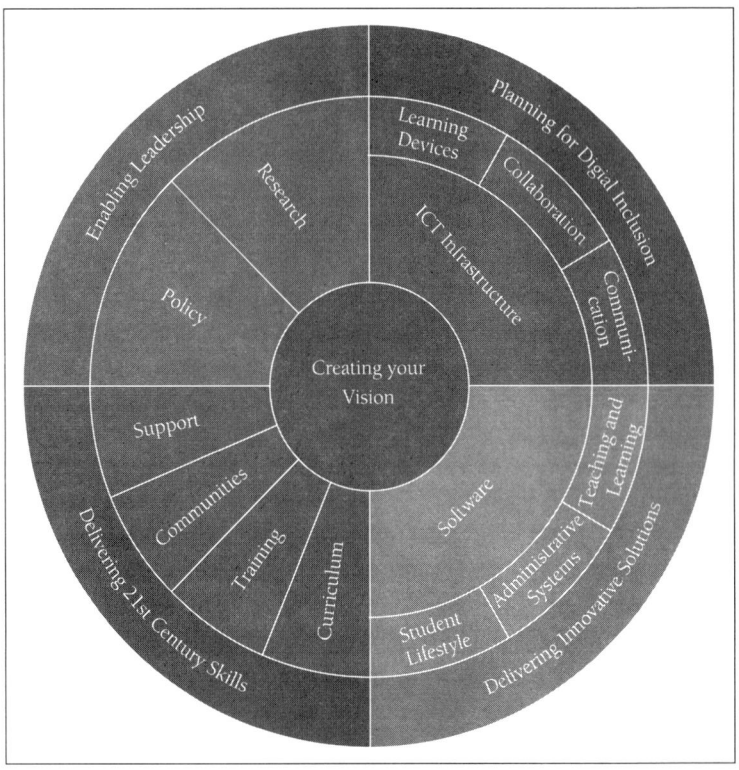

Source: http://www.microsoft.com/education/demos/roadmap/index.html
(accessed March 3, 2014).

for national elite teacher training, provincial teacher training, regional project management and project coordination.

IT Teacher Training

Training Plans

Phase I of the project planned to provide basic, intermediate, and advanced training to 12,100 IT teachers in central and western provinces in the five years from 2003 to 2008, and establish a representative

Figure 10.2
Structure of the PiL Project

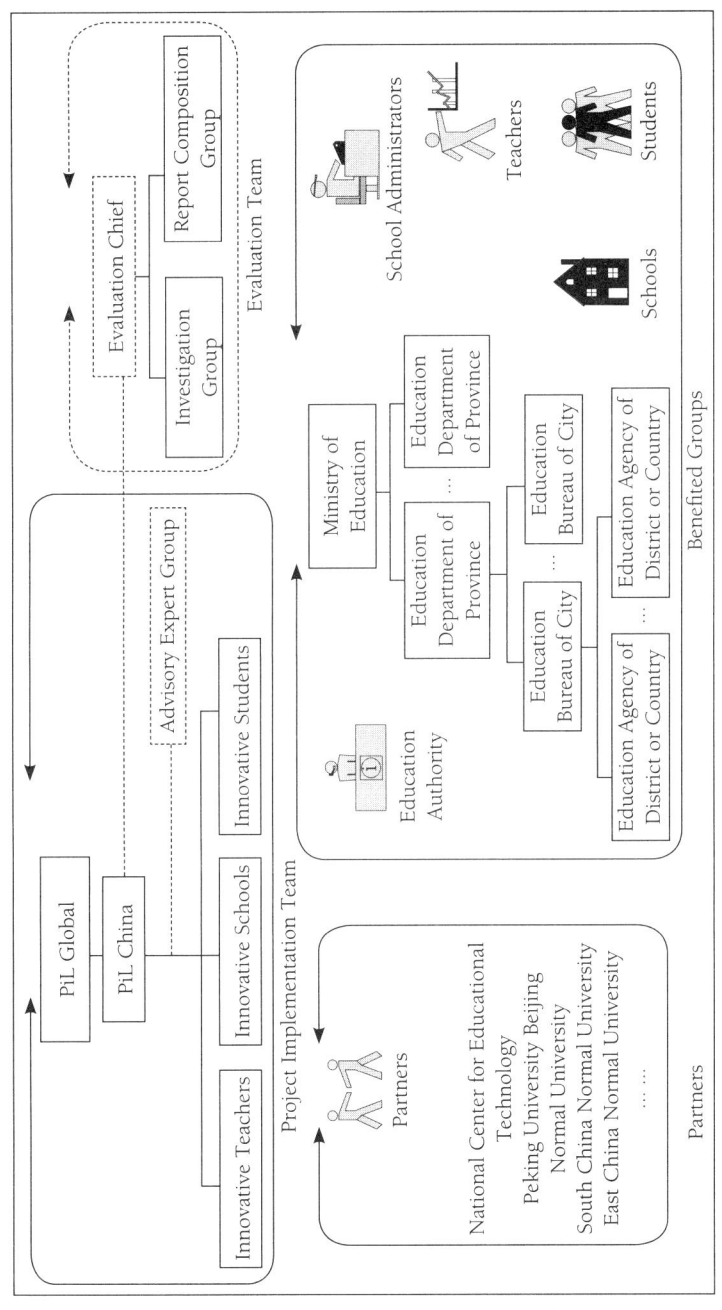

Source: Author.

training mode, training procedure and curriculum. Phase II offered training to 50,000 national-level and provincial-level elite teachers and IT teachers. After the training, IT teachers would meet national intermediate educational technology standards and be able to work to improve the educational technology capability of other teachers to improve the teaching quality of both IT courses and subject courses.

In order to ensure quality of the large-scale training, the project team adopted a training procedure of "3+1": "3" represented one name list, one activity and one story, and "1" symbolized one report (see Figure 10.3).

The project established a three-level training system, in which National Center for Educational Technology was responsible for advanced training, provincial training centers for intermediate training for teachers in the province, and district/county-level training centers for basic training by making full use of the existing teacher training system (see Figure 10.4).

Multiple parties were involved in the project for research, development, implementation, and evaluation (see Figure 10.5).

Under the guidance of Ministry of Education, Microsoft (China) cooperated with partners to plan application and promotion of the distance education platform. School of Educational Technology, Beijing Normal University, presided over promotion of the "Innovative Teachers Networks" platform. CCID Department of Distance Education was responsible for development of VCT resources. Microsoft (China) was in charge of application and promotion of online resource center for basic training and e-learning platform (LMS) (see Figure 10.6).

Training Activities

During the training, IT teachers need to:

- Participate in theoretical study, cooperation and interaction, case study, practice and reflection, and professional development seminars. By doing so, they can get experience both pertinent to their daily work and feel the charm of using educational concepts and information technologies to support teaching innovation.
- Select a teaching topic, finish the corresponding teaching design, and gradually generate a series of works as the training progressed.

Figure 10.3
"3+1" Training Procedure for Teachers

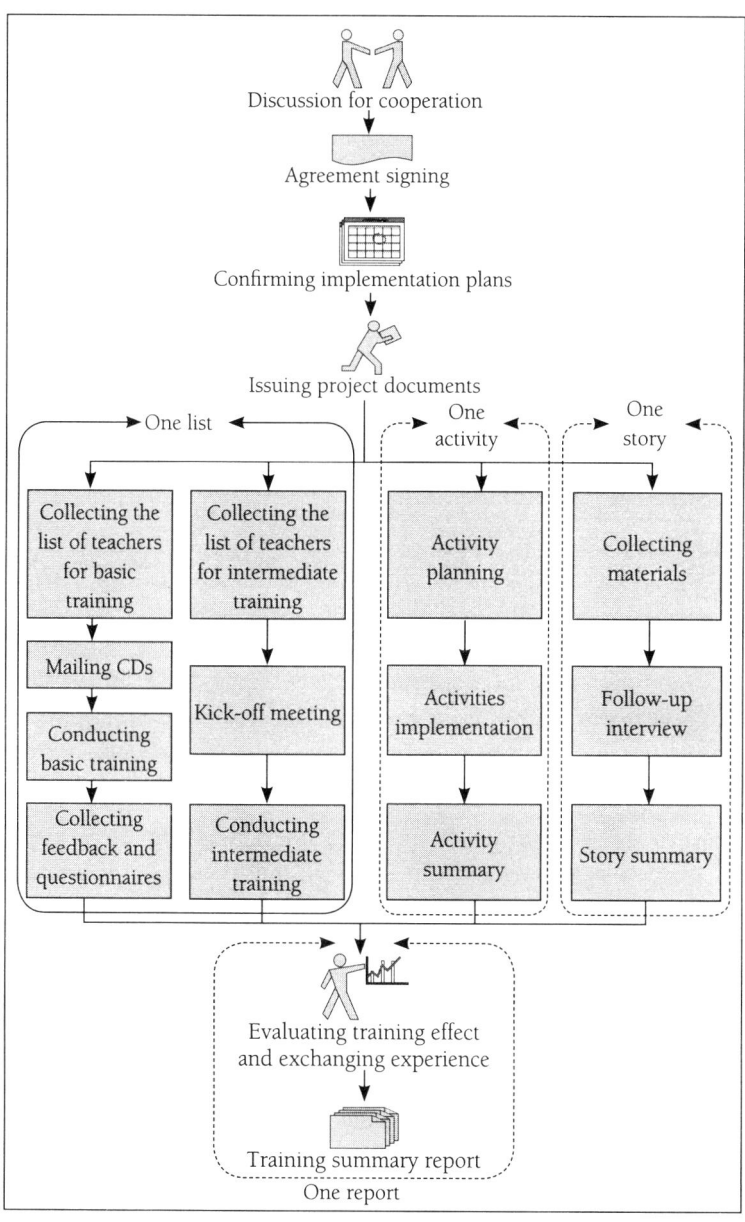

Source: Author.

Figure 10.4

Three-level Training System and Corresponding Trainees and Training Modes

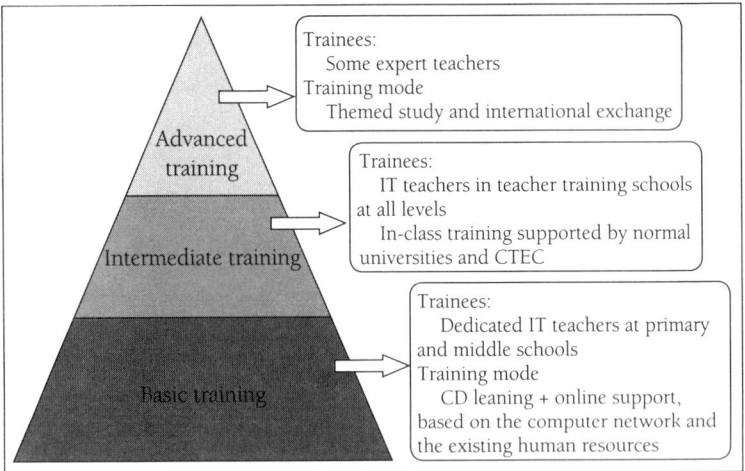

Source: Author.

- Learn and use a PowerPoint template for sharing teaching design and teaching experience provided by the project, that is, virtual classroom tour (VCT), to experience its convenience and support.

Development of Advanced Courses

Advanced courses were divided into eight units: information acquisition, information processing and expression, information resource management, information technology and society, multimedia application, network application, program design, and artificial intelligence. Each unit included modules of knowledge deepening, teaching method discussion, learning resources, and technical practice (see Figure 10.7).

A training strategy of "infiltrating professional development culture into professional development activities by starting with theme games and relying on professional development community for support" was adopted in the training (see Figure 10.8). Questionnaires, field visits, interviews, and video analysis showed that IT teachers recognized

Figure 10.5
"Course Development" Organization and Communication

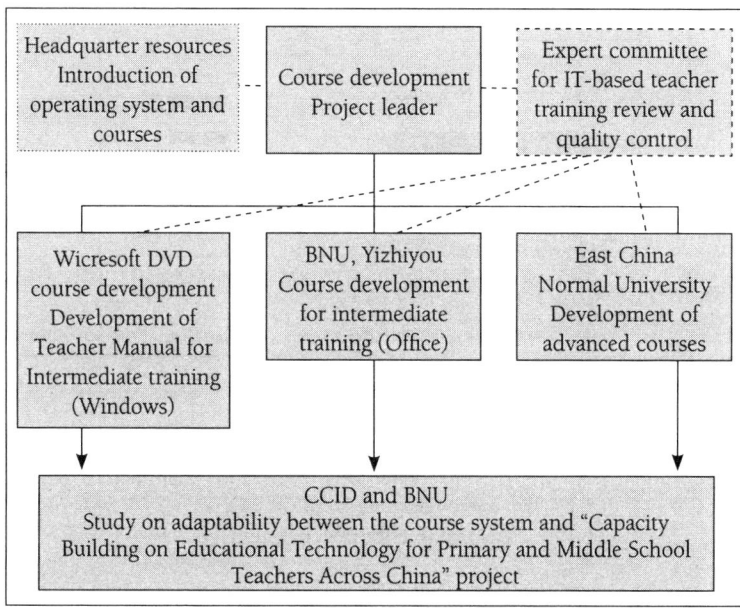

Source: Author.

application of new concepts, new knowledge, new skills, and new methods as well as the learning support.

Training Platforms and Resources

The project launched a group of platforms for teacher training, learning, and communication, including 21st Century Learning Center, Innovative Teachers Networks, Virtual Classroom Tour and Resource Center.

- 21st Century Learning Center was a personalized learning management platform for middle and primary school IT teachers nationwide jointly developed by the PiL team and one of its partners, CCID. It aims to help IT teachers learn more IT knowledge and skills through self-teaching and self-testing by offering them a

Figure 10.6
"Distance Learning Solutions" Organization and Communication

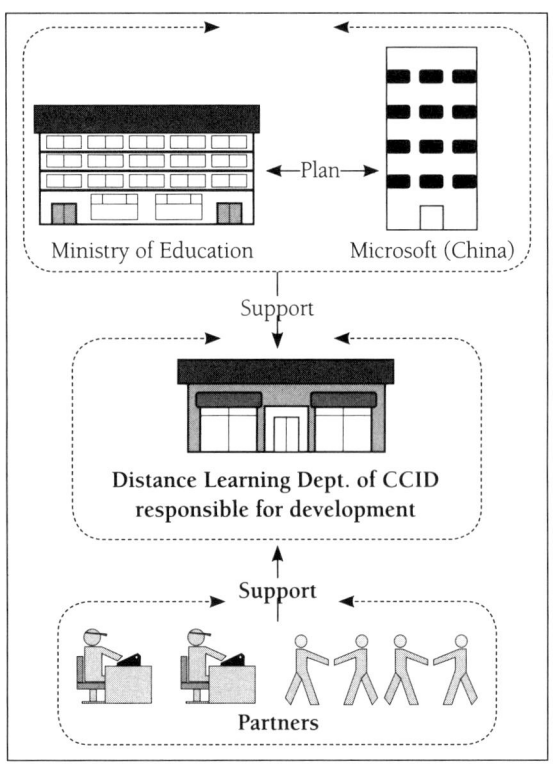

Source: Author.

large number of courses catering to their learning and work needs online. Priority was given to helping rural teachers to share rich teaching and learning resources via the Internet.

- Innovative Teachers Networks (ITN) portal website was intended to provide opportunities and tools for information exchange, resource sharing, and professional development for all education practitioners who are willing to join.
- Virtual Classroom Tour was a teaching practice exhibition template that the Innovative Teacher Project invited renowned education

Figure 10.7
Structure of Each Course Unit

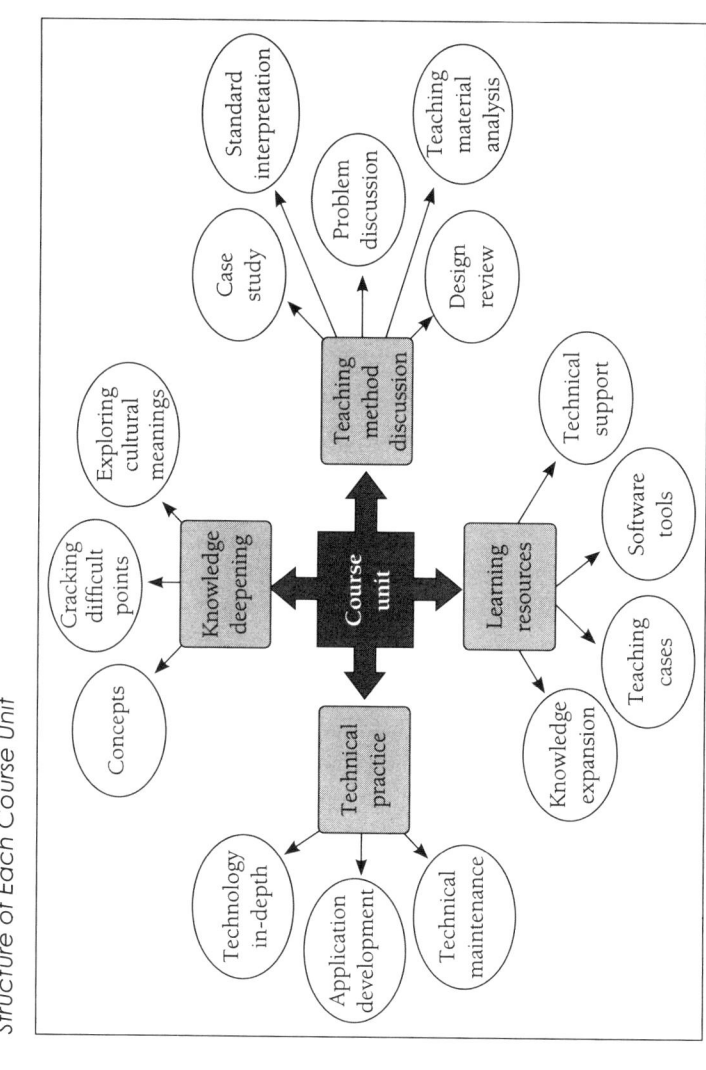

Source: Author.

Figure 10.8
Strategy for IT Teacher Training

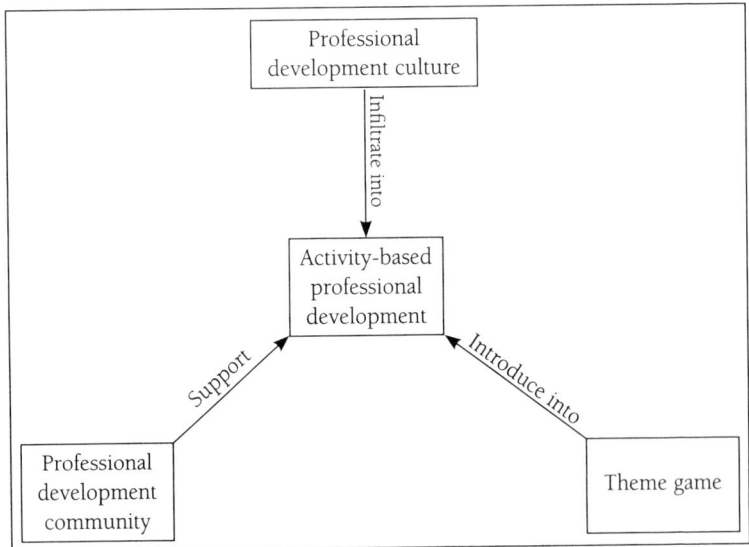

Source: Author.

experts and educational technology experts to specially develop for teachers. It consisted of six functional modules: overview, teaching plans, teaching implementation and reflection, teaching resources, teaching evaluation, and profile of schools and teachers. VCT helps teachers learn how to effectively design and summarize their innovative cases and share them with others.

- Resource Center, a platform driven by users, enabled users to upload, manage, use, and evaluate resources to minimize expenses on resource design and management. With resource items organized and managed with labels, users can easily get the most popular and valuable items. Communication through the system was convenient and fast with pal recommendation, finding a friend and other functions. Resources covered different types such as teaching cases, courseware, materials, papers, teaching games, teaching tools, and books.

Voluntary Teaching

In 2005, the first PiL volunteer program engaged 37 graduate students majored in educational technology to visit 11 places throughout the country for voluntary teaching. In 2006, the second volunteer program adopted an innovative "1+X+Y" model. It consisted of three volunteer groups: graduate students, teachers, and enterprise representatives. Besides educational technology training, the volunteers offered local teachers, students, and parents other IT-related training based on their own specialties to benefit the participants (see Figure 10.9). A total

Figure 10.9
Design of PiL Volunteer Program

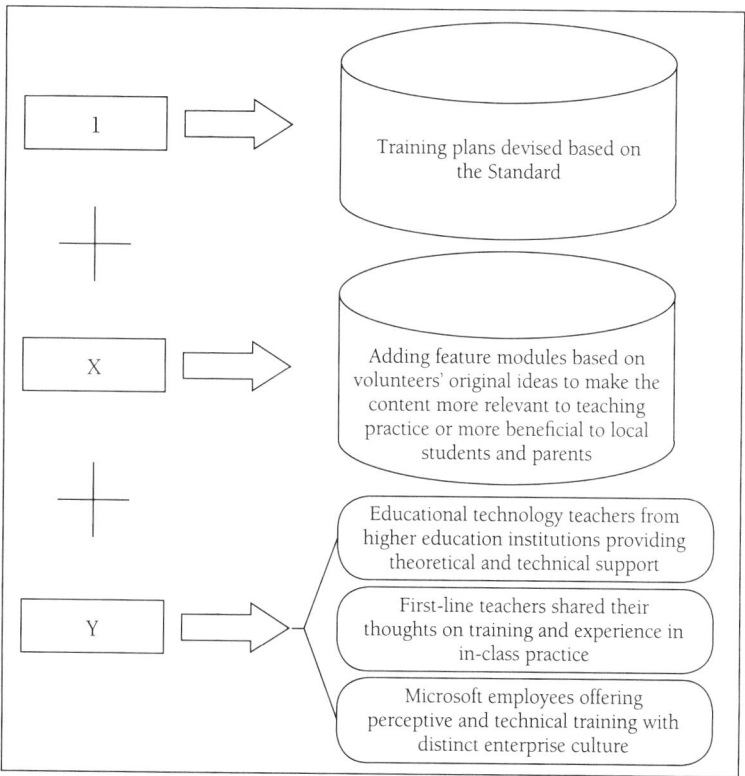

Source: Author.

of 30 volunteers from 14 higher education institutions, 10 Microsoft employees, and 10 teachers from key middle and primary schools participated in the program.

Subject Teacher Training

Training Plans

In order to facilitate the implementation of the Capacity Building on Educational Technology Project of MoE, subject teacher training was launched to offer educational technology training to 100,000 teachers of subjects other than IT in primary and middle schools, including 1,000 tutors. By relying on 100 eligible county-level teacher training agencies nationwide and using an online platform, the training adopted a mixed mode that combined online training and face-to-face training (see Figure 10.10).

After the training, participating teachers should meet national intermediate educational technology standards, be able to organize demonstration educational activities and promote the IT integration in subject teaching, and be capable of using multiple teaching methods and skills. Training courses consisted of nine modules according to the *National Educational Technology Standards for Primary and Secondary Schools (Trial)* (see Figure 10.11).

Subject teacher training was divided into several phases, including start-up, national-level training, basic training and wrap-up. Responsibilities were clearly divided between related implementation teams and supporting teams (see Figure 10.12).

National Center for Educational Technology (Coordination Group) appropriated funds according to the progress of the training based on the funding limits that Microsoft (China) confirmed for Innovative Teachers Training of PiL Phase II. The funds were mainly used to subsidize elite teacher training, subject teacher training, and teaching management.

Figure 10.10
Workflow of Teacher Training

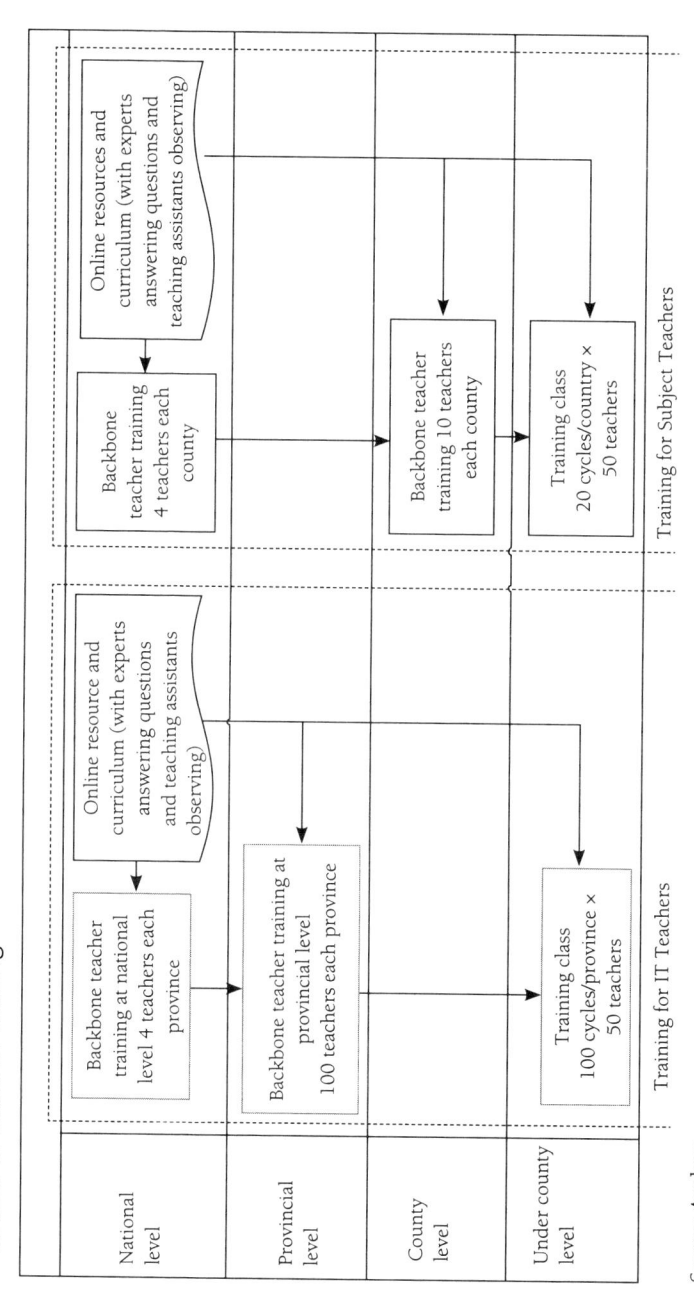

Source: Author.

Figure 10.11
Framework of Training Courses

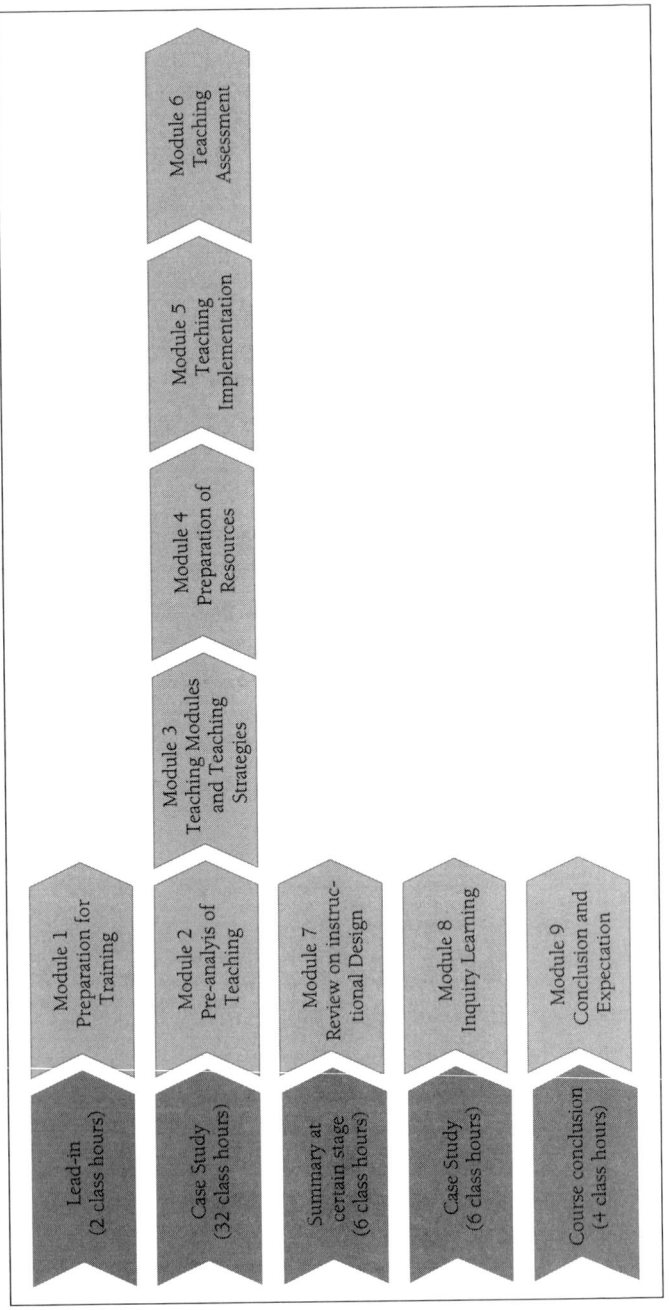

Demand Investigation

At the expert preparation meeting, methods were set for baseline investigation, monitoring, and evaluation, responsibilities were divided between relevant personnel, and the implementation content, methods, and directions were confirmed, as well as evaluation plans were determined. At the review meeting for training materials and online curriculum, participants discussed the preparation of supporting materials and online curriculum for IT teachers and subject teachers, respectively.

The PiL team set up a special expert investigation panel to select typical county- or city-level targets for field visit and in-depth investigation. Through reports, questionnaires, field interviews, and on-site surveys (see Figure 10.13), the panel understood the attitudes of local teachers toward the training and their current ability, analyzed the progress and results of the training, and proposed measures to address the problems identified.

Following surveys in selected counties, the panel confirmed the standards on selecting project counties for subject teacher training as follows:

- They should be well prepared to organize intermediate educational technology training for primary and middle school teachers.
- They should be able to provide intermediate educational technology training for at least 1,000 teachers in the coming four years.
- They should have suitable places for educational technology training, with appropriate equipment available to support online learning, and sound conditions to support the use, maintenance and management of the equipment during project implementation.
- They should be able to secure support from county-level teacher training institutions and audiovisual education authorities to ensure smooth progress of the project.
- They should be able to send at least 10 elite teachers to national-level training and ensure sufficient time and energy to organize and tutor 1,000 local teachers to finish online learning.
- Their educational authorities should be fully aware of the importance of the project, have the initiative to organize intermediate educational technology training, and be able to set up leadership groups and establish a forceful support system.

Figure 10.12
Workflow of Subject Teacher Training

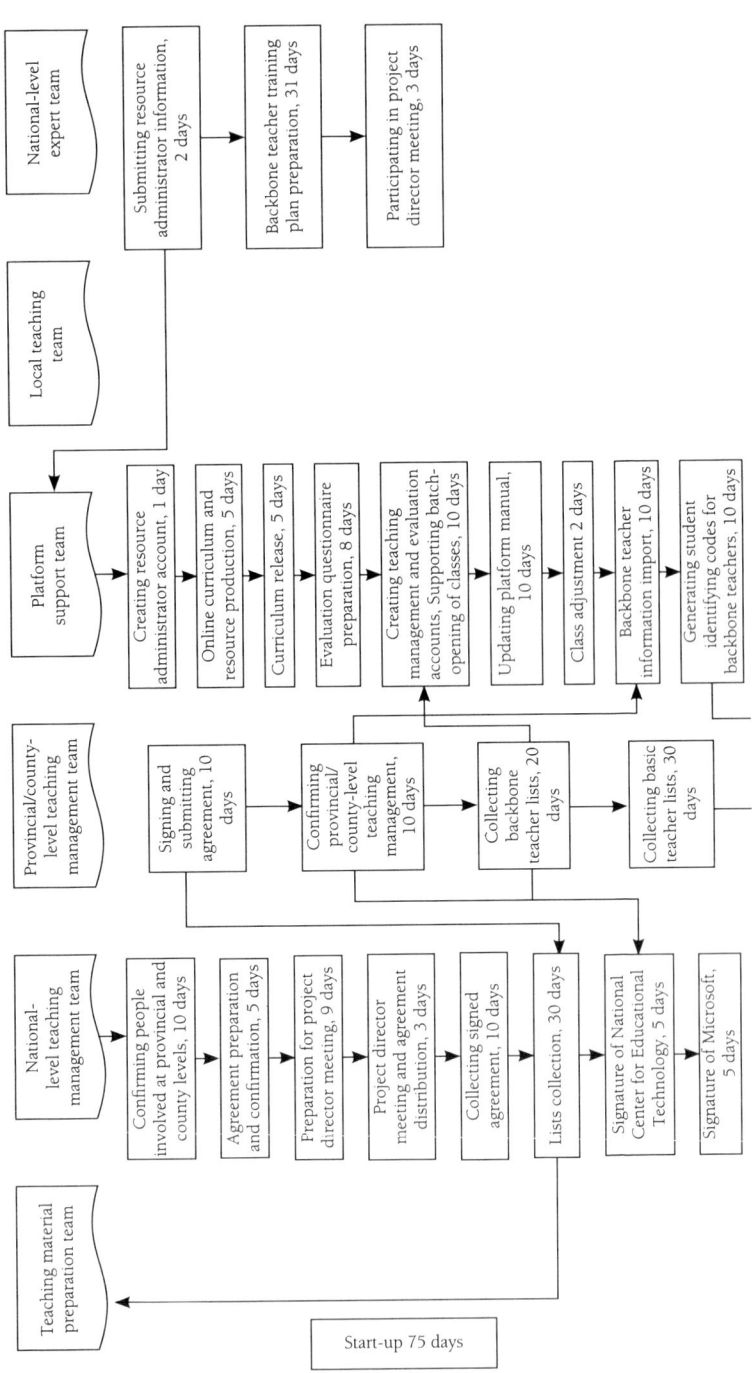

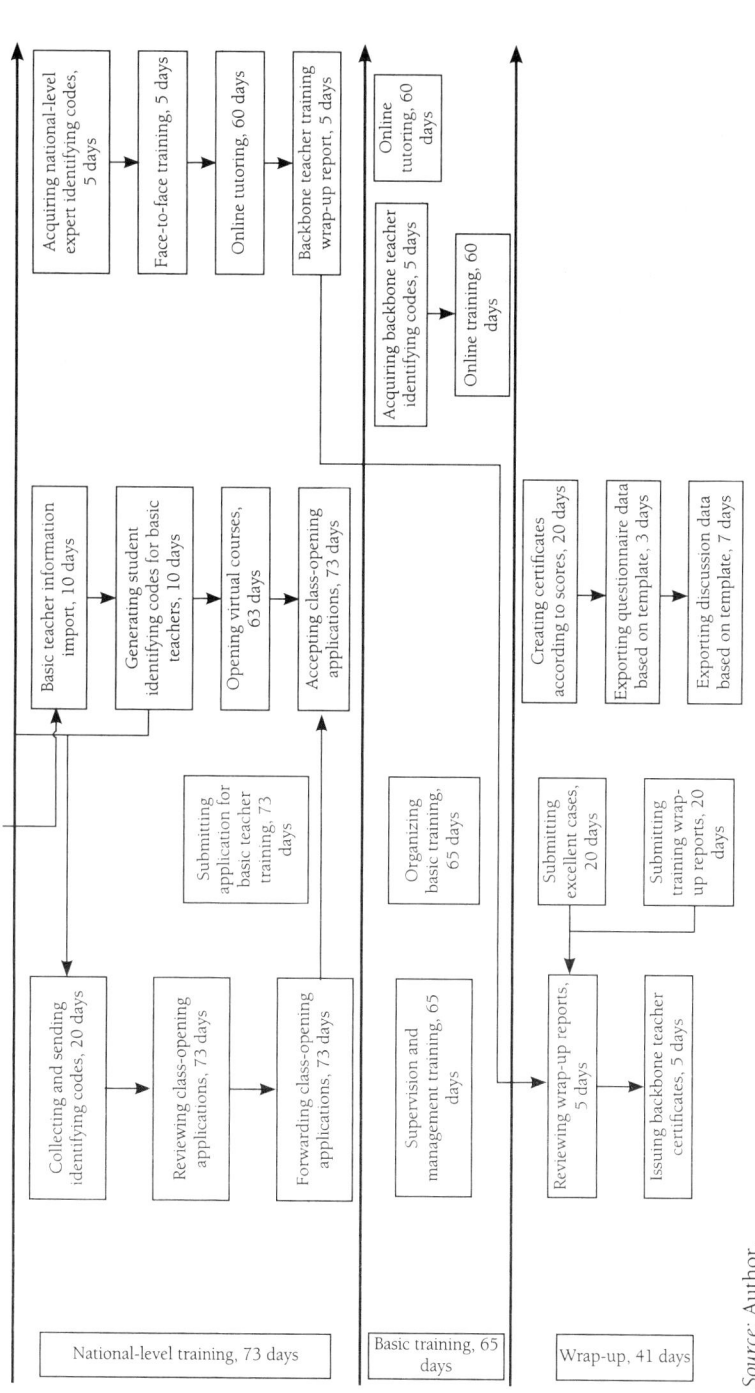

National-level training, 73 days

Collecting and sending identifying codes, 20 days → Reviewing class-opening applications, 73 days → Forwarding class-opening applications, 73 days

Submitting application for basic teacher training, 73 days

Basic teacher information import, 10 days → Generating student identifying codes for basic teachers, 10 days → Opening virtual courses, 63 days → Accepting class-opening applications, 73 days

Acquiring national-level expert identifying codes, 5 days → Face-to-face training, 5 days → Online tutoring, 60 days → Backbone teacher training wrap-up report, 5 days

Basic training, 65 days

Supervision and management training, 65 days

Organizing basic training, 65 days

Acquiring backbone teacher identifying codes, 5 days → Online training, 60 days

Online tutoring, 60 days

Wrap-up, 41 days

Reviewing wrap-up reports, 5 days

Issuing backbone teacher certificates, 5 days

Submitting excellent cases, 20 days

Submitting training wrap-up reports, 20 days

Creating certificates according to scores, 20 days → Exporting questionnaire data based on template, 3 days → Exporting discussion data based on template, 7 days

Source: Author.

Figure 10.13
Pictures of Field Investigation

Source: Author.

National-level Training

National-level subject teacher training was organized by National Center for Educational Technology with the support of MoE and educational authorities of each target area of the project. Expert teams were responsible for online teaching and face-to-face training. Each project county recommended four national-level elite teachers to participate and finish no less than 50 hours of online learning and 5 days of face-to-face training, including online teaching and tutoring and innovative teacher training corresponding to intermediate educational technology. Innovative teacher training adopted a mixed model, involving not only face-to-face teaching but also self-teaching via the Internet and communication with classmates (see Figure 10.14).

Generally speaking, the Innovative Teachers project benefited the participating teachers in the following aspects: It broadened their horizon and deepened their understanding of IT integration in teaching. New educational and teaching theories changed the teaching concepts

Figure 10.14
National-level Training for Subject Teachers from 100 Counties

Source: Author.

for many trained teachers, building up their awareness that teachers should promote students to learn and students should be the main body in learning activities, and facilitating their practice in this regard. The participants learned to use many modern IT tools, such as mind map, VCT, and resource websites, which were of great help to their teaching. By learning from model cases and communicating with peer teachers, they greatly improved their teaching skills.

Innovative Teacher Competition and Innovative Education Seminar

The Innovative Teacher Competition aimed to improve teachers' educational technology capacity, enhance communication among teachers, and promote middle and primary school teachers' teaching ability to develop and teaching skills to improve by applying Microsoft project-based and research-based learning and teaching templates (see Figure 10.15). The 4th, 5th, 6th, and 7th Innovative Teachers Competition was held

Figure 10.15
Innovative Teachers Competition 2010

Source: Author.

during PiL Phase II, and 852 teachers participated in the competitions. Winners of Excellence Awards also attended the 5th and 6th Microsoft Global Innovative Education Conference.

In May 2011, MoE and Microsoft (China) jointly organized China IT-based Education and Innovative Education Seminar. Educational experts from around the world, officials of Chinese educational authorities, and representative teachers gathered to discuss the importance of information technology in promoting innovative education, and share successful experience of using innovative technologies to promote teaching reform. Awards of the Innovative Students Competition and the Innovative Teachers Competition were granted.

Building of Training Platforms and Resources

Innovative teacher training combined the latest Microsoft technologies and teacher training in China in a creative way, and designed teaching materials in line with our syllabus. The training won great support from educational technology centers at various levels and of various types. The online curriculum, teaching materials and training platforms developed passed expert review, and teachers who fulfilled the training were regarded as up to the standard of intermediate education technology level.

Supplementary materials were developed to cater to the needs of different trainees. For instance, *Supplementary Materials for Subject Teachers* and *Online Curriculum for Subject Teachers* were developed for subject teachers of 100 counties, and online courses for subject teacher training and IT training were also developed.

Platforms were developed to support Innovative Teacher training according to the demand.

- Organizers uploaded and managed teaching resources to the teaching management platform, and conducted teaching management and statistics check on the platform.
- Trainers and learners used the platform for teaching and learning, as well as for checking the progress of learning through homework and tests. Trainers monitored and guided learners in the learning process.

- The interactive learning platform (discussion groups) was synchronized with the learning platform to provide scenarios for trainers to organize discussions.

Project Evaluation

The evaluation team consisted of educational technology experts, senior researchers, and practitioners from the Research Center of Knowledge Engineering, Beijing Normal University. It adopted the 5th version Context-Input-Process-Product (CIPP) evaluation model (see Figure 10.16),[1] and the evaluation focused on five aspects of the project: that is, product, impact, effectiveness, sustainability, and transportability.

Basically Fulfilling the Set Tasks

In terms of the number of participating teachers, innovative teacher training has basically fulfilled the set tasks. As revealed in some blog posts

Figure 10.16
Fifth Version CIPP Evaluation Model

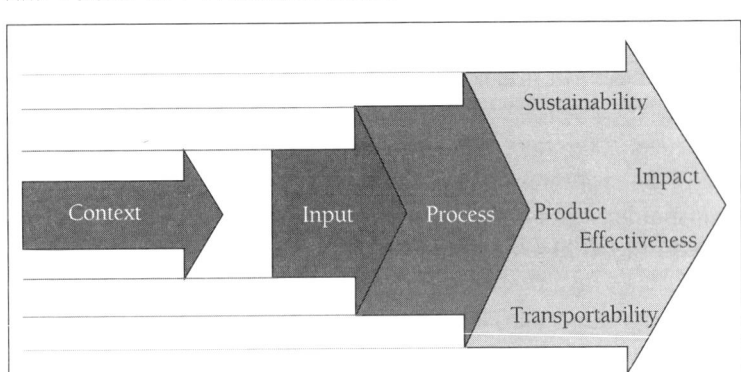

Source: Author.

[1] See CIPP Evaluation Model Checklist, Daniel L. Stufflebeam, July 2009 for details of the model, published online at http://www.wmich.edu/evalctr/checklists/cippchecklist.htm.

published by teachers trained during the training, participant experience was good, the training methods and content were well received, trainees learned a lot, and believed the training greatly facilitated their personal development and work in the future.

Innovative teacher training served as a demonstration project. The evaluation team interviewed project leaders of each province, and the result showed that the training had greatly promoted the local teacher team building. Moreover, the team also conducted phone interviews with selected project management staff at provincial level, and all those interviewed showed positive opinion toward the experience of PiL teacher training, believing that this helped them accumulate experience for other training and could be helpful to other similar work.

Exploring Online Training Mode for Teachers

Unlike the traditional method of issuing CDs, innovative teacher training adopted a mixed training mode that combined online training and face-to-face training. It turned out that primary and middle school teachers accept such a mode well and acquired rich experience in using online platforms for learning.

Standardizing the Training Procedure and Management

Related parties signed agreements to specify responsibilities of each party to ensure smooth progress of the project. Each area already formulated a relatively complete set of training plans prior to the actual implementation, and specified arrangement in terms of training objectives, targets, content, implementation, and supporting measures.

Different types of management documents were formed during the training, including task description, technical feedback mechanism for the platform, innovative teacher training platform manual, procedures for subject teacher and IT teacher training, overall project schedule, and a variety of report templates. Teams were set up and responsibilities clearly defined to ensure successful execution of the project.

Promoting Teachers to Use IT Tools Effectively with the Help of Microsoft

Innovative teacher training project fully tapped into the advantage of Microsoft in information technologies, and provided different teacher groups with frequently used IT tools needed by each group, such as VCT, Visio, Math and Zplusz. For IT teachers, training was focused on effective maintenance of campus network, firewall, server technical support, and IT support. As a frontrunner in the global software industry, Microsoft was able to assist the teachers in every way they needed.

Learning from Peers Abroad and Enhancing International Exchange

Innovative teacher training project conducted exchanges at various levels and cooperation with Microsoft in different fields. In January 2011, MoE awarded Microsoft (China) Co. Ltd the honorary certificate of "Outstanding Contribution," which was the fourth year in a row for Microsoft to win the honor.

Summary

The project also met some challenges during its implementation.

- Teachers in different environment, from different academic background or with different teaching experience had their own teaching style and preferences. How to integrate such personal features with professional development of teachers and find a win–win training mode?
- Teachers' initiative for participation had a direct impact on the progress and effectiveness of the project, and exterior incentives alone could not keep an enduring interest in learning. How to improve the participation initiative of the teachers?
- How to use individual demonstration cases to promote the problem-solving ability of the teachers?
- How to upgrade the teachers' teaching concepts and methods, and how to help them change their learning concepts, their role in

the teaching–learning process and their learning methods to drive IT-based school development?
- How to address the conflict between work and learning which occurred to many teachers during the training?

The project also need be improved in terms of online training mode for teachers and its organization and implementation. For instance, trainers need be able to provide better guidance; case study used for online courses should integrate theories better into practice; learning tasks and content should be more reasonably arranged for participating teachers; and technical support for the online training platforms should be enhanced.

With a large geographical coverage, scattered population, insufficient funds, and conflict between work and learning in rural areas, teacher training in rural China faces various challenges. Relying on modern distance education to overcome the barriers of time and space enabled teachers in different areas to share quality education resources. This is an effective approach to conduct large-scale continuing education for teachers and considerably improve the overall competence of teachers, especially those in rural areas. Innovative teacher training has had considerable success in its exploration for the online training mode and organization methods, and is expected to play a bigger role in large-scale teacher training programs. Microsoft should continue to follow China's teacher training policies, such as the National Training Program for Primary and Secondary School Teachers implemented in 2010, and launch a new round of teacher training project.

11

Success Factors and Lessons Learned from Cases on iERD in Asia, Africa, and Latin America

Eilean von Lautz-Cauzanet

Introduction

It is widely assumed that the benefits of information and communication technology (ICT) can impact positively on the development of information-poor rural and remote areas. The power of ICT to connect these areas with the world's information society and to break down barriers to knowledge and information exchange has led to an overall enthusiasm within the iERD debate (Chapman and Slaymaker, 2002). Subsequently, a multitude of projects that use ICT in order to improve the livelihood of rural inhabitants have been launched, seeking to exploit the apparently unlimited potential of ICT in order to tackle challenges related to rural areas (FAO, 2012).

While these projects used in the beginning, mainly electronic broadcast technologies such as TV and radio, Internet, and mobile-based technologies, have emerged during the past two decades. ICT now include computer-based applications and communication tools, such as social media, digital information repositories (online or offline), digital photography, video, and mobile phones (Balaji et al., 2007).

Through ICT, a large number of iERD projects seek to provide farmers with the information they need in order to adapt their decision making to an increasingly knowledge-intensive agricultural sector. Furthermore, many projects see in ICT the opportunity to develop rural areas by providing schools with quality education or imparting ICT training to rural inhabitants in view of developing their professional perspectives.

However, there is a large number of inefficient and failing initiatives that could not reach their objectives despite an enthusiast project start and availability of ICT. In this regard, it appears even more important to understand how successful projects have actually achieved to improve the livelihood of rural inhabitants. For this purpose, 12 projects and initiatives from Asia, Africa, and Latin America have been selected and analyzed in separate case studies.

Success Factors

A closer look at their functioning reveals three overarching characteristics that contributed significantly to their respective success.

Content Relevancy and User-centered ICT

Successful projects are aware of the importance of implementing a project in line with the users' social reality and accordingly define their objectives and the content to be delivered. Hence, they recognize the importance of embedding the use of the respective ICT in the socioeconomic context of the community and adapt its mechanisms to the needs and skills of rural inhabitants.

Complementary Project Partners and Inclusive Management

Successful projects have no difficulties to embed the project efficiently in the rural as multiple stakeholders with complementary strengths and resources are involved in the planning and implementation process. The associated integration of local inhabitants in the management of the project allows them to enhance the process of integration, stimulate the actual use of the project's services, and subsequently, achieve their skills development.

Training and Development-based Sustainability Strategies

Successful projects are dynamic and invest in their sustainability through training and support activities that connect users to the project and enable them to permanently develop their skills. The willingness to continuously innovate the project through the adaptation of ICT and the delivered content to the emerging needs of users, as well efforts to increase the number of beneficiaries, contribute to the project's longevity and relevance for rural populations.

These three characteristics are interdependent and directly affect each other (see Figure 11.1). Furthermore, they have in common the objective to enhance a relationship between the initial project launching entities and the respective target group of the project, which is based on proximity and mutual understanding. It is this proximity that confers a high degree of efficiency to each of the analyzed projects.

Lessons Learned

In the following, how these characteristics contribute to the success of the analyzed iERD projects will be detailed.

Figure 11.1
Three Success Characteristics of Selected Projects

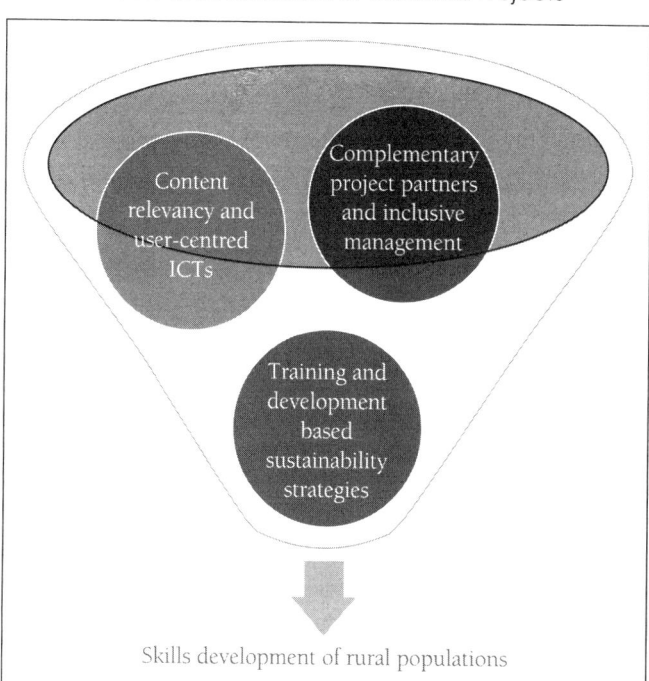

Source: Author.

Relevance of Defined Objectives and Associated ICT

Concordance between Objectives and User's Social Reality

The first success criterion of all analyzed projects is the great effort made to define objectives that take into consideration the socioeconomic context of the target area. All initiatives are characterized by a great understanding of rural challenges and the specific needs of the area in which the pilot project is implemented. This is an important element as the relevance of a project and its objectives depend on the extent to which a project is capable of producing a major and necessary change for beneficiaries (IICA, 2009). In other words, it is important to design projects activities and strategies that focus on the most relevant areas for these beneficiaries in order to effectively and efficiently implement an iERD project.

Furthermore, designing relevant objectives according to the main challenges of rural populations does also have a major impact on the attitude that future users will have toward the project: Potential beneficiaries who feel that the project understands their problems will be more likely to believe in its potential outputs and be more receptive to its services and tools.

For example, the analyzed successful projects could identify relevant challenges in rural development by defining relevant and realistic objectives that take into consideration these challenges and aims to tackle the latter:

1. *The Weak Position of Small Farmers within the Agricultural Value Chain Process.* The projects Tradenet, e-Krishi; MEDA as well as the Mbire podcasting project, Cocoa Link and Farmerline have all identified successfully the main problems that lead to the weak position of farmers—lack of information concerning product prices and information on weather, agricultural practices, and market behaviors. The projects aim also to help small farmers to identify potential buyers. All cited projects have defined objectives that tackle the consequences of these issues—decrease the dependence on middlemen, avoid loss of time and money spent during the search of agricultural information, offer fair product prices, and increase farmers' decision-making capacity and efficiency.

2. *The Disadvantaged Situation of Rural Students and Teachers.* The projects Telesecundaria, Text2Teach, and e-Bario analyzed in the case studies have successfully identified the main elements that disadvantage rural students in comparison to their urban peers: shortage of quality education material, lack of access to updated information and difficulties to exchange best practices with teachers and students networks, discrepancy between rural life and educational content, and migration to urban areas. In this regard, these successful projects have defined the following objectives: improve academic achievements, increase students and teachers

motivation, decrease dropout and absenteeism rates, and create professional perspectives for students in rural areas.

3. Overall Underdevelopment and Marginalization of Rural Areas and Their Inhabitants. e-Bario, Mahiti Manthana, RSITC, and Réseau Femmes En Action are considered successful projects with regard to addressing the reasons that contribute to the underdevelopment of rural areas and the marginalization of rural inhabitants: lack of information and communication infrastructures; low ICT skills; higher rates of illiteracy and higher social vulnerability and exclusion, particularly of women, in comparison to urban areas. In order to eliminate these problems and contribute to the development of rural areas, the cited projects seek to enhance the communication of rural inhabitants with other communities and urban areas; provide them with access to information in the area of education, health, and professional opportunities; stimulate local business and marketing opportunities; enable them to empower themselves.

The *e-Krishi* platform offers 30 categories of agricultural information and a high amount of subcategories providing up-to-date crop price information and advisory on how to cultivate crops according to the location of each farmer. The information is retrieved from a large-scale server managed by a delivery system of an online agricultural information portal. The platform is accessible online and in each of the dedicated e-Krishi centers that are never more than 3 km away from a farmer. There farmer can also find over 30 different types of print material accessible in the local language that helps them how to use the platform (in addition to the training they receive) and provides agricultural information that is adapted to their needs. Finally, farmers can also call a toll-free agricultural information center, available in their local language.

Concordance between ICT and User's Social Reality

The analyzed successful projects were not only able to identify relevant objectives, but also they could choose their respective ICT in accordance with the social reality of rural inhabitants. Indeed, it is important to select cautiously the ICT equipments and infrastructures and ensure that these are suitable for the local community and concord with the defined objectives of the project (Badsar et al., 2011). All analyzed projects seem to have chosen their respective ICT in accordance to the question: "How could our target group *benefit* the most from ICT?" instead of asking simply "How can they learn to *use ICT*?" This question is of high importance, as the way rural inhabitants access the respective ICT, and its information delivery mechanism impacts directly on the users' willingness to use the ICT (Glendenning and Ficarelli, 2011).

In order to ensure that these users are indeed receptive to the project, the selected ICT and the conveyed information should be packaged in a context-specific manner: The geographical distance between the target group and the ICT should be as short as possible or even inexistent, as for example through mobile technologies, in order to facilitate as much as possible the access to the respective ICT. Furthermore, the ICT information delivery mechanism itself (e.g., an online trading platform or educational videos) must be easily available and usable, and be adapted to the ICT skills of users whose ICT skills are often much lower compared to urban populations. It is also recommended to design an ICT delivery mechanism in the local language of the community, or at least explain its use in the local language (Glendenning and Ficarelli, 2011). These efforts to offer easy to use technologies can be considered as important success factor for an iERD project, as user-friendly technologies are quicker to adopt than complex ones. Interestingly, ICT such as television or radio is often wrongly considered as outdated tools, which can be as efficient or even more efficient then "new" technologies, as users have been familiar with these for years. Another advantage is also their accessibility to nonliterate populations (Higgins and Izushi, 2002). Also, easy-to-use technologies should be combined with print material and a human interface, particularly at the initial stages of an iERD initiative. This association increases the accessibility of the used ICT and avoids disconnectedness between project and end users (Ballantyne, 2002).

In terms of content, context specificity means that the information and content delivered by the ICT has ideally been locally collected and/ or is adapted to the social reality of users. In the case of projects that provide agricultural information, it is reported that individual relate better to content that is locally produced (Glendenning and Ficarelli, 2011). Besides, context-specific information is reported to be more resource intensive, as it varies spatially, temporally, and may have different degrees of specificity, particularly at the farm level. In the area of education, for example, context specificity can be ensured through delivering educational content that is in line with the national content and diploma requirements, but imparted through activities and subjects that take into consideration the rural reality of students.

Complementary Partnerships

The capacity of a project to address the needs of rural populations and provide adapted solutions depends also on the entities that are involved in the project and their respective capacities. A look at successful iERD projects shows that a majority is launched or supported by partnerships who were willing to donate their strengths and efforts to a cause related to rural development. These partnerships, which include often local, national, and international private commercial enterprises, as well as nongovernment organizations (NGOs), not-for-profit trusts, philanthropic organizations, and development agencies, can benefit iERD project in multiple ways through their association (Pillay and Hearn, 2009).

Text2Teach was initially designed by the so-called Bridge It Alliance (Nokia, the International Youth Foundation, Pearson and UNDP), which combine their expertise in technology, training, and content development in the area of mobile learning. On a national level, the project received financial and conceptual support from USAID, Nokia Philippines, the Department of Education and SEAMEO—Innotech, an intergovernmental organization, as well as the Philippine IT companies PMSI and Chikka Asia. Thanks to this multiple stakeholder partnership, the project could set up a large-scale ICT infrastructure, including mobile phones, TVs, and storage servers and implement the project rapidly in a progressively increasing amount of schools throughout the country. It further allows the project to modernize regularly the used ICT tools. Finally, the Ayala foundation, because of their experience in working on the grassroots level, was chosen to monitor the project and impart ICT training in the field. The foundation is the main interlocutor for teachers and participating schools and their presence ensures the smooth implementation of the project.

Firstly, these partnerships can accelerate the pace of progress of an iERD initiative, through the association of different albeit complementary interests and strengths, creating a collective knowledge that enriches the project and increase its efficiency. For example, a project will benefit from a partnership that involves an NGO with experience in project management and is familiar with working on the field and delivering services to the grassroots. Furthermore, partners with expertise in rural development, as for example dedicated public agencies, universities or Think Tanks can be a valuable partner for iERD projects, as they are familiar with analyzing rural challenges in the long term and hence capable of designing a project that will take into consideration the specificities of rural issues. These partners can avoid discrepancies between the used ICT and the social reality of the project's target group, and design a project that is based on long-term research, increasing a project's chances of efficiency and sustainability.

Furthermore, the analyzed successful projects and international research findings also show that iERD projects benefit from partnerships composed of entities with subject expertise and actors capable and willing to provide the technological infrastructure, as for example large IT companies within a corporate social responsibility program. Their involvement is important for many iERD projects, as they can equip the project with computers, mobile phones, software, and high-quality Internet connection even in very remote areas, as well as provide data hosting and storage spaces. Their involvement can impact positively on the overall quality of the project and help to reduce project costs (Pillay and Hearn, 2009; de Silva, 2008). Furthermore, these alliances can also enlarge the project's area of influence and enable it to reach more easily the respective target group, for example, through established mobile networks. Finally, iERD projects do also benefit from their technical expertise that allows modernizing and innovating the project's ICT infrastructure and tools.

Then, the involvement of partners with publicly acknowledged legitimacy and large decision-making power—in these cases as for example ministries of agriculture or education—can also benefit a project. These entities are more likely to have the capacity to implement changes in public institutions such as schools and to monitor a project on a large-scale level. Their support also allows enlarging the catchment area of an iERD project, as it can, for example, benefit from governmental funds that have been created to fund rural development.

Finally, it is recommended that partnerships take into considerations previous initiatives that have taken place in the targeted area, in order to learn from their experiences and, if possible, reuse existing infrastructures. These partnerships should also integrate the project within existing systems of local information exchange and flow in rural communities, which increases the overall efficiency of the project (Roman and Colle, 2003). However, the added value of partnerships with complementing interests can only be fully exploited if there are clear agreements between all involved entities, for example, concerning the implementation framework or the excludability of target groups. Also, roles and responsibilities must be clearly defined in ways that accommodate different expectations of all parties (FAO, 2012; Pillay and Hearn, 2009).

A Participatory Planning and Management Approach

A look at successful iERD project and international research findings confirms that projects that have adopted a participatory approach during the planning and implementation phase increase the efficiency and effectiveness of the entire initiative. A large number of successful projects adopt a specific component of this participatory approach, the so-called Participatory Action Research or Participatory Rural Appraisal. This approach is based "on the collaboration of those affected by the issue being studied, for purposes of education and taking action or effecting change" (University of Berkeley, 2005). Furthermore, within this approach, the organization of needs assessment surveys in the households of a community or through the practical experiences, as well as community discussions and workshops, aims to incorporate the knowledge and opinions of rural inhabitants in the planning and management of a development project.

There are several advantages and benefits of adopting a participatory approach: Firstly, the overall community development can be enhanced through strategies that promote equitable and collaborative participation (Farr and Papandrea, 2006). More concretely, the organization of needs assessments or data gathering in collaboration with the local community and the respective target group creates a co-learning process: Researchers and project coordinators will be able to identify already existing social structures, processes, and knowledge, which in turn will increase their capacity to design relevant and efficient project objectives, activities, and timeframes, and avoid discrepancies between the project and the community's social reality (Glendenning and Ficarelli, 2011). Simultaneously, the importance of the community's knowledge is acknowledged through this participatory approach, giving them a first insight in the overall project objectives and stimulating their willingness to commit to and take part in future activities.

The active involvement of future beneficiaries in the preparation process of an iERD project also contributes to a relationship based on mutual understanding and respect between the local community and the project team, which enhances the integration of the project in the socio-cultural context of the community and increases the efficiency of the project implementation. This integration can be even enhanced through the distribution of responsibilities and tasks during the preparation of the project, showing the community that they are supposed to take ownership of the project in the long term: Again, this is a motivating factor that contributes to the success of the project.

> The projects *Coca Link* and *e-Bario* have both included the local community in the planning and implementation phase: While local inhabitants supported the Cocoa Link staff during the registration process of farmers, the volunteers from the Bario community collaborated with the project staff during the initial needs assessment and community discussions were organized in order to take into consideration their needs and opinions. Furthermore, Cocoa Link has recruited local inhabitants among their field staff in order to ensure a close collaboration with the community. In Bario, local inhabitants are represented in the steering committee of the project and volunteers manage the computer laboratory and telecenter as well as the ICT training.

It is important to underline the importance of adopting a participatory approach that focuses not only on the respective target group, but also on the community as a whole. Indeed, a project will increase its chances of success if local and regional decision makers can be convinced about the projects utility, even if they are not the main beneficiaries of the project. It is crucial to respect and adapt to local hierarchies and to integrate these decision makers, as their support is indispensable to reach the actual target groups and necessary for the overall smooth project implementation. Here, the associated presence of a local champion can be very useful and contribute to the local acceptance toward an iERD initiative (Pillay and Hearn, 2009).

However, a participatory approach should ideally not be limited to the planning phase of a project. Integrating the knowledge of the target group and the whole community in the actual management of the iERD project through collaborative partnerships increases the long-term success of the latter. Concretely, this involvement can, for example, be institutionalized through the creation of project management committees on the local, municipal, and regional level. These management or monitoring entities should systematically involve community representatives, interest groups, and enterprises as their integration and support strengthen the legitimacy of the project. In addition, collaborative management entities increase the community's feeling of ownership and accountability within a knowledge production process (University of Berkeley, 2005). These partnerships are crucial, as proactive attitudes among the community are indispensable for the sustainability of an iERD project. Furthermore, the distribution of managerial positions of the iERD project to members of the respective target group, as well as local private and public actors of the community, enriches the organized activities and services. It also contributes to the project's capacity to innovate and develop itself further in accordance with local needs.

User Centered Training and Support Activities

An iERD project that has defined realistic objectives in line with the social reality of the respective target group is based on solid and complementary partnerships and adopts participatory planning and management methods, and it has fulfilled some of the most significant criteria in view of achieving effectiveness and sustainability. However, these factors can only generate the desired effects if the project can guarantee that the target group will be actually *able* to use the respective ICT tool. It is therefore not surprising to see that successful iERD projects spent significant efforts on training and support activities that accompany users and enable them to access, assess, apply, and act upon the information provided by the ICT projects (Higgins and Izushi, 2002).

The nature of this training depends on the ICT used and objective of the iERD project, as well as on user skills. It is crucial to design a training that takes into consideration the often low ICT skills of rural inhabitants. In this regard, projects that use relatively complex technologies must obviously organize more extensive and continuous training sessions than those that select easy-to-use ICT which are already familiar to the users.

For example, a project that is willing to launch a community telecenter through which rural inhabitants can access the Internet and enhance their professional opportunities must train the rural community how to use various software and align the ICT courses to the respective needs of the user. This kind of project will need to impart more training sessions than a project that focuses on a smaller target group and selects an ICT to which this target group is already familiar with, for example, a project that allows farmers to receive market price information on their mobile phones. Both projects can achieve their objectives and impact positively on the livelihood of the respective target groups, given that an adapted training has been imparted.

Training should ideally be imparted by locally known actors, as for example local NGOs or field staff with a regular presence in the community. This proximity contributes to a relationship based on trust between project staff and beneficiaries. Ideally, the training should also train volunteer future trainers in order to create local inhabitants to take ownership of the training sessions and increase the feeling of ownership.

> The *Mahiti Manthana* project imparts various training sessions to marginalized women and the field staff on how to use the software associated to video and radio productions. The mid-term objective is to train women to act as trainers for future members. However, ICT training is not only imparted to the target group (women) but also organized for representatives of the community who participate in workshops dealing with general awareness of ICT and its potential for social projects. More generally, the local women initiative Mahila Samakhya supports continuously each information center and provides them with technical as well as conceptual advice.

As regards training methods of iERD projects, both research findings and a look at successful projects show that group working and practical simulations are valuable approaches of ICT training (Craig et al., 2005). Indeed, learning in groups allows enhancing an active and independent learning process. Furthermore, the organization of workshops that, for example, bring together teachers or farmers from different villages of the same community facilitates the creation of networks. The latter can be very helpful for mutual support and increase the capacity of participants to help themselves at a later stage.

For rural inhabitants, who seek to use the respective ICT tool in order to increase their professional opportunities, empower themselves or improve the quality of their daily life, it is crucial to impart training based on practical experiences and which is tailored to their social reality. This approach increases their motivation and the perception that the acquired skills will actually have an impact and improve their lives. Also, linking the training to real-life experiences will decrease the probability that the training is perceived as additional workload. This is particularly true for iERD projects that train, for example, teachers to use ICT-based teaching methods.

A look at successful iERD project also shows the advantages of training users not only how to use ICT for a specific purpose, but also to include technical components and troubleshooting in the training. This increases their capacity to overcome technical difficulties and ideally develop autonomously new ways of usage and implementation.

In any case, ICT training should aim to promote self-help and personal responsibility in the learning process, so that participants feel they *own* the process and sustain their activities. It is important that the training allows them to gradually gain knowledge in increase their self-confidence in the meantime and at their own pace (Higgins and Izushi, 2002). This is particularly important as rushed training will hinder the efficient and smooth implementation of the project and decrease the likelihood that the community or respective target group will to take ownership of an iERD project.

Besides imparting adapted training, iERD projects should provide continuously support activities and assistance to ICT users and project beneficiaries, both in terms of technical advice and concerning administrative issues, as technical and administrative difficulties hinder the smooth implementation of an ICT project. It also enables users in the long term to make their own decisions on how to improve the implementation of these ICT in *their* project. In the long term, this support should not be provided by project staff, but by local actors who have been progressively prepared for that role. Again, this is an important factor allowing the community to take over and manage the project.

It is important to underline the importance of continuity to impart training and organize support activities. Continuity is central to both the empowerment process and maintaining the dynamism of the initiative through development of human potential of the community (Craig et al., 2005).

Development Strategies for Sustainability

The ultimate goal of all iERD projects is not only to achieve its planned objectives, but also to launch a project capable of bringing the intended change in a sustainable manner. This is directly linked to the degree of social sustainability of the project, commonly defined as the project's capacity to bring the intended change after the end of a pilot phase. Social sustainability is achieved when the community has fully accepted and ideally taken ownership of the project (Badsar et al., 2011).

Obviously, the criteria analyzed in the previous sections contribute to the sustainability of an iERD project. However, a key factor contributing to sustainability is a project's capacity to constantly evolve. For this purpose, successful ICT projects adopt development strategies that stimulate the project's capacity to grow and innovate.

One of the major components of these strategies is a precise evaluation of the project, continuously or at defined moments, which includes consultation and feedback from users on the applicability and relevance of the acquired skills and offered services, as well as on the use of the respective ICT. This allows assessing the short- and medium-term impact of the project and permits to examine the need of additional resources. This examination in turn allows the project to conduct adjustments and corrections, both in terms of management and ICT use, and to increase the overall quality of offered services and delivered information.

Furthermore, consulting the community and particularly the project's target group in view of assessing their needs enables the project to evolve with this target group and adapt its services and functioning accordingly. This is crucial for the project's sustainability, because a project must be perceived as useful and relevant in order to survive after the first period of curiosity.

Another key component of a development strategy consists in the analysis of possibilities to innovate and diversify the project, both in view of the respective ICT and organized activities or services. Successful projects do analyze the rapid evolution of ICT and eventually replace the respective ICT tool by a more innovative one. This allows the projects to increase their efficiency, and enriches its activities and services, increasing its overall attractiveness and importance to the community in the meantime.

> After two years of implementation, the governmental program *Telesecundaria* conducted a first evaluation of the impact the video based lessons had on academic achievements. Two more evaluations followed, analyzing the degree to which the target group could be reached and the degree of integration of Telesecundaria schools in their respective communities. After seven years, MoE started an innovation process of the ICT material and aligned its content to hitherto to the new national curriculum. In terms of expansion, the initiative increased the number of Telesecundaria schools from 40 to 650 in six years.

Finally, successful iERD projects have also often adopted development strategies that are characterized by the effort to expand progressively the project's sphere of impact, in order to offer an increased number of inhabitants the opportunity to participate and benefit from the project. This is particularly important as projects that allow only some groups to gain benefit from an iERD initiative increase their chances to fail in the long term (Kumar and Best, 2006).

Policy Recommendations

Initiatives that desire to use ICT in order to improve the livelihood of rural populations through ICT should make sure that they have a sound understanding of the challenges that these populations face, and more generally, be aware of the socioeconomic background and habits of the respective target group. Indeed, rural challenges can be very diverse even within one community: Rural women do not face the same challenges as farmers, neither do these need the same support as teachers or students in rural areas. Understanding the unique social reality in which the future target group of an iERD project lives, works, and learns is a key condition for successful iERD projects, and can be considered as starting point of the process that leads to the definition of realistic and relevant objectives. Indeed, this understanding affects directly the project's chances to actually reach rural populations and improve their livelihoods.

It is also important to adopt a flexible and user-tailored approach with regards to the type of ICT that is chosen and the manner it will be used by the respective target group. iERD projects must make sure that the selected technology is coherent with the social reality and objectives of the initiatives and to be aware that one technology can be used in multiple ways. These are influenced by factors such as e-readiness, literacy, or signal coverage. In other words, projects must adapt the content delivery mechanism of ICT to the skills, habits, and environment of the beneficiaries.

Furthermore, iERD projects must ensure that they actually have the capacity to exploit fully the advantages of iERD projects. For this purpose, it is recommended that these initiatives involve multiple stakeholders from whose expertise and material as well as financial resources the project will benefit. Ideally, these partnerships should be composed of experts in the area of content development, IT providers, and experts, as well as entities who are familiar with the challenges of the respective target group and community, and have gained experiences in managing projects on the grassroots level. These partnerships increase the projects efficiency chances.

In addition, iERD projects should actively include the community's perspectives, opinions, and ideas in the planning and management process. For example, this can be done through participatory needs assessments and the creation of management committees composed of local volunteers. A participatory approach is recommendable as it ensures that the project will not drift away from relevant objectives and stimulates a feeling of ownership that, in the end, contributes significantly to a project's longevity.

Indeed, projects should consider their respective target group as actors of their own change and progressively enable them to fulfill this role. For this purpose, it is indispensable that the target group regularly receives training in order to be able to actually use and benefit from the ICT-based services of the project. This training should be user centered, this is say, tailored to the needs, interests and skills of the target group. In addition, continuous support must be provided in order to avoid a slowdown of activities, for example, related to technical or administrative issues. This support should be locally accessible through a field presence of implementing entities and ideally be provided by local inhabitants trained for this purpose.

Finally, iERD initiatives should develop strategies that stimulate their sustainability and systematically conduct evaluations of results, conduct needs assessments in order to ensure coherent project activities and exploit the potential of new and innovating ICT tools for their project objectives. This permits to diversify activities and services and extend the project's overall sphere of influence. The latter impacts directly on the project's sustainability, as all iERD projects are positioned in an interdependent relationship toward their beneficiaries.

Appendix: Summary Tables of the Cases on iERD from Asia, Africa, and Latin America

Table A11.1
Characteristics of Context-specific ICT within Successful iERD Projects

Project	*Adaptation of ICT to the Rural Context*
e-Bario	While the computer laboratory and associated learning software was available in English to students and teachers, the ICT material was translated into the national language Bahasa in order to reach the whole community, who did not always speak English. Both in the computer laboratory and community center managers were always present in order to provide advice and answer questions. The delivered content focused especially on rural needs: Improve access to educational information and enhance collaboration with peers; provide skills that enable the rural populations to decrease their marginalization, e.g. through tourism

Table A11.1 continued

Table A11.1 continued

Project	Adaptation of ICT to the Rural Context
e-Krishi	The e-Krishi platform offers 30 categories of agricultural information and a high amount of subcategories providing up-to-date crop price information and advisory on how to cultivate crops according to the location of each farmer. The information is retrieved from a large-scale server managed by a delivery system of an online agricultural information portal. The platform is accessible online and in each of the dedicated e-Krishi centers that are never more than 3 km away from a farmer. There farmer can also find over 30 different types of print material accessible in the local language that helps them how to use the platform (in addition to the training they receive) and provides agricultural information that is adapted to their needs. Finally, farmers can also call a toll-free agricultural information center, available in their local language
Mahiti Manthana	Mahiti Manthana has established many information centers with Internet, telephone, and fax access close to participating villages. As the majority of women are illiterate and unable to read websites, a literate woman is chosen to access, for example, governmental websites and contact local governments. She then transfers the information to the rest of the group and helps them during the application procedure for governmental services. Furthermore, the project implements nontextual ICT activities as film and radio producing which are easily usable and learnable by illiterate women. The content itself of each of these activities deals also with subjects that help women to empower themselves. Finally, the project staff uses online data management systems and email communication in order to increase the cooperation between women of different villages and assembly their voices and increase their bargaining efficiency within decision-making processes
MEDA	The platform is—albeit produced by foreign IT firms—available in Spanish. Furthermore, farmers can conduct their water transactions in a dedicated local office where a project coordinator is continuously present and helps them during the transaction process. They receive price information, in Spanish too, via a simple SMS on their mobile phone

Table A11.1 continued

Table A11.1 continued

Project	Adaptation of ICT to the Rural Context
RSITC	The project chose software (Microsoft Unlimited Potential) that was developed in order to increase digital inclusion in disadvantaged socioeconomic environments such as rural areas. The software facilitates collaborative activities and is embedded in ICT training that varies its focus according to the needs of participants (farmers, women etc.). A permanent administration and IT team is present in each RSITC in order to answer questions. Software, computers and activities are all accessible in Spanish
Telesecundaria	Telesecundaria uses televisions, educational videos and printed work material in order to provide rural students with quality education. The videos are extremely easy to use and their integration into the lesson is guided through learning books that help to organize in accordance with the videos activities that focus on the rural life of students
Text2Teach	Text2Teach aims to increase the quality in disadvantaged regions as for example rural and remote areas. It stores educational videos, which have been previously aligned to the national curriculum, on an online server that organizes the videos according to subjects and grades. Teachers can easily download these educational videos via simple mobile phones directly from the server and organize a screening during the lesson. They use dedicated printed workbooks in order to embed the videos efficiently in the lessons
Tradenet	Staff from the Sri Lankan project Tradenet collects several times per day price information on products from the five markets used by a majority of farmers participating in the project. The information is send firstly to a server that stores and reorganizes the data before sending it in a single SMS to the subscribers of the project. Those can choose in which language they wish to receive the information. They can also use their mobile phone to post directly offers via their WAP enabled mobile phones in their chosen language on an online platform which matches offers and demands automatically

Table A11.1 continued

Table A11.1 continued

Project	Adaptation of ICT to the Rural Context
The Mbire podcasting project	The project conveys agricultural information (e.g., the adequate use of fertilizers) via podcasts on portable MP3 devices. This technology allows reaching farmers with low literacy levels. The content is developed by local actors and accessible in the local languages
Cocoa Link	Cocoa Link provides farmers via SMS with information on farming practice, disease prevention, postharvest production and crop marketing, but also on social issues as child labor and farm safety. Farmers can send their question and receive SMS or call with the answer to their question. Farmers can choose if they want to receive the SMS in local language or English. They also receive SMS about farmer meetings and literacy courses
Réseau Femmes en Action	RFEA provides female farmers and rural women, in general, with agricultural information via permanent cybercafés, radio broadcasting sessions and a mobile based information network. The information is made available in the local language (Mooré among others). Offline material is available in the cybercafés
Farmerline	Specific information related to fisheries is send via SMS to farmers on their mobiles phones. (A needs assessment confirmed that the target group is literate and possesses mobile phones, but lacks precise agricultural information. The content is adapted to interests of rural students (e.g., rural administrative management)

Source: Author.

Table A11.2
Role Distribution within Partnerships of Successful ICTRD Projects

Project and Target Area	Main Partners and Role
e-Krishi	• Kerala IT Mission (State government): *Conceptualization, design, monitoring* • Ministry of Agricultural Development: *Funding* • National Institute for Smart Government (Nonprofit company): *ICT capacity building, field support* • C-DIT (IT company): *Technical support* • UNDP (International organization): *Policy advice, funding* • Akshaya project (NGO): *Provision of ICT equipment*
e-Bario	• University of Sarawak: *Conceptualization, design, monitor, and research* • COMPUSERV (IT company): *ICT training, design of educational ICT program* • International Development and Research Council (Canadian aid program): *Funding* • Government of Malaysia: *Funding*
Mahiti Manthana	• IT for Change (NGO): *Conceptualization, design, monitoring* • Mahila Samakhya (National empowerment project): *Monitoring, local support, ICT training* • UNDP (International organization): *Policy advice, funding*
MEDA	• Pontifical Catholic University of Chile and University for Development: *Conceptualization, design, monitoring, research* • Zoltner Consulting Group and DataDyne (IT specialized nonprofit company): *Provision of ICT infrastructure* • Corporation for the Promotion of Production (Chilean government): *Funding* • National Society of Mining, National Association of Enterprises for Sanitary Services, the Chilean Commodity Exchange, National Commission on Irrigation: *Subject expertise*
RSITC	• Foundation for Agricultural Innovation (Chilean government): *Conceptualization, design, monitoring, funding* • Committee for Democratization of Information Technologies (NGO): *Monitoring, ICT training*

Table A11.2 continued

Table A11.2 continued

Project and Target Area	Main Partners and Role
Telesecundaria	• Chilean Ministry of Education: *Conceptualization, design, monitoring, funding* • World Bank: *Funding*
Text2Teach	• BridgeIT alliance (NPO): *Conceptualization, design, monitoring* • Ayala Foundation: *Monitoring, technical support, ICT training* • Department of Education (national and regional level): *Content development, monitoring, ICT training* • SEAMEO-Innotech (Intergovernmental organization): *Content development* • PMSI (IT company): *Provision of ICT/satellite infrastructure* • Nokia Philippines (IT company): *Funding, ICT equipment* • USAID (aid program): *Funding* • UNDP (International organization): *Funding*
Tradenet	• LIRNE Asia (Think Tank): *Conceptualization, design, monitoring, research* • DIALOG (IT company): *Provision of ICT equipment and tools, funding, field support* • GoviGnaanaSeva (NGO): *Conceptualization, design, local support*
The Mbire podcasting project	• HIVOS (NGO): *Conceptualization, design* • Practical Action (NGO): *Conceptualization, design* • Lower Guruve Development Association (NGO): *Monitoring, local support* • AGRITEX, Tsetse, Health, Vet Control (Agricultural Ministry agencies): *Content development*
Cocoa Link	• World Cocoa Foundation (NPO): *Conceptualization, design* • World Education (NPO): *Conceptualization, design, content development* • Ghana Cocoa Board (Government of Ghana): *Local support, content development* • CENCOSAD (NGO): *Training* • DreamOval (IT company): *Provision of ICT equipment* • The Hershey Company (Social corporate program): *Funding* • USAID (Aid program): *Funding*

Table A11.2 continued

Table A11.2 continued

Project and Target Area	Main Partners and Role
Réseau Femmes en Action	• Réseau Femmes en Action (NGO): *Monitoring* • The Technical Center for Agricultural and Rural Cooperation (CTA) at Wegenigen University (the Netherlands): *Conceptualization, design of ICT component* • Africa Rice (FAO agency): *Content development* • Radiodiffusion Television Burkina (National broadcaster): *Content development, IT equipment*
Farmerline	• Two graduates of Kwame Nkrumah University of Science and Technology (Founder of the company Farmerline): *Conceptualization, design, monitoring,* • Lecturer from Kwame Nkrumah University of Science and Technology: *Content development, design* • Fisheries commission (Government of Ghana): *Content development*

ICTRD: Indian Council for Technical Research and Development.
Source: Author.

Table A11.3
Participatory Approaches during the Preparation and Implementation of Successful iERD Projects

Project	Preparation Phase	Implementation Phase
e-Krishi	• e-Krishi field coordinators question farmers who articulate their needs • Face to face meetings with farmers are organized in 102 Panchayats (Indian type of village councils) and five municipalities: the project is presented and farmers can ask questions and make suggestions • Organization of 14 road shows, managed by heads of the e-Krishi centers who explain to farmers of their respective the project's objectives	• Creation of a District Implementation Office that involves district government representatives, agricultural representatives and local NGOs • On the village level, so called Bhoomi clubs meet on a monthly basis to follow-up the implementation of e-Krishi. The club is headed by the respective chief of the village and composed of village members that administrate also the local budget of each e-Krishi center. The Bhoomi clubs work directly with the project field coordinators who are the link to the district level management committee
E-Bario	• The data collection in view of a needs assessment was conducted in collaboration with local volunteers • Community discussions are organized during which inhabitants express concerns and opinions, and inhabitants are recruited for the management of the project	• Under the auspices of the community council of elders, the project is managed by a steering committee composed of members of the research team who launched the project, the local project coordinator (volunteer from the community) a telecenter manager (volunteer from the community), technical assistants and various appointed members of the community • A volunteer from the community is trained in order to implement and manage the ICT literacy training • Five community volunteers are in charge of managing the telecenter

Mahiti Manthana	• Organization of needs assessments in cooperation with women from the existing empowerment project and project staff • Organization of group discussions and experiences with future beneficiaries within their respective community • Consultation of local decision makers, particularly males, and NGOs	• The management committee of each information center is composed of local women and local empowerment NGOs and in charge of decisions related to fees, activity planning evaluation of previous activities and conflict resolution • In each information center, one young women of the community is in charge of information transfer and continuous data collection • Women are taught to be trainers and organize independently the video and radio based activities • Local government institutions and the district administration are mandated to provide content for the project activities
MEDA	• The local water user associations were responsible for leveraging data about farmers • Practical experiences were organized in order to test and improve the elaborated trade mechanism and familiarize farmers with the future functioning of the platform	• A local agricultural engineer was in charge of managing the office which provided farmers with access to the trade platform and helped them to use it • Local water user associations have major responsibilities within the online trade mechanism (content, transaction etc.)
RSTIC	• Farmer cooperatives were selected on a voluntary basis	• Each community telecenter is managed by an administration team and an IT team • ICT training imparted by trained local inhabitants

Table A11.3 continued

Table A11.3 continued

Project	Preparation Phase	Implementation Phase
Telesecundaria		• In every Telesecundaria school, five teachers, and one coordinating teacher are responsible for the implementation of the project • Participating schools are flexible in view of space and time management. • Local decision making and autonomous initiatives are encouraged, particularly through the Networks of Pedagogical Management that bring together Telesecundaria teachers on a municipal level • Local enterprises are involved in the educational activities of each school
Text2Teach	• Local Departments of Education (DepEds) act as local advocates and explain the projects objectives to Local Government Units (LGU), in order to convince them to finance the project in their area • The willingness to integrate the project in the local level is emphasized through the involvement of LGUs, DepEds, villages chiefs, and representatives of the parents association at each launch of new Text2Teach schools	• On the regional/municipal level, local government units and local Departments of Education take ownership of the project as they finance the project and impart training to teachers • Teachers are trained how to develop a sustainable plan for their respective school, involving public, private and civil society actors of the respective community • Teachers are encouraged to use their phones for communication with their peers, in order to create progressively a Text2Teach community and exchange best practices via SMS

Project		
Tradenet	• Local enumerators were in charge of conducting interviews with farmers in view of a needs assessment • Practical experiences were developed in order to test and develop further the designed trading platform	• The price information collectors are local inhabitants • So called *infomediaries*, recruited among local social entrepreneurs, discuss and explain the objective of the project and gain the trust of farmers
The Mbire podcasting project		• Local inhabitants act as Local Animators and manage the podcast platforms and community meetings • So-called lead farmers and the local animators organize training sessions
Cocoa Link	• Local inhabitants supports the NGO staff during the registration process of farmers • Community discussion are organized during which farmers learn about the project, can ask questions and make suggestions	• The project staff on the local level is recruited among community inhabitants
Réseau Femmes en Action		• Participants are requested to "recruit" women to listen to the broadcasts
Farmerline	• Local workshops consisting in service demonstrations, opinion gathering, market research farmer reaction are organized. Their reaction is analyzed and impacts on the implementation phase	• The technical coordinators are local inhabitants • During regular meetings with local Farming Associations the project identifies the current need of information

Source: Author.

Table A11.4
Training and Support Activities

Project	Training Characteristics	Informal Support and Assistance
e-Krishi	• Trained coordinators of e-Krishi centers train farmers basis how to use e-Krishi portal. The project could build on the ICT training imparted by a previous project	• The Indian Institute for Information Technologies and Management, one of the launching entities of the project, provides technological support to e-Krishi centers
e-Bario	• A local volunteer was trained by an IT company first and then trained during three months the teachers of the school which had been equipped with a computer laboratory. They learned ICT based teaching and learning methods, methods of distance learning, how to integrate ICT for administrative purposes, as well as technical aspects of ICT including troubleshooting and maintenance of the VSAT technologies • ICT courses were imparted by the locally trained volunteer to primary and secondary students on a continuous and compulsory basis with a focus on educational ICT use • Five local volunteers were trained in order to act as permanent ICT advisors within the community laboratory, where they imparted training adapted to local needs: Use of ICT for professional purposes and communication with peers as well as access to health and governmental information	• The telecenter manager arranges ad hoc training workshops with external experts in order to allow local inhabitants to acquire advanced skills in one specific IT area • One teacher per school is the focal point for ad hoc questions and advice. He in turn can address the steering committee for additional support

Mahiti Manthana	• Field staff of the project as well as members of local governments participated in training on general principles of radio use • Women of each information center participated on a voluntary basis in training on video and radio recording, editing and courses concerning scriptwriting and the choice of subjects. They received also training on the technical aspects and of the used ICT and associated software • Representatives of the community participated also in training, albeit they were not the main target group of the project: Two workshops on general awareness of ICT and their potential for social projects were organized for them	• The already existing initiative Mahila Samakhya supports locally each information center and provides content as well as technical advice • Local governments support the activities of the project and provide content information
MEDA	• Farmers enrolled in training sessions in a local office in order to learn how to conduct online water auctions and transactions	• Today the office is open on a daily basis and allows farmers without Internet access not only to conduct transactions but provides them also with advice on the functioning of the platform
RSITC	• A NGO specialized in ICT training (CDI) and implementing partner of the project trained the educators and IT specialists of each the Rural School of Information Technologies and Citizenship. Training focused on issues related to the digital gap and the construction of citizenship, social and educative practices and non-formal education. These local educators in turn trained all participants of the farmer cooperatives according to their needs and interests	• CDI visited the RSITCs every two months during the first year of the project during which the trainers could ask questions. Three workshops of were organized by CDI in order to improve the administrative and educative methodologies. If a new member joins the administration team he/she is imparted with the same training as the rest of the team. Also, the RSITC meet once a year other telecenters in order to exchange best practices

Table A11.4 continued

Table A11.4 *continued*

Project	Training Characteristics	Informal Support and Assistance
Telesecundaria	• Participating schools received administrative training and new Telesecundaria teachers are imparted in three workshops with practical content, pedagogical and technological training. Focus on inclusion of local resources	• The Association of Professional for Quality Education provides continuous technical assistance and training sessions concerning the integration of educational videos in the lesson. Teachers are can obtain support via the coordinating Telesecundaria teacher and self-help is encouraged through the Pedagogical Management Networks
Text2Teach	• Local education officers train teachers through group work and simulations how to integrate properly the educational videos in their lessons and use local resources in association with the videos. Staff from the Ayala Foundation imparts practical training that focuses on technical aspects and troubleshooting. The training lasts three days	• Teachers and schools can reach the online Text2Teach helpdesk via the project's mobile or call the regional Facebook groups tend to enhance the exchange of best practices and autonomous mutual help
Tradenet	• The so called *infomediaries* explained the functioning of the projects. However, as the majority of Philippines are familiar with the use of mobile phones even in rural areas no extensive training was needed. Only a small group of farmers participating in an action research experiment were provided with training	• Farmers can ask for additional help via their mobile phones, the online website or call the call center

Mbire podcasting project	• The five Community Animators and four local agents (project staff recruited among the community) receive technical training on podcasting devices in order to be able to organize the podcast sessions and train in turn the farmers	• Farmers can ask local staff agents and Community Animators for support
Cocoa Link	• Almost the half of all registered farmers and their families participate in training that focuses for example on literacy and numeracy, the application of new technologies to increase crop yields, or on basic business concepts	
Réseau Femmes en Action	• The target group can enroll training sessions on agricultural practices and information	• The personnel (around 20 persons) are permanently present on the field and can be approached for questions or advice
Farmerline	• Local inhabitants are trained to be technical coordinators	

Source: Author.

Table A11.5
Development and Enhancement Strategies of Successful iERD Projects

Project	Development Strategy
e-Krishi	• Evaluation through questionnaires by the implementing agency and UNDP focusing on amount of registered farmers and their characteristics; impact of the trade platform on farmer's business activities income and dependency on middlemen; overall dynamism of agricultural productions and trade • Continues development and update of services and information on the trade website: e.g., enlarged crop advisory, launch of a bilingual trade website, improvement of the farmer database • After the pilot phase, the project launched in nine other districts ICT of the state
E-Bario	• Continuous evaluation in parallel to the implementation of the pilot phase focusing on improvement of overall ICT skills and their impact on teaching and learning methods; reduction of the digital gap between rural and urban students; use of ICT infrastructure and skills for personal and professional activities; impact on the development of local economy • After the pilot phase second telecenter was build an online radio station was launched and associated activities designed; an ICT based science laboratory created • The community uses the project to organize yearly an international fair on rural telecenters • The project has equipped other public spaces of the community with VSAT technologies
Mahiti Manthana	• UNDP evaluation on: Amount and content of produced videos and radio programs; impact of ICT based activities on self-confidence and Impact on access of information on women's and their family's livelihood; impact on women's position in their respective community; Impact on communication between self-help groups; • Increased creation of local management committees and in parallel increased organization of ICT-based activities capable to reach more villages

Table A11.5 continued

Table A11.5 continued

Project	Development Strategy
	• Development of an associated project focusing on adolescent girls in cooperation with UNICEF
MEDA	• Evaluation of the project in parallel to the pilot phase on the amount of transactions; average prices; farmers' dependence on middlemen; farmer's characteristics; farmers' preferences on amount of SMS to receive; users perception on the relevance of the platform; • The project will enlarge the trading options on the website • The project will expand its services to other water basins in order to offer more farmers to trade the water of their respective catchment area
RSITC	• Evaluation of ICT skills and use of ICT for professional and personal purposes before and after the ICT course cycle • A modified version of the pilot project was launched in six further regions of the country
Telesecundaria	• After 2 years of implementation, the profile of Telesecundaria students were analyzed by the national project team in order to assess if the project was actually capable to attract its target group (e.g., dropout students) • Evaluation by the national project team of Telesecundaria students achievements in the SABER assessment in order to evaluate the academic impact of Telesecundaria • Conduction of a study focusing on the degree of integration of Telesecundaria schools in their rural communities, including consultations to include Telesecundaria teachers observations and opinions in the assessment • After 7 years of implementation MoE started an innovation process of the ICT material and an alignment process of the content in order to adapt the latter to the national curriculum
Text2Teach	• After each phase, a third-party evaluation was conducted by, respectively, the National Institute for Science and Mathematics Educational Development, the Demographic Research and Development Foundation and a team of external consultants. Evaluations focused on academic achievements, student's profile, teachers' feedback on

Table A11.5 continued

Table A11.5 continued

Project	Development Strategy
	workload and cooperation with peers as well as on impact on the relationship between schools and local decision makers • In 2005, 2008, and 2011, the distributed ICT material was replaced by more innovative technologies and adaptation of learning material to the national curriculum • Continuous expansion of the project to new Text2Teach schools: After the first phase, 80 schools were participating in the project, the target amount of schools to participate by 2014 is 850
Tradenet	• Conduction of an interim and final assessment in 2010 focusing on impact of the platform on farmer's income, their behavior and decision making, the interaction with other stakeholders of the agricultural value chain, agricultural skills, amount of registered farmers • Improvement of the data collection system in 2010 • Expansion of information of product prices at local fares after some months of implementation • Expansion to other markets to be realized soon
The Mbire podcasting project	• Conduction of an final assessment after the pilot phase • Expansion of the project to district of Bindura and further 50,000 smallholders in Mangwe • Bulilima • Planned extension to the project to three more districts • Introduction of SMS based agricultural information service after the pilot phase: lead farmers receive information on their mobile phones and transfer it to other farmers
Cocoa Link	• Currently: Expansion to the project to other regions • Development of voice message system for illiterate farmers who cannot read SMS • Development of agricultural videos integrated in farmer training on good practices and during community sessions: farmers are informed via SMS about these events
Réseau Femmes en Action	• Expansion of beneficiaries and activities planned

Table A11.5 continued

Table A11.5 continued

Project	Development Strategy
Farmerline	• The technical platform is continuously enhanced • The project will offer a subscription system that is adapted to new subscribers, experienced subscribers and expert subscribers • It is planned to collaborate with local farmer association for the advertising of the project and to use of local representatives to recruit users

Source: Author.

Bibliography

Badsar, Mohammad, Bahaman, Abu Samah, Musa, Abu Hassan, Osman, Nizam Bin, & Shaffri, Hayrol Azril Mohd. (2011). Social Sustainability of Information and Communication Technology (ICT) Telecentres in Rural Communities in Malaysia. *Australian Journal of Basic and Applied Sciences*, 5(12): 2929–2938.

Balaji, V., Meera S.N., & Dixit, S. (2007). ICT-enabled Knowledge Sharing in Support of Extension: Addressing the Agrarian Challenges of the Developing World Threatened by Climate Change, with a Case Study of India. *SATe Journal*, 4(1): 18.

Ballantyne, P. (2002). Collecting and Propagating Local Development Content. Synthesis and Conclusions. Retrieved from www.iicd.org/.../collecting-and-propagating-local-development-content-synthesis-and-conclusions/report7. pdf (accessed March 12, 2013).

Chapman, R., & Slaymaker, T. (2002). ICT and Rural Development: Review of the Literature, Current Interventions and Opportunities for Action. Working Paper 192. London: Overseas Development Institute.

Craig, G., Derounian J., & Garbutt, R. (2005). Training for Rural Community Activists. Retrieved from .http://www.iacdglobal.org/files/rpt190406RuralTrainingForCommunityDevelopmentActivists.pdf (accessed March 13, 2013).

De Silva, H. (2008). Scoping Study: ICT and Rural Livelihoods South Asia Component. ICT for Rural Livelihoods Research Scoping Report. New Delhi: International Development Research Center.

FAO. (2012). Mobile Technologies for Food Security, Agriculture and Rural Development: Role of the Public Sector. Retrieved from http://www.fao.org/docrep/017/i3074e/i3074e.pdf (accessed March 12, 2013).

Farr, P., & Papandrea, P. (2006). Sustainability of Community Online Access Centres. *Governance of Communication Networks* (pp. 165–185). Heidelberg: Springer.

Garforth, C., Angell, B., Archer, J., & Green, K. (2003). Improving Farmers' Access to Advice on Land Management: Lessons from Case Studies in Developed Countries. Network Paper Nr. 125, p. 18. London: Agricultural Research and Extension Network, Overseas Development Institute.

Glendenning, C., & Ficarelli P. (2011). Information Development, Content Development and Management Processes of ICT Initiatives in Indian Agriculture. Retrieved from http://idv.sagepub.com/content/27/4/301 (accessed March 12, 2013).

Higgins, R., & Izushi, H. (2003). The Digital Divide and ICT Learning in Rural Communities: Examples of Good Practice Service Delivery. *Local Economy*, 17(2):111–122.

Inter-American Institute for Cooperation on Agriculture (IICA). (2009). National Experiences for the Improvement of Agriculture and Rural Life.. San José: Inter-American Institute for Cooperation on Agriculture.

Kumar, R., & Best, M. (2006). Social Impact and Diffusion of Telecenter Use: A Study from the Sustainable Access in Rural India Project. *The Journal of Community Informatics*, 2(3). Retrieved from http://ci-journal.net/index.php/ciej/article/view/328/268 (accessed March 4, 2014).

Pillay H., & Hearn G. (2009). Public-Private Partnerships in ICT for Education. In Shahid Akhtar & Patricia Arinto (Eds.). *Digital Review of Asia Pacific* (pp. 77–87). New Delhi: SAGE.

Roman, R., & Colle, R. (2003). Content Creation for ICT Development Projects: Integrating Normative Approaches and Community Demand. *Information Technology for Development*, 10: 85–94.

UNESCAP. (2009). Best Practices of Telecentre/Knowledge Networking in India. Retrieved from http://www.unescap.org/idd/events/2009_RW-AP%20 Knowledge-hubs/Presentation%20in%20PDF/India-Shailendra-Presentation.pdf (accessed March 12, 2013).

University of Berkeley. (2005). Definitions, Goals and Principles of Participatory Action Research. Retrieved from http://www.cnr.berkeley.edu/community_forestry/Fellowships/parinfo/PAR%20Definitions.pdf (accessed March 13, 2013).

12

e-Bario: Telecenters for Remote and Rural Communities (Malaysia)

Eilean von Lautz-Cauzanet

Overview

The e-Bario project, launched by a research team of the University Malaysia Sarawak, seeks to develop remote rural areas and tackle the issues related to their isolation. For this purpose, a community telecenter and computer laboratories were established in the community of Bario, and information and communication technology (ICT) training imparted to the rural population. The project has increased the overall quality of life, stimulated the local economy and empowered the rural community. These achievements as well as the highly inclusive and participatory approach adopted throughout the planning, and implementation phases have contributed to e-Bario's international popularity and therefore replicated in other countries.

Project Background

Malaysia, upper-middle income and multisector economy, seeks to become a fully developed nation with an emphasis on knowledge-based economy by the year 2020. In the late 1990s, the country started to show increasing interest in the potential of ICT for national development and claimed that one of its objectives was the presence of a computer with Internet connection in every Malaysian household. However, in 1999 around 39% of the total population lived in rural areas and faced major difficulties to access modern ICT or even basic infrastructures.[1] In this context, the University Malaysia Sarawak (UNIMAS) decided in 1999 to launch a pilot project, which aimed to deliver equal access to ICT to remote and marginalized populations through the construction of a community telecenter and computer laboratories with Internet access.

The pilot project took place in Bario, an extremely isolated and remote district in the state of Sarawak, where a majority of communities are unserved by road and have almost nonexistent telecommunications services. The district of Bario is composed of 12 communities with a population of around 1000 people, a majority of them belongs to the indigenous tribe of Kelabits. As the Bario district, due to its significant lack of infrastructures, rurality, and remoteness, was very much concerned by the *digital gap*, it was selected by UNIMAS in order to confront the pilot project to a particularly challenging environment.

Impact of Existing Similar Projects

The pilot project was inspired by various other projects that had been developed in order to provide rural communities with ICT components or Internet access. Initiatives such as the project *Village Information Shops* developed by MS Swaminathan Research Center (MSSRF) in India, or the *Digital Town Centers* in Costa Rica inspired and encouraged UNIMAS to conduct their own project.

---

[1] The annual growth of the rural population has been decreasing throughout the last decade. In 2011, around 27% of the population lived in rural areas (World Bank).

The Participatory Action Research
The PAR Model argues for close cooperation with local stakeholders and inhabitants in order to ensure the flow of information, to empower the local community to control their development and create a feeling of responsibility (Songan and Yeo, 2006). Empowerment is considered as crucial for the effective management and sustainability of the telecenter. Through the creation of a bond of trust with the community, their aspirations, hopes and expectation of ICT use can be efficiently detected. It also allows identifying local leaders that represent the community's aspiration and have the capacity to mobilize local resources. These "vision carriers" are essential for the sustainability of the project. This approach, according to Anderson, comes along with high importance of ICT awareness strategies and training in order to ensure that the new infrastructure will be successfully integrated into the community and not be rejected by its inhabitants because of lacking comprehension.

Planning Process

Within the University of Malaysia Sarawak, a research team composed of members from different faculties, among which one team member was originally from Bario, had to determine the approach of the planning and implementation process.[2] As there was not a similar project in Malaysia or abroad, the choice of the project approach appeared to be as decisive as challenging. Finally, the research time decided to adopt the Participatory Action Research (PAR) model for the pilot project. This approach, initially developed in the late 1940s by Lewin at the Massachusetts Institute of Technology, has since been further developed by various researchers, for example, Paulo Freire. Here, the researchers of UNIMAS based themselves on experiences from Anderson, who previously analyzed the potential of the PAR model for the construction of telecenters in rural areas. More concretely, adopting this model to a telecenter project means to take into consideration the socioeconomic and political context of the community in which a telecenter will be launched, and to put the main focus on future beneficiaries, not solely on the technology they will use.

[2] Faculty of Information Technology; the Faculty of Cognitive Science and Human Development; the Faculty of Information Technology, the Faculty of Science, the Faculty of Education and the Faculty of Engineering.

Elaboration of an Implementation Framework

Once the theoretical approach had been defined, the planning process moved further to the creation of an implementation framework. This framework is composed of three phases and seven steps, in which the PAR approach is clearly reflected.

The first phase consists in the preparation phase and starts with a feasibility and needs assessment as well the elaboration of baseline studies in order to determine whether the project will meet the requirements and detect the community's major needs. These assessments and studies have to be conducted in close cooperation between the project team and the rural inhabitants. The goal of this participatory assessment is to guarantee the realistic approach of local needs and engage the community from the beginning of the project (see Figure 12.1).

The second step of the preparation phase consists in the mobilization of the community. For this purpose, community discussions must be organized for rural inhabitants involved in organizational entities. At this stage, the decision concerning the concrete objectives and activities

Figure 12.1
Implementation Framework

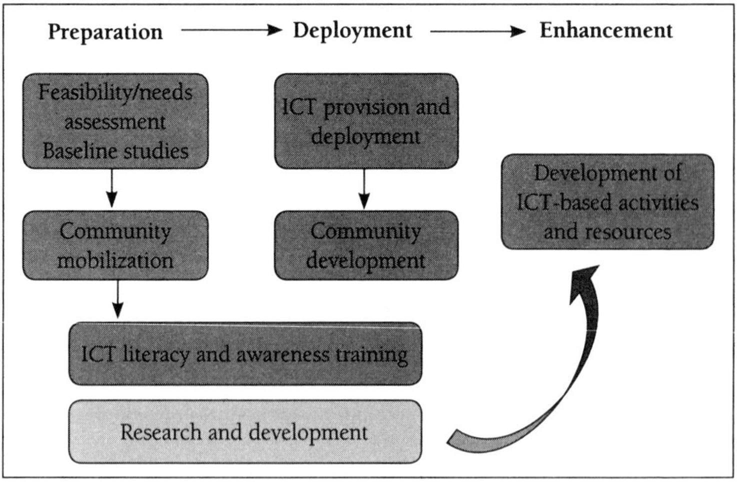

Source: Author.

of the telecenter and computer laboratories should be made. The preparation phase ends with the start of ICT literacy and awareness training for the respective beneficiaries of the IT infrastructure. This ICT training starts right after the installation of the IT infrastructure and continues throughout the implementation of the project. During the phase of deployment, ICT are used in the computer laboratory and the community telecenter and activities launched that contribute to an increasing inclusion and development of the community.

Finally, the project is supposed to be progressively owned and managed by the local community without major support from the UNIMAS research team. During this phase of enhancement, new ICT-based activities and resources are supposed to be developed. This phase seeks also to develop sustainability strategies for the new infrastructures and their management.

During the whole pilot phase of the implementation process, researchers are in charge of conducting impact studies and detect areas in which further development should or can be stimulated. This step shall contribute to the enhancement phase and its objectives.

Definition of Objectives

Based on this implementation framework, the research team defined the objectives the project should meet:

1. Increase the rural community's ability to communicate with the rest of the world as well as strengthen and promote interaction within the community.
2. Increase the access to information on areas such as education, health, agricultural practices, government, as well entertainment and cultural activities.
3. Online promotion of the local culture of the community and its different villages; development of light industries, for example, tourism.
4. Identification of new opportunities regarding the use of ICT for rural community development; development of action-oriented ICT strategies in accordance with these findings.

IT Infrastructure

In terms of infrastructure, it was decided to set up a computer laboratory in a school that enjoyed a daytime electricity supply and had five computers. Subsequently, a community telecenter was launched. The setting up of a computer laboratory was supposed to serve as training location for those who would manage and use then to serve as the community telecenter. In view of equipping these facilities with an Internet connection, the research team decided to install solar-powered very small aperture terminals (VSAT). They allow establishing high-speed satellite connection and are particularly adapted to isolated areas such as Bario, which are also too distant from fiber backbones and their terrain is too rough for line of sight required between terrestrial microwave antennas.

Organizational Structures and Responsibilities

In light of a participatory approach and action, it was decided to institutionalize the involvement of local community. The following organizations and roles were created:

- The *steering committee* is composed of the UNIMAS research team, members, the project coordinator, a telecenter manager, technical assistants, and various appointed members of the community. Under the auspices of the Council of Elders and supported by the research team, it manages and coordinates the project: It is in charge of setting the directions, guidelines, and strategies of the telecenter and the computer laboratory. In addition, it develops policies and procedures related to the usage of the IT facilities and appoint the management committee.
- The *management committee* is led by a coordinator who oversees the day-to-day operations of the telecenter in order to achieve the goals set by the steering committee.
- The *project coordinator* is the local coordinator in Bario. They are also in charge of implementing the IT literacy training at the secondary school.
- The *telecenter manager* is an IT literate person who helps users in the telecenter, manages IT courses. They are supported by technical assistants.

- *The computer teacher* is in charge of supervising the activities in the computer laboratory during dedicated free access hours.

The objective of this role distribution was to diminish reluctance toward the projects and create willingness to take ownership of the project, which would contribute to the sustainability of the project.

Implementation Process

In the following sections, the actors of the implementation process as well as the difficulties they faced throughout this process will be presented. The different steps of the implementation are then exposed.

Actors of the Implementation Process

1. *University Malaysia Sarawak (UNIMAS)*: At the beginning of the project, the research group from the UNIMAS was composed of seven members. The team was in charge of following the implementation process according to the previously designed framework. They were in charge of the feasibility and baseline studies and had to report back to the funding organization, as well as to media in general.

   Difficulties faced: Due to teaching duties and other activities related to their position as academics, the research team could work only part time on the project, for example, weekends, breaks between semesters, or holidays. Therefore, the project activity was not always regular and continuous. The research team also had to face logistical challenges related to Bario's isolation and lack of transportation. This created difficulties during the transfer of the equipment to Bario, as well as to general communication problems with the community at the beginning of the project.

2. *Community steering committee*: This large committee is in charge of strategic planning (see "Organizational Structures and Responsibilities")

3. *Management committee*: This committee, composed of members of the research team, oversees the daily activities in the telecenter (see "Organizational Structures and Responsibilities")

Difficulties faced: During the initial ICT training of the community, it appeared that the local inhabitants had difficulty in understanding the English manuals. These had to be translated to the national language Bahasa Malaysia.[3]

4. *COMPUSERV*: This local enterprise from Kuching developed the IT literacy program and imparted initial training to the project coordinator.

5. *Project coordinator*: Trained by COMPUSERV, the project coordinator implements the IT literacy courses in the computer laboratory.

6. *Computer teacher*: The computer teacher supervises the ICT-based learning activities and is the focal point for students who wish the provided ICT material. They are also the focal point for teachers who wish to use ICT-based teaching methodologies.

    Difficulties faced: During the implementation of the ICT-based learning activities, the project assessed the effectiveness of language software. Results showed that this software hindered more the learning process than supporting it and the software was changed.

7. The *school principal* supervises the advancement and activities of the computer laboratory and works in close cooperation with the steering committee.

Participatory Data Gathering and Community Mobilization

As decided during the planning of the project, the research team started to gather data related to the community and elaborated baseline studies concerning the socioeconomic situation of Bario as well as attitudes and awareness toward ICT. More concretely, the research team, together with local voluntary inhabitants, conducted surveys in 140 out of 242 household in Bario in September and October 1999. The collected data for these baseline studies were supposed to answer important questions in view of the actual implementation of the future ICT infrastructures, for example:

---

[3] Official language in Malaysia.

- Which are the most effective technology options for this particular geographical, social, and cultural environment?
- Which kind of business models can foster smart partnerships between public and private entities and the rural community, so that future ICT-based infrastructures and activities are implemented with realistic objectives and supported by economically viable investments?
- How can the rural community be encouraged to participate actively in the process of community relevant information and knowledge production?
- How can modern ICT learning material be efficiently adapted to a rural and remote population with low levels of education?
- How should telecenter services be me marketed in these rural and remote locations and what are the expected effects of their introduction?

In order to gather information that would permit to answer these questions, the baseline study focused on the following areas:

- Profile of the respondent (e.g., age, sex, ethnic group, religion, occupation, education)
- Family background (e.g., average income, expenditure, ages, where the children work)
- Land ownership
- Socioeconomic activities (e.g., source of income and type of activity)
- Marketing facilities
- Facilities and amenities (e.g., existence of electricity supply, existence of TV or telephone)
- Health (e.g., sanitary infrastructure, source of drinking water, access to medical treatments)
- Patterns of communication (e.g., channel and source of information, type of information the respondent would like to receive)
- Knowledge about ICT (e.g., possession and use of computers and Internet, purpose of use)
- Role and decision making (e.g., role within the community)

The research revealed that a majority of the local population is composed of farmers who depend on rice agriculture and do not have 24 hour electricity supply: They rely on personally owned generators, gravity-feed water system, and rain water. None of the inhabitants reported to have access to public telephone or Internet connection, no one had their own telephone or Internet connection. However, around 79% of the households reported to have their own radio and 30% a television.

The surveys revealed further that the community of Bario considered one of their most important objective is the possibility to communicate with their family as well as have better access to information. Discussions with the research team made them realize further that the use of new technologies could also improve their livelihood through the stimulation of the local industry. Finally, 12 teachers were selected for a study assessing their attitude and anxiety levels toward the use of IT. The study revealed that only a minority was using the already existing four computers at their school. Teachers reported that this was, among others, due to a high student–teacher–computer ratio and inadequate computers and software for teaching. However, a majority of them were excited to be involved in a computer laboratory project and expected major benefits both for teaching and learning practices.

These conclusions were taken into consideration the question on which services and activities the computer laboratory and community telecenter should focus.

Launching of the Computer Laboratory

In May 2000, a computer laboratory with 16 computers and printers was set up at the secondary school, and another with 10 computers and printers at a primary school. Various peripherals as well as software were progressively installed. During the first two months, there were no Internet connection available, but in September the research team had finalized the negotiations with Telecom Malaysia, which agreed to provide the computer laboratory with Internet access and telephone lines. In the meantime, COMPUSERV, in charge of developing an IT literacy program, had trained a volunteer from the community—the new project coordinator—to implement the IT literacy training at the secondary school. Right after the installation of Internet teachers and students enrolled in this IT literacy training. The training schedule started first with the teachers, who had received a three-month intensive training.

Afterwards, around 148 students from secondary schools and primary school (standard 5 and 6) in Bario started their training. For this purpose, they were divided into groups of 10 persons who met every Monday from 2 pm to 5 pm (secondary school students) and Saturdays from 8 am to 10 am (primary school students). In addition to this IT literacy training, all students had access to the computer laboratory under the supervision of the computer teacher. The training included word processing, keyboard usage, e-mailing, browsing the web, and the management of technologies, including trouble shooting. The training process was conducted in association with other agencies like SHELL, OSEAN, University of Cambridge, and Engineers without Borders UK. However, training sessions were not limited to computing technologies, they included the maintenance of renewable energy supply and the VSATs system, including its network and configuration.

It was quickly decided by the local authorities that ICT and computer courses had to be compulsory for all students, particularly because of the need to consider ICT training as ongoing process. Concretely, the following activities were initiated through the computer laboratory:

- *IT Literacy Training.* Students and teacher learn basic and advanced use of computers and Internet services.
- *ICT-based Teaching and Learning Methodologies.* A significant amount of subjects within the curriculum are taught through the use of computers and educational software, both for collective and individual exercises, for example, PowerPoint presentations, mathematical and language software.
- *Distance and Network Learning.* Students enroll and access courses from institutions abroad and obtain additional certifications or enroll in interactive language courses from distant institutions.
- *School Administration and Communication.* Via email and telephone, teachers communicate with their peers and exchange best practices. Computers are used for internal management purposes, for example, the creation of schedules and timetables.

Community Telecenters: From an Installed to an Operational Status

The creation of the computer laboratory served as preparing step of the core part of the project, the community telecenter. In order to prepare the community for the use of the telecenter, a research assistant trained the community at the computer laboratory for their future use of the telecenter. For this purpose, the manual used during the IT literacy program at the secondary school was adapted and translated into Bahasa Malaysia. During these training activities, five volunteer inhabitants were identified as IT trainers in order to support future training activities. In parallel to these IT courses held in the computer laboratory, the creation and preparation of the community telecenter began:

Firstly, the location was chosen: The steering committee decided to set up the telecenter nearby the shops as these were frequently visited. Volunteers willing to act as telecenter manager or assistant in charge of maintaining and managing the telecenters were recruited, and the telecenters equipped with power supply, telephone booths, and Internet connection via four VSAT dishes, computers, printers, a copy and a fax machine. The telecenter started, progressively, to be used by the community for the following services and activities.

- Telephone
- E-mail services
- Photocopying, scanning, printing
- Internet browsing (in view of finding specific information, e.g., for business)
- Word processing (e.g., for application letters)
- Desktop publishing (e.g., for newsletters, flyers, business cards)
- Creation of brochures and logos
- Graphic and web design
- Binding, laminating, photocopying (of school materials, professional materials, booklets)
- Video conferencing
- IT courses (ongoing)

A telecenter manger is in charge of registering and introducing new users to the telecenters and its equipment. He/she arranges tutorial assistance when needed and helps those who wish to enroll in distance courses. The telecenter manager also arranges training in various ICT-related areas via local ICT trainers or IT professional who are hired for this purpose (e.g., for advanced graphic design courses).

Distribution of Funds during the Pilot Project

The pilot project was funded by an external donor (IDRC) and a national grant: The International Development Research Center (IDRC) of the Canadian government funded the project with RM 620,000 (around USD 202,429) and the Malaysian government, under the Demonstrator Application Grant Scheme, granted the project with additional RM 200,000 (around USD 65,300).

The majority of the funds were disbursed for the installation of the solar panels and the computer equipment. VSAT equipment and ICT literacy components were the second largest investment. Finally, the transportation of the materials and equipments that could be undertaken only via charter flights accounted a tenth of the funds. Local salaries and the allowances for the research team and their travel to Bario accounted also for almost 10% of the budget (Figure 12.2).

Supervision Process

There is a clear communication channel between different entities of the project: The telecenter manager is in constant contact with the steering committee. Every month, they provide written reports to the committee concerning usage, activities, and achievements of the telecenter. At the school laboratory level, regular reports provided by the school principal inform the steering committee about implemented and new activities. The UNIMAS research team regularly visits the project.

The management committee supervises the daily activities in the telecenter and is also in regular contact with the telecenter manager. Moreover, the project manager on the field supervises the adequate spending of the resources and reports back to the steering committee and

Figure 12.2
Distribution of Funds (Year 2000–2003)

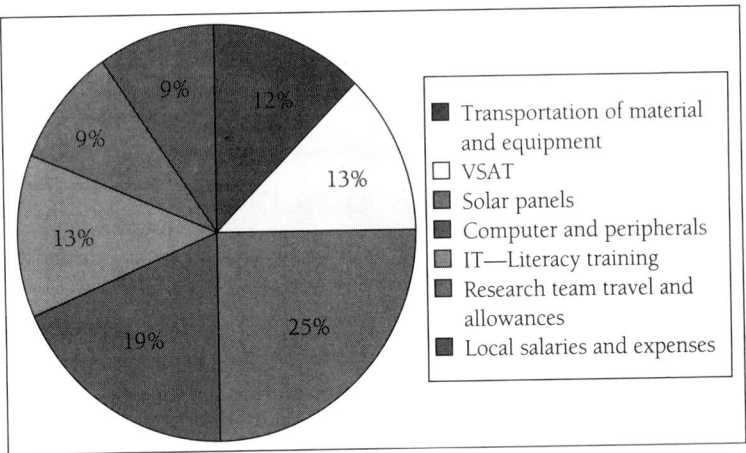

Source: Data from Dr Alvin W. Leo and his team.

the research team. Finally, the research team had to report back to the funding agencies and report for which purposes the funds were spent.

Achievement and Impact

From March 2001 to June 2002, the research team analyzed the evolution of the project in view of assessing its impact on the community of Bario. The evaluation conducted by UNIMAS revealed that the pilot project had a significant and positive impact on the socioeconomic environment in the following areas.

Improvement of Skills and Knowledge

All lodger owners achieved to be fully computer literate after having participated in IT courses provided at the telecenter. They reported to use their acquired skills to communicate via email with potential clients and manage reservations via the Internet. Teachers reported that thanks to the Internet connection, it could improve their teaching practices as they had access to innovative materials and could exchange with their colleagues in other departments. On the students' side, the digital gap between them and their peers in urban areas could be eliminated or at least reduced, thanks to the compulsory ICT and Internet courses. The principal of the secondary school reported further that thanks to the Internet connection, it had finally been fully integrated in school-related communications: for example, the principal reported that departmental school meetings are not missed anymore as it used to happen earlier due to delayed postal delivery.

Development of the Local Economy

The presence of telecenters and the new acquired ICT skills of the community had an important impact on the local economy: A website of the community was created (e-bario.com) in order to promote tourism. The main coordinator, who took part in a web design course at the telecenter, supervised the development of the website. The members of the steering committee contributed to different contents of the website and quickly, more than 200 visitors per month consulted the website. Another website (kelabit.org) was created that focuses on organizing trekking tours, bookings can be done via the website. Thanks to these portals and the fact that the e-Bario project contributed in general to the popularity of the community and the tourist industry has also grown: Lodges and tourist accommodations have increased from three before the start of the project to 20 after the pilot phase. Lodgers reported to receive more than 50 enquiries per year. Furthermore, since October 1, 2003, there are two flights per day from and to Bario instead of only one flight. The local community benefits directly from this improved accessibility. For example, some inhabitants reported that thanks to this indirect consequence of the project, they are even able to easily access important infrastructures as hospitals or doctors (Figure 12.3).

The report also revealed that another impact of the presence of computer laboratory and the telecenters was creation of incentives for young people to stay in their community instead of moving to urban areas in order to seek employment. Thanks to increased demand in tourism

Figure 12.3
Total Visitors Coming to Bario According to the Lodgers' Visitor Book from 1997 to 2006

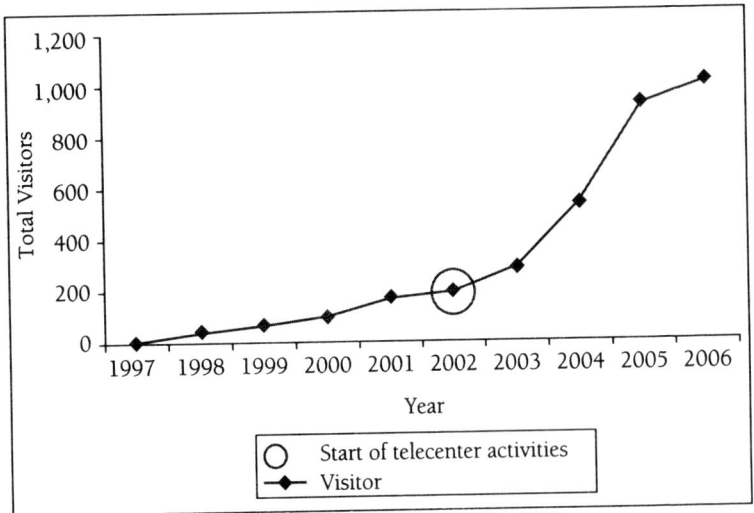

Source: Data from Dr Alvin W. Leo and his team.

industry, they can now find employment opportunities in this area, for example, work as tourist guides or in hotels.

Furthermore, the report mentions that thanks to the telecenter, inhabitants of the community felt more connected to the rest of the country and could be informed in time, for example, when a family member had fallen ill.

Financial Sustainability

The project achieved to be financially sustainable to cover technical support costs, salaries, connection costs, and unforeseen expenses through leasing the telecenters for workshops, information hubs etc. Also, each student pays a small fee (RM 40, around 13 USD) per year in order to have access to the computer lab. One could also pay with the "Bario Rice," local rice which is usually exported. Furthermore, an IT club (Kelab IT) has been created: The club seeks to promote ICT awareness and offers IT training sessions, against a small fee or Bario Rice. These fees also contribute to cover the costs of the whole e-Bario project.

Awards

The achievements of the project have been acknowledged by various awards:

- Silver Medal, Internal UNIMAS R&D Expo 2012, Indigenous Technological Innovation in Malaysia: Reducing Vulnerability and Marginalization among Malaysia's Indigenous Peoples (2012)
- Gold Medal of the Commonwealth Association of Public Administration and Management (CAPAM) International Innovations Awards in Sydney (2006)
- Mondialogo Award—Berlin (2005)
- eAsia Award—Taipei (2004)
- Anugerah Perdana Teknologi Maklumat Kuala Lumpur (2003)
- Industry Innovators Award for Systems Development & Applications from the Society of Satellite Professionals International—Washington, DC (2002)
- Award for one of the Top Seven Intelligent Communities by the World Teleport Association—New York (2001)

Post-pilot Project Phase

In 2004, the research team from UNIMAS had officially transferred the ICT equipment to the management entities of the project on the local level, including the IT literacy training components to the local directorate of education. This was an important step toward the autonomous management of e-Bario by its rural inhabitants.

Today, the community is still highly involved in the maintenance of the project, for example, maintenance activities and providing resources, and an agenda for the development of ICT-based activities and information delivery has been developed. This agenda has led to various new initiatives: for example, a second community telecenter has been launched and equipped with 10 computers, printers, and copy and fax machines. It is often used for activities related to the local economy, such as preparation of lodgers meetings, creation of agendas, or minutes of the meeting. Furthermore, a joint project between e-Bario and the Institute of Social Informatics and Technology Innovation of the University Malaysia Sarawak, called *e-Bario Innovation Network Village*, has been initiated. It operates as a living laboratory and incubator to conceive, implement, test, develop, and commercialize innovative applications of ICT and renewable sources of energy. Examples of initiatives are the new community radio and aerial photography technologies for community mapping (Figure 12.4).

The community also organizes regularly the *e-Bario Knowledge Fair*: This conference showcases the use of ICT for rural development and is conducted in conjunction with the local community, bringing together researchers, practitioners, and policy makers with the residents of Bario and the wider Kelabit ethnic community (Universiti Malaysia Sarawak, 2001).

Finally, since the end of the pilot phase, three more VSATs have been installed in the district: one for the clinic and immigration department and their services, and the second one at the airport in order to facilitate airline bookings and the third one (Celcom) in order to enable mobile telephony coverage.

Figure 12.4
The New Community Radio

Source: www.ebario.com

Impact on Policies and Projects

The e-Bario project has had not only a positive impact on the local community, it also influenced national policies and projects in Malaysia and abroad. The project had contributed to increased awareness of the potential that ICT could have for rural development, particularly for isolated communities that did not have access to other forms of infrastructure. The government of Malaysia has since encouraged the expansion of the project to other rural locations in and outside of Sarawak. The project e-Bedian, for example, builds on the e-Bario experience (Institute of Social Informatics and Technological Innovations, 2012). Besides, the following impacts are related to the implementation of e-Bario and its components:

- Since 2002, the Malaysian Telekom Agency has used the VSAT infrastructure to connect over 400 schools to the Internet
- The Demonstrator Application Grant Scheme changed its funding and evaluation procedures in support projects more efficiently
- Other projects in Malaysia have replicated the e-Bario model in Malaysia (e-Bedian, e-Lamai)
- The projects *PANGAEA* and *J3* were initiated after the success of e-Bario and focus on rural locations in Ecuador, Thailand, and Micronesia
- In 2009, after the application from e-Bario to broadcast their own radio, the government released a new rule that permits all communities to receive a license for radio broadcasting

Conclusion

The e-Bario project achieved to integrate ICT infrastructures and services, as well as provided ICT training to students and inhabitants of an extremely remote area in Malaysia. This project has not only increased the population's access to information and services and also improved the quality of education. The e-Bario has also stimulated the local economy and impacted positively on the livelihoods of the rural inhabitants.

Today, e-Bario is an example of how a project can successfully be trans-form from a top–down initiative to a project fully owned by the local community.

This success is based on the combination of various factors, which would not have been effective if applied in an isolated way.

Firstly, the planning of the pilot project is strikingly inclusive and characterized by a significant effort to gain the community's trust, to adapt the project to the population needs, and to include these in the design of the whole project. Indeed, the conduction of baseline surveys and needs assessment surveys, associated with community discussions in order to disseminate the idea of the project and familiarize future users with e-Bari, can be considered a foundation for the subsequent smooth implementation of e-Bario. This inclusive approach is also highly visible during the implementation of the project itself. The decision to *institu-tionalize* community ownership through the integration of community members at each stage of the management levels has created a proactive attitude among users of e-Bario and enhanced the project's efficiency, taking continuously into consideration their needs, opinions, and ideas.

Another factor of success lies in organizing training, adapted to the respective user groups (e.g., translation of guides into Bahasa) that accompanied the launch of the computer laboratory and the telecenter. This training made sure that each member of the community would actually be able to get the best possible benefit from using these ICT. The fact that this ICT training and the services offered by both instal-lations were tailored to rural needs, allowed the community to develop capacities and activities that in the end improved not only their IT skills, but also had a major impact on their livelihood.

Furthermore, the fact that e-Bario started as an experimental research project explains the continuous assessment and evaluation of the project. This effort to analyze and support best practices allowed in the end to enhance and further adapt the project to the needs of the rural commu-nity, for example, launching a rural radio station in addition to the first ICT installations. This is a crucial element given that the sustainability of a project depends also on its capacity to adapt to changes and evolve.

The project has proven its replicability both in Malaysia and abroad. The fact that e-Bario had chosen a "worst-case scenario" both in view of the selected location (lack of transportation, electricity and communication infrastructures) and the target group (low level of education, initial reluctance, and mistrust) appears to be an important guarantee factor that this project could actually be replicated in many rural areas of developing countries facing similar challenges.

Bibliography

Defense Technical Information Center. (2004). A Comparison on the Implementation Approaches for the e-Bario and e-Bedian Projects. Retrieved from http://www.dtic.mil/cgi-bin/GetTRDoc?AD=ADA438157 (accessed December 17, 2012).

Institute of Social Informatics and Technological Innovations (ISITI). (2012). Lesson's Learnt from e-Bario and e-Bedian Implementation. Retrieved from http://www.isiti.unimas.my/images/pdf_scholar/Lessons%20Learnt%20 from%20E%20Bario%20and%20E%20Bedian%20Projects.pdf (accessed December 17, 2012).

Songan, P., & Yeo, A. (2006). *Guidebook on Developing Community e-Centers in Rural areas: Based on the Malaysian Experience.* New York: United Nations Economic and Social Commission for Asia and the Pacific.

Universiti Malaysia Sarawak (UNIMAS). (2001). Challenges and Opportunities in Introducing Information and Communication Technologies to the Kelabit Community of North Central Borneo. Retrieved from http://www.unimas.my/ebario/paperwork2.html (accessed November 20, 2012).

Important Websites

http://www.unimas.my/ebario/Main_index.htm
http://ebario.com/
http://www.pemandu.gov.my/

13

e-Krishi: The Online Platform for Small Farmers (India)

Eilean von Lautz-Cauzanet

Overview

The e-agriculture project e-Krishi[1] was launched in 2006 by the IT State Mission Kerala in cooperation with the Kerala Agricultural Department and the National Institute for Smart Government. This community-inclusive and award-winning project supports small farmers through an Internet platform that provides them with agricultural information and allows them to conduct online transactions. Since the launch of the project, over 10,000 farmers have registered on the website. Through e-Krishi they could increase the quality of their products and obtain fair prices.

[1] *Krishi* means agriculture in Hindi.

Project Background

India is the world's largest democracy and fourth-largest economy in purchasing power parity terms. According to the World Bank the country is an agricultural powerhouse, producing, for example, the world largest amount of milk, pulses, and spices. Even though the growth of rural population is decreasing, nearly three-quarters of India's families still depend on rural incomes (2011 National Census; World Bank, 2012). In the district Malappuram, which is located in Kerala, region of the pilot project presented here, a majority of the population depends on agriculture: 50% of the working population work as cultivators or agricultural laborers and 20% depend indirectly on agricultural activities.[2] Compared to other states, farmers are more disadvantaged in Kerala as there is no so-called Agricultural Produce Market Act.[3] This act has been launched in many states in order to provide regulation of agricultural products and fixes the creation of Agricultural Produce Market Committees supervising the application of these regulations. The absence of this regulation in Kerala penalizes particularly small farmers, as they lack real-time and updated information regarding market prices, access to quality assurance, logistics, warehousing, commodity trading, pesticides and other activities, and resources. Subsequently, they have difficulty to produce in a market-oriented way and are vulnerable toward middlemen and money lenders. This situation is even more difficult as the majority of small farmers cultivate nontraditional perishables, for example, vegetables, herbs, and medicinal plants. In this area, there is a lack of institution support for trade, compared to the very organized sectors of trade, such as tea, coffee, or pulses.

In order to tackle this problem, the IT State Mission—Kerala, the Kerala Agricultural Department, and the National Institute for Smart Government (NISG) have launched the pilot project e-Krishi,

---

[2] http://www.undp.org/content/dam/india/docs/terminal_evaluation_of_information_and_communication_technology_for_development_project.pdf (accessed March 15, 2013).

[3] http://www.msamb.com/english/apmc/default.htm (accessed March 10, 2013).

implemented from 2006 to 2009 in Malappuram. This project seeks to improve the bargaining capacity of farmers through an Internet platform, accessible online and in already existing e-centers, allowing small farmers to access information and contact various stakeholders in view of facilitating their agriculture activities.

Impact of Existing Similar Projects

e-Krishi builds on two initiatives: firstly, the Akshayae center initiative, a successful and well-accepted project launched in 2002 with the creation of 350 telecenters. The project objective was to increase e-literacy among the population and use ICT as tool for inclusion of the rural population. These Akshaya e-centers are never more than 3 km away from a farmer's location serve as the local service provider of government services and are equipped with 5 to 10 PCs, an Internet connection to the Kerala State Wide Area Network (KSWAN), webcams, scanners, and printers. Each center is managed by at least two coordinators who have received ICT training.

These Akshaya centers are organized according to a social entrepreneur model: Each e-center is owned by a private entrepreneur who is selected by a state-level committee, which is supposed to guarantee the selection of an entrepreneur willing to serve the local community. This entrepreneur is in charge of investing in the infrastructure and is responsible for the successful operation of the center. He or she receives support from the state regarding the procurement of materials at lower costs, loans, and Internet connection. e-Krishire uses the infrastructure of the Akshaya centers (location, IT infrastructure, IT-trained personnel, and organizational structure) and renames those selected for the e-Krishi project into e-Krishi telecenters. The second source of inspiration for the e-Krishi project was the Karshaka Information System Services and Networking (KISSAN) initiative, an integrated, multi-model delivery system of online agricultural information for farmers created in 2003. e-Krishi reused the concept of offering updated information to farmers and developed it further. As the KISSAN project did not provide farmers with the possibility to avoid middlemen, a dedicated portal was developed in order to fulfill this gap.

Planning Process

In 2005, the Kerala State IT Mission, the National Institute for Smart Government, and the Agricultural Department started the planning process for a project that should facilitate the agricultural information flow and the transaction management of small farmers.

> Kerala State Information Technology Mission (KSITM) is an autonomous nodal IT implementation agency for Department of Information Technology, Government of Kerala. It provides managerial support to various initiatives of the department. Among these figure activities related to ICT dissemination to bridge the digital divide, e-Governance, and developing human resources for IT.

As the Akshaya project had been developed successfully in rural areas, it was decided to use 146 of their existing e-centers and their infrastructures for the future pilot project. This explains also the choice of Malappuram district for the implementation of the pilot project.

The planning process was composed of four main steps, each developed in order to guarantee the successful implementation of the project:

1. Definition of the organizational structure
2. Development of a communication and publicity strategy
3. Collection of data and development of the e-Krishi website
4. Definition of objectives

Definition of the Organizational Structure

One of the first steps of the planning process consisted in the definition of the organizational structure: In order to guarantee the efficient development and implementation of the project, it was decided that the project should have its coordinating entity on state, district, block, and village level (Figure 13.1):

- On the *state level* (Kerala), the head of e-Krishi coordinates the e-Krishi implementation within a state-level committee. This committee is headed by the Secretary of IT Department of the

Figure 13.1
Organizational Structure

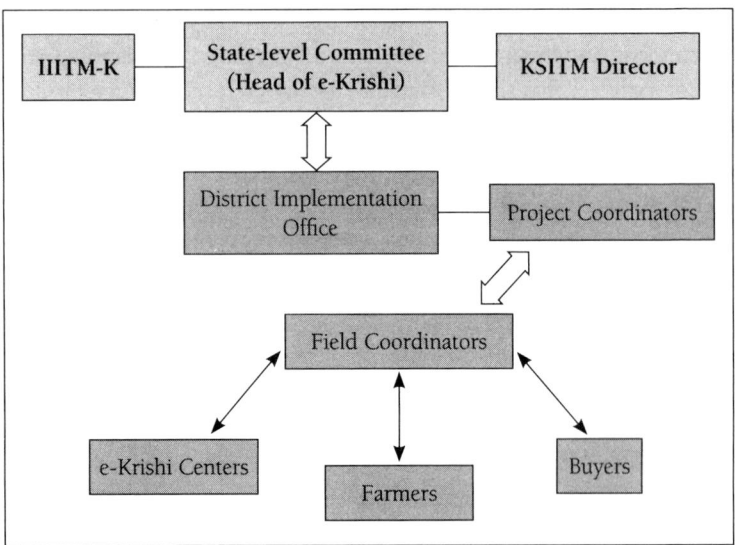

Source: Author.

Government of Kerala and is composed of 12 members. They work in close cooperation with the KSITM director and the Indian Institute of Information Technology and Management, Kerala (IIITM-K).

- On the *district level* (Malappuram), the so-called District Implementation Office is created. It is headed by a chairman, the President of all Panchayats[4] in the district. The committee is assisted by an information coordinator in charge of coordinating the collection of agricultural information, a principal agricultural officer, and three deputy directors, each in charge of one of the three agricultural resorts: animal husbandry, diary, and fisheries. Furthermore, the committee is composed of a manager from the Vegetable and Fruit Promotion Council Kerala (VFPCK), a district officer from the Kerala Sericulture Cooperative Federation (SERIFED), the head of the Self-development Center

---

[4] Panchayats are elected by local governments at the village level.

for Popularization of Agricultural Research and Technology Programs,[5] and the women empowerment project *Kudumbasree,* as well as the head of Cashew Research Center. They are assisted by a district secretary from the Akshaya project. Finally, the National Bank for Agriculture and Rural Development (NABARD) is also part of the committee.

Still on the district level, the project coordinators are in charge of selecting Akshaya centers for the e-Krishi program, depending on their performance: frequency of Internet usage, electronic transactions within the centers, imparted courses, and variety of ICT-based activities and interaction with the local self-government and other line departments.

These project coordinators organize farmers and buyers meeting in the district and manage the capacity-training programs imparted in different Akshaya centers. Finally, they consolidate the data collected by the field coordinators.

- On the *block level*, these 14 field coordinators work directly with the entrepreneurs of the e-Krishi centers. They distribute questionnaires and collect field data on farmers and buyers, as well as conduct market studies on various agricultural products. They support the organization of Bhoomi Clubs (see next section) and support farmers who wish to conduct soil testing—against a small fee—analyzed later on the e-Krishi website.

- In all of the 102 *Panchayats* and 5 municipalities, Bhoomi Clubs are formed. These clubs composed of chief of the village council, the so-called Panchayat president, who is also the chief of the Bhoomi club, the agricultural officer of the Panchayat, fulfilling the role of an official advisor. Various members of the local community are regularly invited, as well as the leading farmers who endorse the role of secretary, joint secretary, and treasurer within the Bhoomi Club. They meet once in a month in order to discuss issues related to the implementation of e-Krishi in their village. The objective of the creation of Bhoomi clubs is to adopt a participatory approach right from the project initiation stage and ensure the sustainability of the project.

[5] Each district has one of these centers.

Development of a Communication and Publicity Strategy

The second step of the planning phase consisted in the development of a multitier communication and publicity strategy, in order to broadcast the new project. This strategy consisted in:

- Distribution of informative leaflets and brochures among farmers in English and Malayalam[6]
- Publication of articles in newspapers and participation in radio programs
- Organization of press conferences at each visit of NISG members on the field
- Face-to-face interaction with farmers, organized in 102 Panchayats and 5 municipalities at Farmer's Day (August 17)
- A compulsory orientation session for registered farmers on the adequate use of the website services
- Organization of 14 road shows, managed by the e-Krishi entrepreneurs, and the Bhoomi club members in 14 blocks of the district. At these events, they explained the objective of the e-Krishi website with the help of CDs, presentations, and leaflets.

Collection of Data and Development of the e-Krishi Website

The next step of the planning and preparation phase consisted in the elaboration of farm data questionnaires which had to be fulfilled by local farmers in order to adapt the future website to their needs. As defined in the organizational structure, it was decided that field coordinators would be in charge of meeting with farmers and combine the gathering of this data with a pedagogical approach, for example, explaining the purpose of this data collection and the advantages of the future project. The collected information would then be transferred to the project coordinators, in charge of consolidating the information and preparing it, after verification by an agricultural officer, for uploading to the e-Krishi website.

---

[6] Malayalam is the language predominantly spoken in Kerala.

It was decided that the IIITM-K would develop this website and develop successively the following services:

1. Provide a web-based platform (portal) for advertising (postings) of their commodities and attract potential buyers
2. Create a matching system that is capable of identifying potential buyers on selected commodities
3. Develop quality videos on agricultural practices and disseminate these through e-centers and on the website
4. Online advice on selection of planting materials
5. Offer the possibility to contact with soil-testing labs
6. Provide fertilizer recommendation based on soil test and crop specificities
7. Provide online advisory services on agricultural disease management
8. Provide seasonal alerts on disease outbreaks
9. Establish a trade call center for trade-related enquiries
10. Identify location specific production of agricultural commodities
11. Establish a data-collection mechanism to capture local market price
12. Provide web-enabled market and price information on various agricultural commodities from selected markets
13. Collect and aggregate all relevant information on various schemes, subsidies, and loans from various agencies and provide through the portal

Definition of Objectives

The final component of the planning phase was the definition of objectives to achieve during the pilot implementation phase (2006–2009).

1. Identify farmer groups in order to enhance registration and postings by farmers on the e-Krishi portal
2. Identify potential traders and agents to explore market opportunities
3. Use ICT to reach farmers and provide them with information that allows them to enhance their productivity and the quality of their products

4. Enhance the awareness among farmers in order to enable them to negotiate on a fair basis with middlemen
5. Establish active enrollment of agricultural input providers (seeds, plantlets, fertilizers, technology providers, etc.)

Project Implementation

The project was officially launched in January 2006 in 146 Akshaya centers, selected for the pilot project and renamed e-Krishi centers.

In the following, the main implementing agencies and the difficulties they faced throughout the implementation of the project will be presented.

Actors of the Implementation Process

1. *Kerala State IT Mission.* KSITM coordinated all the e-Krishi activities with the help of the e-Krishi Head at state level.
2. *Department of Agriculture.* Officials from the Department of Agriculture were in charge of creating direct linkages of farmers with e-Krishi centers. At the beginning of the project, they provided together with the Virtual University for Agricultural Trade the first market information in order to attract farmers to join the project.
3. *Indian Institute for Information Technologies and Management, Kerala.* IIITM-K provided consultation and technological support.
4. *District implementation committee.* The committee is among others responsible for the implementation of the project on a district level and in charge of organizing meetings with different agricultural stakeholders.

    Difficulties faced: During the farmer–buyers meetings, it appeared that many stakeholders were firstly reluctant to use the presented e-Krishi center and portal, given that the innovative character of the project. Also, the strong dependence on middlemen could not be eliminated immediately. Organizing various meetings and the presence of field coordinators were therefore necessary.

5. *Virtual University for Agricultural Trade.* Together with the experts from the Agricultural Department and the KISSAN Data

Center, it provides the website with agricultural information—collected at various farming institutions, departments, and farmer questionnaires.

Difficulties faced: Most of the big enterprises were not interested in small quantities of agriculture products, so it was initially difficult to convince them of the utility of the website. Thanks to the virtual aggregation facility of the website, this issue could be resolved.

6. *Agricultural banks.* The National Bank for Agriculture and Rural Development, the South Malabar Grameen Bank, the Canara Bank, and different cooperatives provided loans and financial assistance to farmers via the e-Krishi.

7. *Panchayats.* They are in charge of gathering funds and support for the project and the Akshaya centers.

8. *Akshaya center.* The Akshaya project provided e-Krishi with the IT infrastructure and location for the e-Krishi pilot project. In their location were imparted training session and digital as well as print material put at disposal.

   Difficulties faced: During the implementation of the pilot project, it appeared that users of the e-Krishi portal and center had difficulties in relying only on digital information and the Internet. Many users asked for print material in order to be able to access the information at home. Printed material, albeit less detailed than the digital component, has been therefore provided. Furthermore, the Akshaya center realized that many buyers and agricultural stakeholders were not used to using IT-based trade applications. Therefore, specific training for these stakeholders had to be developed.

9. *Bhoomi clubs.* The Bhoomi clubs are in charge of locating products suitable for marketing via the project and supporting the project on the village level.

Implementation Process

In early 2006, 146 Akshaya centers for the e-Krishi project were selected on criteria of distance to farmer communities, amount of members, quality of infrastructure, and existence of IT trained staff. As defined in the implementation framework, the field coordinators visited the farmers and collected information in the following areas:

- Acreage by product
- Name and age of plants
- Used seeds
- Harvest schedule and expected quantity per month

Apart from farmers, the following stakeholders registered on the platform during the pilot phase:

- Agriculture buyers and exporters
- Agriculture product manufacturers
- Agriculture input providers: seeds, plantlets, fertilizers, pesticides
- Agricultural experts from universities
- Test laboratories
- Agricultural equipments suppliers
- Quality graders
- Warehousing
- Logistics providers
- Banks
- Insurers
- Documentation specialists
- Accountants, legal support
- Payment gateway services
- Government offices/resources, agricultural institutions
- NGOs

e-Krishi Website

The website itself is accessible via Internet. However, given the fact that a majority of small farmers does not have their own Internet access, the e-Krishi centers serve as support location. Thanks to the collected information as well as the information accessible through the IT infrastructure, the following services could be launched on the website during the implementation phase:

Online Trade Portal

The online trade platform can be considered as the heart of the program: On the portal, traders can post their demands and offer for each category of a product.

- Livestock
- Logistic services
- Nursery
- Organic fertilizers
- Plastic culture
- Pulses
- Fodder crops
- Medicinal plants
- Insurance Services
- Financial services

- Chemical fertilizers
- Vegetables
- Tubers
- Legal services
- Agro-forestry
- Cereals and millets
- Commercial crops
- Oil seeds
- Quality certifiers
- Government services

- Other crops
- Eggs
- Flowers
- Fruits
- Poultry
- Aquaculture
- Vegetables
- Condiments/spices
- Laboratory services

Within each of these categories, registered users can indicate the type of product and its quantity needed. Farmers desire to sell their products can post in turn their offers on the website. As they have precise information on their current value of their products, they can expect to sell for a fair price. Buyers and sellers can effectively search for advertisement and requirement postings. Thanks to the indicated location, they can also find the nearest buyer or provider. The aggregation application allows them to buy the same product in the meantime from various farmers, which allows them to satisfy their demands of often large quantities of a specific product (Figure 13.2).

Information Applications

Furthermore, the portal provides farmers and agricultural stakeholders with a multitude of updated and accurate information on products and practices, available in the *Market Advisory* section. This information is directly accessed from the KISSAN server (Figure 13.3).

- *Crop information.* Users can access information on more than 80 crops cultivated in Kerala via a KISSAN managed information website. More precisely, they can access information concerning a crop's characteristic, the selection criteria, the amount of seeds to be used per hectare, how to prepare the field. Furthermore, recommendations concerning water, weed, and nutrient management, as well as information concerning adapted plant protection strategies and harvesting methods and results to expect, are provided.

354 EILEAN VON LAUTZ-CAUZANET

Figure 13.2

Sellers Corner at the Trade Center Platform on the e-Krishi Website and Advertising Example

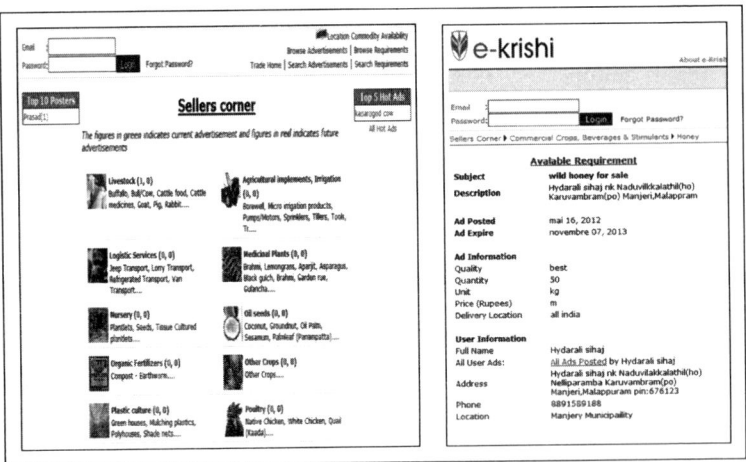

Source: www.ekrishi.org

- *Fertilizer recommendation.* Farmers can ask the nearest district soil-testing laboratory in the state to conduct a soil analysis. These laboratories are connected via broadband to the KISSAN Kerala server and update the results of the soil testing. Farmers can then, thanks to an attributed identification number generated by the laboratory's software, access the results of their soil testing and related recommendations.

- *Planting material availability.* Through this application, farmers can obtain information on planting material in their area. Information is provides on all major planting material produced on district level: around 160 crops and their varieties.

- *Fertilizers and pesticides.* In order to avoid the inadequate use of chemical fertilizers—and useless expenditures for farmers—this application informs about different fertilizers and pesticides and proposes alternatives. It provides them also with information of the licensed retail outlets. Users can check the availability of fertilizers in their location online.

Figure 13.3
Planting Material Availability Tool

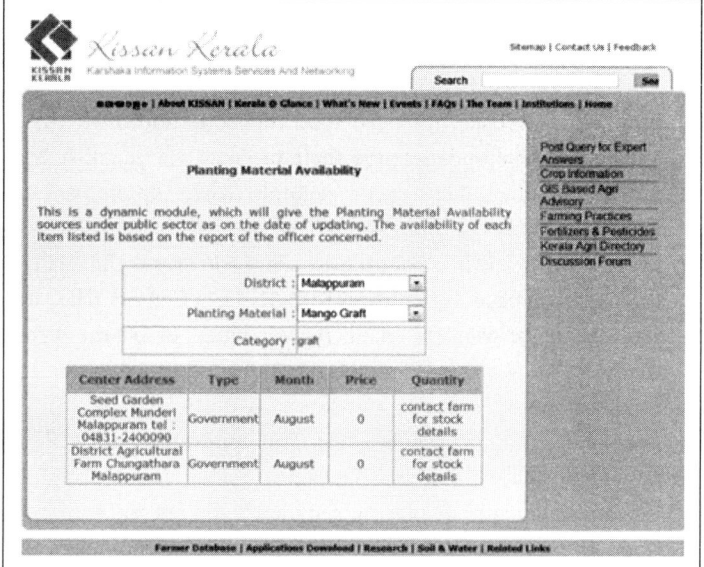

Source: www.ekrishi.org

- *Weather information.* The portal provides weather reports for over 330 localities in Kerala. Users can select their locality and are redirected to the website www.fallingrain.com, which provides them with information on temperature, percentage of cloud coverage, and amount of precipitation (cm³/ last 3 hours).
- *Market prices.* One of the key tools of the Internet portal is *Agri Market Info.* Via this tool, farmers are redirected to the website of the Vegetable and Fruit Promotion Council Kerala. Users can choose to access the information on price on a specific market in Kerala or access the average price of a product in Kerala.
- *KISSAN information channel.* The *Agri Video Channel* is a YouTube-based Internet channel with videos on agricultural practices, developed by IITM-K. More than 100 videos dealing with agricultural information are available.

Online Advisory

The section Online Advisory is composed of various tools that seek to optimize and enhance the farmers' production possibilities:

- *Ask an Expert.* If farmers do not find the answer to their question on the website, they can send their question using the Ask and Expert tool and describe their problem via email. It is also possible to attach pictures, for example, when the problem deals with the disease of their animals. The email is then treated by experts and scientists from the Kerala Agricultural University, or the Department of Agriculture (KISSAN Data Center). The farmer receives the answer via email, regular letter, or on the website, thanks to an access code which the user receives when the email has been sent.
- *Location specific market information.* This application uses a GIS web based information system—a system capable of capturing, storing, analyzing, and displaying geographically referenced information—in order to provide farmers with crop practices depending on a specific location. It helps farmers to optimize their production and allows rationalizing the demand–supply process of crops.
- *Farming practices.* Within this application, farmers can access a high number farming practices and detailed recommendations, for example, recommendations concerning plant protection measures: In this case, the farmer will learn which products exist, how to use and store them. The provided information is very clear and describes, for example, how to handle a sprayer for chemical pesticides.
- *Discussion forum.* In the forum, farmers can exchange directly best practices and experiences with their peers and agricultural stakeholders.

Offline Material

The e-Krishi centers are supplied with around 30 different educational materials, for example, books, booklets, and magazines in the local language. Furthermore, CDs dealing with agricultural practices as well as copies of the online farming videos are provided. The material focuses on topics related to various sectors of agriculture: animal husbandry, fisheries etc. It is donated by the Kerala Agricultural University and the Farm Information Bureau, the Central Plantation Research Institute, and the TBGIRI (Tropical Botanical Garden and Research Institute, part of the Kerala government science and technology department).

Call Center

e-Krishi also launched a call center with a toll-free information number. The call center is supposed to provide, similar to the *Ask an Expert* application, farmers with answers to their farming related questions. The call center also allows illiterate farmers to access information. The Kerala-based call center is composed of 3 agricultural graduates and supported by more than 120 agricultural experts.

e-Krishi Training

Under the Akshaya project, at least one person of each family in the Malappuram district had followed courses on how to use computers and the Internet, which facilitated the implementation of e-Krishi. However, training was imparted by trained staff of the Akshaya centers. Users received around 10 to 15 hours of practical computer training. This training was divided in order to suit different target groups:

- *Training for farmers.* At the e-Krishi centers, farmers can not only access the Internet in view of using the e-Krishi portal and its services, they can also enroll for courses of management and skill development training, and follow courses related to specific agricultural sectors.
- *Training for the whole e-Krishi community.* Training is also imparted to the business community, the e-Krishi entrepreneurs, field coordinators, members of the local self-government, officers of the Department of Agriculture, and members of different self-help groups.

Midway Evaluation of the Portal
In 2008, a midway survey conducted in 32 centers revealed that there were already 14,443 farmers registered in these 32 e-Krishi centers, which equals around 451 farmers per center. They posted 18,353 postings in the trade portal and agriculture products worth INR 5.57 million had been sold. Apart from Areca nuts, all products could be sold at higher prices via e-Krishi than via middlemen. The survey revealed also that 48% of the registered farmers owned around 1.5 to 3 hectares. Seventy percent of them were more than 7 km away from the next market place. Those farmers who were more than 15 km away from the local market were the ones who transacted most on the platform.

Role of ICT throughout the Process

ICT are used in two different ways fulfill two different roles throughout the e-Krishi project:

- *ICT-based data platform.* ICT-based data platforms of the KISSAN Data Center are used as leverage in order to collect and transform agricultural raw data into usable information. This phase is composed of the so called "processing" and "cognition" steps. The ICT systems serve here as the technical basis and background of the project. Their role is important as they are continuously solicited in order to actualize the data stock.
- *ICT tools.* In contrast to the ICT systems, ICT tools are visible and actively used by the users of the portal via different applications available. These ICT applications (the website and its applications) have the role of transforming collected data into context-based knowledge for farmers: They are used as dynamic tools, able to combine various information sources (e.g., combine location information with crop information in order to formulate a related recommendation) and explain what the collected data actually shows. ICT tools are supposed to guide farmers from the knowledge state to the understanding state, which means to enable them how to use their knowledge, and to foresee the results of actions based on this use (Figure 13.4).

Figure 13.4
Role of ICT

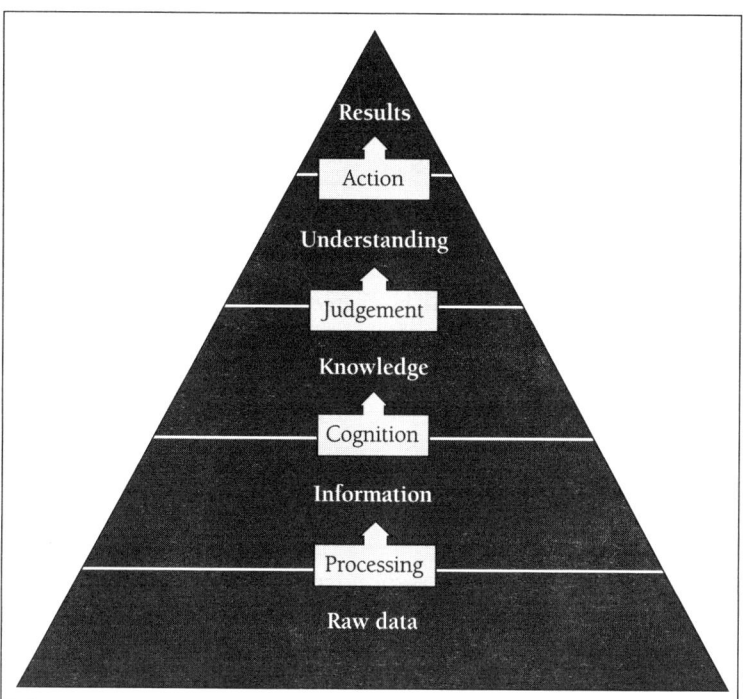

Source: Author.

Distribution of Funds

The e-Krishi project was funded by United Nations Development Programme (UNDP) within the nationwide project ICT for development from 2006 to 2009 with around INR 146 million (USD 267,963). Concretely, these funds were mainly disbursed for the following activities:

- Activities implemented within the communication strategy
- Training imparted to e-Krishi users
- Development of the website

- Development of the call center facility
- Administrative expenditures

Since 2009, IIITM- K has been funding the project.

Supervision Process

A clear supervision process between different organizations and stakeholders of the project has been defined:

The Kerala IT Mission was in charge of looking after the project management of the project and received therefore regular feedback from the State Implementation Committee, who met every 6 months in order to discuss collected information and feedback from the District Implementation Committee. The state-level committee is in charge of supervising the activities in various departments and report back to the Kerala IT Mission. The District Implementation Committee is in charge of evaluating the project every quarter, based on field visits in each e-Krishi center and on statistical reports from the KISSAN server. In the meantime, the IIITM-K supervises website-related matters and intervenes directly at the technical support center (C-DIT).

Concretely, this supervision is based on result-based management (RBM) reports. These are sent during the first week of every month to the respective supervising entity. Furthermore, the project coordinator drafts a monthly review of the Bhoomi clubs and the field coordinators of the project. e-Krishi center entrepreneurs are also supervised: Their performance is reviewed and they are categorized into grades ranging from A to E, depending on the quality of their activities. They can be disqualified if they do not follow the regulations defined by the government, for example, if social obligations are not fulfilled.

Achievement and Impact

In the year 2010, the pilot phase ended, achievements were assessed on the basis of questionnaires that tend to evaluate the extent to which the previously fixed objectives had been achieved:

Identify Farmer Groups in order to Enhance Registration and Postings by Farmers on the e-Krishi Portal

The pilot project achieved to set up 145 e-Krishi centers and to develop a functioning e-Krishi portal. During the pilot phase (2006–2009) over 10,000 farmers registered and took part in different activities provided by the centers and used the services of the portal. Around 15,000 persons in the district of Malappuram posted offers or demands on the trade portal.

Identification of Potential Traders and Agents to Explore Market Opportunities

In 2010, 408 buyers/retailers/wholesalers/exporters and 62 institutional buyers as well as two NGOs had registered. They reported that they had benefited from the e-Krishi platform particularly because of its capacity to aggregate different items posted by the farmers.

Use ICT to Reach Farmers and Provide Them with Information that Allows them to Enhance Their Productivity and the Quality of Their Products

After one year of implementation, the e-Krishi website counted already 100,000 visits among which 50% were farmers. Furthermore, 5,000 queries could be answered through the *Ask an Expert* application. Concretely, 10% of the farmers in the targeted district could be reached. The 2010 evaluation of UNDP reported further that experts, scientists, and officials from other institutions did also take part in the project. Farmers reported that they were able to increase their productivity and the quality of their product, thanks to the information and guidance application on the website.

Enhance the Awareness among Farmers in Order to Enable Them to Negotiate on a Fair Basis with Middlemen

In over 14 blocks and 567 locations, information meetings had been organized. Furthermore, the national radio station *All India Radio* consecrated four programs on the pilot project. Farmers reported that they decided to register on the website after these information sessions. They reported further that the combination of registered external buyers and the knowledge of market prices allowed them be in a better position regarding their middlemen.

Furthermore, the project generated impacts in the following areas:

- *Conversion of fallow lands.* In 2007, the Government of Kerala, encouraged by the Civil Supply Corporation, decided to buy the entire paddy production in the Malappuram district through the e-Krishi trade portal. This production had almost been ceased because of the low prices and had increased the amount of fallow lands. Thanks to this e-Krishi based intervention, the price for paddy cultivation increased and farmers are encouraged to post their paddy offers on the trade center.

- *Revival of closed down units (Mushrooms).* The Department of Agriculture decided to launch e-Krishi courses on mushroom cultivation. In this area, there were a lack of marketing support, which resulted in a lack of buyers and the closing down of production units. Thanks to the e-Krishi project, these units could be revived as farmers were accompanied and directly put in contact with buyers via the e-Krishi portal and centers. A memorandum of agreement regarding quantity, price, and frequency of supply were signed between buyers and sellers of the website.

- *Improved access to advice on disease management.* The toll-free call centers allowed farmers to get advice on urgent strategies on pest and disease management. It was not the case earlier as the remoteness of many farmers and the unavailability of immediate support led to the loss of harvests.

- *Better access to business opportunities.* Thanks to e-Krishi, farmers were able to use the provided information on crops and harvesting in order to adapt their products on the buyers requirements. This allowed them to obtain a better price for their product. Furthermore, groups of farmers producing one project were formed within some e-Krishi centers, which allowed them to attract bigger major buyers.

- *Comprehensive database of marketable commodities.* The comprehensive databank of the trade center encouraged farmers to post even small product quantities, as it allows buyers to have an overview of the global amount of a product depending on the locality from which they seek to buy.

- *Improved access to price and market infrastructure.* e-Krishi managed to provide on its portal daily updated market prices. Moreover, the toll-free call center was widely used, particularly by farmers desiring to sell small quantities of products which had not been listed in the market price application. Through the e-Krishi call center, these farmers could be put in contact with buyers and processors.

Furthermore, one of the funding agencies, UNDP, conducted an evaluation of the project on five parameters: relevance, effectiveness, efficiency, results/impacts, and sustainability. These were based on subparameters evaluated in six categories of highly satisfactory (6 points), satisfactory (5 points), moderately satisfactory (4 points), moderately unsatisfactory (3 points), unsatisfactory (2 points), and highly unsatisfactory (1 point). This evaluation came to the conclusion that the project objectives were fulfilled to a satisfactory or highly satisfactory extent (Figure 13.5).

Figure 13.5
Project Evaluation

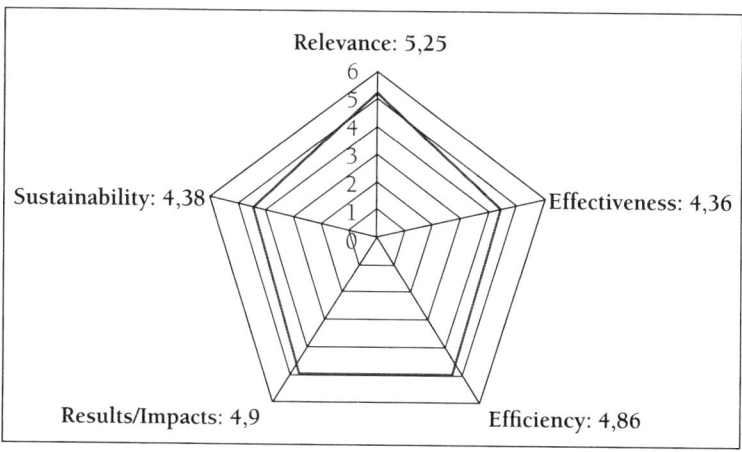

Source: UNDP.

Finally, UNDP (2010) also indicates that e-Krishi achieved to contribute to the development of rural areas as it provided support in multiple areas relevant for small farmers:

- Bridge the digital divide
- Citizen-centric service delivery
- Public–private partnership
- Capacity building
- Change management
- Business process reengineering
- Knowledge/experience sharing

Awards

Since the implementation of the project, e-Krishi has won several prizes for its achievements:

- 2008/2009: One of the winners of the CSI-Nihilent E-Governance Awards
- 2010: e-Krishi is mentioned as being one of the reasons why Akshaya wins the Manthan Award South Asia
- 2010/2011: National Award on E-Governance (Silver Medal)

Post-pilot Phase

After the successful piloting in Malappuram, KSITM decided to develop e-Krishi in 9 other districts, and via 1200 Akshaya centers. The government of Kerala agreed to finance the project after the end of the UNDP funding in June 2009. More recently, the Department of Agriculture (Government of Kerala) has taken ownership of the project in association with the National Informatics Center. They seek to develop an advanced farmer database across the state, offer a bilingual trading portal, and enhance the whole project further.

Conclusion

The e-K0rishi project has achieved to improve the position of small farmers within the agricultural value chain through the use of an online platform that provides them with important access to agricultural information and facilitates the trade of their products for fair prices.

The success of the e-Krishi project appears to be based on several factors: Firstly, the fact that the project built up on existing, successfully functioning infrastructures provided by the Akshaya and KISSAN project, conferred a high degree of stability to the planning and implementation process. The cooperation with a field project that was familiar with working on the grassroots level increased the efficiency of the project. It also diminished the cost of the project as e-Krishi could benefit from existing centers and their equipment. This partnership proves the efficiency of improving existing projects and tools, instead of launching completely new ones.

Furthermore, the participatory approach of the projects has also contributed much to the project's success. Thanks to the close cooperation with local groups and integration of the Panchayats during the planning and implementation process, the project was able to attain a high degree of credibility and increased the trust and receptiveness of rural inhabitants. The inclusion of local decision makers in the key committees of the project is a key example of this approach. Associated to this, a well-planned communication strategy was crucial for the project as it could also decrease the reluctance and hesitation of many farmers regarding the project and its pretended outcomes. Indeed, the absence of ownership and lack of a communication and broadcast can lead to the failure of innovative projects without any precursor in the region, as its success depends on the community's willingness to use and commit to the project.

Another success factor is the large-scale ICT training imparted by e-Krishi. The focus on farmer's needs and the continuous support by local trainers increased the efficiency of the project as farmers were increasingly able to use the platform. Also, this training was characterized by an effort of proximity, as it was imparted in different centers close to where farmers lived and worked. This proximity was another crucial aspect of the project, as the project aimed to be perceived as tool that facilitates their trade and is not related to additional efforts.

Finally, the fact that the project has planned from the beginning a demand driven strategy—the more the platform was used, the more new online services were developed and the platform adapt to the users' demands—contributed to the popularity of the project. In the long term, this strategy also increases the projects sustainability chances, proving its capacity to innovate and evolve together with its users.

The post-pilot phase has already proven that the project would spread out quickly in other districts and states of the country and there is clear willingness to expand the provided services. Online platforms offering small farmers to trade their products are also increasingly developed in developing countries, albeit not always successful. It is important to mention that for this kind of project, the importance of basic infrastructure, such as electricity, and the lack of data centers containing up-to-date agricultural information may complicate their implementation to some extent. This is particularly true for those countries with a low Internet penetration and ICT connectivity. However, depending on the effort invested in order to tackle these problems, and given the modern possibilities to access Internet via solar- and satellite-based technologies, these challenges are not insuperable and therefore not a fatality.

Bibliography

Indian Institute of Information Technology and Management, Kerala (IITM-K). (2007). "IT Enabled Strategic Framework for Agriculture: The KISSAN-Kerala Approach." Retrieved from http://www.iiitmk.ac.in/edugrid/download/Strategy-Agri-2-082k7.pdf (accessed November 28, 2012).

Information for Development. (2007). Interview with Anvar Sadath. Retrieved from http://i4d.eletsonline.com/?p=11560 (accessed November 28, 2012).

National Institute for Smart Government. (2006). Efficient Programme Monitoring. Retrieved from http://www.nisg.org/knowledgecentre_docs/D08010008.pdf (accessed November 28, 2012).

UNDP India. (2010). Terminal Evaluation of Information and Communication Technology for Development. pp. 86–101.

Important Websites

www.ekrishi.org
www.keralaitmission.org

14

Mahiti Manthana: ICT for Empowerment of Rural Women (India)

Eilean von Lautz-Cauzanet

Overview

The project Mahiti Manthana, launched in 2005 by the Indian NGO IT for Change, seeks to empower rural women through ICT. More precisely, women can access information on governmental services through rural telecenters. Furthermore, radio- and video-based activities help women to learn more about subjects crucial for empowerment. The participatory and collective approach, as well as the development of nontextual tools for mainly illiterate women, has had a positive impact on their self-confidence. Finally, Mahiti Manthana has also permitted women to assembly their voices through ICT-based organization, and increased their legitimacy within rural communities.

Project Background

Despite a strong economy and its status as world's largest democracy, India faces challenges regarding gender equity: the country ranked only

129th out of 146 countries within the Gender Inequality Index in 2011 and occupied the 105th position out of 135 countries within Global Gender Gap ranking, published by the World Economic Forum (2012). Particularly in rural areas, women are more vulnerable to issues such as illiteracy or malnutrition (World Bank). In Karnataka, 9th biggest state of India and location of the project presented here, over 40% of women in rural areas are illiterate (National Census, 2011).

Both governmental and nongovernmental organizations play an important role to tackle the problems related to the vulnerability of rural women and to move them away from a state of dependency. The adoption of empowerment strategies is widespread. These often imply the creation and support of self-help groups in view of promoting capacity building to assist rural communities in their efforts to utilize resources, access information, enhance self-awareness, and experience leadership (*International Journal of Rural Management*, 2006). In this context, the NGO IT for Change developed in cooperation with the governmental project Mahila Samakhya, the project Mahiti Manthana (in English: knowledge processes), which aims to empower and mobilize rural women in self-help groups through organizing collective and ICT-based activities.

Impacts of Existing Projects

Mahiti Manthana builds on the pan-Indian program Mahila Samakhya, set up by the Indian Ministry of Human Resource Development in 1989 to empower rural women through self-help group activities. The project is active in 60 districts in 10 states. In Karnataka, Mahila Samakhya is present in nine districts. The project focuses on areas such as education, health, legal literacy, self-governance, and community linkages to governmental institutions. The main strategy was the creation and support of women self-help groups (*sanghas*[1]). These self-help groups aim to provide women with those skills that help them to resolve daily issues. Women have access to the so-called resources centers where they meet and organize collective activities. Debates on gender issues and the promotion of women's leadership on the local level are major strategies

---

[1] Sangha means group.

of this project. However, in early 2005, the project expressed the need to introduce innovative methods in order to continue to contribute to women's empowerment.

In response to this need to innovate, the NGO IT for Change, more precisely its field center in Karnataka (Center for Community Informatics and Development), developed in 2005 the project Mahiti Manthana in collaboration with the Mahila Samakhya. Mahiti Manthana seeks to develop ICT-based activities and support the development of ICT-based knowledge management within the existing project Mahila Samakhya. More precisely, it was decided to introduce collective video and radio activities and create telecenters that would serve as information and meeting centers for rural *sangha* women.

Both Mahila Samakhya and IT for Change agreed that the introduction of ICT-based tools and methodologies should be embedded in a dedicated ICT strategy in order to guarantee its success in the long term, particularly in light of the innovative character of the project.

Planning Process

The planning process involved coordinating members of Mahila Samakhya-Karnataka and IT for Change.

The planning process can be subdivided into six progressive steps:

1. Definition of the location for the pilot project
2. Identification of information and services need
3. Development of an ICT strategy
4. Development of a risk and mitigation strategy
5. Definition of the project management approach
6. Definition of project's components/objectives

Firstly, it was decided to launch the pilot project in one location and then expand it progressively to other locations that had already been involved in the Mahila Samakhya initiative. For the pilot phase, the three taluks (subdistricts) within the district of Mysore in Karnataka state were chosen: Nanjangud, Hunsur, and H.D. Kote. This selection was based on the fact that these taluks had been classified in 2002 by the High Power

Committee for the Redressal of Regional Imbalances as particularly in backward location. In addition, Mahila Samakhya had already implemented their self-help group project in 56 to 59 villages of these taluks, and a better receptivity toward Mahiti Manthana was expected.

In order to guarantee that the new implementation would be effective and correspond to the member's needs, IT for Chance elaborated **baseline surveys** in order to assess the socioeconomic profile of *sangha* women, their involvement in Mahila Samakhya and their level of exposure to ICT. These surveys were carried out between September and November 2005 by IT for Change project staff and volunteers from the faculty of sociology at the Mysore University in 19 villages within the three selected taluks.

The baselines surveys revealed that more than 50% of the self-help group members were from disadvantaged castes and a majority (77%) had never attended school. Furthermore, around 62% of these women worked as agricultural laborers and a large majority (92%) did not possess land in their own name. In addition, 87% of self-help groups women lived in households with a daily income of around 100 rupees (approximately USD 2) per day for a family of at least five persons. Finally, more than a third of these households were not equipped with electricity and 80% do not have access to private water supply.

Furthermore, the surveys also revealed some problems related to the functioning and organization of the Mahila Samakhya initiative: Interviewees reported among others an insufficient presence of Mahila Samakhya staff at the village level and showed that some *sangha* women did not know to which committees they belonged to within Mahila Samakhya. In addition, surveys revealed a lack of communication between different villages and *sangha* women, as well as a need to include the *Dalit* (*untouchables*) community actively in the new Mahiti Manthana project.

Subsequently—and in parallel to the process of designing the video and radio components of the ICT strategy—a *needs assessment* was conducted together with *sangha* women and staff from Mahila Samakhya. The purpose of this assessment was to identify the main needs on which Mahiti Manthana should focus and to identify how *sangha* women perceived empowerment and disempowerment. Six villages, two from each taluk, were selected and two-and-half hours were spent in each village for group discussions and activity-based exercises (e.g., storytelling). This needs assessment came to the conclusion that the main needs of the self-help groups were

- a greater access to information about governmental services,
- effective intraorganizational flow of information between villages, district levels, and the state office of the project,
- innovative training activities that contribute to women's empowerment and the general motivation of participants,
- integration of female adolescents into self-help groups, and
- need for training and knowledge resources.

These results were taken into consideration during the design process of the *ICT strategy*, which defined the role and objectives of ICT within the implementation framework, as well as their objectives. More precisely, the strategy determined that ICT should contribute to the

- integration of ICT in view of diminishing the dependence of learning processes on physically present persons,
- enhancement of collective activities through ICT-based activities,
- promotion of the role of the self-help groups as local knowledge institutions for rural women,
- introduction of ICT-based horizontal and vertical communication within the project, and
- introduce ICT-based training and pedagogy methodologies.

Given the innovative character of Mahiti Manthana, IT for Change decided to associate a *risk and mitigation strategy* to the project. This strategy focused on two major challenges:

1. *Acceptance of ICT on the coordinating level of the project.* The project, on which Mahiti Manthana builds on (Mahila Samakhya), was based on a human resource intensive work strategy without digital platforms. The primary risk was a low level of acceptance of ICT as new development and communication tool and a subsequent lack of ownership. To mitigate this risk, it was decided to embed ICT in participatory methodologies and structures,

combined with regular consultations with the coordinating members of the project and demonstration of benefits related to ICT used. It was decided to adopt this "hand holding" approach, particularly at the beginning of the pilot project.

2. *Sociocultural aspects and acceptance of ICT within the self-help groups.* The challenge of acceptance on the members' side was even greater, particularly in light of the fact that most members were illiterate. Also, sociocultural challenges as the perception that low castes had no reason to use ICT, and a patriarchic reluctance to let women learn how to use these had to be considered. Therefore, it was decided to involve the community in the creation process of the new project, for example, through collective information sessions.

In light of this challenging project context, an adapted *project management approach* was developed: This community-based approach implied that from the beginning of the project planning process, meetings with local governments (Panchayat), grassroots NGOs, and various departments within the district were organized in order to inform them about the initiative and seek for their support. During the implementation phase, this approach implied the continuous involvement of local decision makers and the use of local expertise for content development of the ICT-based activities. Moreover, this approach implied that on the medium term, *sangha* women would be managing collectively the activities and interact with decision makers outside of the self-help groups, without depending on support of project coordinators.

The approach also consisted in using local expertise for content development, delivery, and interaction with local government organization. For example, it was decided that the content of the ICT-based activities (see section "Project Implementation") shall be created by local inhabitants and the members of the self-help groups.

The final step of the planning process consisted in the definition of the *projects components*, which can also be considered as the objectives of the new projects. As the Mahiti Manthana project was built on the foundations of Mahila Samakhya in Karnataka and its activities in Karnataka, the final objective—empowerment of rural women—remained unchanged. However, Mahiti Manthana's added value consisted in the development of seven specific activity components, all based on ICT, and considered as innovative tools in view of achieving this final objective:

1. Meet and develop knowledge and capacity needs of *sangha* women
2. Promote their communication and identity—building skills: *Use ICT in view of stronger self-confidence and acknowledge the legitimacy of their opinion in the villages*
3. Address information and communication needs of adolescent girls: *Use ICT to integrate and support vulnerable female adolescents*
4. Build and develop capacities of Mahila Samakhya coordinating personnel: *Use ICT in order to improve their managerial efficiency*
5. Enhance the intraorganizational information and communication process as well as the knowledge management of the project: *Use of ICT for effective communication*
6. Provide access to legal information and expertise: *Use ICT to access information that improves their livelihoods*
7. Strengthen linkages to governmental agencies: *Use ICT to interact with these agencies and create partnerships*

It was decided that these objectives should be achieved on the implementation of ICT based, self-managed activities. More precisely, it was decided that the three main components of the projects would consist in collective video and radio activities as well as ICT-based information transfer through telecenters (see Figure 14.1).

Project Implementation

Based on the findings and decisions made during the planning process, IT for Change started the implementation of its project Mahiti Manthana.

In the following, the actors of the implementation process as well as eventual challenges they faced will be presented.

Actors of the Implementation Process

1. *IT for Change.* The Indian NGO, through its field center, was in charge of conceptualizing, planning, designing, managing, and monitoring global aspects of the project.

Figure 14.1
Main ICT Components of Mahiti Manthana

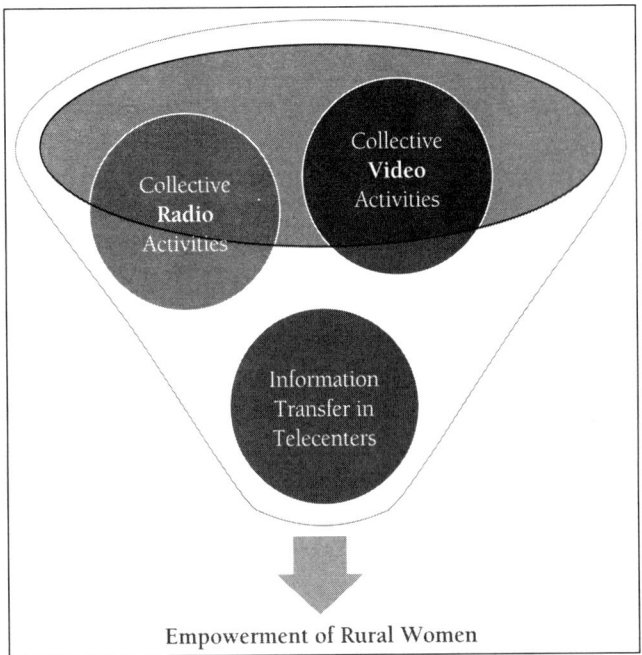

Source: Author.

Difficulties faced: The lack of infrastructures and difficulties to acquire appropriate locations for telecenter led to delays regarding the launch of telecenters.

2. *Mahila Samakhya, Karnataka.* This governmental initiative was responsible for the promotion of the ownership process through the involvement of its personnel on the field. Their work experience with self-groups explains their role domain experts in charge of internal evaluation. The project coordinators of this project were in charge of coordinating and sustaining Mahiti Manthana after the pilot phase, without IT for Change, and replicate the pilot experience in other states and districts.

Difficulties faced: In some cases, it was difficult to work with existing sangha groups as these, and particularly the leading sangha women, had already various responsibilities and tasks to fulfill. It was necessary to convince them about the project's utility and, subsequently, convince them to contribute to Mahiti Manthana.

3. *District administration.* The district administration of Mysore played a key role in the implementation process as it was in charge of creating and supporting links between *sanghas* and the governmental department, as well as the project field team of Mahiti Manthana. It provided content for the project activities.

4. *Panchayat Raj Institutions.* Even though no official implementation role was conferred to these local governments, they were actively involved as one of the project's objectives was to strengthen the relationship between *sanghas* and local governments. These local governments are in charge of supporting the activities of different resource centers of Mahiti Manthana.

Implementation Process

The implementation process of the pilot phase started in late 2005 to early 2006 and lasted until 2009.

Creation of Telecenters and the Concept of the "Self-help Group Classroom"

Up from 2006, four *Namma Mahiti Kendras* (*Our Information Centers*), in the following referred to as telecenters, and two hub centers (small telecenters depending on the main telecenters) for mainly illiterate women were created, serving as local knowledge institution for the surrounding villages.

Within these centers, the concept of "*sangha* shaale" ("self-help group classroom") is implemented: This concept involves organizing meetings of all *sangha* women within these telecenters. As they owned the telecenters and manage the activities of the "self-help group classroom," they are both members and coordinators of their telecenters. Even the creation of the telecenters is based on the negotiations between the *sangha* women with local, mainly masculine, power elites, in view of obtaining physical space, electricity and, if possible, Internet connection. This participatory approach, as defined during the planning process, is supposed to guarantee the participation of *sangha* women at all stages of interventions and to ascertain the support of village opinion leaders. It seeks to impact on the balance of power between men, local elite, and government officials.

At each telecenter, a young woman—trained by *sangha* women and the field center of IT for Change—acts as information intermediary between the telecenters, the villages and local departments. This young woman, also called *sakhi* (friend) is in charge of stimulating the dialogue with the government departments within the district in order to tackle issues such as lack of institutional transparency. Furthermore, her role is supposed to stimulate self-confidence and serve as example for leadership of young and adolescent women.

One of the main activities within these self-help group classrooms is the transfer of information to different categories of women in the villages. This transfer is done in association with constant identification of needs within the local population. This collection is conducted by adolescent volunteers. Small and marginal farmers, women headed households, *Dalit* populations, youth, disabled, and disadvantaged women are the main populations in need for support and information concerning governmental services, and therefore the target groups for this information transfer service. At telecenters level, information concerning entitlements and various governmental services, retrieved via the Internet (email) or directly from the websites of various departments, are directed by *sangha* women to the respectively concerned group category. However, women are not only informed about these governmental services but also received practical support when it comes to correctly fulfilling the application forms for a governmental service. For example, through these telecenters and their services, all pregnant women in the villages surrounding the telecenters are informed about the state government nutrition program for pregnant women provided by the *Anganawadi* centers.[2] They receive support during the application phase and receive their 6 kg rice provision. Also, children of villages surrounding the telecenters are fully covered by the *Anganawadi* centers, thanks to the same information process. Furthermore, women are informed about vaccinations dates in the Public Health Centers and are mobilized

---

[2] Child health centers which are part of the Indian public healthcare system.

by the *sangha* women to attend these dates. If they desire, they can even use themselves the computers in order to browse the Internet for information, supported by the coordinators or other *sangha* women. Another example of implementation is the transfer of information to *Dalit* women concerning the specific state livelihood programs conducted by the departments.

The concept of self-help group classrooms encourages also women leadership: *Sangha* attend the *gram sabhas* (village assemblies which are organized twice a year and are open to all women and men who are over 18) and report back to other women about decisions and debates taken place during these assemblies. They inform women about their rights and possibilities and encourage them to attend these assemblies, which are mainly dominated by men. Information on the elected representatives, for example, names, telephone numbers etc. are collected and made available for the community. Coalitions of different groups (e.g., young women) have also been formed in order to efficiently represent their interests.

Furthermore, the organizational structure is supposed to reflect the participatory approach of the project: The *Namma Mahiti Kendras* Management Committee is composed of women from self-help groups within the Mahila Samakhya project was well as other women empowerment initiatives as for example *Sthree Shakti*. The committee, which meets every month, is in charge of decisions concerning, for example, user fees, the choice and planning of activities and their content, review of completed activities, or conflict resolutions.

Radio- and Video-based Activities for Women

Besides offering rural and vulnerable women the possibility to access important information through the use of Internet and computers, Mahiti Manthana also organizes activities based on video and radio technologies in view of achieving the overarching goal of empowering rural women. The self-help group classroom concept seeks to work with technologies that go beyond text and written word based knowledge processes (see Table 14.1).

Video-based activities are one core activity of the project and have been implemented through the development of a toolkit, composed of various

Table 14.1

ICT Equipment of the Mahiti Manthana

Telecenter Equipment	*Video Equipment*	*Radio Equipment*
• Standard Personal Computer • Internet provided by BSNL (dial-up connection) • Digital cameras: Sony Cybershot 7.2. Mega Pixel)	• Minivid DV Sony PD 170 • Panasonic Handy Cam GS35 • 3 high-ends systems with DVD RW drives, two external hard drives of 250 GB • Sennheiser ME45 Boom Microphone and wireless lapel microphone • Reflector • Tripod • Video software: Adobe Premiere Pro 1.5 for video editing, Adobe Audition for audio editing and Adobe Encore for DVD authoring	• Microphones: Shure SM 58 • Microphones: Shure SM 58 • Recorders and systems: Field recordings via Edirol R09 Portable Recorders. • Two high end PC systems (1GB RAM, Intel P4, DVD RW drives and 80 GB HDDs) • Sony MDR – XD 100 headphones for clear monitoring of audio quality and levels. • Mixer: Yamaha MW10 Mixer and its CuBase software. • Software: Adobe Audition for audio editing/Audacity

Source: Author.

films accessible at each telecenter. More precisely, *sangha* women produce films on

- subjects relevant to the members and beneficiaries of the self-help group, such as:

  o Health (e.g., a film on the social and biological aspects of the menstruation process)
  o Literacy (e.g., a film on women's experience in a 48-day literacy camp held in Hunsur for *sangha* women)
  o Role plays related to gender conflicts
  o Functioning of the Gram Panchayats (local governments) and *gram sabhas* (assemblies)

o Movies on departments in charge of sericulture, agriculture, health, bank links (e.g., a filmed interview with the bank department in order to learn how to obtain a microcredit or use effectively certain crops

o Adolescent issues (e.g., a film on issues of choice in marriage)

- organizational aspects of the project for the main coordinators:

o Peer-to-peer learning and information sharing between different telecenters (use of telephone and email in order to update other self-help groups)

o Success stories of the projects

o Organizational practices

The Mahila Samakhya personnel are in charge of training *sangha* women how to produce films. These are supposed to teach in turn other *sangha* women the use of video technologies in order to guarantee the participatory approach of the methodology. In light of this approach, *sangha* women organize collective screening of films, followed by debates on what has been shown. More generally, these videos seek to impact on women's role and condition within the society through the creation of debates. During the pilot phase, the demand for screening and producing these films were steadily increasing, which lead to the creation of seven digital libraries in the state at block level (telecenters) and at village levels (hub centers), accessible for all *sangha* women.

ICT as dynamic and stimulating tool

The project does not aim to transform rural women into ICT experts, but to enable them to use ICT as tools, which facilitate their empowerment in the public sphere. Here, ICT do not only facilitate their communication possibilities, but also stimulate the dialogue and self-reflection on their social condition, as their utilizations leads to questions as: "How should we interpret phenomena? How do we ascribe meaning? How do we represent situations and issues?"

Radio-based activities are the second core component within this empowerment project for rural women: Mahiti Manthana has launched a weekly broadcast radio program, the so-called *Kelu Sakhi* (*Listen, my friend*) program. The radio programs are produced and recorded in a recording studio set up in the project office of Mahiti Manthana. A group of *sangha* women has taken ownership of this activity and produced the program with support from project coordinators. *Sangha* women choose collectively the content of the weekly programs. These programs focus mainly on the following areas:

- Issues pertaining to poverty, dowry, women rights, education, and health
- Campaigns on dysfunctions within the village assemblies
- Availability of new governmental services
- Ongoing and future activities within the self-help groups and invitation to contribute to the radio program
- Presentation of self-help group success stories—sharing of best practices and member motivation

The project uses the university radio channel *Gyan Vani* FM of the Karnataka State Open University, which accepted to air the program every Monday and Thursday morning, at no charge. The broadcasts cover the district of Mysore and can reach dispersed self-help groups. *Sangha* women meet in the telecenters that serve as dynamic space of dialogue: Members listen collectively to the broadcast of the program, discuss and reflect the respective subject afterwards. At this occasion, they also debate on possibilities to improve future programs.

The radio program has adopted an inclusive stance and its programs focus on the daily realities of different castes and categories of women, trying to contribute to a shift of attitude toward the most marginalized ones. More generally, the initiative seeks to help *sangha* women in the region to articulate their collective identity as members of a larger women's empowerment group, and to contribute to their identity-building process. Indeed, an increasing number of women decided to join the self-help groups within the Mahiti Manthana project and showed high interest to learn how to produce or at least contribute to the radio program (see Figure 14.2). The program also aims to increase the acknowledgement and legitimacy of their opinion within the community.

In order to reach a larger number of women, the radio program is broadcasted in the dialect spoken in the three taluks of the pilot project. Also, the program never uses names that give information on the religion or caste a character belongs to. Each program lasts maximum seven minutes in order to avoid a lack of attentiveness and is articulated in a clear, pedagogical way.

Introduction of Training Sessions

Training activities were another important component of the implementation process. The training, designed by IT for Change and Mahila Samakhya members, focused on different subjects depending on the respective target group. Training activities that dealt with advanced techniques were imparted by a team of experts who had been recruited for the project.

The following training activities were imparted:

1. Two workshops on general awareness of ICT and their potential for social projects were organized for representatives of the

Figure 14.2
Collective Listening Session

Source: IT for Change.

community. These workshops focused particularly on the radio initiative, and external experts were consulted for this purpose.

2. Training on general principles of radio use was imparted to the field staff of the project, as well as to staff of local governments.

3. Training of video recording techniques was imparted on voluntary basis to all *sangha* women. This training focuses on the basic principles of recording as well as on the process of editing, scripting, and choosing a drama format.

4. Equipment training, also imparted to all voluntary *sangha* women, focused more generally on the technical aspects of the equipment they used for the video and radio activities: connections, cables, software courses are part of this training.

5. For those willing to contribute either to the video or radio activities, the so-called ideation training was designed. These courses accompany *sangha* women through the whole production cycle: from the choice of a topic relevant for the project and teaches them various possibilities to approach and present the issue. Participants of this training met weekly.

6. Additional training focused on the learning of software like *Audacity*.

Supervision and Monitoring Process

The project monitoring was supported through an online content management system. This system allowed to record and exchange information between different telecenters and stakeholder of Mahiti Manthana and to supervise the actual evolution of the project in terms of

- the amount of villages and districts involved,
- the profile of *sangha* members,
- meetings held and the content,
- training programs,
- content viewing,
- content generation,
- the amount and frequency of ICT interaction with governmental agencies,

- ICT deployment, and
- ICT usage.

For each of these items, activities, efforts, and resources, as well as costs and timelines were recorded. On a regular basis, IT for Change and project coordinators conducted assessments of these indicators in order to understand the impact of the project on their members and to detect the most successful activities or possible problems.

Furthermore, the IT for Change team as well as a dedicated board, composed of a government official, an independent film maker, a technical experts, and a feminist activist researcher, met every quarter from 2005 to 2009 in order to conduct internal evaluations. These reviews allowed to guarantee that the project was constantly implemented and further developed.

Funding

The project was funded by UNDP and the Government of India with the project budget was INR 1,04,98,000 for the period 2005–2010. Funds were routed through the NGO National Institute for Smart Government.

Achievement and Impact

After the end of the pilot phase, UNDP conducted an evaluation of the project and came out with the following conclusions:

Telecenter Usage

Five telecenters and two subcenters were established. Each one covers around 5 to 6 villages and is accessed by the community in view of obtaining information and services offered by different governmental departments, for example, entitlements and schemes. The increased participation and interest of the community pressured the departments to be more transparent, accountable, and adopt a citizen-centered approach. Users reported that thanks to these telecenters, they could now easily and quickly access information and could reduce time and costs related to visits to the respective departments. Moreover, seven management committees for the telecenters were established and led by *sangha* women, who reported to feel empowered thanks to their new responsibilities. Furthermore, the request from many villages outside of those which were already involved in the project led to the creation of activities that could reach more than six villages.

Finally, some women who had been trained at the centers joined later local assemblies. Their increased importance for local governments also appeared during elections, when they were approached by political parties.

Development of Video Activities

During the pilot phase, 3 films directed by Mahila Samakhya staff and created by *sangha* women were produced. Around 17 productions without any help from staff members were produced. Over 180 collective viewing sessions of these films were organized by *sangha* women. Today, at many events of Mahila Samakhya video technologies and screenings are used. In each telecenter, one *sangha* woman has been elected to manage the video resources, and *sangha* women are considered in their villages as interlocutors for community screenings. An unforeseen impact of the video-based activities was the large utilization of the videos outside of the women self-help groups, for example, by men who wished to know more about local governance issues and services offered by different departments.

Development of Radio Activities

The weekly broadcasted program has become an inherent part of the university radio channel. The training of radio technologies has led to autonomous content creation for these weekly sessions. The majority of the radio sessions deal with subjects related to health, legal rights, education, social problems, gender and governance. Furthermore, 150 folk songs have been recorded and broadcasted during 2006 and 2009.

There are also unforeseen outcomes of this activity: The radio broadcast reaches areas outside of the district. This enlarged audience has reported to be enthusiastic about the program and other self-help groups (non-Mahiti Manthana/Mahila Samakhya) of the project have started radio training programs for their members after having listened to the broadcast. Finally, many women reported that their husbands, initially reluctant to let their wives take part in radio activities or collective listening sessions, were now proud that they were part of this project.

Impact on Learning Processes, Empowerment, and Communication Channels

From September to November 2010, an impact study conducted by IT for Change assessed the impacts of the pilot phase. This assessment was also developed in order to analyze the extent to which Mahiti Manthana had transformed preexisting collective learning-action process of Mahila Samakhya *sangha* women. Regarding the impact of the radio program, the in-depth interviews with *sangha* women revealed that the collective listening sessions were now regular part of their meetings and systematically followed by debates. They reported that these sessions had enhanced the dialog within the community.

Furthermore, *Dalit* women reported how important it was that non-*Dalit* women acknowledged their work and that this recognition impacted positively on their self-confidence.

The surveys revealed further that the video-based activities could increase women's awareness about public services, for example, how to access bank loans, the functioning of the local governments, and the availability of governmental entitlements. They reported further that the video-based activities allowed them to acquire the capacity to challenge mainstream discourses and enabled them to question the local power elite. Other women reported, for example, that the videos made them realize how important it was to send their children to school. Apart from the impact related to video content, the surveys also revealed that learning how to use a video camera and the associated software, as well as to speak in a film, for example, boosted their self-confidence. In addition, the creation and diffusion of videos impacted positively on the dialog between geographically dispersed women and motivated other women to be more actively involved in *sangha* self-help group activities.

Furthermore, the assessment showed that the instauration of telecenters within the communities and their services contributed to the creation of linkages between *sangha* women, non-*sangha* women and marginalized groups in the community. Women reported to appreciate the fact that they could now access important information on services provided by governmental departments through the *sakhi* intermediary at each telecenter. In general, the creation of *sakhis* impacted positively on the information flow: the surveys revealed that government officials passed over the information promptly to the intermediaries, which was not the case before when a *sangha* woman requested information. Other positive impacts of the telecenters include the introduction of services, such as photocopying and photography, freely available for all women.

The assessment observed also positive impact on the functioning of intraorganizational communication channels. Before the launch of the project, all communications between the committees and *sangha* women were based on postcards; the introduction of radio-based information diminished this mean of communication. In the meantime, the attendance at *sangha* meetings and activities improved as women were informed on time by the radio program. Finally, the surveys revealed that the resource persons of Mahila Samakhya could actually improve their ICT skills and learned how to record, plan and, edit radio programs, as well as shoot and edit videos. Most importantly, the surveys revealed a strong degree of ownership as many women referred, for example, to Mahiti Manthana as "our project."

Finally, UNDP evaluated the project according to five parameters: relevance, effectiveness, efficiency, results, and sustainability (see Figure 14.3). These were based on subparameters evaluated according to six levels: highly satisfactory (6 points), satisfactory (5 points), moderately satisfactory (4 points), moderately satisfactory (3 points), unsatisfactory (2 points) and highly unsatisfactory (1 point).They came to the conclusion that the project achieved mainly satisfactory and highly satisfactory results.

Post-pilot Phase

The success of the pilot phase led to the creation of a new project in Mysore district: IT for Change, Mahila Samakhya Karnataka and UNICEF launched in July 2009, a project which focuses on adolescent girls. The

Figure 14.3
UNDP Evaluation

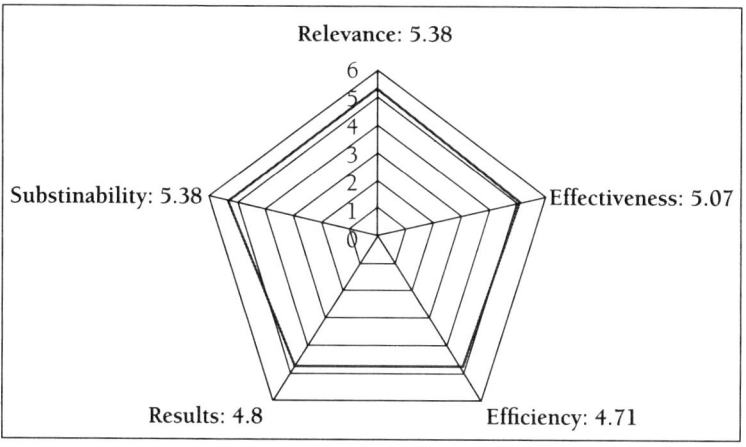

Source: UNDP (2009).

project addresses the learning needs of out-of-school adolescent girls through innovative uses of video, radio, photography, and computing technologies. Based on a social constructivist approach, girls are encouraged to explore and question their social and cultural environment. Furthermore, the project launched another IT project called "Women Gov," which aims to enhance women's participation in governmental structures through digital technologies.

Conclusion

Mahiti Manthana has successfully achieved designing of ICT-based activities for women within rural self-help groups and transforming the existing collective learning-action processes of the existing initiative Mahila Samakhya through the introduction of ICT-based activities in these learning processes. The project also achieved in enhancing the intra-organizational information and communication processes of the existing initiative. Most importantly, Mahiti Manthana carved out a space for rural women in the public sphere, allowed them to occupy audible positions in their communities, and impacted positively on existing power constellations.

There are several important factors that contributed to this success. Firstly, Mahiti Manthana's ICT strategy embedded nontextual tools and ICT-based material and activities in the learning processes of rural women. The use of tools that are both innovative and usable by illiterate women is one of the major key success factors of the project. As shown by the final assessments, rural women could not only increase their knowledge and access a higher amount of quality information and governmental services but also learn how to use innovative ICT tools that are not even handled by the majority of the male population. This increased considerably their self-confidence and self-esteem and led to an overall feeling of empowerment. The importance of adapting ICT to the overarching objective of a project clearly shows here.

Furthermore, the ICT strategy and functioning of the entire Mahiti Manthana project features a highly participative approach: From the beginning, the project was strengthened through an intensive participatory planning process (baselines surveys, needs assessment, consultation of local decision makers and NGOs) that led to strong community support. Most importantly, the constant involvement of the target group—rural women—during the implementation process of the project contributed to the widespread feeling of ownership that could be ascertained in the final assessments. The fact that these women were actually the actors of their change, allowed them to experience leadership and develop subsequently a feeling of responsibility and accountability.

Furthermore, the training that was extensively delivered to rural women allowed them to progressively expand their skills, and adopt sometimes the role of trainers themselves. This training was crucial in order to ensure that women could benefit as expected from the activities and can be considered as major success factor.

Summarizing the above, it can be said that combining a collective learning and organization process with a highly participatory approach contributed to the creation of a space in which vulnerable rural women can develop their capacities and actively empower themselves. It is this feeling of ownership that appears to be decisive for guaranteeing the project's sustainability. In the long term, this sustainability may be challenged by factors such as the necessity to acquire infrastructures for telecenters, which in turn depends on sustainable funding mechanisms. In addition, it is important to keep in mind that the project is being implemented under challenging social conditions: The project needs to align constantly to the specific needs of these rural women whose socioeconomic reality is conditioned by factors like castes, religion, and social class.

Bibliography

Dollar, M., Moyle, L., & Biswas, S.N. (2006). Personal and Economical Empowerment of Rural Indian Women: A Self-help Group Approach. *International Journal of Rural Management*, 2: 245–266.

Gurumurthy, A., Sing, P.J., & Kalley A. (2010). Mahiti Manthana Reimagining a Women's Empowerment Programme through Digital Technologies, IT for Change, 2010. Retrieved from http://www.itforchange.net/sites/default/files/ITfC/Mahiti%20Mantana-%20website.pdf (accessed February 4, 2013).

Gurumurthy, Anita, Singh, Parminder Jeet, Kalley, Aparna, Arakali, Chinmayi & Thimmaiah, Krupa. (2010). Digitizing a Feminist Stratagem What Mahiti Manthana Has Taught us about Women's Empowerment. Retrieved from http://www.isiswomen.org/index.php?option=com_content&view=article&id=1474&Itemid=206 (accessed February 4, 2013).

IT for Change. (2007). Mahiti Manthana—Institutionalizing ICT for Women's Collectives.

———. (2007). Using New ICT Possibilities to Strengthen Mahila Samakhya – A Policy Note Based on Emerging Insights from the Pilot Project Mahiti Manthana. Retrieved from http://www.itforchange.net/sites/default/files/ITfC/ict_for_ms-plan_updated2.pdf (accessed January 30, 2013).

Mahiti Manthana's Participation at the Stockholm Challenge. (2010). Retrieved from http://event.stockholmchallenge.org/project/2008/Education/Mahiti-Manthana (accessed January 30, 2013).

National Institute for Smart Government. (2010). Mahiti Manthana—Brief Outline of the Project. Retrieved from http://www.nisg.org/docs/Project_Mahiti_Manthana.pdf (accessed February 1, 2013).

UNDP India. (2010). Terminal Evaluation of Information and Communication Technology for Development. pp. 192–202.

Important Websites

IT for Change: www.itforchange.net

Data on India/World Bank: http://data.worldbank.org/country/india

Data on Karnataka/National Census 2011:http://www.census2011.co.in/census/
state/karnataka.html

Human Development Report/UNDP: http://hdr.undp.org/en/media/HDR_2011_
EN_Complete.pdf

Global Gender Gap Report/World Economic Forum: http://www3.weforum.org/
docs/WEF_GenderGap_Report_2012.pdf

15

Text2Teach: Mobile-based Video Lessons for Philippine Schools (Philippines)

Eilean von Lautz-Cauzanet

Overview

Text2Teach is the Philippine's pilot version of the global mobile learning program, BridgeIT, launched in 2003. This project provides selected schools with an information and communication technology (ICT) package that permits teachers to screen videos that have been previously downloaded on a mobile phone. The solidity of the public–private partnerships, close cooperation with local decision-makers and the easy-to-use technologies have contributed to the overall positive impacts of the project, such as lower dropout and absenteeism rates, improved performances at national assessments, and increased motivation. Although not focusing exclusively on rural areas, Text2Teach manages to support rural schools in an efficient and sustainable manner.

Project Background

Despite the significant economic growth that the Philippine economy has experienced in recent years, the country struggles to decrease the national poverty rate. In rural areas, where 51% of the Philippine population lived in 2011, the majority of the population is still poor (The International Fund for Agricultural Development-IFAD). The low population density in these rural areas led in turn to further challenges, particularly visible in the education sector: Many areas lack schools, classrooms as well as adequate teaching and learning material.

In order to tackle these problems, MoE has launched several initiatives and programs, among which figure also plans to use ICT in order to impact positively on the quality and access to education. The First Philippine Education Technology Master Plan, for example, was launched in 1996 and followed by two plans in 2005 and 2011. Another ICT initiative was the national program LINK, launched in order to enhance the connectivity of schools and provide teachers with ICT training.

For the general use of ICT in the Philippines, the expansion during the past decade has been consistent. While the number of people with a mobile cellular subscription was around 24 people out of 100 in 2003, this figure attained 92 people in 2011. Today, the Philippines are even sometimes called "the world's texting capital": Over 13 million cellular phones send around two million SMS every day (Figure 15.1). The amount of Filipinos using the Internet has also increased, particularly since 2009. The expansion process, however, appears to be slower compared to the figures of mobile phone use (Figure 15.2).

In this context, the project BridgeIT, the result of a partnership between the Pearson Foundation, Nokia, the International Youth Foundation, and United Nations Development Program (UNDP), approached the Ayala Foundation in 2003 to pilot BridgeIT in the Philippines. BridgeIT had developed a program in which teacher's access to quality education material could be improved through the creation of videos that are downloadable on traditional mobile phones. These can then be connected to a television and shown during the lesson. The project combines mobile technology and wireless technologies in order to deliver educational programs to those teachers and students who are

Figure 15.1
Mobile Cellular Subscriptions (Per 100 People)

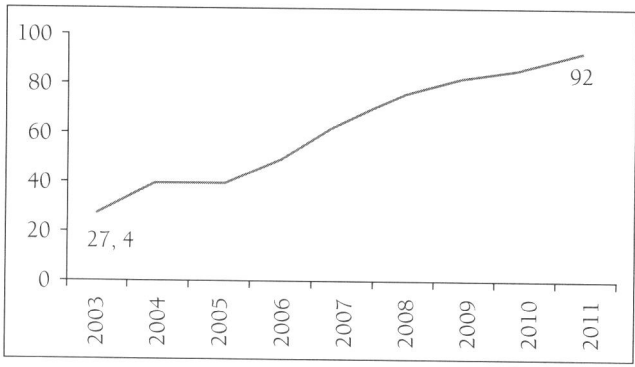

Source: World Bank (2012).

Figure 15.2
Internet Users (Per 100 People)

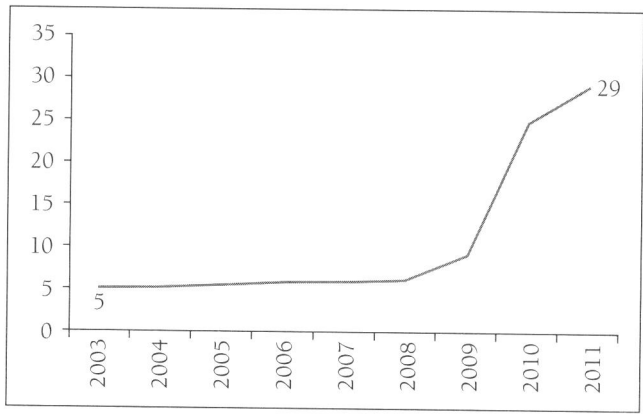

Source: World Bank (2012).

often deprived from access to quality education material, for example, in rural areas.

This decision to implement BridgeIT in the Philippines was based on the fact that the country already had a robust mobile technology infrastructure and because of the population's extensive use of mobile phones.

As SMS are commonly referred to as "text" in the Philippines, the project adopted the name Text2Teach for the Philippine BridgeIT version.

Project Planning

The planning process of implementing BridgeIT in the Philippines started in 2003 with the creation of a national alliance.

Launching a National Alliance

The decision to implement BridgeIT in the Philippines was followed by negotiations with national stakeholders in view of creating a Philippine-specific alliance. The Ayala Foundation could convince the following stakeholders to be main actors of the project:

- SEAMEO Innotech, the organization of Southeast Asian Ministries of Education Organization–Innotech—their regional center is based in the Philippines.
- PMSI, a satellite provider and the SMS software provider Chikka Asia, an Internet-based instant messaging application.

Most importantly, MoE accepted to be a member of the Text2Teach Philippine implementation team. The National Secretary of Education was chosen as permanent member of the Text2Teach steering committee and the project was subsequently incorporated in the National ICT for Education Strategy. This involvement signified that the project could count on the support of MoE both in terms of funding and organizational support.

This national alliance then started the planning of the first pilot phase. These steps, which will be discussed in the following, were later repeated at each of the project's expansion phases.

Identification of Text2Teach Areas and Design of an Inclusive Cost-sharing Partnership

In order to guarantee the success and sustainability of the project, the Text2Teach alliance adopted a local inclusion approach and developed a cost-sharing arrangement scheme. This scheme seeks to enhance community ownership through financial contribution by the local department of education (DepEd) offices and the so-called local government units (LGU).[1] For this purpose, visits to the regional DepEd offices were organized in order to explain them the educational benefits of the project. These DepEd offices in turn acted as local advocates and supported the Text2Teach proposals that were send to the LGUs. The collaboration with these LGUs was and is crucial for the project as they provide material and financial support to the schools in their respective areas. In order to inform the LGUs about the project and explain them the necessity to fund future Text2Teach schools, visits to the local school boards, which are part of each LGU, were organized.

In order to validate the selection of a future Text2Teach area, the following conditions had also to be fulfilled:

- Presence of Globe Telecom's mobile phone signal
- Commitment of LGU and local DepEd office to support the Text2Teach project in 10 to 12 schools
- Selected areas must be under–resourced areas and show low national test scores performances (e.g., in rural areas)

This partnership process and the fulfillment of the necessary criteria could be first achieved in the regions surrounding the cities of Quezon, Bantagas, and Cotobato. Later (see section "Project Implementation"), further regions and municipalities followed.

Community Launch

After having signed a memorandum of agreement with the local DepEd office, the planning process culminates with the release of funds provided by the LGU, made official during a community launch ceremony (Figure 15.3). This community launch is attended by LGUs, local DepEd offices, village chiefs, representatives of the parents association of each

---

[1] The Philippines started a process of decentralization in 1991. Local Government Units are composed of an executive, legislative and judiciary branches, as well as an assembly. They enjoy, to a certain extent, local autonomy, for example, they can decide to finance school projects.

Figure 15.3
Community Launch Ceremony

Source: Text2Teach.

Text2Teach school, as well as representatives from the Text2Teach alliance. This ceremony is also the opportunity to underline the importance of the local community for the project.

Reception and Adaptation of Text2Teach Material

After the community launch, Text2Teach schools receive their IT equipment.[2] In phase 1, the delivered package was composed of:

- Mobile phones (dual-band GSM900/1800 – Nokia 33 15 in 2003) and prepaid cards allowing teachers to use the phone for free
- CRT televisions
- Digital Satellite Recorder (Media Master)
- Access to a Nokia managed sever (260 S system setup) through which mobile phones can access the educational videos
- Library of educational videos developed by the Pearson Foundation and later local stakeholders
- Teacher guides for grades 5 and 6, as well as user manuals

---

[2] This equipment evolved later in phase 2 and 3.

MoE supervised the selection process of the material (selection of videos and design of teacher guides) to the basic education curriculum. This effort was made in order to guarantee concordance between the curriculum taught in Text2teach schools and traditional schools. Furthermore, this adaptation aimed to offer teachers the convenience of scheduling and integrating the program into their lesson plans. This should also avoid a feeling of additional workload.

Design of an Implementation Plan and Definition of Objectives

At this stage of the planning process, an implementation framework was designed. It was composed of five steps—later repeated during each expansion phase:

- School validation
- Delivery of the equipment to the schools
- Teacher training
- Classroom implementation
- Evaluation

Finally, the project defined the following objectives that the project should achieve:

- Encourage cooperation among the public, private, and civil society sectors at the local levels
- Complement the national curriculum with high quality educational content delivered through a mobile network
- Increase the performance of Text2Teach students at the National Achievement Test (NAT)
- Increase student's motivation and engagement in the classroom
- Decrease absenteeism and dropout rates
- Provide teachers with easily accessible quality content for their lessons without increasing their workload

Target Level and Groups

The target groups of the project are grade 5 and 6 students and teachers in both urban and rural areas. This decision was based on two reasons:

Firstly, students learn from grade 1 to 4 in their mother tongue and start using English during the lessons only in grade 5. Given that the Text2Teach material is mainly in English, it was decided to introduce the project only at grade 5. Furthermore, it was hoped that the project would positively impact on the students' motivation to pursue their studies in high school.

Project Implementation

In the following, the main actors of the project as well as eventual difficulties related to their activities or tasks will be presented.

Implementing Agencies

1. *Ayala Foundation.* In charge of the local coordination of the project, the foundation is in charge of mobilizing resources and project partners. It is also in charge in selecting future Text2Teach schools. The Ayala Foundation provides also technical support through a help desk reachable via the mobile phones.

2. *Department of Education.* Also called DepEd, the Department of Education defines the curriculum-based objectives of the program and verifies the concordance of the educational material with these objectives. It is further in charge of organizing and monitoring the teacher training component of the project. For this purpose, it is in charge of introducing the Text2Teach program in selected schools and coordinates the introduction of the program with the LGUs.

3. *Pearson Foundation.* This NGO funded the content review of the educational material and contributed to the development of new educational video materials and teacher guides.

   Difficulties faced: Some teachers found the videos produced difficult to understand, as some narrators were speaking too fast or with an accent difficult to understand for Philippine teachers and students. Furthermore, some videos did not suit the Philippine social reality and were considered as unhelpful. For this reason, local video productions were launched at a later point.

4. *Nokia Philippines*. Nokia Philippines is the largest fund provider from the private sector and provided the schools with the mobile phones and later with the NED software (Nokia Education Delivery) used for the project.

   Difficulties faced: Some teachers regretted that there were only one mobile phone and TV set per school, limiting sometimes organizing Text2Teach lessons as teachers had to share the infrastructures. However, some schools could gather additional funding in order to buy additional televisions and increase the availability of Text2Teach rooms.

5. *UNDP*. The United Nations Development Program is—until 2005—in charge of documenting lessons learned and best practices in order to facilitate the replication of the project.

6. *SEAMEO-Innotech*. The Southeast Asian Ministries of Education Organization-Innotech, a regional center for educational innovation and technology content is, during phases 2 and 3, in charge of content development of the project and teacher training (phase 3). It is part of the education and livelihood skills alliance, which funded partly the teacher guides.

7. *USAID*. This US agency funds the second phase of the project and allowed the extension of Text2Teach to further schools.

8. *PMSI*. This satellite provider was in charge of transmitting the videos on the mobile phones until 2007.

Implementation Process

In order to achieve operational efficiency, Text2Teach is implemented in clusters of 10 to 12 schools in each municipality. This collective approach was chosen in order to increase the willingness of the LGUs to fund the project and convince local DepEd to support the project. Finally, the clustering of Text2Teach schools should also facilitate the later evaluation of the project.

School Selection

The project starts with the selection of the schools that would participate in the project.

Schools willing to participate in the Text2Teach program receive a detailed questionnaire to be filled up by the principals and teachers and

Figure 15.4
Visit to a Rural School during the Selection Process

Source: Text2Teach (2011).

are then interviewed. These interviews focus on the fulfillment of the following criteria (Figure 15.4):

- Commitment and support of the local government and community
- Readiness of the schools for ICT-enabled instructions
- Commitment of schools to support and sustain the project
- School performance indicators
- School's accessibility to electrical power
- Strength of mobile phone signals
- School's ability to provide security for equipment
- History of community support to earlier and/or existing projects
- Similar interventions within the school
- Clustering of schools by city or municipality

Teacher Training

In order to ensure the adequate use and understanding of the mobile-based teaching tool, the so-called training of trainers (TOT) is organized.

The training is managed by the project team and the central Department of Education, more precisely the Bureau of Elementary Education, which trains supervisors from local DepEd offices. This pool of teacher trainers is in charge of organizing the teacher training of selected schools. While these trainers are in charge of the curriculum component of the training, staff from the Ayala Foundation provides teachers with the technical training with regards to a proper use of Text2Teach technologies (Figure 15.5).

Teachers and principals from each selected school are trained in an intensive three days training course. The courses are delivered within the respective schools. Teachers and principals receive training on:

- The historical overview of the project and plans for the future.
- The appropriate introduction of the Text2Teach videos in the lesson, in concordance with the curriculum and based on the teacher's guides: Teachers learn how to associate various activities to different videos related to the subjects of the curriculum. Furthermore, they learn to integrate the videos actively in the student's learning process. The training focuses on possibilities to

Figure 15.5
Teachers during Their Training

Source: Text2Teach (2011).

stimulate the learner's interest and enhance learning approaches based on exploration and collaboration.

- Technological components (e.g., how to connect the mobile phone to the television, how to choose and download videos, trouble-shooting, etc.)

The training session are accompanied by practical simulations and activities in which teacher have to demonstrate lessons and activities. The training also focuses on the importance of community involvement and trained teachers to develop a sustainable plan for their respective schools. During the courses, teachers are encouraged to use their phones for communication with their peers, in order to create progressively a Text2Teach community and exchange best practices via SMS and in some regions, via Facebook groups. The training is also supposed to strengthen teacher's receptivity and motivation to use the new teaching tool. In addition, it seeks to increase teachers' self-confidence with regard to ICT use and to enhance their professional development.

Content and Pedagogical Approach

Text2Teach videos are available for four subjects:

- English
- Mathematics
- Sciences
- Values (phase 3)

For each subjects, videos and associated teaching guides are adapted to the national curriculum. Students are supposed to learn the same content as their peers in traditional schools, but in a more efficient manner. The pedagogical approach of Text2Teach is based on the learner-centered approach as it has been defined by MoE in the curriculum of basic education. For the pedagogical component of Text2Teach, this means concretely that each video screening is based on pre-viewing activities, as for example the request to brainstorm during a sciences class together about the meaning of puberty. Furthermore, after the collective video sessions, activities, such as group works, are organized. The teacher is supposed to serve as a tutor who guides students through their video-based learning process. At a later stage of the project, a subject dealing with values was introduced, which came along with the production of cultural sensitive videos. For example, some English videos focused on peace education subjects and take into consideration the cultural reality of the Philippines, including Muslim, Christians and Indigenous protagonists. The teacher's guide offers teachers lesson plans for each subject and grade and proposes the associated videos. Furthermore, the guide is supposed to support the pedagogical component of the lesson through providing examples of activities (e.g., group discussion, collective projects) that the teacher can organize in concordance with the subject and video.

Evolution of the ICT Framework

Phase 1: BridgeIT–Text2Teach Pilot Phase (2003–2005)

The first phase of the program started in 40 schools that were selected in the municipalities of Quezon, Bantagas, and Cotobato. At this very first stage, the project was officially named Text2Teach. In 2004, the project started to be piloted in further 41 schools in Oriental Mindoro, Antique, and Cagayan de Oro.

During the period 2004–2005, teachers had the possibility to choose among 120 educational videos of five minutes each. More precisely, teachers could order educational videos from a Nokia-managed server. For this purpose, teachers had to send the catalogue number of the desired video through the Chikka SMS server. This provider used the Globe's GSM network to connect to the multimedia server of the text to teach portal. Videos were then delivered via PMSI satellite and could be downloaded to a digital video recorder connected to a CRT-TV set in the school. Teachers could also use the mobile phone to access the Text2Teach helpdesk or to communicate with other teachers, for example, in order to compare experiences or notes via SMS or exchange via Facebook groups' information on updates, events, or post pictures (Figure 15.6).

Phase 2: USAID-funded Text2Teach (2005–2007)

From 2005 to 2007, another 124 public schools in the so-called region 12, also called SoCCSKSarGen[3] and the Autonomous Region of Muslim

---

[3] Acronym that stands for the region's four provinces and one of its cities: South Cotabato, Cotabato, Sultan Kudarat, Sarangani, and General Santos City.

Figure 15.6
Text2Teach ICT Infrastructure during Phase 1

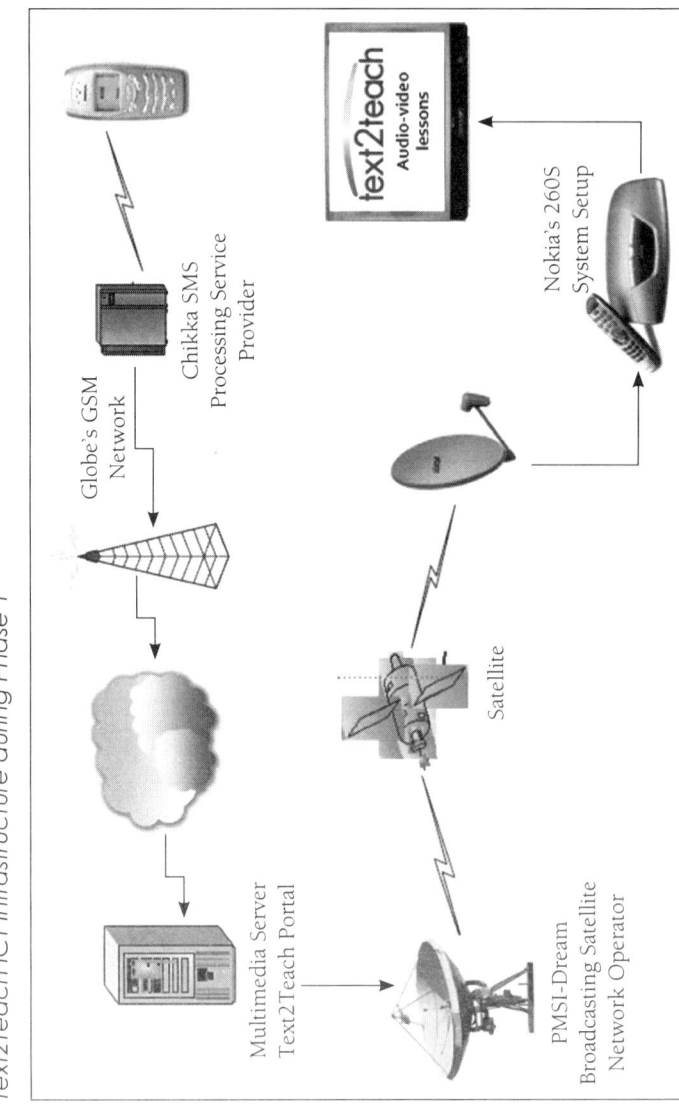

Source: Ayala Foundation (2011).

Mindanao (ARMM) joined the Text2Teach project. During this phase, USAID funded the project through the Education and Livelihood Skills Alliance (ELSA). Teachers had now the possibility to choose among 400 videos, preloaded on the mobile phone (Figure 15.7).

The second phase of the Text2Teach project was followed by a revision of the videos in order to actualize the content according to the national curriculum and its recent evolutions. For this purpose, 23 education specialists from the Department of Education reviewed all videos in order to detect outdated or inefficient videos and teacher guides. Furthermore, the Ayala Foundation approached Philippine scriptwriters and organized workshops, bringing together the scriptwriters and specialists from the DepEd in order to produce videos that were tailored to the needs of the Philippine curriculum. The final production of these videos was managed by:

- Filipinas Heritage Library (FHL)
- Ramon Magsaysay Award Foundation (RMAF)

Figure 15.7
Mobile Connected Video Screening

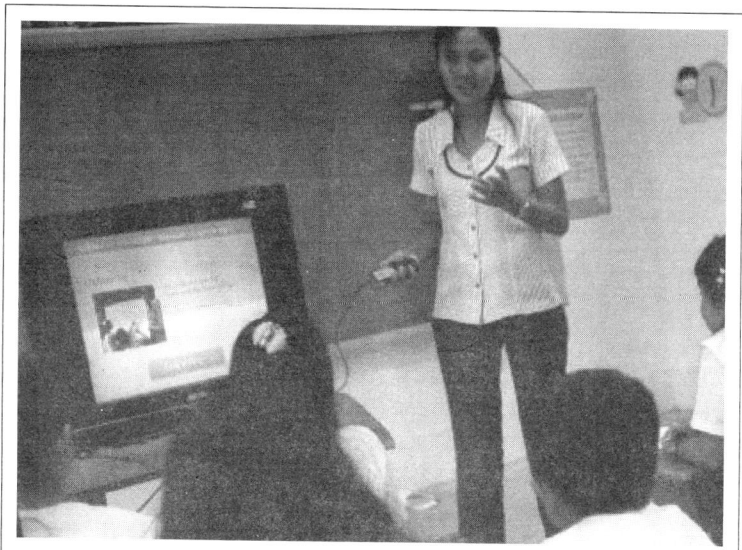

Source: Text2Teach (2011).

- Overmind Stress Productions
- Asia American Initiative and YouthGOAL, Inc.
- Young Leaders Alliance Alumni

Phase 3: Nokia Education Delivery Text2Teach (2008–2011)

In order to provide better connectivity to particularly remote schools, it was decided to replace the satellite dish, as well as the Media Master and hitherto used mobile phones. Concretely, schools were provided with 8 GB Nokia N95 mobile phones, loaded with Nokia Education Delivery software (Figure 15.8). Through Globe's 3G infrastructures, teachers could now download a video in less than 15 minutes. Furthermore, they could store and catalogue the videos in their mobile phones for future users. In order to screen the videos during a lesson, teachers connected the mobile phone directly to the new 29-inch flat screen TV or digital projector (Figure 15.9). The third phase of the project also increased its video offer: teacher could now choose among 900 videos.

Distribution of Funds

Costs of the project were progressively increasing throughout the phases and the expansion of the project. The third phase, for example, was funded with PHP 354 millions (~USD 871,000) by the Text2Teach alliance (private sector) and with PHP 105 million (~USD 258,000) by

Figure 15.8
Mobile Phone with NED Software

Source: Text2Teach (2011).

Figure 15.9
Text2Tech ICT Infrastructure during Phase 3

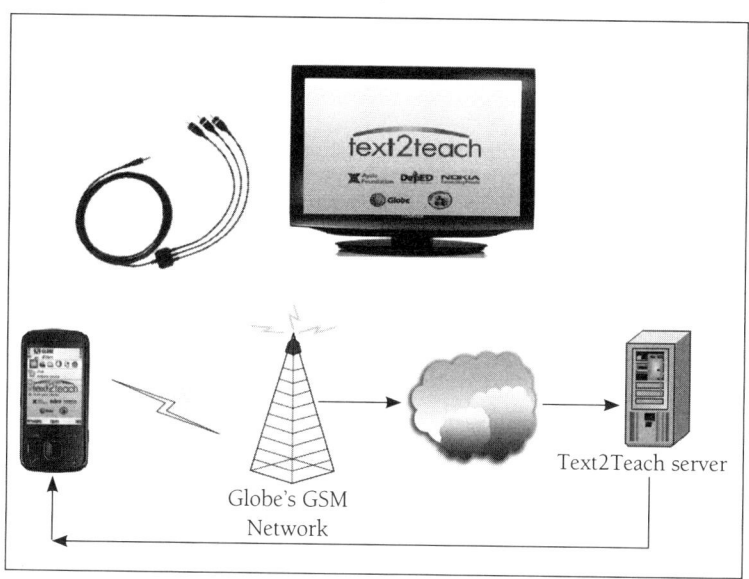

Source: Ayala Foundation (2011).

Figure 15.10
Main Funding Agencies

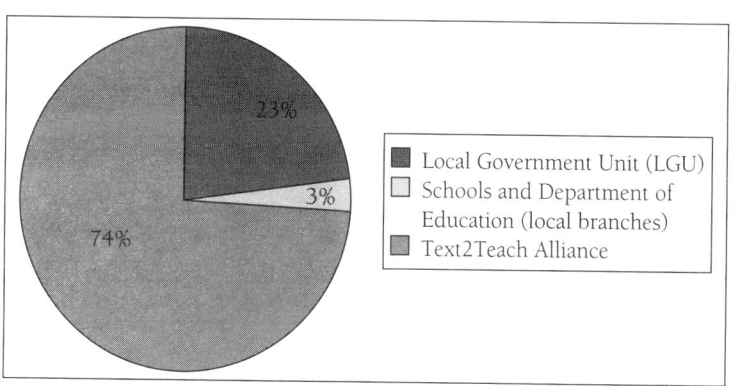

Source: Text2Teach (2012).

Figure 15.11
Average Distribution of Funds

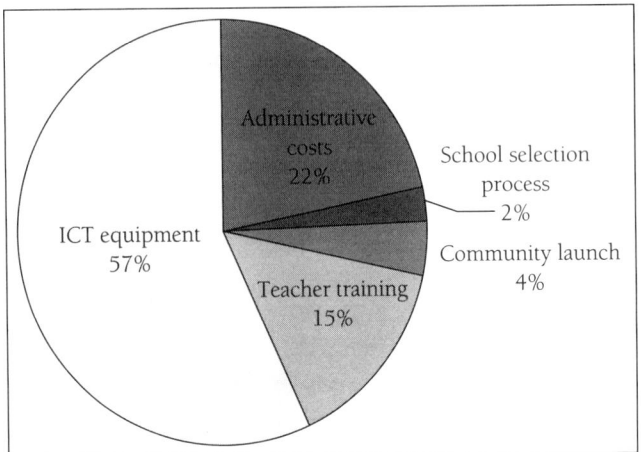

Source: Text2Teach (2012).

the LGUs and local DepEd offices (public sector) (Figure 15.10). These funds were mainly spent for ICT equipment, administrative funds, and teacher training. Other costs included those related to the community launch and cooperation with the local community and decision-makers and the subsequent school selection process (Figure 15.11).

Supervision

A supervision process was implemented in order to guarantee the efficiency of the project. More precisely, the Ayala Foundation provides LGUs and local DepEd offices with completion reports containing the details of how their funds were used. Furthermore, a monitoring system was set up in order to evaluate the usage and impact of Text2Teach: For this purposes, teachers and principals elaborate feedback reports for this purpose. Finally, third-party evaluations are organized in order to evaluate the overall impact of the project after each phase.

Achievement

Third-party evaluation studies were conducted for each of the phases by the following entities:

- Phase 1: National Institute for Science and Mathematics Educational Development (NISMED)
- Phase 2: Demographic Research and Development Foundation (DRDF)
- Phase 3: Monitoring and evaluation by team of external consultants

Thanks to these evaluations, the projects achievements are quantifiable today. By the end of the third phase, the project had achieved to:

- Launch 440 Text2Teach schools
- Train 1,476 primary school teachers
- Involve 976,000 students (rural and urban)

See Figure 15.12.

The evaluations also revealed the positive impact of Text2Teach more precisely:

- Reduced dropout rates
- More regular school attendance—lower absenteeism
- Increased learning gains: improved NAT results in mathematics, English and sciences
- Increased scores at test conducted as post-viewing evaluation activities
- Improvement of students' behavior: increased discipline and motivation, students became more engaged in school activities
- Improved teacher competence and attitudes towards using technology as a teaching tool
- Teachers felt disburden during the preparation of their lessons
- Teachers felt more connected to their peers, particularly in rural areas
- Positive attitude on the community/school officials/parents side toward ICT use in the classroom and advocated the project in other schools

Figure 15.12
Number of Text2Teach Schools Out of All Public Elementary Schools (2011)

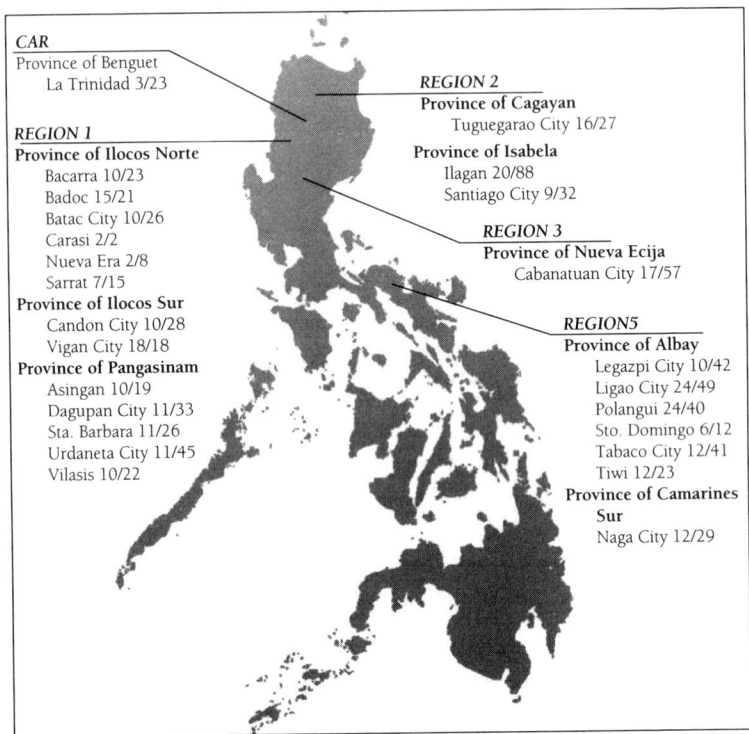

Source: Text2Teach (2011).

- More efficient communication between teachers, thanks to the mobile phones, including efficient dissemination of information and opportunities
- Improved relationship between local decision makers and schools

Post-pilot Phase

The fourth phase of the project started in 2011 and seeks to increase the number of Text2Teach schools to 850. It is also planned to review and produce new videos and teachers' guides. Video content focusing on environmental issues, responsible citizenship, and disaster preparedness are also planned to be covered by the new videos. In terms of ICT development, the fourth phase will include the Nokia Data Gathering (NDG) software that allows collecting data in a fast and cost-effective manner even from remote locations. For example, this software will allow sending questionnaires directly to teachers in different Text2Teach schools.

Conclusion

Text2Teach has been able to achieve its objective to improve the access to quality education through mobile phones and ICT-enabled framework that allowed teachers to download and screen videos during their lessons. While videos stimulated the motivation and learning outcomes of students, the use of interconnected mobile phones provided teachers with pedagogical supports and quality content for their lessons.

Text2Teach has particularly changed the daily routine of selected schools in remote areas that are deprived from adequate teaching material and infrastructure. Globally, one can say that the project achieved its objectives: It lowered absenteeism and dropout rates and improved the overall performances of students who were particularly vulnerable to school failure.

To analyze the success of this project, various factors appear to have clearly contributed to the achievement of Text2Teach.

Firstly, strong and solid partnerships between the public and the private sector have significantly contributed to the project's efficiency. The rapid expansion and development of Text2Teach would have been impossible without the involvement of local enterprises willing to take part in the project and produce videos for Text2Teach in cooperation with educational experts. These partnerships allowed not only increasing the number but also the quality of available videos and permitted to adapt their content to the evolutions of the national curriculum. This effort to constantly update and improve the project has stimulated the interest on the user side and avoided the lack of interest that some projects face after a first time of enthusiasm and curiosity.

This public–private partnership approach, which included the systematic involvement of the local DepEd offices and LGUs allowed not only leveraging additional funding, thanks to the cost-sharing arrangement scheme. Most importantly, it contributed to the project's sustainability, creating a feeling of ownership, and responsibility toward Text2Teach in the respective communities. The community support, which could be enhanced through the culturally sensitive content of the videos, is one the most crucial success factors of the project and also considerably increases its chances of longevity in the long term.

Furthermore, Text2Teach is also characterized by a continuous effort to monitor and evaluate the project. The instauration of a helpdesk for teachers, the reports provided by the Ayala Foundation on the utilization of the funds and finally the overall impact evaluations conducted after each phase contributed to the success of the project. More precisely, these organizational efforts created a relationship of proximity between management entities and beneficiaries, which in turn increased efficiency of the project in general and impacted positively on motivation of teachers to use the new tool. It further allowed to adopt a rigorous process of content review and development, and to adapt to new opportunities related to the development of ICT, and challenges, such as moving from a satellite-based to a NED-based software.

The key success factor, however, lies in the choice of the used technology. The mobile phones are extremely easy to use and facilitated the teaching instead of complicating it. A three-day intensive training only sufficed to train teachers how to use the mobile phones and download videos. Given the considerable impact of the project, and compared to training periods of other ICT-based projects, this is an important element. It proves that successful ICT for development projects do not necessarily rely on complex and brand new technologies: a mobile phone, a cable, and a television can suffice. It leads us to the conclusion that choosing technologies to which users can adapt quickly increases their global receptivity toward the project and the long-term efficiency of the latter. Most importantly, the ICT framework could prove its efficiency in rural areas, albeit the project did not exclusively focus on these.

A Tanzanian version of BridgeIT has been launched in Tanzania and demonstrates the project's replicability and flexibility to adapt to challenges that are simultaneously similar and different to those rural areas faced in the Philippines. In order to replicate and expand the project further, it appears to be recommendable to tackle eventual weaknesses of the project, for example, the limitation in terms of subject (mathematics, English, and sciences), the dependence on a specific telecom provider, and the risk to face technological obsolescence as well as constant need of financial support in view of covering the costs related to the mobile use.

Bibliography

Ayala Foundation. (2011). Text2Teach. Guide for Text2Teach Schools Validation.
———. (2011). Text2Teach. Internal Guidelines for Text2Teach Teacher's Training.
———. (2011). Text2Teach. Internal Summary of the Content Development Process.
———. (2011). Text2Teach. Phase III Accomplishment Report.
———. (2012). Text2Teach. Power Point Presentation on Phases 1 to 4.
Josh Weinstein (2010). The Problem of Rural Education in the Philippines. Retrieved from http://joshweinstein.wordpress.com/2010/03/02/the-problem-of-education-in-the-philippines (accessed February 18, 2013).
Ramos, Angelo Juan, Nangit, Genevieve, Ranga, Adelina I., & Triñona, Jerome. (2007). "ICT-Enabled Distance Education in Community Development in the Philippines," *Distance Education,* 28:2; ProQuest Education Journal. Retrieved from http://unpan1.un.org/intradoc/groups/public/documents/unpan/unpan037291.pdf (accessed February 18, 2013).
The World Bank. (2012). Mobile Applications for Agriculture and Rural Development. Retrieved from http://siteresources.worldbank.org/INFORMATIONANDCOMMUNICATIONANDTECHNOLOGIES/Resources/MobileApplications_for_ARD.pdf (accessed February 18, 2013).
UNESCO Bangkok. (2004). *Integrating ICT in Education: Lessons Learned.* Bangkok.
UNESCO. (2011). Mobile Learning for Teachers in Asia. Retrieved from http://unesdoc.unesco.org/images/0021/002162/216284E.pdf (accessed February 18, 2013).
United Nations. (2004). *NOKIA and Pearson BridgeIT Partnership.* Retrieved from http://business.un.org/fr/documents/276 (accessed February 18, 2013).

16

Tradenet: The Mobile Trade Platform for Small Farmers (Sri Lanka)

Eilean von Lautz-Cauzanet

Overview

Tradenet was launched by Dialog and the think-tank LIRNE*asia* in 2009. The project aims to reduce those costs of small farmers that are related to information search during the agricultural value chain farmers can access price information via SMS, the dedicated website or call center and even trade their products for a fair price via this platform. The project has already shown positive impacts on farmer livelihoods, including reduced price vulnerability, higher income, and decreased dependency on middlemen.

Project Background

Since the end of the armed conflict in 2009, Sri Lanka's economy has shown a growth of 8% both in 2010 and 2011 and poverty rates have decreased from 15% in 2006–2007 to 9% in 2009–2010. The agricultural sector is of great significance for the country, as it employs almost 33% of all Sri Lankan employees (World Bank, 2009b).

However, a closer look at this sector reveals challenges: According to the Sri Lankan Department of Census and Statistics, 82% of the population living below the national poverty line lives in rural areas. In reality, the poverty headcount ratio at rural poverty line accounts for 9% of the rural population (Word Bank, 2009b). The majority of the rural poor are engaged in the agricultural sector. Around 37% of agricultural land is used by the plantation sector, covering export cash crops, such as tea, rubber, and coconut. On the other hand, a significant share of landowners are small farmers, who rarely own more than 8 m^2 of land, and cultivate mainly field crops, such as maize, chili, onion, and other fruits and vegetables. These crops are traded at one of the eight major markets, of which the Dambulla market is the largest with the value of daily traded products attains almost 4.5 million USD. The market is divided into 144 stalls owned by middlemen and traders. These middlemen obviously take commissions from farmers for their services, which can affect negatively particularly small farmers. Furthermore, Sri Lankan markets are characterized by the absence of auction mechanisms as they exist, for example, in India. In Sri Lanka, prices are determined by individual negotiations, which leads to high information asymmetry. Furthermore, the use of forward contracts has not been very successful in Sri Lanka, despite the introduction of tripartite forward agreements by the Central Bank in 1999 in order to reduce price volatility. Forward contracts are often broken (by both sellers and buyers) depending on the spot price on the contract's delivery date. This price volatility and information asymmetry disadvantages again particularly small farmers, who face major challenges to participate effectively in agricultural markets. In order to obtain information on crops and market prices, farmers have to visit markets or meet farmers who have been to the market before. They can also obtain information on the average prices provided by the Dambulla market, which are published in newspapers, radio, and TV on a daily basis. However, these prices are not concise, given the issue of price volatility. In consequence, a majority of small farmers sell their products for smaller prices than expected. In addition, they are unable to take efficient decisions regarding their crop planting and harvesting schedules or to adapt their production to market demands. Their lack of information and an efficient production planning also restricts their possibilities to engage financial instruments, such as forward contracts. Subsequently, they cannot access crop insurance and working capital loans for which they use their products as collateral.

In light of these challenges, the project Tradenet was developed in 2009 in order to increase price transparency by creating an online price information platform that informs farmers via SMS about market prices on a real-time basis and to permit them to trade their products via the platform.

Impact of Similar Projects

The Tradenet project is inspired by two existing projects: Firstly, the Govi Gnana Seva initiative (in English: Farmer Knowledge System), a nonprofit organization, which was developed in 2002 by the economist Harish de Silva and supported by the ICT Agency of Sri Lanka, funded the project through World Bank funds. This initiative consisted in tackling the issue of information asymmetry through the collection of price information at the Dambulla market, conducted by dedicated investigators. This then transferred the information to a server, and prices were disseminated via local screens, newspapers, radio, or television. Tradenet aimed to expand the functionalities of Govi Gnana Seva in order to offer more price information from various markets on a real-time basis.

The second initiative which inspired Tradenet was the Cell Bazar project in Bangladesh. This project offered a mobile platform, able to match offers and demands from users interested in trading agricultural and nonagricultural products. The use of mobile phones for information delivery and efficient trading should be reused for the Sri Lankans Tradenet project.

Planning Process

Involved in international research on the impact of ICT, particularly mobile phone on the efficiency of agricultural markets, the 2004 created think-tank LIRNE*asia* elaborated in 2008 a study funded by the

International Development Research Center (IDRC) on the role of ICT in reducing those costs that were related to information search, one of the major challenges for small farmers. This study can be considered as the first step within the design process of Tradenet.

Preparatory Study on the Potential of ICT to Reduce Costs Related to Information Search

For this study, LIRNE*asia* established firstly the meaning of information search costs. These costs were defined to be part of transaction costs, which in turn are part of the total costs that each farmer has to incur. Concretely, a cost that could be reduced by the use of an alternative source in order to obtain the same information, for example, a telephone call, is an information search cost. On the contrary, costs related to a visit in view of buying, for example, fertilizers are defined as observable transaction costs.

Then, LIRNE*asia* started the selection of small farmers who were all selling their products at the Dambulla market. These farmers depend on the *Farmer Knowledge Service* in order to buy and sell products. It is important to mention here that a governmental distribution system offers low prices for fertilizers to rice farmers and some plantation farmers, but not vegetable farmers. This has contributed to a perverse incentive for vegetable farmers, who spent time and money to search for opportunities to purchase these fertilizers, despite their ineligibility.

In order to guarantee the representativeness of the study, 314 farmers were chosen from 10 out of 89 farmer associations, who cultivated tomatoes, onion, aubergine (eggplant), or chili. The study focused on the costs at each of the seven phases of the agricultural value chain: (a) deciding, (b) seeding, (c) preparing and planting, (d) growing, (e) harvesting, (f) packing and storing, and (g) selling (see Figure 16.1).

Figure 16.1
Phases of the Agricultural Value Chain

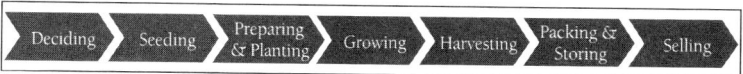

Source: World Bank (2009a).

Enumerators recruited from the Dambulla Agriculture Technical College conducted interviews at the farmer's homes under the supervision of the *Farmer Knowledge System* staff. Questions covered the whole agricultural value-chain process and aimed to identify the information search related costs at each of these steps.

The study revealed that 15.2% of all costs the interviewees reported to have were due to transaction costs occurring during the seven phases, and that a majority of these transaction costs were due to information research (see Figure 16.2).

The interviews revealed further that in terms of high information search costs, the growing phase ranks first followed by the decision phase, the selling phase, and the preparation phase: During the growing

Figure 16.2
Breakdown of Total Information Search Cost by Stage

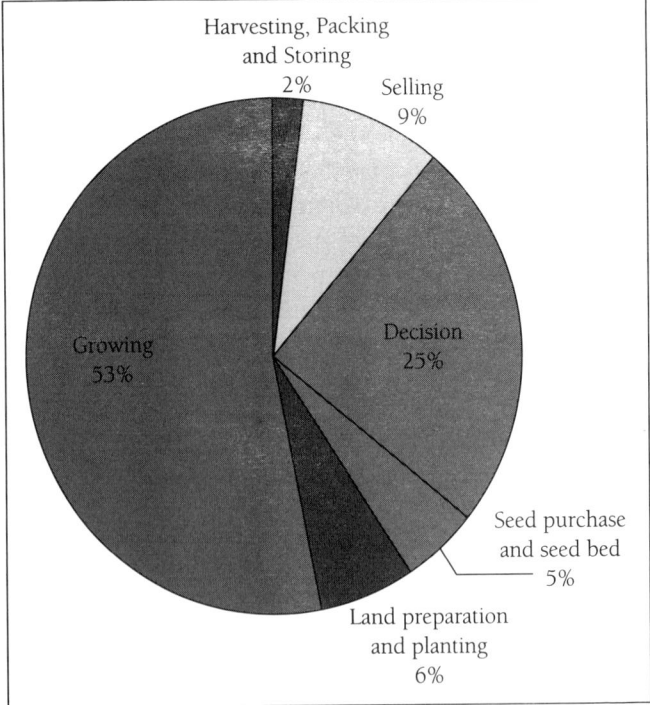

Source: Adapted from de Silva and Ratnadiwakara (2008).

phase, the high amount of costs related to information search were directly linked to the costs occurred during the growing phase, because of the governmental distribution procedure of fertilizers.

During the decision phase, farmers incurred costs related to information search as they had to visit farmers associations and neighbors, for example, in order to decide which crop to grow. During this phase, farmers also had to face additional information costs as they were obliged to organize visits to banks and rural finance institutions in order to obtain information, application forms and guarantors, indispensable in view of financial support. Furthermore, information search costs during the selling phase were related to the obligation to compare prices at various markets and provided by different traders as well as the necessity to find means of transportation to the market. Finally, farmers incurred costs during the preparation phase as they had to look for agricultural equipment or search for information on seeding types.

Potential Impact of ICT

This LIRNE*asia* study revealed that small farmers hardly ever used phones to obtain the information they were looking for during different phases of the agricultural value chain process. Only 0.2% of the total costs related to information search was related to phone calls. In comparison, it was found that farmers traveled around 24 times to markets and agricultural stakeholders in order to obtain information, fertilizers, or ideal prices for their products and that these visits cost them around USD 52. Assuming that around half of these visits could be replaced by phone calls, the researchers came to the conclusion that costs related to information search could indeed be considerably diminished. They based their hypothesis by referring on similar experiences and studies, which revealed that fishermen who used mobile phones for information search could diminish their costs.

Partnership with Dialog and Design of Tradenet

The finding that ICT could actually have a positive impact on farmer's producing and trading opportunities, convinced LIRNE*asia* to put the research results into practice. For this purpose, Dialog Axiata PLC, the largest mobile phone operator in Sri Lanka, accepted to participate in this project, and USAID and IDRC provided parts of the funds necessary for the design of the project.

On the base of their research findings, the research team, composed of both Dialog and LIRNE*asia* personnel, decided to create an online platform that would bring farmers, enterprises of varying sizes, aggregators, and trade associations or cooperatives together. More precisely, they designed a platform that:

- allows the delivery of spot and forward agricultural commodity price information via mobile phones and enable farmers to integrate supply and demand information for their agricultural production
- is a repository for price information from the three biggest markets in Sri Lanka: Dambulla, Meegoda, and Narahenpita
- encompasses the collation, comparison, qualification, and dissemination of information that is indispensable for efficient trading
- allows farmers and buyers to conclude both spot and forward contracts
- reaches a large number of stakeholders and diminish information arbitrage; particularly small farmers who live in rural areas with a low Internet penetration rate but high mobile phone penetration rate (m-readiness) are supposed to be reached by these technologies.

Defining Objectives

Finally, the planning phase culminated with the definition of the objectives that the use of the platform should achieve:

- Increase the financial capital of farmers by reducing their vulnerability related to price trends.
- Enhance their decision-making capacities by offering them the possibility to leverage a large amount of adequate information.
- Contribute to the social and functional network of farmers

- Increase their physical capital by reducing crop wastage resulting from their inability to sell harvested crops during periods of over-supply in the market.

Project Implementation

In the following section, the main actors of the implementation process, their role as well as eventual difficulties they faced will be presented.

Implementing Agencies

1. *Dialog.* Dialog designed, supported by LIRNE*asia*, the Tradenet project and provided the technical and ICT framework of the platform through which the agricultural market information was disseminated. Dialog is in charge of coordinating the platform activities.

   Difficulties faced: The patchy phone reception in some areas limited the use of the mobile-based alert and trading system. Furthermore, LIRNEasia desired to establish a timeline defining the moment Tradenet would become available to farmers using other operators than Tradenet. Firstly, this was not possible due to telecommunication regulations. However, even after the end of this restriction, Tradenet was reluctant to offer the service to users of other operators.

2. LIRNE*asia*. The think-tank provided research on how to improve the data collection system and expand the outreach of the platform to more markets.

3. Govi Gnana Seva (GGS). The nonprofit organization GoviGnanaSeva worked together with Dialog and was in charge of collecting the price information at the three dedicated markets. Under the supervision of a manager, around eight information collectors were in charge of gathering real-time price information and transfer these via WAP (Wireless Application Protocol)-enabled mobile phones to the Tradenet server.

4. *IDRC and USAID.* both funded the research conducted by LIRNE*asia* in view of expanding the platform to three other markets than those involved during the pilot phase. They also

launched the idea to charge a small fee for the use of the platform and funded the survey (see Action Research Project) in which this possibility was assessed.

Implementation Process

In December 2009, the Tradenet was officially launched during an opening ceremony at the launched at the Meegoda market. The same month, famers start to benefit from the following services.

Information and Trade Services

The portal offered farmers three different possibilities to obtain information on prices. Firstly, they could connect on the TradeNet portal and access real-time information on agricultural products. These were collected by the initiative *Farmer Knowledge System*, which assimilates the real-time market prices through WAP-enabled mobile handsets (see Figure 16.3). Thanks to this system, Tradenet provided information on prices of over 200 agricultural products, all sold at these three markets: The Dambulla Market, covering almost 80% of the wholesale trades in the country, and the Meegoda and Narahenpita markets. Farmers who subscribed to the information alert service could obtained up to five SMS per day—either on a daily or hourly basis—with real-time price alerts

Figure 16.3
An Employee of GGS Captures the Price at the Market

Source: Lokanathan et al. (2011).

Figure 16.4
An SMS Market Price Alert

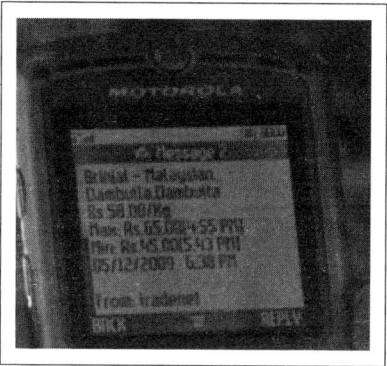

Source: Lokanathan et al. (2011).

for five fruits and vegetables traded at one of these three markets (see Figure 16.4). Phones handling using the so-called *Unicode* system allow users to choose if he/she wishes to receive the SMS in English, Sinhala, or Tamil. Furthermore, phones without the Unicode system obtained the SMS in Singlish.[1]

The online platform aims to establish a fair environment for trade that offers opportunities for efficient and inclusive trade. For this purpose, the project offered three main possibilities to access the platform in order to post offers or demands (see Figure 16.5): Firstly, buyers and sellers can use their mobiles phones and register via WAP and USSD (Unstructured Supplementary Service Data) to the platform's services and start posting their offers. The functioning of these services can be compared with accessing a website, as users had to start and end the Tradenet session on their mobile phone. The second possibility to access the Tradenet platform is via an Internet connected computer: Farmers could connect directly on the website, register, post offers or demands, and access price information. Finally, they also had the option to call directly the Tradenet call center, where a (human) operator registered their offers and transferred them to the website.

---

[1] Singlish is an English-based creole language.

Figure 16.5
Process and Use of the Tradenet Portal

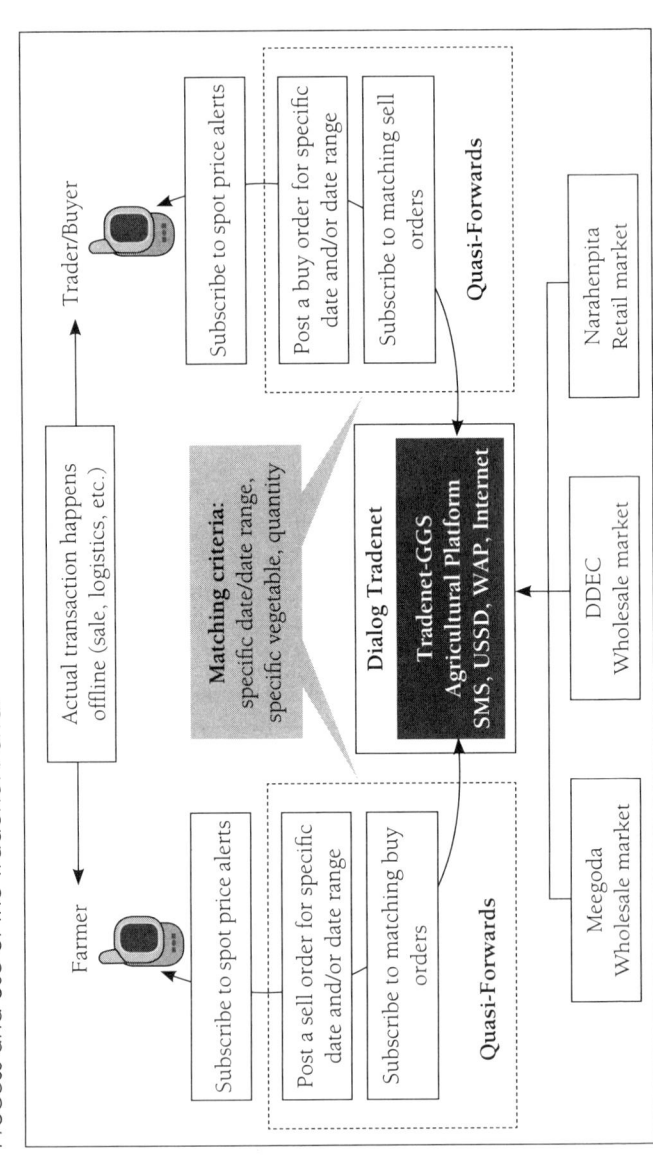

All offers and demands were then analyzed by an intelligent supply and demand matching system, which takes into consideration the preferences of each profile (e.g., price, quantity, category, geographical location). Once the respective offers and demands had been matched, the system alerted the respective users via SMS. These SMS also contained the contact details of each trade partner in view of facilitating their offline interaction.

Then, farmers could also trade agricultural products they plan to harvest in the future for a fixed price. Here, the platform acted similar to a forward exchange market of agricultural products. In contrast to formal forward contracts, which have to be concluded prior to cultivation, the platform allowed farmers to establish "quasi" forward contracts prior to the harvesting phase. At this stage farmers have a high degree of certainty concerning the amount of products they are able to sell. This system is supposed to stabilize the prices as each of these "quasi" forward contracts appears in the Tradenet platform, within a publicly accessible section on forward prices. Finally, buyers and sellers proceed to the actual transaction offline.

The "Infomediary"

In order to ensure the efficient functioning of the online trade cycle, it appeared to the project coordinators essential that farmers trust and understand the functioning and potential benefits of Tradenet. For this purpose, a "last mile" approach was adopted and a network of the so-called Infomediaries was created. The task of the project coordinator here is to explain and present various ICT-based services and functionalities of the project. Infomediaries are social entrepreneurs convinced of the potential of the project and who act in their local community. This network is supposed to contribute to the adoption of the project within small farmer communities.

Dialog and the International Finance Corporation conducted workshops and training sessions in all region of Sri Lanka. These "entrepreneurship empowerment" workshops trained 5,000 entrepreneurs for their role within the Infomediary network. For example, they were given training on social etiquettes, public speaking, and community engagement. Furthermore, Infomediaries were provided with a distinctive branding that brings prominence in the community to his or her role as a "digital services evangelist." The GSMA's m-women initiative collaborated with Dialog for this purpose in order to sensitize Infomediaries on female farmer's needs.

Conduction of an Action Research Project

In order to test the impacts of the online platform on the farmer's livelihood, LIRNE*asia* organized an Action Research Project from December 2009 to September 2010 (see Figure 16.6). The experience involved farmers from similar socioeconomic conditions: Participants had a monthly income which was below USD 200, owned less than 6 m² of cultivated land and cultivated the similar crops as their peers. Furthermore, they were all around 10–15 km away from the Dambulla market. Participants were subdivided into two groups. The first group was composed of 61 farmers who would use the Tradenet platform for their decision making regarding the cultivation and trade of crops. The second group was composed of 31 farmers who were supposed to not use Tradenet for decision making or trade. This group served as control group and was not informed about the existence of Tradenet. They were only approached by the research team during the three assessments. However, around six farmers left the control group after having heard from the project via hearsay or advertisement.

Figure 16.6
Information Session for ARP Participants

Source: Lokanathan et al. (2011).

Both groups took part in an initial baseline study, which started before the official launch of Tradenet, as well as an interim assessment for both groups after the sale of the crops from the first crop cycle, and a final assessment after the sale of the crops of the second crop cycle. Each assessment was composed of surveys, conducted in order to identify income and expenditure changes, as well as behavioral changes during the entire agricultural value chain process.

The group using Tradenet participated in an in-depth training workshop immediately after the baseline study. During this workshop, they were explained how to use properly the website with their mobile phones, the Internet or the call center. They also received a phone credit of 200 Sri Lankan Rupees (around USD 180) per month in order to be able to call the call center, and 14 farmers whose mobile phone were working with another provider than DIALOG received a DIALOG simcard. As the baseline study revealed that some farmers were selling only a small amount of their productions at weekly fairs instead of selling at the Dambulla market, the field staff of GGS decided to collect and disseminate the prices of these fairs on a regular basis via phone calls, even though they were not displayed via Tradenet. The survey were also used in order to evaluate the willingness of farmers to pay a small fee for use of Tradenet and which amount they were willing to disburse. For this purpose, farmers were asked to indicate the highest amount (between LKR 0 and LKR 5) they would pay for each price alert.

Distribution of Funds

The project was partly funded by the Sri Lankan government, USAID, and parts of the research by IDRC.

The total cost of the project design was around LKR 8 million (~USD 64,000) and mainly spent on technology development. The total costs include further the research conducted during the planning phase, as well as the employment of eight price collectors and a manger within the Govi Gnana Seva initiative, and the costs related to the mobile handsets used for the price collection. Around LKR 1 million (USD 8,000) per year operational cost was financed by DIALOG via an exclusive content provision agreement.

Post-pilot Phase

Since July 2010, the data collection system has been improved and the introduction of more markets is planned to be realized soon. This would also extend the number of farmers who can benefit from the platform. Furthermore, the platform started to offer the possibility to trade all goods and services, not only agricultural products.

Since 2011, the Tradenet project charges subscribers for using m-ARD apps based on the number of transactions conducted and shares some features with the premium model.

Achievement and Impact

The interim and final assessment conducted by LIRNE*asia* in cooperation with DIALOG revealed positive impact of the use of Tradenet in the following areas:

- *Higher income.* Farmers who used during the 10 months of the Action Research Project Tradenet could increase obtain prices for their products that were approximately 23.4% higher than the daily average kilo price.
- *Extended social networks.* Around 81% of the group reported that they had used Tradenet and that increased their interactions with traders, other groups of farmers (26.4%), relatives (17.1%), and neighbors (34%).
- *Increased knowledge.* According to the surveys, farmers could increase their knowledge and understanding of price trends by over 131% during these 10 months. Around 50% of the participating farmers had subscribed to SMS alerts concerning vegetables they were not cultivating but wished to extend their knowledge on other crops. This led to the demand of crop advisory and extension services. Another unexpected effect was the learning of vegetable names in English, as some farmers had subscribed accidentally to receive their SMS alerts in English and decided finally to keep this

configuration. Five farmers decided to buy mobile phones in order to benefit from this service.

- *Reduced vulnerability.* The surveys revealed also that the use of Tradenet contributed to a lower vulnerability regarding price volatility, as farmers were able to monitor prices in real time.

- *Impact on decision making.* Tradenet users could take into consideration the real-time price information to choose when to cultivate, harvest, and sell their products, as well as decide which crops to cultivate. They reported further that their bargaining power had increased as traders were aware that they were receiving accurate price information and had therefore fewer incentives to offer low prices.

- *Impact on structures and procedures.* As farmers depend often from traders in order to obtain emergency and working capital loans without interests, they rarely try to bargain with them in view of obtaining better prices. The survey revealed that traders used the price information received via the SMS system as benchmark price when they determined their price the next day, which allowed farmers to obtain fair prices for their products. Given the short duration of the Action Research Project, only 14 "quasi" forward contracts had been concluded, as many farmer reported to be afraid of price volatility. Subsequently, they were reluctant to determine a price for future productions on the platform, even though the price was further negotiable offline.

Furthermore, evaluations conducted by LIRNE*asia* and DIALOG revealed that the amount of farmers who registered on the platform was steadily increasing. In late 2011, the amount of farmers registered on the Tradenet platform attained around 10,000. So far nearly 1,500 farmers have subscribed for the agricultural market information service via SMS, and the call center receives nearly 50 calls per day from farmers willing to trade products or obtain price information.

Assessments also revealed challenges, particularly regarding the use of forward contracts. The evaluation showed that farmers needed to increase their trust in price stability and transparency before actively using this option.

Awards

The projects achievements have been recognized by the following awards:

- Mobile Global Awards (2010)
- M-billionth award in the m-inclusion category for innovation excellence in using mobiles and ICT's for development (2010)

Conclusion

The Tradenet project proves the significant impact that ICT—in this case a platform based on WAP, USSD, telephony, and Internet—can have on the agricultural value chain process of farmers. Indeed, the platform which offers small farmers the possibility to access price information via SMS and to trade their products has enabled them to increase their income and reinforce their position toward middlemen. In addition, the project also impacted on their overall behavior during the agricultural value chain process. The fact that farmers started to show interest in other crops and associated seeding and harvesting techniques shows that the project did not only achieve to optimize farmer's market participation, but also were able to stimulate their decision making and offer them new opportunities to develop their production.

There are multiple factors that contributed to the success of Tradenet. Firstly, the combination of expertise from the private sector (Dialog) and the research sector (LIRNEasia) is certainly one of the key success factors of the project. The large-scale mobile operator's ownership of the project made it possible to implement a project capable to reach a large number of beneficiaries through the existing network of Tradenet subscribers. Furthermore, it allowed further to offer farmers a platform accessible through a range of technologies and at low cost. Secondly, the fact that the project was funded and accompanied by a strong research component contributed to a planning and implementation process that took into consideration the reality and needs of farmers. This effort in turn allowed the design of a realistic and efficient platform. In addition, the research component is essential for the project's sustainability as it allowed to identify needs for adjustments, for example, the necessity to offer price information on products sold at smaller markets than the three main markets of the platform. More generally, this partnership proves that despite some disagreements that can occur between private enterprise and a research entity, an efficient cooperation with clear role distribution can generate a win-win situation.

Another success factor is the involvement of GGS, which had been on the markets for years in view of collecting price information. This involvement did certainly strengthen the pilot project from the beginning. The added value of building on existing projects instead of recreating entirely new ones clearly appears here.

Finally, another reason of Tradenet's success is the effort spent on explaining the functioning and benefits of the platform to farmers: The work done by the intermediaries allowed to create a climate of trust and receptivity, indispensable for the smooth functioning of the project.

In the long term, the project may have to adapt and enlarge services due to new demands, such as crop advisory, or to cover more markets. Other challenges may be the above-mentioned restriction of the platform of users without a Dialog simcard. However, the successful adaption to these demands should contribute to the project's longevity. Furthermore, the project's chances of sustainability appears to be relatively good, thanks to the significant support provided by DIALOG, the fact that users have to pay a small fee (LKR 3) to access the call center, and in light of future plans to charge SMS price alerts on a monthly basis.

Given the importance of the agricultural sector and large number of small independent farmers in many developing countries, it seems that there is a strong demand to adopt the lessons learned from the Tradenet project for similar projects in developing countries. Projects like *Lima Links* in Zambia seem to prove the replicability of Tradenet in countries facing the same challenges as Sri Lanka's small farmers. However, particularly rural areas in developing countries are still unconnected to mobile networks. This reminds us that providing access to mobile networks is the first and most crucial step to use mobile technologies for the development of rural areas.

Bibliography

Da Silva, H., & Ratnadiwakara D. (2008). Using ICT to Reduce Transaction Costs in Agriculture through Better Communication: A Case Study from Sri Lanka. Retrieved from http://www.lirneasia.net/wp-content/uploads/2008/11/transactioncosts.pdf (accessed February 6, 2013).

IDRC. (2011). Strengthening Rural Livelihoods: The Impact of Information and Communication Technologies in Asia. Retrieved from http://www.gsma.com/mobilefordevelopment/strengthening-rural-livelihoods-the-impact-of-information-and-communication-technologies-in-asia (accessed February 5, 2013).

Lokanathan, S., de Silva, H., & Fernando, I. (2011). Price Transparency in Agricultural Produce Markets: Sri Lanka. In D.J. Grimshaw & S. Kala (Eds), *Strengthening Rural Livelihoods: The Impact of Information and Communication Technologies in Asia* (pp. 15–32). Retrieved from http://www.indiaenvironmentportal.org.in/files/strengthening%20rural%20livelihood.pdf (accessed March 5, 2013).

Tradenet. (2009). Dialog Tradenet – GGS Partnership set to Revolutionise Agri Market Access Retrieved from http://www.dialog.lk/news/dialog-tradenet-ggs-partnership-set-to-revolutionise-agri-market-access (accessed February 5, 2013).

Wijayasuriya, H., & De Soyza, M. (2012). Dialog Tradenet and Creating Shared Value: Bridging Divides with Inclusive mCommerce. *Innovations*, 7(4): 43–51.

World Bank. (2009a). Srilanka Data. Retrieved from http://data.worldbank.org/country/sri-lanka (accessed March 5, 2013).

———. (2009b). Srilanka Overview. Retrieved from http://www.worldbank.org/en/country/srilanka/overview (acccessed March 5, 2013).

———. (2012). *Mobile Applications for Agriculture and Rural Development.* Retrieved from http://siteresources.worldbank.org/INFORMATIONANDCOMMUNICATIONANDTECHNOLOGIES/Resources/MobileApplications_for_ARD.pdf (accessed February 6, 2013).

17

MEDA: An Online Platform for Water Trade and Information (Chile)

Eilean von Lautz-Cauzanet

Overview

The electronic water market project (MEDA: Mercado Electrónico Del Agua) was developed in 2009 by the Pontificia Universidad Católicade Chile and Universidad del Desarrollo. The project offers small farmers the possibility to trade water volumes via an online platform based on an automatic matching mechanism for offers and demands and an online payment system that guarantees both sellers and buyers a secured transaction. Furthermore, an SMS-based information service provides them with information on average prices of water. Among the positive impacts figure lower price volatility, fairer prices, and higher market transparency. These results are also the consequence of a highly participatory planning phase, involving key decision makers, and a highly supportive attitude toward farmers during the implementation of the pilot project.

Project Background

In Chile, around 11% of the population lives in rural areas (World Bank, 2012), with a majority of them working in the agricultural sector. These populations are often disadvantaged compared to urban areas: almost 10% lives below the national poverty line and 72% does not have access to ICT and Internet. The figure is even higher when it comes to lack of home-based Internet access.

Access to Additional Water Resources: A Challenge for Small Farmers

Among the variety of challenges that these rural populations and particularly farmers face, the most frequently figured include drought seasons and the associated need to acquire additional water for soil irrigation. In order to regulate the acquisition and transaction of water resources, the Chilean government adopted the National Water Act in 1981. This act established a comprehensive system of tradable water rights. More precisely, it created a system for water distribution, which is supposed to function like a market that allows acquiring or selling water resources, according to a price generated by the interaction of offer and demand. The water resources, stored in regional water reservoirs and dams, are managed by the so-called water user associations. The Water Act also allowed a spot market for transactions of water volumes and a permanent transactions market for buying and selling water rights. Water rights confer ownership of a certain proportion of water available in the reservoir and can be valid for a certain period of time as well as can be a lifelong right. The actual volume of the proportion of water rights holder depend on the total availability of water in the reservoir defines the amount. Even though the possession of these water rights is often related to the possession of agricultural land, a farmer desires to acquire water rights can buy these from rights holders, because of the private property status of water rights.

The functioning of the Limarí spot water market is based on agricultural cycles. Therefore, the distribution of water starts at the beginning of the cropping season in May. Firstly, a private committee, integrated by representatives of different water user associations attributes under the supervision of the National Direction of Irrigation a proportion of the available water to each water user association of the dam or reservoir. The size of the proportion is based on negotiations conducted at the time the dam was built. The actual volume of water to be distributed to the water user associations depends on the total volume stored in the basin. Once the water distribution among different water user associations has been done, they distribute the water, in turn, to the respective rights holders.

After this distribution process, the main activity of the so-called spot market starts. This market includes the high number of farmers who have no water rights and buy the needed amount of water on an ad hoc basis, for example, depending on the characteristics of their crops or the size of their lands. In order to meet their additional needs of water, they can buy water from water right holders who do not need the totality of the water obtained through their water right.

The prices of the water within the spot market are influenced by the factors such as drought seasons, offer, and demand. Depending on the price of the water, farmers can optimize their decision on how to use this resource for their agricultural activities. In other words, the availability and capacity to acquire water has a major impact on their agricultural production.

Despite the objectives of these markets to distribute in a regulated and fair way, water resources among farmers remain some challenges: Firstly, many farmers have difficulty in obtaining water rights because of a long administrative procedure. A large number of transactions within the spot markets are therefore conducted in an unofficial way. The main constraint, however, is the water availability, and the fact that most of the available water has already been granted diminishes the availability of water rights. Furthermore, many farmers have only insufficient access to information regarding the trade of water. Particularly farmers in very rural areas with basic infrastructures and unfamiliar with water trade are disadvantaged. They lack information concerning volume prices, potential sellers, and buyers and are uncertain regarding the outcome of the transaction. More precisely, they do not have the guaranty that they will be paid, neither know the exact date of the transaction. Furthermore, farmers with water rights acquired before 1981 have to regularize their water rights when they wish to sell them. Many farmers, however, are not aware of the associated procedure—they are supposed to contact the respective water user association or the General Direction of Waters— and have to pay a lawyer or middlemen for this purpose. This lack of information hinders them from efficient decision making, for example, when it comes to the decision at which moment they can buy water for a lower price. Furthermore, this information asymmetry leads to under- or overestimation of their water right values and the related price of water. This lack of transparency benefits overall large-scale enterprises, for them it is easier to invest in lawyers and middlemen in view of obtaining information on water prices. It allows them to speculate with water and disadvantage small farmers even more.

In light of these dysfunctions, the electronic water market project, in the following referred to as MEDA (in Spanish: Mercado Electrónico Del Agua) was launched in 2008 by the Pontificia Universidad Católica de Chile and the Universidaddel Desarrollo. The project focused on two areas: the Limari valley and the Maipo valley. The objective of this project was to contribute to the efficiency and transparency of the water market by means of a website that offers an up-to-date and secured online exchange system. This online market is supposed to reduce the costs related to the search of buyers or sellers and provide price information that allows the conduction of fair transactions of water. Moreover, the website includes a system that is supposed to guarantee both buyers and sellers the delivery of the acquired water and the respective payment for sellers. Finally, MEDA seeks to contribute to an efficient distribution of water within a dedicated market and increase the farmers' certainty regarding the planning of their investments.

Impact of Existing Projects

The project MEDA is based on research conducted by the academics from the MEDA research team, who had analyzed the water market system in the area of Li0mari in 2002 and revealed that more than 27% of water rights were exchanged independent of land transfers. This research concluded that there was a demand to create a water market based on active mechanism for water allocation. They developed the hypothesis that offering a space for private decision making would allow the proper management of water resources.

Furthermore, the MEDA project was inspired by a project of the University of California and various environmental groups, who had successfully implemented a website for water trade and significantly contributed to an increase of water transactions in this area. Finally, the Australian website *Waterfind*, which facilitates the buying and selling of both permanent and temporary water across the major irrigation regions in Australia reinforced the conviction that a similar project could be implemented in Chile.

Project Planning

The project was launched by the Pontificia Universidad Catolica de Chile in collaboration with the Universidad del Desarrollo and financed by the Corporation for the Promotion of Production—CORFO, a public sector organization dedicated to the promotion of entrepreneurship, innovation and growth.[1]

The actual planning and preparation phase began in January 2008 under the auspices of the General Directorate of Waters in parallel to the national debate how to deal with the challenges related to drought periods in the country in an efficient way.

In order to guarantee that the project would contribute in an efficient way to an improved functioning of the water market, the research groups—composed of researcher from the Pontifical Catholic University of Chile and the General Direction of Waters—decided to involve stakeholders from the public and private sphere in the planning and later implementation process of the project. For this purpose, a strategic alliance was launched, which was composed of water intensive production sectors (National Society of Mining and the National Association of Enterprises for Sanitary Services) as well as the Chilean Commodity Exchange, the University for Development, the Pontifical Catholic University of Chile and National Commission on Irrigation, responsible for the development of public policies in the area of soil irrigation in Chile.

---

[1] Corporación de Fomento de la Producción.

The planning phase consisted in the choice of locations in which the future project could be tested, a needs assessment and the realization of economic experiences in order to test and optimize the implementation phase. It was split into three phases: During the first phase (April to August 2008), surveys were conducted among users of in two water basins. During the second phase (August 2008 to January 2009), field experiences were conducted within the *Sistema Palomadamn* association of Limari. The third phase consisted in the design of the project website and its services.

Phase I: Choice of Test Locations and Conduction of Surveys

Limari and Maipo and their respective water basins were chosen in order to analyze the needs the future project should respond to and to which the MEDA website should adapt its functioning. The choice of these locations was based on the fact that the characteristics of the water markets and users differed from each other:

The water basin area of Limari is located 472 km north of the Chilean capital Santiago de Chile. The area is composed of 65,000 hectares of watered soil, which are mainly used for traditional field fruits (e.g., potatoes), horticultural productions, and grapes. Various profiles of farmers can be found in Limari: There are both garden owners and medium-sized farms and large-scale enterprises that specialized in fruit exportations.

The water basin is managed by the so-called Paloma System, a committee of water user associations of the three dams and basins of this area: Camarico, Cogotí, and Recoleta (Figure 17.1). A sophisticated water conduction infrastructure and the committees of the water basins have contributed to an active water market, including water rights as well temporary ad hoc water acquisition (*spot* market). The transactions of water within the *spot* market of the Limari water market are higher than those concerning water rights and the majority of transactions, within both market types, are realized between farmers.

In collaboration with the water user associations, the project team selected graduated agronomists from the regional university (University of La Serena) to conduct 300 surveys in Limari from May to August 2008. The survey focused on users of both water basins and their

Figure 17.1
Water Basin of the Paloma System

Source: Christi et al. (2002).

markets and was composed of questions that tended to evaluate their profile and needs. A majority of the surveys were conducted in the community of Ovalle (89%). The surveys covered 435 land plots and revealed that 58% of the interviewees had faced water deficits in past seasons. Furthermore, interviewees reported that 40% of their decisions to cultivate nonpermanent crops every season were directly taken due to this deficit.

Regarding the participation of interviewees in the water market, 30% of interviewees declared to buy or sell water within the ad hoc water acquisition market (*spot* market). Around 18% declared that they had conducted transaction of water rights in the past. The surveys revealed further high price volatility and water appropriation prices that attained sometimes 6 million Chilean Pesos (~USD 12,700) per water right.

In the case of Maipo, the water basin covers almost the whole metropolitan region (Figure 17.2). Around 246,447 hectares within the area of the water basin is composed of agriculture soil for permanent crops, for example, fruit crops around 22,916 hectares are used in rotation for forage crops plantation. The principal source of water in this region is the Maipo River and Mapuche River, covering around 70% of the demand of drinkable water and 90% of the demands for irrigation water. In contrast

Figure 17.2
Maipo Area

Source: www.sobrechile.com

to Limari, this water basin offers only a market of water rights. The profile of participants differs also from those in Limari: not only farmers but also private production sectors are involved in water transactions.

The conduction of surveys among users of the water basin of Maipo took place in parallel to the survey process in Limari. With the support from the water user associations of the two main river dams, 405 interviewees took part in the surveys. Surveys revealed strong water demands, particularly for technology-based irrigation systems used by 70% of interviewees.

Furthermore, surveys revealed that 13% of the interviewees had already bought or sold water rights. In the case of Maipo, water rights had been sold together with a dedicated land. However, despite this "package" sale, a specific price for the respective water right was defined for each transaction. Around 14 interviewees stated that they would like to buy water rights independent from soil acquisition. Finally, the surveys also revealed that a majority of respondents had insufficient knowledge concerning the functioning of the market of water rights; neither knew the actual values and the process related to the acquisition or sell of these.

Phase II: Testing and Preparation of Transaction Mechanisms

During the second phase of the planning process, three field experiences were organized in Limari in order to complement the information obtained through the conducted surveys and to test and prepare a future online *spot* market. These field experiences, which included farmers and beneficiaries from the water basin of the Paloma System, were also organized in order to test the efficiency of transaction mechanisms for the future electronic water trade platform and its impact on the water market itself.

The first experience took place in August 2008. A water market focusing on the trade of ad hoc acquisition of water (spot market) was organized in a dedicated office in Ovalle. The experience revealed that farmers decided to buy water when they knew its origin and preferred to buy from nearby sellers. Furthermore, farmers preferred to buy from those sellers who guaranteed a fixed date on which the acquired water would be available. This first experience led to the decision that the future electronic platform should indeed offer clear information on actual water availability, its origin and the date of the possible transaction. At this point, it was decided that the future platforms should offer distinct markets for the respective water user associations.

The second experience took place in January 2008 and aimed to test the offer and demand behavior within an auction system based on sealed-bid and uniform-price procedure, also known as clearing price auction. In this case, every farmer who wished to buy water indicated the volume needed and the price he was willing to pay in a sealed envelope, 24 hours in advance of the water market. On the sellers price, the available water volume and the minimum price was indicated in another envelope. Sellers wishing to participate had to provide a certificate from the respective water user association of the dam indicating the actual amount of available water in the water basin the day of the auction. On the buyers' side, farmers had to make a direct deposit in a bank and to have it at MEDA research team disposal in view of a future payment. In the following, the project team aligned the respective offers and demands and compared the lowest selling price with the highest purchase price. The transactions started with the highest bidder first. The market closed when the selling prices were higher than the purchase price. Once the market was closed, a fair price of water was calculated on the average of purchase and selling price. At the time the market reopened, farmers desire to sell or buy water could refer to this price when formulating their demands and offers. The mechanism's transparency, guarantee concerning availability and payment, and particularly the possibility to generate a fair price for participants led to the decision to include it in the future website. Indeed, the research team detected that, within this kind of market, each seller receives at least the same or a higher price for its offer, and buyers would pay the price or even less than they are willing to pay. Compared to previous prices within the hitherto active water market, the average prices of this clearing price auction were lower and the increasing demand seamed to prove the benefits of a transparent transaction system.

Furthermore, this experience was also conducted in view of familiarizing farmers with the mechanism of the future online market and aimed to demonstrate the advantages they may benefit from.

The third and final experience developed this market mechanism further and added an auction of options to buy a determined volume of water for a fixed price for at a later point. Concretely, farmers apprehensive of additional water requirement after the winter—and raining—season can buy certain amount of water in advance, at the latest until September (winter season) for a fixed price and receive the water during the summer season. In case there is a drought period, this auction allowed farmers to reduce the risks to pay high prices for ad hoc water needs, for example, during a drought periods.

The experiences were conducted in a computer laboratory launched for this purpose in Ovalle at 20 interconnected computers. The experimental auction was developed via software for experimental economics, enabling among other double auctions: Z-Tree. This allowed farmers to familiarize themselves not only with the use of new water market mechanism, but also with the use of computer for this purpose. Farmers reported to be enthusiastic about the conditions in which they could conduct their transactions. In parallel, training sessions were organized in special meetings, focusing on the functioning of double auction mechanisms. Around 310 farmers attended these training sessions.

Phase III: Design of the Online Market Platform

On the basis of the collected information and taking into consideration the lessons learned from the conducted experiences, the MEDA project team designed the actual MEDA online market platform. The main water user associations of the dams were involved in this final step of the planning phase.

Firstly, it was decided that the MEDA online market provide separate water markets for each of the dams and their water user associations in the area of Maipo and Limari, in order to provide buyers with transparency in terms of water origins.

In view of offering sellers a payment security—established through the deposal system during the experiences—it was decided to involve user organizations and commercial banks in the MEDA project. These banks inform MEDA when they have received the deposit, covering the totality of the purchase price. MEDA in turn informs the bank about the sellers who will receive the deposit. This procedure allows sellers and buyers to remain anonymous.

Furthermore, the role of the water user associations were defined: Their tasks consist in validating the registration of farmers willing to conduct transaction with the MEDA online market, to inform MEDA about registered and authorized farmers and to verify whether farmers offering a dedicated volume of water or options for future selling actually possess this volume. For this purpose, the water user associations oblige to seller to immobilize the volume of water to be sold, in order to avoid untrue offers. The committees debit and credit the accounts of users, based on information they receive from MEDA concerning conducted transactions.

The final step consisted in the development of the MEDA platform software and was done by experts from the Institute for Social and Economic Research of the University of Alaska Anchorage who had previously developed the Python Experimental Economics Toolkit, which provides services and user interfaces, such as parameter management, client–server communication, status monitoring, and output data management. For MEDA, this toolkit was further developed, which signifies the development of interfaces for all users of the platform, including buyers and sellers, water user associations and coordinators of the

Figure 17.3
Functioning of MEDA

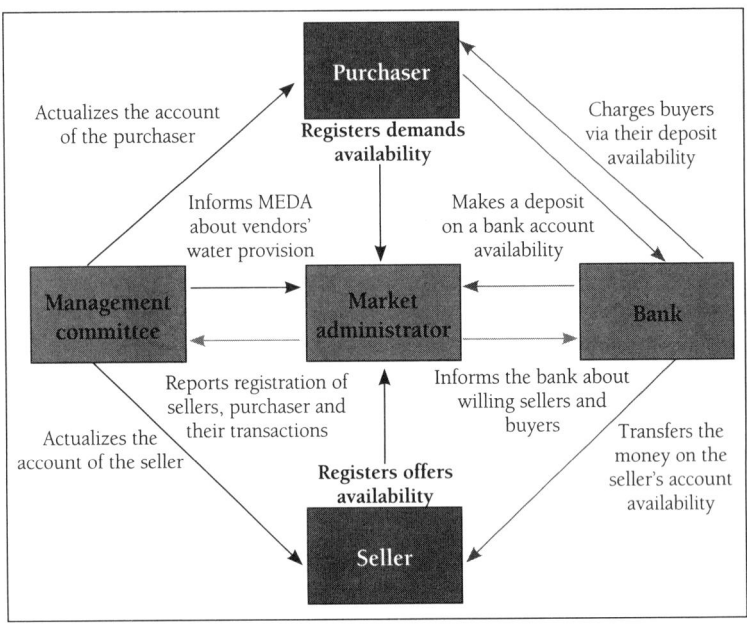

Source: Alevy et al. (2011).

MEDA project. Furthermore, the software had to be adapted in order to create a secured exchange and transaction system (Figure 17.3).

Project Implementation

In the following, different entities involved in the implementation of the MEDA website will be presented.

Actors of the Implementation Process

- *Pontificia Universidad Catolica de Chile and Universidad del Desarrollo.* A research team from respectively the Faculty of Economics and Business and the Faculty of Agronomy and Forrest Engineering initiated the project and was responsible for the coordination of MEDA throughout the planning and implementation phase.

- *MEDA field office coordinator.* An agricultural engineer who had contributed to the conduction of the surveys and experiences was in charge of explaining the functioning of the MEDA platform to farmers and if needed, help them to conduct their transactions.
- *Water user associations.* The water user associations of the Camarico canal, the Recoleta reservoir and the Cogotí reservoir credit or debit the water accounts of their respective users, depending on the information they receive from MEDA.
- *Zoltner Consulting Group.* The Zoltner Consulting Group is specialized in the use of ICT for agricultural development. It developed together with DataDyne the platform for the SMS information system in view of explaining and enhancing the use of the MEDA website.

Implementation Process

The MEDA Office and Training Center

The MEDA website was officially launched in September 2010 for users of the water basin of the Paloma System. In order to establish a climate of confidence and to establish a visible face of the project, a MEDA office was opened in September 2010 in the nearby city of Ovalle. This office was equipped with computers and farmers had the possibility to enroll in a one to one training sessions in order to deepen their skills with regards to the conduction of online transactions. Around 290 farmers took part in these training sessions.

Users were further offered the possibility to take part in both the market of water rights and the market of water volume transactions. During the first weeks, the online market operated once a week.

In the following the functioning of the MEDA website and its services during the pilot phase will be described.

User Registration

A farmer willing to participate in the MEDA market has to create a user account via the project website (www.mercadoelectronicodelagua.cl) and indicate the water user association to which he belongs. He has then to mandate via an online form for MEDA to be involved in future water transactions.

Registration and Mandate Process

If the user is interested in buying water, he must make a deposit in a *servipag* office[2] or its associated banks. If he is already a client of one of these banks, he can make the deposit via the payment on the MEDA website. This deposit must be made before 2 pm the day before the auction starts. The market platform opens (during the pilot phase) twice a week from 8.30 am and closes and clears at 4 pm.

Throughout the market duration, the farmer can use parts or the total of his deposit. Furthermore, he can withdraw the unspent parts of the deposit once the auction is closed or use it for future transactions.

In case the user is a seller, he mandates MEDA to offer the amount of water for the price fixed by the seller. As decided during the planning phase of the project, this mandate allows MEDA to verify via the respective water user association the actual availability of his offer. Once this availability is confirmed, the vendor is obliged to guarantee that this availability does not change until the auction has been closed. In case he desires to sell options for water acquisitions, he is obliged to guarantee that the amount fixed in the option is available until the date of the proper transaction.

Once the farmer has provided all necessary information to take part in the water auction, he can choose on the website whether he wishes to participate in the spot market, either in the market of options for water acquisition or in water rights market.

Start of the Online Spot Market

In case a farmer wishes to participate in the *spot* market, he must indicate the volume of water he wishes to sell or buy. This operation generates each time a purchase or sells order and every user is allowed to realize various orders during one auction on the auction dialog box of the MEDA website. On the same dialog box a seller can see the amount of water he can sell and a purchase check for his available budget. During this period, users can make their bids. Once the auction is closed, the

---

[2] Servipag is an online payment system.

MEDA system determines for each water user association the adequate price according to the sealed-bid and uniform-price procedure elaborated during the planning phase. Finally, the MEDA website informs every participant in the "User account" section about the amount of water he purchased or sold and the price of the respective transaction.

Market of Water Rights

Given that national regulations prohibit the online transaction of water rights, the MEDA website offers an "electronic whiteboard" tool through which interested sellers and purchasers can indicate their intention to sell or buy water rights.

For this purpose, participants have to provide various information, for example, on the source of the water, the location of the water uptake area, the quantity of water associated to the water right, the type of the water right (permanent, temporary, alternate, for consumptive purposes or not) and exercise of the right (continuous or discontinuous).

This "electronic whiteboard" also includes a search engine through which participants can precise their search on the basis of criteria, for example, geographical proximity or the source of water. Users can then obtain detailed information of those water rights that fulfill their criteria and can localize them online.

If the user finds an offer or demand that meets his requirements, he can contact the respective purchaser or seller via the system which will then manage the transaction.

The SMS Information System

The high affluent farmers seeking for information in the Ovalle offices led to the creation of a SMS-based information system, launched in February 2011. The objective was to provide farmers with information concerning the use and functioning of the MEDA website in an efficient way. This system, based on a platform for multiple text messaging, had been created by the Zoltner Consulting Group and DataDyne.

During almost two months, 405 users, belonging to the four respective locations concerned by the MEDA project, received text messages containing information concerning the functioning of the MEDA online market and the average price for water at each of the water basins. The popularity of the initiative increased the demands of farmers desire to register for this initiative. Another interesting immediate effect was the fact that the questions asked at the Ovalle office were much more concise than before the introduction of the SMS information system.

Funds

The pilot project was funded—in stages—with USD 793,400. CORFO provided the majority of the funds, followed by Chilean Commodity Exchange, the University of Development and the Pontifical University and the National Mining Association as well as the National Association of Enterprises for Sanitary Services (Figure 17.4).

These funds were mainly used for the costs related to human resources throughout the planning and implementation phases. Furthermore, 18% of available funds were used for operational costs (e.g., rent on an office in Ovalle), followed by costs related to the administration of the project (10%). Around 6% of the funds were spent for the equipment for the project (e.g., computers), followed by efforts to promote the project (5%, e.g., via the radio or newspapers). Costs related to farmer's training during the planning phase used around 5% of the project (Figure 17.5).

Figure 17.4
Main Funding Agencies

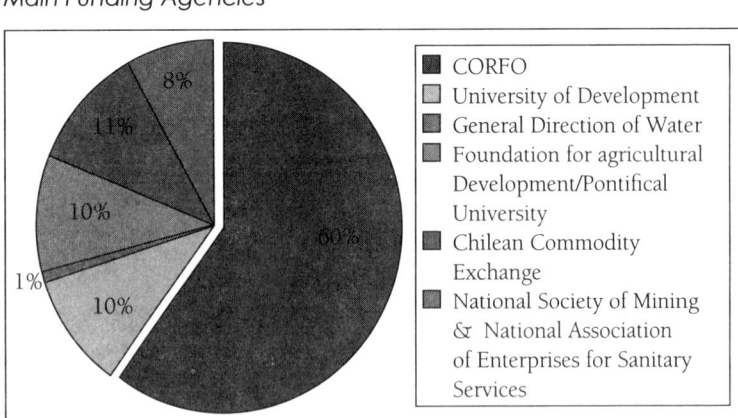

Source: Data provided by Oscar Cristi.

Figure 17.5
Distribution of Funds

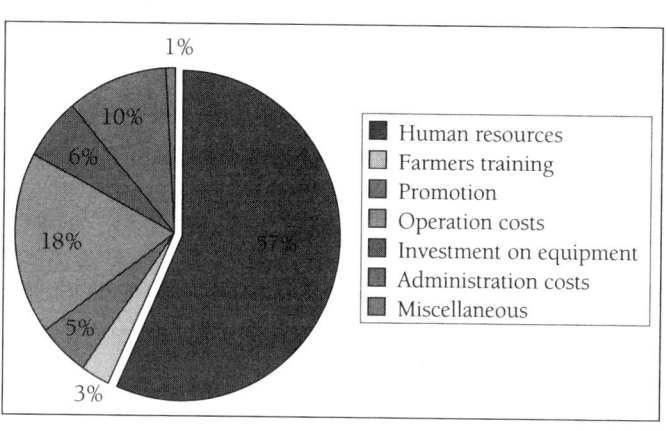

Source: Data provided by Oscar Cristi.

Since December 2012, MEDA charges a fee on a fixed-percentage basis per transaction. This fee is split between the buyer and the seller and is supposed to contribute to the project's sustainability in the long term.

Achievement

The MEDA project was constantly evaluated in order to assess the progress and impact of the electronic market. Theses evaluations came to the following conclusions:

From September 2010 to April 2011—year of another drought period, which makes the comparison with prices before the launch of MEDA difficult—the MEDA online market led to 22 online transaction conducted by 26 sellers and 18 buyers. In total, the value of the online transferred water attained USD 41,310,850. The majority of these transactions took place between January and April 2011. The average price generated by the MEDA auction was USD 82.5:1 m³. This price is much likely to be lower than average prices during drought seasons before the launch of MEDA.

From September 2011 to April 2012, the amount of transactions more than doubled to 50 online transactions, conducted between 40 sellers and 24 buyers. The majority of the transactions took place between November and April. Around 2,214,334 m³ of water were transacted and the total value of these transactions attained USD 204,894,740. The price for water during this year varied between USD 75 and USD 160 per 1 m³ (average USD 117.5/m³).

The evaluation also revealed a positive reception and impact of the SMS information system. Around 62% of those farmers who had received the SMS with price alerts considered the indicated price as valuable reference. Around 16% reported that the price alerts helped them to conduct transactions via the MEDA platform. Furthermore, 53% declared to be in favor of a daily SMS alert. Out of the 26% who did not agree with a daily SMS alert reported to prefer to receive an SMS with price information once a week (60%), while 40% preferred to receive two alerts per months. In June 2012, over 600 farmers were benefitted from the SMS information system.

Regarding the characteristics of participants, the analysis revealed that the majority of sellers were farmers planting traditional annual crops, those who were capable of deciding every season on the superficies of land they wish to cultivate, as well as stock farmers. However, some sellers were shareholders from other sectors than agriculture. The profile of buyers varied between small agriculture enterprises, owner of agricultural land, and growers of vegetables. Furthermore, the evaluations revealed that the majority of transactions were conducted by users from the water basin of the Cogotí water user association. In 2010–2011, 3% of their users took part in the MEDA online market, and in the year 2011–2012, this figure doubled and attained 6%.

More generally, MEDA is considered today as the only online sources of information regarding water volume prices in the region. Evaluations reported that even farmers outside of the MEDA system and its associated water basins were using the platform for information purposes.

Post-pilot Phase

Thanks to funds provided by National Irrigation Commission, MEDA is still active today. Provided that the transactions within the MEDA market continue growing, the project is supposed to relay on self-financing in late 2013.

On a mid-term perspective, the project seeks to increase training possibilities for farmers in order to enhance the market for water appropriation options—none of the transaction concerned options between 2010 and 2012—and familiarize them further with the use of the online market. In the long term, the project seeks to convince farmers to use the online market possibilities just as much, if not predominantly, for their transactions within the spot market. Furthermore, MEDA also plans to expand its transaction platform to other water basins and their respective user associations.

This expansion comes along with a closer cooperation with these water user organizations. The project also seeks to promote the use of the "electronic whiteboard" among potential users throughout the whole country. For this purpose, it is hoped that national legislations will allow the platform to trade water rights online.

Conclusion

The MEDA project has achieved in offering farmers the possibility to obtain valuable information enabling them to optimize their decision-making regarding the moment of acquisition and origin of the source, which decreases their dependence from middlemen or lawyers helping them to conduct transactions, for example, acquiring water rights. Furthermore, farmers were able to acquire water for fair prices via the online platform and obtained better prices right after the launch of the platform.

Despite relative recentness of the project, it appears clearly that the positive results achieved so far are due to a combination of factors that have strengthened the project from the start: The planning phase, characterized by the decision to involve stakeholders and decision makers within the area of national irrigation policies, strengthened the project in terms of legitimacy and expertise and, most of all, provided the necessary funding for the planning and implementation of the project. Furthermore, the strong research component on which the project was based, allowed developing a project based on the verification of established hypothesis through investigation and research.

These efforts to adapt the project to the real life and needs of farmers through the conduction of surveys and economic experiences can be considered as key success factor, as these contributed in the meantime the project's dissemination, convinced farmers of MEDA's added value and familiarized them with the use of ICT for water transactions. The fact that the water user associations were in charge of the data leverage process is another crucial element: The integration of the main organizations for water transactions was inevitable and indispensable for a smooth functioning of the project. Here, MEDA teaches an important lesson about the significance of a planning phase that uses participatory methods during the project design process.

The proximity to users and a hand-holding approach, institutionalized through the creation of a MEDA office where farmers are trained and supported during their transactions, reflects these efforts also during the implementation of the project. Indeed, particularly innovative projects which require adaptation efforts on the user side and training need to be properly embedded in the local community. The fact that MEDA adopted this attitude has certainly contributed to these rapidly achieved positive results.

Current plans to develop and extent the project appear realistic given the enthusiasm that the platform possibilities generated among farmers and the fact that the National Irrigation Commission has taken ownership of the project since. However, the sustainability of the project will obviously depend on the success of this development and on available funds that are indispensable for the extension of ICT-based services, such as the platform's data collection or the SMS information system.

Bibliography

Alevy, J., Melo, O., & Cristi, O. (2011). Proyecto Mercado Electrónico del Agua en Chile (Draft).

Cristi, O. et al. (2002). Markets for Water Used for Irrigation: An Application to the Paloma System of the Limarí Water Basin—Chile. Draft Version Prepared for the World Bank Training Seminar on Water Rights, March 27–28, Santiago de Chile.

Electronic Water Market (2011a). Mercado electrónico del agua para pequeños agricultores - Un Piloto Móvil Exitoso. [Electronic Water Market for Small Farmers – A Successful Pilot Project] Retrieved from http://www.e-agriculture.org/es/blog/mercado-electr%C3%B3nico-del-agua-para-peque%C3%B1los-agricultores (accessed February 8, 2013).

Electronic Water Market. (2011b). La iniciativa apoya el Mercado Electrónico del Agua (MEDA) que contribuye a la modernización y mejoramiento del mercado de aguas en Chile mediante un mecanismo de intercambio online. [The Initiative Supports the Electronic Water Market that Contributes to the Modernization and Improvement of the Water Market in Chile through an Online Exchange Mechanism] Retrieved from http://www3.cnr.cl/opensite_det_20110921195328.aspx (accessed February 8, 2013).

———. (2012). Transacciones en Mercado Electrónico del Agua superan los $53 millones en marzo-junio de 2012 [Transactions of the Electronic Water Market Exceed $ 53 Million in March – June 2012] Retrieved from http://www.estrategia.cl/detalle_noticia.php?cod=62345 (accessed February 8, 2013).

Oficina de Estudios y Políticas Agrarias. (2010). Análisis del mercado del agua de riego en Chile:una revisión crítica a través del caso de laRegión de Valparaíso [Analysis of the Rain Water Market in Chile: A Critical Revision Based on the Case in the Valparaiso Region]. Retrieved from http://www.odepa.gob.cl/odepaweb/servicios-informacion/publica/Analisis_agua_riego_Valparaiso.pdf (accessed February 8, 2013).

World Bank. (2012). Data on Chile. Retrieved from http://data.worldbank.org/country/chile (accessed March 6, 2012).

Important Websites

http://www.mercadoelectronicodelagua.cl/
Data on Chile/World Bank: http://data.worldbank.org/country/chile

18

Rural Schools of Information Technologies and Citizenship (Chile)

Eilean von Lautz-Cauzanet

Overview

The pilot project Rural Schools of Information Technologies and Citizenship (RSITC) was launched in 2006 in the region of Valparaiso and La Araucania by the Ministry of Agriculture and the Brazilian NGO Committee for Democratization of Information Technologies. This initiative has achieved to increase information and communication technology (ICT) skills among the rural population through the construction of rural telecenters that offer courses tailored to participants' needs. Adapted training sessions, continuous support to each RSITC and a participatory management approach are the main success factors of this project.

Project Background

Chile is the first South American country to join the Organization for Economic Co-operation and Development (OCDE) and one of the fastest growing Latin-American economies. Despite significant progress in terms of poverty reduction, inequality remains a considerable challenge for the country, especially in rural areas where 11% of its population lives (2010). In 2009, 12.9% of the rural population lived below the national rural poverty line (World Bank, 2012)

These population of people are also the first to be deprived of access to ICT and Internet connections: According to the Chilean Ministry of Agriculture, in 2010 only 38% of small farmers had access to computers. Of this, only 25% were using the Internet and only 9% had home-based Internet access. These figures appear to be rather low, especially when compared to medium-sized producers, 63% of which have home-based Internet access (Foundation for Agricultural Innovation [FAI], 2010).

In light of the integration of digital technologies into farmer organizations, technologies that are seen as an efficient tool to support economic and societal development, and as an opportunity to empower small farmers through rural digital alphabetization programs, the FAI, part of the Ministry of Agriculture, launched the *Model of Digital Inclusion*. One of its components is the pilot project *Rural Schools of Information Technologies and Citizenship*.

The project seeks to develop ICT skills among the rural population through participation in ICT courses that are adapted to the participants' needs. The pilot project includes two cooperatives that are both located in remote and rural areas: Firstly, there is the Cooperative of Rabbit Breeding in the municipality San Esteban, in the region of Valparaiso, which is composed of 10 small enterprises. Secondly, there is the Farmer Cooperative Pocoyan, composed of 20 farmers, mainly specialized in cattle breeding and located in the region of La Araucania.

Impact of Existing Similar Projects

The *Program of Farmers Training and Digital* Access,[1] launched by the Institute for Agricultural Development,[2] had previously laid this focus on

---

[1] Spanish: Programa de profesionalización y acceso digital campesino.
[2] Spanish: Instituto de DesarolloAgropecuario.

rural areas, and had already sought to modernize and strengthen skills of small farmers to enable them to innovate and improve their land management. These farmers took part in training courses in urban zones, or mobile telecenters, which taught them how to use Word, Excel, and the Internet. This project also distributed computers to farmers across the country. Furthermore, the project *Schools for Information Technologies and Citizenship* (SITC) was implemented 33 times in Chile by the NGO Committee for Democratization of Information Technologies (CDI), and was a major source of inspiration for the project RSITC. The objective of the RSITC was to collaborate with local communities and to create schools or centers where one could learn how to use new technologies. However, this project did not focus specifically on rural communities and their needs. It became apparent quickly that the already existing *Schools of Information Technologies and Citizenship* could not be adapted on a one-to-one basis for rural areas. Despite this, the lessons learned and the information collected during these previous experiences contributed to the designing of the pilot project *Rural Schools of Information Technologies and Citizenship*.

> *The Committee for the Democratization of Information Technologies* is a Brazilian NGO founded in 1995. Its objective is the promotion of educative activities through the use of ICT to reintegrate community members who have low incomes and to decrease digital exclusion. The organization works in 9 different countries and has launched 753 *Schools of Information Technologies and Citizenship*.

Planning Process

> The Foundation for Agricultural Innovation is part of the Ministry of Agriculture. Its objective is the promotion and development of an innovative culture within the agro-forestry sector. The purpose is to strengthen the sector's competiveness, increase life standards for rural families, and to empower local employees and enterprises.

In 2006, the FAI started the planning process for its Rural Schools of Information Technologies and Citizenship. The objective of this first step was to collect all available information concerning the characteristics of ICT access and its use by farmers in the country. It also aimed to identify existing public initiatives that were already dealing with the digital gap in rural areas. This collection of information was conducted by the Centre for Human Development, a consulting firm, and was financed by the Study Office of Agriculture Policies. The final report ("Vision of the access and use of new information technologies by farmers") gave the following conclusions: Farmers declared that they had no or insufficient access to ICT infrastructures. This situation was even worse for very young and old farmers, or for those with only low levels of education and income. The notion of telecenter was not known. Regarding the use of ICT, farmers declared that the software they used most was Word and Excel, although only at a basic level, that is, for book-keeping. The use of Internet was limited to email. Furthermore, farmers reported that there was a lack quality training opportunities. Low levels of education, elderly farmers, or farmers with low incomes found even less training possibilities.

Development of the Implementation Plan

Regarding the long experience of CDI in the domain of ICT training, the FAI mandated the NGO to implement the pilot project. Together, the FAI and CDI defined the responsibilities that should fall on each entity if involved in the planning and implementation of a RSITC (see Figure 18.1):

- The *support organization* is in charge of providing the resources for the development and implementation of the project and it has to supervise the execution of the activities and the meeting of previously fixed deadlines. This organization can be a public or private entity as well as a public–private partnership. It takes part in the preparation and implementation phases until the project can finance and manage itself.
- The *promoting organization* is in charge of resource management, training of educators, and supporting the executing organizations throughout the process. It coordinates participants and manages the preparation phase of the project. Furthermore, it transfers its

Figure 18.1
Entities Involved in the Planning and Creation of an RSITC

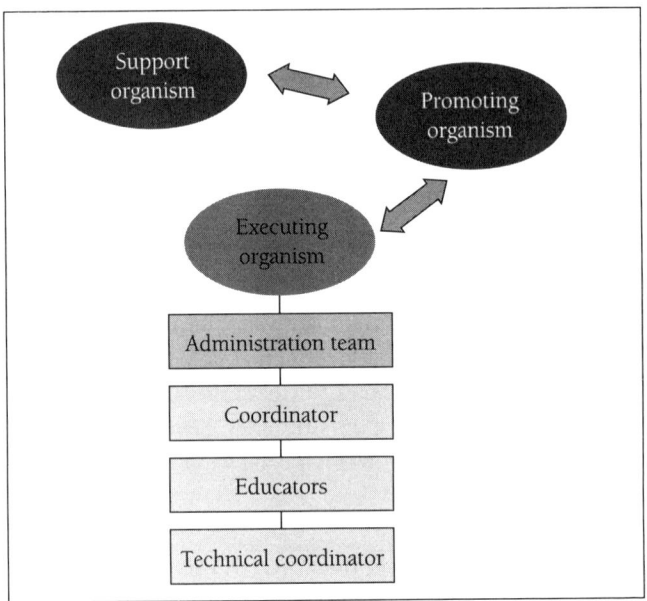

Source: Author.

knowledge to the executing organization. The promoting organization can be an NGO, a member of ATACH (Association of Active Chilean Telecenters), a university or a public as well as a private institution. The promoting organization is in charge of selecting the executing organization, based on broadcasting activities, in order to inform possible candidates about the project. The promoting organization has to pay field visits to applying candidates—which are supposed to be farmer organizations—and give advice on and during the application process. It supervises the selected executing organization and also fulfills the role of connecting the executing and the support organization. The promoting organization also aids, on an ad hoc basis, the support organization, for example, in order to find additional resources. Within the promoting organization, a field coordinator and a technical coordinator are in charge of visiting the rural communities and they provide assistance if needed.

- The *executing organization* fulfills the role of implementing every step in the field. The executing organization must have a well-defined organizational structure, exist long enough to prove a certain degree of sustainability and be well integrated in the local community. This organization must also prove that there is already a dedicated group of employees or persons ready to take over the implementation of the rural RSITC.

This group, also called the *administration team* is composed of a coordinator, an educator and a technological coordinator, which have the following roles:

- The *coordinator* has the fundamental role of designing, together with the rest of the administration team, the adequate schedule and timetable of the RSITC. Also, he/she must organize the broadcasting, enrollment, and graduation processes while coordinating various initiatives that will allow, in the long term, the self-management and sustainability of the RSITC. The coordinator is the intermediary between the executing organization, the educators, and the local community, and is also the promoting organization of the project.
- The *educators* are in charge of teaching ICT classes. They are usually very experienced in this area and have already worked in community projects. It is important that they are integrated into the community.
- The *technological coordinator* is an ICT expert and an important element in each RSITC, constantly in contact with the promoting organization.

In order to guarantee a fluid communication, the FAI and CDI decided that every RSITC project must start with a fixed calendar of meetings, a communication protocol, as well as a calendar of planned activities and investments. The objective of this strategy is the optimization of human and economic resources and to guarantee an efficient implementation of the project.

Regarding the objectives of the implementation plan, FAI and CDI decided to define five separate phases (see Figure 18.2): (1) selection of

Figure 18.2

Planning and Implementation Process

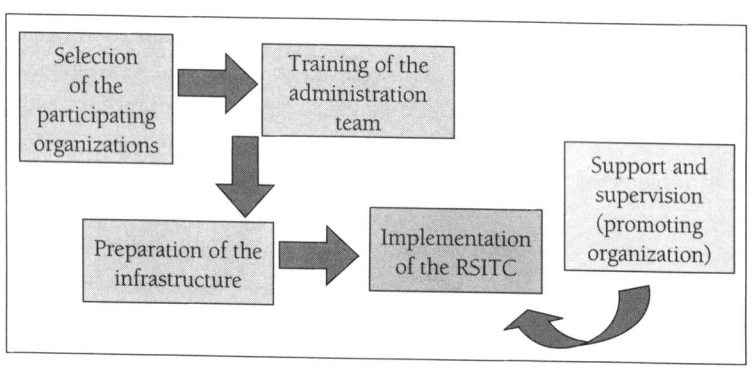

Source: Author.

the participating organizations, (2) training of the administration team, (3) preparation of the infrastructure, (4) implementation of the RSITC, and (5) support and supervision.

The first step consists of the *selection of participating organizations* (e.g., as in the following case, two cooperatives). This phase itself is subdivided in five progressive steps:

1. *Investigation within a chosen area and advertising of the planned project.* Firstly, a review of all organizations in a selected geographical area must be conducted in order to ensure that these organizations are indeed farmer's organizations and, therefore, representative of a rural region. Secondly, a communication strategy is launched in order to adapt the advertising to the selected rural area and application forms are distributed to interested farmer organizations.

2. *Fulfillment of the application forms.* Interested farmer organizations fill out the application forms, which focus on criteria related to previous experience of the organization and its administration team, as well the motivation and interest in taking part in a RSITC project.

3. *Pre-selection.* The promoting organization conducts a preselection based on these criteria (defined in step 2) and selects

stable organizations that have several years of experience, that are well integrated and accepted by the local community, and have an administration team that has worked on community projects, occupied positions where leadership was necessary and have at least some ICT skills.

4. *Field visits.* The promoting organization pays field visits to pre-selected organizations in order to assess the feasibility of a RSITC in the respective area. Feasibility is dependent on the location, existing basic infrastructures and the administration team.

5. *Selection of the executing organization and presentation of the agreement.* The promoting organization selects neutral farmer organizations willing to work, without exception, for the whole rural community. Furthermore, they must have an adequate location where to build an RSITC, a well-organized administration team. The selected RSITC must commit to take part in all activities recommended by the promotion organization (seminars, meetings, training sessions etc.), and be ready to adapt opening hours in a way that allows for the maximum benefit to participants from the RSITC.

After this selection step, the training process of the administration team and the educators begins. This training is delivered during courses, which take place at the promoting organization, by professionals from social, pedagogical, and technological domains. They are trained in the following areas: challenges related to the digital gap, educative and social practices, nonformal education, origins and functioning of a RSITC, and roles of the administration team. Educators, particularly those who have not been professional teachers before, enroll in special classes in order to prepare them and to increase their self-confidence. After the course, they receive an official ICT training certificate.

Hereupon, the promoting organization launches the infrastructure preparation process of the RSITC: the supporting organization finances, eventually with other partners, the construction of the RSITC. In the meantime, the administration team approaches eventual partners willing to provide material on a voluntary basis or provide financial support. Furthermore, the classrooms are equipped with computers and networks.

Finally, a reinforcement workshop for the administration team and the educators is organized in order to strengthen their pedagogical and ICT skills.

Then, the actual implementation of the project takes place: Together with the supporting organization, the project is again broadcasted and the registration of interested participants starts. An inauguration ceremony marks the beginning of the classes. The schedules for the inauguration are adapted to the rural community. After the completion of a certain number of courses, participants receive their certificate during a graduation ceremony.

Throughout the implementation phase, the promoting organization provides technical, organizational, methodological, and pedagogical support to the RSITC. Meetings and workshops are regularly organized, particularly in view of allowing the RSITC to work in a sustainable and independent way as soon as possible.

In order to guarantee the efficiency of the project, a communication strategy is developed and implemented to inform the community about the advantages of the project. Local enterprises and leader must regularly be invited. Furthermore, a follow-up strategy takes place: During the first year of implementation, a member of the promoting organization pays regular visits to the RSITC in order to assess its functioning and to detect potential issues. Finally, a sustainability strategy is developed.

In order to guarantee regular and balanced activities within the RSITC, specific courses are organized for advanced participants, children, and housewives. Strategic alliances are built with enterprises, as well as public institutions, which can rent the classrooms to use the ICT installations for meetings or training sessions.

Project Implementation

Actors of the Implementation Process

Based on this project design and planning, the FAI started, together with CDI, the implementation phase. In the following, the involved actors, as well as the challenges they faced throughout the process, are presented:

1. *Foundation for Agricultural Innovation.* The FAI, which is also part of the Ministry of Agriculture, conceptualized, designed, and monitored the project.

   Difficulty faced: While the FAI had no experience related to the work of educational telecenters, the CDI had no experience regarding the work in rural areas. This led to some communication difficulties between the two entities regarding the definition of objectives.

2. *Committee for the Democratization of Information Technologies.* This NGO is mandated by the FAI and is actively involved in the implementation process, particularly in view of providing training and support to the RSITC.

   Difficulty faced: During the selection process, CDI focused only rural cooperatives. Unfortunately, many cooperatives did not receive the invitations to informative meetings, owing to mail delivery problems in the targeted regions. This delayed the selection process, as CDI had to launch new invitations, for example, via telephone.

3. *Farmer Cooperative Pocoyan* is one of the two farmer organizations that have been selected for the implementation of a RSITC on their land. It provides an administration team in charge of implementation on a daily basis.

   Difficulty faced: The cooperative had reported that there was an available warehouse which could serve as a facility for a future RSITC. However, it turned out that the infrastructure was not adapted and a new building had to be built. Additional funds had to be spent and the infrastructure preparation was delayed. Also, their RSITC could not initially be equipped with Internet connection as there were no enterprises, usually in charge of this kind of service, willing to work in this remote area.

4. *Cooperative of Rabbit Breeding of San Esteban* is the second farmer organization selected for the realization of a RSITC and it also provides an administration team for daily implementation of the project.

   Difficulty faced: The building chosen by the cooperative in San Esteban was less adapted for a RSITC than expected. Significant renovations had to be undertaken, which also led to additional fundraising and delays. The restructuring of the administration team had to be undertaken, as some educators had resigned shortly after the course began. This led to a 3 month interruption of classes.

Implementation Process

As defined during the planning phase, the first step of the project implementation involved in the selection of the cooperatives willing to launch an RSITC project.

Firstly, a review of all organizations in the region of Valparaiso and La Araucania was conducted in order to ensure that they were actual farmers' organizations and representative of their rural region. Potential candidates received information letters and were invited to informative meetings. In the region of Valparaiso, this information meeting took place in April and May 2007, in Petorca. The information meeting for farmers' organizations in the region of Araucania took place in Temuco in April of the same year. During these meetings, participants received an application form, which focused on criteria related to previous experience of the organization and its administration team, as well the motivation and interest in taking part in an RSITC project.

FAI and CDI received the applications in April and May 2007 and started the pre-selection process based on the previously defined criteria. They started visiting various farmer organizations. Among these were the Farmer Cooperative Pocoyan, visited in May, and the Cooperative of Rabbit Breeding of San Esteban, visited in June 2007. These two cooperatives fulfilled the criteria and were therefore selected to implement their own RSITC projects.

Training of Educators

In the following, professionals of the CDI started the training process of the administration teams in both cooperatives. The administration team from San Esteban was trained at CDI headquarters in Santiago and the administration team from Pocayan in a school in Toltén near the cooperative. The training was split into specific training for the coordinators, the educators, and the technical coordinators. Coordinators and technical coordinators received 24 hours of training, while educators received 72 hours of training. The training took place during 3 to 6 weeks—depending on the group—and focused on three main areas, as defined during the planning process:

1. The digital gap and the construction of citizenship
2. Social and educative practices
3. Nonformal education

More concretely, participants took part in the following main and subcourses:

The development of an RSITC

- How is a RSTCI generated?
- Functions and objectives of a RSITC
- Roles and functions of the administration team

Pedagogical objectives

- Promote analysis and reflection in areas which are relevant for participants
- Promote the development and the strengthening of community projects and services in social domains
- Strengthening of the sustaining organizations through its integration in the local community

Pedagogical steps of the project

- This course teaches how to develop practical projects with participants.

Microsoft Unlimited Potential Training for educators

- Microsoft Unlimited Potential is a program that seeks to increase digital inclusion and improve the life standards of youngsters and adults who live in disadvantaged socioeconomic environments. It has developed educational software and materials that can be used in collaborative projects, such as the RSITC. Users learn how to use and teach various Unlimited Potential tools (e.g., Office, Windows operational system).

    This training process ended with a certification day, during which, both administration teams presented in public and in presence of

Figure 18.3
Certification of the Administration Team

Source: FIA (2010).

FAI and CDI, the implementation plans they respectively designed (see Figure 18.3): For example, courses they planned to offer at their RSITC, methodologies, opening hours etc. Furthermore, on June 21 and July 9, 2007, the cooperative of Pocoyan and of San Estaban signed the official agreement with CDI.

Launching of the RSITC

The next step involved the construction of the RSTCI. The constructions (Pocoyan) and renovations (San Esteban) started on September 5, 2007. On September 10 and 11, both administration teams attended a meeting of Latin American telecenters, at ECLAC (Economic comisión for Latin America and the Carribean), in order to learn from other experiences and prepare for the implementation of their own telecenters. Shortly after, the administration team of Pocoyan finished the installations of their computers, networks, and webcams in their RSITC, supported by FAI and CDI. It is important to mention here that the RSITC in Pocoyan could not be equipped with Internet access, only with an intranet network.

ICT Courses at the RSITC San Esteban

The RSITC Pocoyan was inaugurated on November 28, 2007. Courses started on March 15, 2008, until October of the same year. The winter weather forced the RSTCI to suspend their courses for several months.

Figure 18.4
ICT Courses at the RSITC San Esteban

Source: FIA (2010).

In the RSTCI of San Esteban, computers, webcams, and Internet access were installed and configured on October 29, 2007 (see Figure 18.4): The administration team arrived on November 10 and installed the networks. Classes started in March 2008 and the first participants graduated in June 2008, but enrolled immediately for another cycle of classes.

The Pedagogical Model and Use of ICT

Courses were organized according to the age, sex, or work interests of the participants. Each course lasted approximately three months and the related classes took place two or three times a week. The scheduling was adapted to the participants profile and their degree of availability. Through the discussion of subjects related to the participants' life or work (e.g., specific courses for apiarists, housewives etc.), they learnt how to use tools, for example, Word, Excel, Power Point, and the Internet. Courses started with a basic level of difficulty and increased progressively, together with the related exercises associated to their work and life.

The project sought to adapt the role of ICT within their courses to the pedagogical model of Paulo Freire, the Brazilian educator and theorist: Freire recommends that in order to achieve sustainable empowerment of vulnerable populations through educational practices, these populations must not be solely passive students but be integrated as active actors in their own learning process. In this perspective, ICT had to be used here as tools that enhance the development of the whole community: More precisely, ICT courses must focus on integrating students in the learning process and convey applicable knowledge, instead of simple information. In the end, this approach is supposed to enable these students to be the actors of their living and working conditions and contribute to a sustainable change in their lives.

> The Chilean pilot project preferred the notion *Rural School of Information Technologies and Citizenship* instead of the generally used notion *telecenter*. According to the FAI, this notion does not sufficiently reflect the participatory approach that ICT are supposed to confer to the learning and teaching process, in comparison to notions as *school* and *citizenship*, which would include this perspective.

Course materials and hours accompanying the software were developed by the RSTIC and were also based on the pedagogy of Paulo Freire: women, for example, would be provided with material featuring exercises focusing on Word and Excel programs in order to enable them to help their children with homework or to help manage their household expenses. On the contrary, farmers would learn how to integrate the same software in their professional activities, for example, communicating with clients and vendors etc. A typical day of an RSTIC could be a course for women during the morning, another for children during the afternoon and courses for adults in general during the evening hours. This would ensure that participants would be able to attend courses. Another objective was to integrate the courses into the life of the participants, instead of forcing participants to change their workday, also in view of guaranteeing the sustainability of the project.

Support Activities during the Implementation Phase

Throughout the whole implementation process, CDI provided support to both RSITCs. Concretely, CDI visited the RSITCs six times during the first 12 months of the project. Each meeting lasted around 1 hour and 30 minutes and aimed to identify challenges and discuss solutions.

Technical support was also provided; for example, if computers could not be repaired within the school, they were sent to CDI who replaced or repaired them. Furthermore, in view of increasing the quality of the RSITCs, three workshops of 8 hours each were organized by CDI in order to improve administrative and educative methodologies. Each new member of the administration team also received specific training when needed. Finally, once a year, both RSITCs met other telecenters in order to exchange best practices.

Distribution of Funds during the Pilot Project

The FAI provided 100% of the necessary funds. Concretely, it provided USD 50,000 for two years of the pilot project and established a framework outlining how these funds should be distributed (see Figure 18.5).

During the first year, funds were mainly invested in the preparation of the project implementation as broadcasting and training activities.

Figure 18.5
Distribution of Funds during the Pilot Project

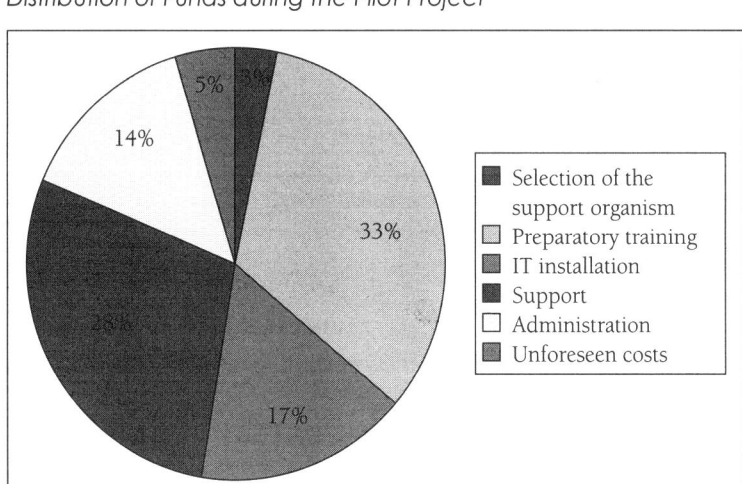

Source: FIA (2010).

During the selection process, 3% of the available funds were spent on the selection of the executing organization, the collecting of information of existing farmers' organizations and cooperatives, the organization of information meetings, the pre-selection of applicants and the field visits to preselected organizations. Preparatory training (training of the administration team, including training sessions for coordinators and educators, implying overall organization of the training, rent of training facilities, material and transportation to the training facilities) used 33% of the allocated budgets, while IT installation, infrastructure and material costs (installation of computers, transfer of the material to the RSITC, etc.) accounted for 33% of the budget.

Each RSITC spent 28% of the budget on support activities. This included the attribution of a scholarship, one workshop each semester, the materials for these workshops, bimonthly visits to the RSITCs for class observations, transportation to the RSITC, technical support and reparations, coordination of trimonthly meetings of the RSITCs and the materials for these meetings. Furthermore, 14% of the budget accounted for administration activities. These activities included the general coordination of the project and institutional support provided by CDI. Finally, unforeseen costs account for approximately 13% of the available budget of the first year.

During the second year of implementation, funds were mainly used for administration and support of the RSITC (see Figure 18.6), for example, training of new staff and renovation of classroom furniture. More precisely, 10% of the budget was invested in training activities, 13% in IT installations and 59% in support activities. Around 14% of the funds accounted for administration costs and 4% had to be spent on unforeseen activities, which is significantly more than during the first year.

Supervision Process

The supervision process is conducted in a hierarchical way: The FAI supervises the work of its subcontracted partner, CDI, which has to report back to FAI, via evaluation and observation reports, billing, etc. CDI, in return, is in charge of supervising and controlling the work of the farmer cooperatives. Within each administration team, the coordinator

Figure 18.6
Percentage of Total Costs for RSITC San Esteban and Pocoyan Second Year

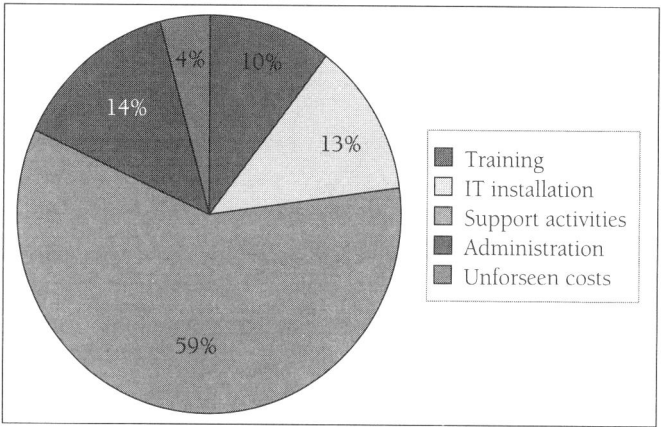

Source: FIA (2010).

supervises the work of the team and reports back to the cooperatives and CDI.

Achievement and Impact

After the first cycle, 20 participants graduated in the RSITC of San Esteban and 15 in the RSITC of Pocoyan. In order to quantify the results and impacts of the RSTIC, impact evaluations were conducted among these participants before and after the course cycles of each RSTIC. More precisely, the objective was to evaluate their ICT skills and their perception of the material used for ICT and citizenship courses, and to analyze the reason for which participants decided to enroll in the courses and how they were using their acquired ICT skills. Firstly, participants had to respond to rather theoretical questions concerning informatics (*What is the difference between hardware and software?*) on a multiple-choice basis. Then, they had to write and format a text in MS-Word, including page numbers, tables etc, create an Excel file including calculations and a graph as well as a PowerPoint presentation with graphs and sound.

Furthermore, their ability to use the Internet was tested: Participants had to write an email, insert links to various web pages as well as attach a file to the email. In the second part of the evaluation, participants were asked to what degree they agreed with given statements (*This course allowed me to improve my economic and social situation*). Also, participants had to explain their motivations for enrolling in RSTIC courses.

The evaluation disclosed results in the following areas.

ICT Skills and Impact

Prior to the course cycle, groups of both RSITC reported that they were not using computers, nor able to use any software or familiar with Internet use. The evaluation identified significant differences between the two groups after completion of the course cycle. Students of the RSITC Pocoyan increased their skills in the use of Word, Excel or PowerPoint but did not increase their ability to use ICT or the Internet for daily activities, which is not surprising as the RSITC Pocoyan was not equipped with Internet access. In comparison, students of the RSITC in San Esteban reported that the newly acquired skills had indeed a major impact on their lives, as they were not only able to use software, but also to communicate, work, and study via the Internet as well as access various websites. The fact that the RSITC San Esteban was equipped with an Internet connection had a major impact on the students' motivation. Also, the administration team in San Esteban was composed of educators with good ICT skills, which helped students in this RSITC to progress quicker than in Pocoyan. Also, more students enrolled for the next cycle than in Pocoyan. Therefore, Pocoyan was later equipped with Internet access in order to tackle this problem.

Regarding the evaluations of Word, Excel, and PowerPoint use, both groups indicated prior to the course that they were not able to carry out the given exercises. After the course, all participants were able to use the three software adequately.

Motivation and Use of Acquired ICT Skills

The majority of both groups indicated that their initial motivation to enroll in RSTIC courses was to learn how to access information, to help their children. Some reported that they enrolled "for professional reasons." After the course cycle, they reported that these expectations had been met and that learning how to use ICT was useful, as they were using their acquired ICT skills mainly for professional purposes, for example, communication via email. The concept of "digital alphabetization" was rather unknown and led to vague answers, for example, "something good," "information." etc. After the cycle, the concept appeared to be well understood and described as "Handling and knowledge of ICT."

Interestingly, the answers to the question "Would you pay for the courses?" did not vary after the completion of the cycle—a majority answered in the negative. This can be due to the fact that many respondents had to deal with difficult economic situations and were reticent to invest in learning that would not lead to immediate benefit. Another explanation could be the fact that some participants found it difficult to integrate the practical aspects of ICT skills in their daily life.

Post-pilot Phase

The RSITC in San Esteban has faced some major challenges with regard to the adequate use of funds and subsequently had to stop the courses for some time. However, over 500 participants have been trained since the launch of the project. Additional renovations had to be made which led to additional costs. Thanks to scholarship programs, educators of both RSITCs continue to receive a salary and the RSITCs achieve high degrees of self-financing and management.

In 2010, eight wireless telecenters have been installed in the region O'Higgins, more precisely in the rural communities of Petorca, Catemu-Panquehue, Peumo-Pichidegua, Nancagua-Placilla, Molina-Río Claro, Maule Sur, and Ñuble. It is expected that there will be around 3,000 regular users.

The pilot project and its positive results have also contributed to the creation of new policy approaches of digital training for rural areas on a national level: In 2009, the Institute of Agriculture Development integrated the mode of RSITCs into its national policy of digital rural development. The pilot project has therefore directly contributed to the creation of a national rural development and education policy.

Conclusion

The RSITC project has achieved to offer ICT courses in very remote areas and helped participants to facilitate their access to information and increase their ICT skills. Various factors have contributed to the success of the project and increased its chances of sustainability in the long term.

A look at the design and planning process reveals significant success factors: Firstly, the strong partnership between a public agency (Foundation of Agricultural Innovation) and the educational NGO (Committee for the Democratization of Information Technologies) has strengthened the project from the beginning of its conception: On one hand, the availability of public funds and independency from external sources made it possible to implement the project rapidly and to provide the schools with a high number of and costly equipment as well as extensive training. On the other hand, the involvement of an NGO with expertise in the field of ICT for education in South America allowed designing and implementing a project that would take into consideration lessons learned from similar experiences and increase its efficiency.

Furthermore, the planning process is characterized by a constant effort to build a strong foundation for the future implementation of the project: The hand-holding approaches, such as organizing support activities for each RSITC allowed strengthening the pilot project from the beginning. However, it is important to mention here the importance to select carefully the implementing entities and to provide long-term administration support to the latter, in order to avoid problems as those faced by the RSITC San Esteban.

Another success factor is the fact that the project has achieved in creating a feeling of ownership and proximity between project coordinators and users during this phase, particularly thanks to the creation and training of administrator teams composed of local inhabitants. This allowed to embed the project in the respective community and to increase the receptivity of the latter toward the new project. This in turn has a significant impact on the project's sustainability, as its success relies obviously on the actual willingness to use the provided services of the RSTIC.

Finally, the last key success factor is the content and setting up of the training sessions, which have been tailored to the social reality of users and focus on availability, needs, and interests of the rural population. It appears here clearly that a key condition for efficiency is defining realistic objectives that try to bring ICT to the user and not the other way around. The actual question to ask is not "How can rural populations learn to use ICT?" but "How can users learn to *benefit* from ICT?"

Despite the existence of many telecenter projects in developing countries, the success factors of the Chilean experience can be considered as important lessons regarding the question how to adapt efficiently ICT projects to their rural context.

Bibliography

Brossard, L.F. (ed.) (2008). Programa FIA: Tecnologías de información y comunicación aplicadas en el mundo rural. [Programm FIA: Information and Communication Technologies Applied to the Rural World], Fundaciónpara la innovación Agraria, Santiago (Serie "FIA Serie" Nr. 4).

CENDEC (2006). Vision of the Access and Use of New Information Technologies by Farmers. Retrieved from http://www.cendec.cl/tecnologias_de_informacion.htm (accessed October 4, 2012).

Chaveau, B.M, & Vergara, S.E. (2011). Proyecto piloto de Escuelas Rurales de Informática y Ciudadanía: un modelo de transformación social en Chile. [Project Pilot of Rural Schools of Information Technologies and Citizenship: A Model of Social Transformation in Chile]. In Cristóbal Cobo Romaní, John W. Moravec (Eds.). *Aprendizaje Invisible. Hacia una nueva ecología de la educación.* Collecció Transmedia XXI. Laboratori de Mitjans Interactius/ Publicacions i Edicions de la Universitat de Barcelona. Barcelona, Spain.

Chile. (2010). Chile Expands Internet Access to Rural Areas. One billion Pesos were Invested to Provide Chilean Farmers with Access to the Web. Retrieved from http://www.thisischile.cl/2778/2/419/Chile-expands-Internet-access-to-rural-areas/Article.aspx (accessed October 30, 2012).

Foundation for Agricultural Innovatio (Fundacion por la Innovacion Agraria). (2010). Retrieved from www.fia.cl (accessed October 4, 2012).

Resultados y lecciones en alfabetización digital rural. Escuelas de Informática y Ciudadanía. Proyecto de Innovación en Regiones V de Valparaíso y IX de La Araucanía. [Results and Lesson in Rural Digital Alphabetisation. Schools of Information Technologies and Citizenship. Project of Innovation in the Regions of Valparaiso and La Araucania]. Fundacionpara la Innovacion Agraria. Santiago, 2010 (Serie Experiencias de Innovación para el Emprendimiento agrario).

STIC. (2009). ProyectoPiloto de Escuelas de Informática y Ciudadanía (EIC): 2006–2009. [Pilot Project of Information Technologies and Citizenship Schools (STIC): 2006–2009]. Fundaciónpara la innovación Agraria, Santiago (Serie Experiencias de Innovación para el Emprendimiento Agrario).

World Bank. (2012). Chile/The World Bank. Retrieved fromhttp://data.worldbank.org/country/chile (accessed September 7, 2012).

Important Websites

Centro para el Desarollo de Capital Humano, www.cendec.cl

Committe de la Democratizacion de la Informatica, www.cdichile.org (accessed October 4, 2012).

Fundacion por la Innovacion Agraria (FIA), www.fia.cl (accessed October 4, 2012).

Instituto Nacional de Desarrollo Agropecuario, www.indap.cl (accessed October 4, 2012).

19

Telesecundaria: An Educational Model for Rural Secondary Schools (Colombia)

Eilean von Lautz-Cauzanet

Overview

The project Telesecundaria was launched by the Colombian Ministry of Education in 2000. Its objective is to offer quality education to secondary school students in rural and remote areas through the integration of video screening in each lesson. For this purpose, schools were equipped with televisions, educational videos, and specific print material for lessons that are adapted to the social reality of rural schools. Apart from introducing systematic video screenings in the classroom, the project's specificity consists in its participative methods that include the local community in the activities of the educational process. Within a few years only, Telesecundaria achieved to improve the academic results of rural students and has strengthened the relationship between rural schools and the local community.

Project Background

Colombia, the fourth largest country of South America, has achieved significant progress in the areas of access and the quality of secondary education, despite the large range of economical and societal problems—among which figures 50 years of civil war. Since 1991, the year of the new National Constitution stipulating that basic secondary education shall be compulsory and free in all public schools, considerable progress could be accomplished. For example, the net enrollment rate in secondary education has increased from 55.4 % in 1998 to 75.9% in 2011 (World Bank, 2012). However, challenges persist, particularly in rural and remote areas of the country: Absenteeism, dropout, and repetition rates are high in remote secondary schools. In 2000, the net enrollment rate for rural areas was only 30% compared to 65% in urban areas and dropout rates were 10.9% compared to 2.5% in Colombian cities. National assessments further confirmed the low quality of education of rural students who consistently performed worse in achievement tests than their urban counterparts. This was not only due to difficult access to education in terms of distance or lack of infrastructures, but also due to low quality of learning processes, lack of adequate pedagogical training of teachers, socioeconomic challenges, and low education levels of families living in rural areas. Furthermore, the rural sector at this time was characterized by a population living mainly below the subsistence level (70%), and the inadequate access to education services was among the leading causes of rural poverty and contributing factors of the burgeoning criminal market and violence among youth (World Bank, 2012).

Aware of the negative impact that this unbalanced situation would have on the countries development, the Rural Education Project was launched in 2000 in order to increase access to quality and basic education up to grade 9. The initiative aimed also to strengthen the delivery of pre-school education for 0–5 year olds, reorganize technical and vocational education in rural areas, and to respond to the needs of agricultural sectors—amongst others—as well as to support the development of social capital through an emphasis on civic values in schools.

The Rural Education Project aimed to strengthen not only the existing national schooling projects, but created also a new project called

Telesecundaria. This project focuses on students aged between 12 and 17, who have finished primary school two or three years ago and were not able to enroll in secondary education because of the challenges related to their rural environment.

Impact of Existing Similar Projects

Telesecundaria was originally a Mexican program that uses satellite television programs in order to improve the access to quality secondary education in rural areas. Students enrolled in the Mexican Telesecundaria had access to formal secondary education based on television programs transmitted via satellite and could obtain the same diplomas as their peers in regular public schools. A classic Telesecundaria lesson in Mexico would be composed of a 15-minute television sequence, followed by exercises in previously distributed workbooks, and developed in concordance with the educational television sequence. During the following 45 minutes, students follow their teachers' instructions. These teachers receive during the weekends or in the afternoon specific training through satellite television programs and guidebooks with teaching strategies as well as learning objectives related to each course. From a technical point of view, the project was based on satellite installations, televisions, combined with specific workbooks. Colombia adopted the Telesecundaria program but adapted the workbooks to Colombian needs, and instead of satellite-based videos, Telesecundaria schools in Colombia received a package of video tapes.

Planning Process

Between 1999 and 2003, experts of the Colombian Ministry of Education analyzed the Telesecundaria Model in view of planning its adaptation in Colombia. Firstly, during a needs and feasibility assessment phase, they canvassed the project planning and implementation process of Telesecundaria in Mexico and the extent to which this development could apply to Colombia. In order to identify indispensable key elements for a successful implementation of Telesecundaria, field visits of one week each to Guatemala and Costa Rica were organized.

Secondly, a cooperation agreement between the Mexican Secretary of Public Education and the Colombian Ministry of Education lead to the installation of an antenna and a decoder in order to receive properly the Mexican satellite signal. The third and key step was to adapt the Mexican Telesecundaria model to the educational policy framework of Colombia, as well as to embed it in the framework of the Rural Education Project and its objective to improve the quality and access of basic secondary education.

In order to guarantee a high degree of conformity of the project's functioning and content and national education standards, a team of five experts from MoE's directorate of research was created. This team was in charge of coordinating Telesecundaria on a national level. Another team composed of 10 internal and external experts, also part of MoE, was created in order to design the educational, pedagogical and didactical components of Telesecundaria. These experts were also responsible of redesigning learning and teaching material associated with this project and had to identify the most pertinent educational television programs related to each area of the curriculum. More precisely, these experts analyzed 3,000 Mexican educational television programs received by the newly installed antenna and selected 2,000 of the most appropriate ones.

Design of Educational Material

The analysis of the Mexican project, its videos and associated material lead to the new design of the so-called *basic concepts, study guides*, and *didactic guides*. These were adapted to Colombian educational system and curriculum.

- *Basic concepts*. The *basic concepts* can be considered as textbooks of Telesecundaria. For each area of the curriculum, there is one *basic concept*. (biology, environmental education, mathematics, technology education, ethics and human values, Spanish, universal history, universal geography, physics, chemistry and climate)
- *Study guides*. The study guides are composed of exercises related to a specific subject studied in the *basic concepts* as well as instructions for experimental and group activities and can be considered

as workbooks. The objective of their use is to stimulate the learning process through these activities.

- *Didactic guides*. These guides tend to guide the teacher how to organize a Telesecundaria lesson and define the role of videos within a lesson. (c.f. implementation phase)

Concretely, the Colombian Telesecundaria model was adapted to the national curriculum, based on the guidelines set by the educational law 115/94, which defines basic standards of the educational system. The teams in charge of the planning process decided to use video tapes instead of satellite transmission, not only because of the high costs of a satellite installation for this program in Colombia, but also in order to benefit from the advantages of video tapes: The possibility to rewind to passed sequences during the lesson confers a higher degree of flexibility and adaptability to the tool and the lesson.

Around 136 educational television programs were elaborated in the areas of history, geography and Colombian values, as it was obviously impossible to use Mexican history modules for the Colombian model. Also, the modules had to be adapted to a secondary level lasting four years in Colombia compared to three years in Mexico.

Finally, a follow-up model was designed: A permanent team, responsible for the sustainable development of the project on the departmental and municipal level was created, an analysis of a sustainability strategy conducted, a network of pedagogical management launched, and the reusability and the evaluation process of all levels examined.

Design of the Implementation Phases

At the end of the planning phase, a schedule for the implementation of the project was designed. This schedule was split up into two phases: The piloting phase (from 2000 to 2003), followed by a phase of expansion (2003 onwards).

It was decided that the main purpose of the first phase should be the assessment of the projects consistency, to test the impact of educational television programs, and their associated print material, as well as to define new pedagogical strategies, which would suit to the Telesecundaria model. In addition, the pilot phase should contribute to the revision and improvement of the overall guidelines of the project and detect areas in which Telesecundaria schools need support.

The second phase had the objective to expand the creation of Telesecundaria schools in rural areas. This expansion should come along with the overall improvement of the project, based on the identification of local issues and needs, the training of teaching and management entities, and an improved organization of logistical aspects, for example, efficient distribution of televisions and videos.

Project Implementation

A chain of implementing entities, from MoE down to the coordinating teacher in the Telesecundaria schools, cooperated in view of an efficient and effective implementation of the project. In the following list will be presented the key actors of the implementation as well as the difficulties they faced throughout the process.

- *National level.* Within MoE, a permanent team of experts is in charge of designing, planning and coordinating Telesecundaria on the national level. It must also ensure that the Telesecundaria Project is in line with national educational policies.

    Difficulty faced. The team did not schedule sufficient time for redesigning and printing the modules before the start of the school year, which led to some delays.

- *Regional level.* A permanent trainer team is in charge of supporting Telesecundaria schools on a regional level. This team focuses on the duplication and sustainability of the project, and created networks of pedagogical management for teachers.

    Difficulty faced. The departments and municipalities were not properly prepared or introduced into the new model before the start of the school year, which led to confusion in some cases.

- *Local level.* Schools of the same geographical area and /or with common interests support themselves within a network. Furthermore, in every Telesecundaria school, five teachers—one teacher per grade—are in charge of coordinating the implementation of the project.

Difficulty faced. Some schools did not choose a coordinating teacher at the beginning of the school year. The absence or change of these teachers interrupted in some cases the development of the learning process, decreased the effectiveness of the program and created distrust in the continuity of the program.

Pilot Phase

Between 2000 and 2003, 41 schools were transformed into Telesecundaria schools in six Colombian departments: Antioquia, Boyacá, Cauca, Cordoba, Cundinamarca, and Valle. Two thousand four hundred and sixty students as well as 200 teachers and principals were concerned by the implementation of the first phase. Concretely, 200 teachers were trained how to teach with Telesecundaria through the participation of four workshops per professional. Around 45 lots of *study guides* and *basic concepts* were printed and delivered to each of the participating schools, along with four didactic guides per school. Furthermore, all schools of the pilot phase were equipped with televisions and recorders, and received also a library, a laboratory, and an assembly of educational video tapes. A national follow up of the installed technologies in repairing or explaining the use of the infrastructure to school teachers was also provided in form of regular visits to Telesecundaria schools in each department.

In the participating departments, trainer teams were created in order to support the implementation, to strengthen the administrative capacities of the program, and to identify success and difficulties in the meantime. Furthermore, efforts were made in order to integrate the Telesecundaria model successfully in the various rural communities: Local decision makers and enterprises were approached in order to explain them the importance of being involved in the educational process of the Telesecundaria school. During this first phase, teachers met regularly peers from other Telesecundaria schools in their region within the so-called Networks of Pedagogical Management, in order to exchange their mutual experiences and practices.

The three years of the pilot phase were also used as an opportunity to analyze the extent to which students would accept and react to their new learning tools.

After three years, the material associated with the educational videos was revised and further adapted to national education policies. This decision was based on the willingness to guarantee a high degree of uniformity of content in secondary schools and to avoid discrepancies between rural and urban schools. More precisely, Telesecundaria's study plans for each area of the curriculum and grade, the educative strategies and the activities proposed in the study guides were adapted.

Expansion Phase

During the second phase, local and regional diagnostics were conducted in order to identify specific problems and adapt Telesecundaria accordingly. As the actual age of participating students were often older than the normal average, videos, material, and activities were adapted to their degree of maturity and interests. Up from 2003, participating schools received administrative and pedagogical training which permitted also to foresee for each school their need of equipment, accompany the implementing teams and teachers, install the necessary spaces for the Telesecundaria model, estimate costs, and distribute the adequate amount of material (*study guides, basic concepts*).

Furthermore, Telesecundaria schools from the same geographical area and with common interests were regrouped within a network and support groups were created. These networks increased their efforts to sensitize the local community regarding the added values of Telesecundaria. In the meantime, they developed common sustainability strategies (e.g., cooperation with local enterprises) and launched a follow-up process of Telesecundaria schools and their organizational and pedagogical management.

Adaptation of the Educational Process to the Rural Environment

The educational process of Telesecundaria seeks not only to support students and encourage flexible learning methodologies, but also to impact positively on the local rural community. In this sense, the educational process was adapted to the social reality of rural communities and based on four major components:

Organizational, Administrative, and Managerial Component

This component aims to encourage the autonomy of participating schools regarding the use of human, economic, and technological resources of their environment. Schools participating in the Telesecundaria project are flexible in view of their space (activities within or outside the school building) and schedule management (duration of lessons, opening hours). Local decision making as well as autonomous initiatives to strengthen inter-institutional relations within the local community are encouraged.

Curriculum and Pedagogy Component

The content- and television-based methodologies of the Telesecundaria lessons (cf. basic concepts) are supposed to confer an active role of students within their own learning process and create a direct link between lessons learned and their life outside of school. Therefore, subjects learned and analyzed during Telesecundaria lessons are embedded with the social, economic, and cultural environment of the community.

Component of Local Integration

The local community, including the families of students in Telesecundaria schools is involved in the day-to-day activities of the school, as many lessons and their topics— presented by an educational TV program and the associated exercises in the study guides—request students to conduct research within their imminent environment. This inclusion of local organisms and enterprises is supposed to have a positive impact on students' motivation and learning results.

Productive Pedagogical Projects

Teachers can organize the so-called Productive Pedagogical Projects (PPP). During these projects, students learn theoretical elements of a theme or subject, thanks to educational television programs. In combination with these lessons, they gain concrete work experiences in cooperation with local enterprises, associations, and meet experts of the rural sector. These projects focus particularly on the sector of the local agroindustry.

The Didactic Model and the Role of Educational Video Screening

A typical Telesecundaria learning session includes a screening of an educational video tape dealing with a subject of one of the nine curriculum areas. In the so-called *basic concepts*, students can contain essential information on the subject that is studied during the lesson. The *study guides* contain exercises and guidance for collective experiences in the area of the studied subject, help students to understand and experience the information conveyed by the program, and the *basic concepts*. Furthermore, teachers are free to include in the learning session the use of regular television programs, in order to include up-to-date information and to represent different ways of how a subject can be presented and analyzed.

In order to guarantee the efficiency of the learning process, including the efficient use of educational videos within this process, the didactic model of Telesecundaria confers a specific role to video screening that varies according to the respective learning phase.

Phase of Questioning: Introducing a Subject

When a teacher wishes to use an educational video in order to introduce a new subject, he or she will chose a brief screening which will be then followed by analyses of information provided by the *basic concepts*, as well as exercises and collective activities. These videos are used in order to introduce a subject and give students a first idea of its importance, functioning, and process. The first phase is supposed to guide students in their efforts to formulate new questions and to approach a subject or issue they are unfamiliar with.

Phase of Exploration

During the phase of exploration, students play around with hypothesizes, possible solutions and answers regarding a specific question, or subject explored in the introducing video. They develop their own theories.

Phase of Contrast

In this phase, students conduct experiences, measurements, observations, gather , and create graphs in order to verify and understand the different theories obtained during the first two learning phases. In this case, the video programs serve as information support. They help students to understand in detail the studied subject. The use of video, in association with the information provided by the *basic concepts* contributes here to the so-called conceptual balance. This balance is achieved after two phases of conceptual unbalance—also called cognitive conflict— during which students are in a process of information gathering and understanding.

Phase of Evaluation

During the phase of evaluation, the students' capacity to apply the learned theoretical concepts to new problems and situations is analyzed. Instead of asking to know by heart the theory, his ability to adapt the theories will be explored, for example during the phase of questioning of another subject studied in the Telesecundaria school.

Teacher Training

In order to guarantee the sustainability of Telesecundaria, the project focused particularly on the support to and development of teachers who are involved in the project. These teachers are supposed to be able to facilitate the process of learning and exploit effectively the possibilities of the model. Also, the project wanted to make sure that they are able to interact positively with students, willing to work with innovative tools, and that they feel empowered and supported by the departmental and municipal trainer team.

Therefore, teachers were accompanied throughout the implementation of the whole project and took part in three qualification workshops, covering the following themes:

- The didactic model of the Telesecundaria
- Learning processes

- Pedagogical strategies
- Use of the *basic concepts*
- Development of learning sessions
- Development of PPP
- Cooperation with the local community

Within the Telesecundaria project, one teacher per grade is in charge of coordinating the development of the model. However, as he/she is obviously not specialized in every area of the curriculum, a rotation model was created in order to train these teachers to coordinate the model for every domain of the curriculum. In addition, the regional trainer teams organized field visits to accompany teachers in their efforts of implementation. These visits allowed verifying progress and difficulties to conduct adjustments if necessary.

Finally, the Association of Professional for Quality Education (ASPROED, in Spanish: *Asociación de Profesionales Pro Calidad de la Educación*) provided during the expansion phase technical assistance and training regarding the use of educational videos. The training took place in 11 rural regions: Antioquia, Arauca, Bolívar, Cesar, Córdoba, Magdalena, Meta, Nariño, Risaralda, Caquetá, and Santander. Around 500 teachers and agents of the trainer team took part in 263 training sessions.

Funding and Costs during the Pilot Phase (2000–2003)

Telesecundaria was part of the second component of the *Rural Education Project*: "Enhancing Access and Quality of Basic Education." The Rural Education Project cost totaled USD 24.2 million and was funded by the World Bank with USD 12.8 million (loan financing).

These funds were invested in the following way: During the planning and preparation phase, USD 296,500 was spent. More precisely, funds were spent for preparing field visits to Mexico, Guatemala, and Costa Rica (USD 5,000), the employment of a coordinator for Telesecundaria within MoE (USD 45 000), and the employment of five curriculum specialists within MoE in view of redesigning *study guides* and *basic concepts*(USD 111, 500). Furthermore, the amount spent for part-time employment of 10 external specialists was USD 100,000, and USD 35,000 were spent for the employment of a technical experts, the investment in a recorder, and a Beta-cam used for the analysis of Mexican videos.

During the first years of the pilot phase, funds were spent in training (USD 100,000 for training of 41 teachers), print, and distribution of print material (USD 130,000), televisions, and video recorders (USD 57,400), installation of a library in each school (USD 53,300), one laboratory per school (USD 61,500), distribution of educational videos (USD 61,500), and technical follow-up activities (USD 6,000)

Achievement and Impact

Rapid Expansion in Terms of Participating Schools

During the first three years (2000–2003), 41 schools implemented the new Telesecundaria model, involving 2,460 students in 41 different municipalities. From 2003 to 2006 (phase of expansion), the amount of Telesecundaria schools and students increased considerably: 20,946 students from 650 schools in 307 municipalities participated in the project. In the Cauca valley, where television screening was transmitted by the Regional TV Telepacífico, in addition to the educational video, 91 Telesecundaria schools were created, involving 8,733 students in 21 municipalities.

Inclusion of Dropout Students

In 2002, a first diagnosis was conducted in order to assess the impact of Telesecundaria. Four hundred nine students (6th grade) were tested in 19 Telesecundaria schools. Students taking part in this evaluation were around two years beneath the regular age and had at least repeated one primary class. Around 25% of them were repeating their 6th grade, 45% had been out of the school system, and 30% were students that had been out of the system before. These figures lead to the conclusion that Telesecundaria achieved to get rural dropout students back into the classroom. In 2004, an evaluation conducted by the MoE revealed that the level of students dropping out of Telesecundaria was lower than before the launch of the project.

Academic Achievements

In terms of academic achievement, achievements of 437 Telesecundaria students (7th grade) in the international SABER[1] assessment were analyzed. Out of these 437 students, 86% were enrolled in Telesecundaria schools from the region of Córdoba, 11% from Boyacá and 3% from the Cauca valley. They obtained better results in mathematics and language than expected and better results than the average of rural students of the same grade who had not participated in a specific support program of the Rural Education Project.

Integration in the Rural Community

An evaluation conducted by MoE in 2004 revealed that PPP had a positive impact on the rural community in which Telesecundaria schools had been launched. Thanks to projects that involved rural actors (e.g., farmers, enterprises, and associations), employment in the agricultural sector could increase its attractiveness in the eyes of Telesecundaria students. The evaluation reported further that the amount of young people migrating to urban areas had decreased.

Improved Teaching and Higher Motivation of Students

The same study revealed further that the rotation system of teachers within Telesecundaria schools contributed successfully to a balance of qualified teachers in all participating schools. Teachers reported that the training and workshops, as well as the didactic guide allowed them to implement effectively the methodology and pedagogical strategy of the Telesecundaria model. The acquired skills as well as the new material allowed them to privilege teamwork and organize exercises which involved the community. According to them, these activities stimulated also the student's motivation and capacity to understand the different

---

[1] System Approach for Better Education Results (World Bank).

subjects of the curriculum. A general positive attitude amongst students towards the innovative methodologies could be observed by teachers.

Post-pilot Phase

In 2010, MoE conducted an evaluation of the material used by the Telesecundaria model, in view to adapt them to the since evolved curriculum guidelines and basic standards of competences for secondary school students.

Conclusion

The governmental top–down and large-scale initiative that Telesecundaria achieved was not only to increase the overall motivation among rural teachers and students, but it has also led to improved academic achievements and decrease dropout rates. Furthermore, the project enhanced the integration of these Telesecundaria schools into their respective communities, which in turn had a positive impact on the migration flux to urban areas.

These achievements and the overall success of the project are based on several success factors. Firstly, the planning process is characterized by a significant effort to adapt the projects to the Colombian curriculum and needs, both in terms of technology choice (videos instead of satellite based screening) and educational content. The willingness to tailor a Colombian version of Telesecundaria, while integrating lessons learned from neighbor countries, has contributed to the program's efficiency and avoided discrepancies between the objectives of the project and its content and tools.

Furthermore, a look at the implementation of the project reveals an organizational structure characterized by an organizational chain that confers a high importance to local decision making. The creation of the so-called Networks of Pedagogical Management on a municipal level, or the creation of Telesecundaria teacher teams on a school level is an example of this participatory management approach. This approach has allowed creating a feeling of ownership and responsibility among the schools, which is particularly for a large-scale project a crucial criterion for efficiency. The integration of local enterprises and decision makers in the educational projects of Telesecundaira (PPP) reinforced the participatory characteristics of the project even more. The creation of a real-life link between the learned theory and active experiences outside of the school and opening hours has contributed to a concept of learning that is not limited to the school building and hours anymore. Given the importance of offer education that is tailored to rural needs, this is a significant success factor of the program.

This success is also due to the choice made in terms of technologies. The fact that TV and videos were easy to use, increased the receptivity on both teacher's and student's side. Their combination with a pedagogy based on flexibility has allowed creating lessons in which students are actors of their learning process, and teachers are tutors within a collective self-learning approach. Again, the learning material that accompany the use of videos offer activities and experiences that take into consideration the rural reality of Telesecundaria students and bridge the gap between what is learned and real life. The fact that the proportion of students leaving their rural community has diminished, teaches an important lessons when it comes to assess the potential of inclusive educational methods for rural development.

Finally, the program puts an emphasis on teacher's training, aware about the importance to train those who are the key actors of the project: Convincing teachers about the project's utility and giving them the impression that the projects helps to optimize their teaching practices was an important success factor of the project.

Thirteen years after the start of Telesecundaria in Colombia and its replication in many South-American countries, the use of television and educational videos cannot be considered as being outdated, despite the massive development of computer- and Internet-based technologies and the new opportunities these create within educational processes. On the contrary, Telesecundaria seems to prove that the use of technologies which may appear today less "innovative" compared to others (e.g., tablets and smartphones) can be very helpful for rural education projects.

These characteristics—and the possibility to use solar-based energy for the use of televisions—are obviously an important point when it comes to the question of the project's replicability in developing countries.

Bibliography

Colombia Ministry of Education. (2006). Horizontes de la Telesecundaria y perspectivas del camino recorrido. [Horizons of Telesecundaria and perspectives of the journey]. Retrieved from http://www.colombiaaprende. edu.co/html/mediateca/1607/articles-82504_archivo.pdf (accessed November 20, 2012).

Fuentes Cardona, M.G., & Quiroz Estrada, R. (2010). Un acercamiento a la reforma de la educación secundaria desde los usos y proposición que los maestros de Telesecundaria dan a los recursos pedagógicos del modelo de 2006 [Anapproach to the reform of secondary education from the perspective of teacher's use of the pedagogical resources from the 2006 model]. Retrieved from http://www.comie.org.mx/congreso/memoriaelectronica/v10/pdf/area_ tematica_02/ponencias/1106-F.pdf (accessed January 16, 2012).

Isaza Ramos, & Mary Luz. (2006). Telesecundaria modelo educativo adaptado a Colombia. [Telesecundaria—educational model adapted to Colombia] Latin America and the Caribbean: Lessons from Best Practices in Promoting Education for all. Retrieved from http://pdfesmanual.com/books/26992/ la_importancia_dada_a_la_educaci%C3%B3n_se_refleja_en_el_monto_. html (accessed January 10, 2013).University of Rosario. (2005). Evaluación de los Modelos Educativos que promueve el Proyecto de Educación Rural del Ministerio de Educación Nacional. [Evaluation of Educational Models promoted by the Rural Education Project of the Ministry of Education]. Retrieved from http://www.mineducacion.gov.co/1621/articles-101945_ archivo_pdf3.pdf (accessed October 16 2012).

World Bank. Colombia—Rural Education Project. Retrieved from http:// documents.worldbank.org/curated/en/2007/06/8130831/colombia-rural-education-project 2007 (accessed January 4, 2012).

20

Sharing Content in Local Language and Voices (Zimbabwe)

Stephen Haggard

Method

This report is based on an extended face-to-face meeting with project leaders (staged in neighboring Zambia because of visa and access difficulties in Zimbabwe) and further exchanges by phone and mail, study of published documents and reviews of literature, and of unpublished data supplied by the project teams. The project staff has verified the accuracy of the text.

Setting

Zimbabwe has few reliable statistics,even for key indicators like GDP per head. In Table 20.1, 2010 data are available for various indicators.

Table 20.1
Zimbabwe Indicators at a Glance

Indicator	Measurement	
Rural Population	(%)	62
Population aged 0–14	(%)	45
Infant Mortality	Deaths age 0–5 per 1000 live births	45
HIV prevalence	% prevalence in adult population	14.3
Tertiary enrollment	GER (%)	6
Literacy rate youth	(%)	99
Literacy rate adult	(%)	92

Source: UNESCO

Zimbabwe Indicators at a Glance

Behind Zimbabwe's current troubles and its unreliably reported political situation, the country has a historic legacy of high literacy and a principled policy commitment to improve the lot of poorer and rural communities. More recently, however, educational attendance has plummeted, with UNICEF reporting up to 80% of rural children not attending schools (UNICEF, 2013). Many international NGOs have effectively withdrawn from the country.

Summary

Sharing Content in Local Languages and Voices (The Mbire podcasting project) involved the use of MP3 portable audio player devices to distribute agricultural knowledge in podcasts to 20,000 smallholder farmers in the district wards of Mbire, initially from October 2008 to March 2009. The pilot phase has smoothly transitioned to local permanent adoption.

The key development themes in this case study are

- localism and self-reliance, from the ICT platform of a stand-alone non-networked battery device, through to the use of local dialects,

- the incorporation of indigenous agricultural knowledge,
- the lead role taken by farmers in disseminating the content,
- sustainability and impact, and
- the generation of capability as opposed to altered functioning in the target communities.

Mbire podcasting qualifies for inclusion in a study of practice in ICT for rural development and education (iERD) on several grounds.

- This project uses stand-alone devices—at a time where ICT-based agricultural development is increasingly run on networked platforms (PC or phone). In doing so, the project challenges the conventional models and raises questions of quality, engagement, and reach in services.
- It is a pioneering and successful use of ICT in apparently unpromising environments, where the usual prerequisites for ICT-based learning do not exist. Literacy is very low while electricity and network signals are entirely absent.
- It extends the standard conceptual frameworks around ICT in rural education and development. The benefits it aims to deliver are not just transferable outputs such as skills, productivity or even knowledge; rather, it aims at improving human capability as the bedrock from which any other benefits can grow.

Project Content and Location

The core activity of the project is the creation and distribution of agricultural extension materials in podcast-recorded formats on the MP3 platform. The project is at the scale of a localized pilot and proof of concept. The technical content is provided by Agricultural Ministry agencies. The packaging of the podcasts in local language versions and distribution in the agricultural areas is by the project team, which is a partnership between a local and an international NGO. The technical content of the podcasts includes livestock and crop production and management, health issues such as cholera, malaria and rabies, and market issues such as sources of seed and other farm inputs. A total of 32 podcasts on this topic range were produced and deployed in the project.

The location for the project, the Mbire district in the Zambezi Valley in Mashonaland central province, in the north-east of Zimbabwe, presents many challenges both for development under any circumstances and in particular for ICT-based projects. Broadcasting, electricity and cell phone coverage are entirely absent. The district is hot, semiarid, and is prone to floods during the rainy season, which presents a pinch point for livestock health as pests and diseases are at their peak, but on the other hands roads are flooded and impassable meaning assistance cannot easily be obtained. Five wards hosted the project (7, 8, 9, 15, and 17). In these wards, the residents are poor communal small-scale farmers, whose main economic activity is rearing cattle. Around 20% are estimated to be nonliterate. To improve their livelihoods, a range of community organizations are engaged in teaching them to grow guar bean to supplement livestock feeds during the dry season, cow peas and sorghum to contribute towards food security. The area is dominated by subsistence agriculture.

Project Partners, Resources, and Roles

The funding partners are

- HIVOS, a development NGO specializing in humanist and technologically oriented projects, originally based in Netherlands but with a Zimbabwe presence; and
- the UK-based NGO, also with a Zimbabwe presence, which specializes in appropriate technology solutions in development.

The project implementing partner was Lower Guruve Development Association (LGDA) in conjunction with project staff from the NGO Practical Action. For this pilot, the LGDA employed and managed five community animators who were dedicated to this project. These animators are natives of each ward and residing in the target wards. They are charged with a role of driving both the knowledge (content) and the distribution (platforms) of the project.

LGDA at its base in Guruve established a Knowledge Node at which all the development agents (AGRITEX, health, Tsetse, Vet Control) could meet and collaborate to assemble content packages and distribute the packages on the ICT platform. The hardware resources for this task at Guruve comprise:

For use at the Knowledge Node:

- new computer desktop and microphone for content recording, conversion to MP3 format and to load content on to portable devices (Figure 20.1)

For use by the Community Animators:

- 7 MP3 devices

From 2008 to 2010, the project used JNC MP3 players in Mbire and Guruve Districts, in Mashonaland Central Province. The devices have 2GB capacity and can hold up to 500 knowledge recordings.

From 2011 to date, the project has been using Sony Walkman MP3 players in Gwanda, Bulilima, and Mangwe Districts of Matabeleland South Province (Figure 20.2). The MP3 device has 2GB capacity and can store up to 500 knowledge recordings.

Figure 20.1
Guruve Knowledge Node: Recording Podcast Content on the Laptop-based Recording Platform

Source: Practical Action (2013).

Figure 20.2
MP3

Source: Practical Action (2013).

Figure 20.3
Speakers

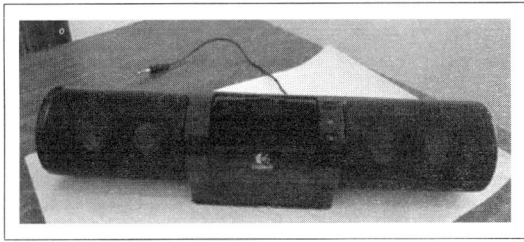

Source: Practical Action (2013).

- Seven broadcast speakers

The speakers used have a standard auxiliary jack cable enabling the connection of the MP3 players. The device uses two AA batteries (Figure 20.3).

- Thirty other MP3 devices for use by farmers
- Two sets of rechargeable batteries for every device.

The cost of each player unit available to use in the field was $150. The choice of Sony's relatively high-cost MP3 technology emerged from trials of a range of MP3 players in early internal pilots. Low-cost generic MP3 players were tested which suffered from high failure rates. The Sony MP3 robustness and reliability, given the need for devices to work unsupported and far from a maintenance base, lead to it being preferred.

Development Background and Previous Experience

The choice of communities and district was influenced by the NGO partners Practical Action's previous three-year project which focused on improving livestock health and product value of resource poor households in the Mbire district. The overall objective of this previous project was to improve the livelihood options of vulnerable rural poor communities in semi-arid areas of Zimbabwe through the improvement of livestock health and product value in resource-poor households in the Mbire district.

In the Mbire district, livestock die due to lack of feed during droughts. Those that survive fetch very low prices on the market or cannot pull the plough because they are in poor condition. In the preceding project, therefore, farmers prioritized a nutritional intervention to improve their livestock feeding systems through use of by-products from adapted crop varieties.

Activities focused mainly on the following:

- Strengthening local production and management of livestock feeds by resource poor farmers.
- Strengthening farmer-to-farmer livestock extension support mechanisms improving livestock feeding practices disseminated at district, provincial, and national levels.

The action directly targeted 38,000 smallholder farmers in the district, and formed a baseline and foundation for the Mbire podcasting project, which targeted methods for delivering agricultural development and extension services.

Focus on Extension Services

Before the Mbire podcasting project, the prior arrangements for agricultural development and extension in the district had been as follows. Four district-based development agents (AGRITEX, Health, Tsetse, and

Vet Control) each worked independently to achieve their own defined objectives in content generation and dissemination. Typically, each agent's representative would, at various villages, call for community meetings on days of their choice. Farmer availability for these sessions was therefore limited. Content formatting, language, and presentation would also follow each agent's choice. Due to inappropriateness of the knowledge formats, dissemination channels, and languages, the proportion of farmers who could benefit seldom exceeded 50%. Impassability of roads in the rainy season at peak agricultural activity time further reduced the extension workers' impacts in the area. Livestock mortality for the average village herd of 120 cows was at the rate of 12 cattle lost to disease per rainy season, with infectious diseases and trypanosomes the main cause of death.

Selection of the ICT platform

The NGO, Practical Action, has a specialist focus on knowledge products in rural development and farmer education in several settings, and already owns Southern Africa's largest digital repository of farmer training content for development applications. Their choice of a podcasting platform therefore reflects an informed analysis of the challenges of using ICT in rural development. Other ICT routes for disseminating agricultural extension content do operate in Zimbabwe and are worth mentioning for context.

State radio infrastructure in Zimbabwe favors urban and cash-oriented communities, and has low penetration and traction in poor and rural areas. For farmers who can receive it, radio content is likely to be incompatible with farming schedules, and hard to listen to as local dialects are not used. Community radio is not encouraged in Zimbabwe's regulatory frameworks, and the broadcasting laws do not allow for NGOs to partner with stations in producing content.

Online formats—websites—do have a role in agricultural extension in Zimbabwe as a "wholesale" channel, which can reach connected experts, development professionals, and agricultural agencies. Practical Action the NGO partner already operates such a channel, but observes that it is not effective beyond an urban knowledge node at reaching farmers in the field.

Podcasting (by which is understood: prerecorded audio files in MP3 or similar format on stand-alone devices) offers advantages of versatility and reach. The platforms can operate anywhere except in water, are valid in urban and rural settings. Content can be cheaply tailored for specific settings and themes.

Project Method

The preconditions for the project team members were:

- ICT skills
- Content—which would have to be specially created

Regarding the ICT skills, the livestock and the crop officer and the projects manager from the implementing partner LGDA, four local development agents' officers, and the five community animators were all given technical training on the podcasting devices. This covered knowledge content generation, packaging, and uploading to various devices for use by community animators.

Regarding the content creation, the 32 knowledge products finally distributed are a fusion of

- technical/scientific agricultural knowledge from the Extension Agents working from Agricultural best practice manuals,
- local indigenous knowledge contributed by area farmers, and
- translation/interpretation by Community Animators to create accessible local language versions.

Content Creation Process

The process for content creation deserves to be described in detail.

Selection of content topics is initially determined by agents in response to their assessment of local farmer need. For the farming communities of Mbire, initial content was themed around specific farming tasks such as deworming of cattle and goats, castration and dehorning of bullocks, and planting of guar, cow peas, and sorghum seeds. An originally planned line of content around marketing was not implemented because the marketing season fell outside the project timeframe.

The content of each podcast starts as a technical brief with a specific theme for its focus, such as assessing yield, use of a medicine, and a specific technique such as dehorning bullocks. A five-minute podcast is the target duration of the media—allowing for short learning sessions with maximum retention of learning.

After translating to local languages and the recording of such knowledge products on the project computer, they are loaded to MP3 players and taken into the wards by the community animators. The back-up battery and charging arrangements for the pilot permit a life of around 14 days for each player device before it needs access to power to recharge.

Content Consumption Process

The social formats for playing the content in village localities are varied, and evolve locally with loose guidance from the community animators.

- At community meetings, the community animator can play the recordings aloud over a loudspeaker.
- At demonstration sessions, trainees use the players with earphones as a live guide to a procedure. These sessions are arranged by lead farmers and by animators.
- A lead farmer can borrow the MP3 player to take home and play to neighbors and friends. This is particularly encouraged as it makes use of networks of kin, family, and neighborhood. One project official described it as "the equivalent of transferring a library with 24/7 opening hours to the village."
- An individual farmer can take a player to consume the podcasts privately using earphones (Figures 20.4 and 20.5).

Figure 20.4
A Lead Farmer Demonstrates the Use of the MP3 Player with
Earphones

Source: Practical Action (2013).

Figure 20.5
Demonstration Session: The Community Animator Is Showing How
Farmers can Follow an Immunization Procedure, While Being
Guided by an MP3 Recording in an Earpiece

Source: Practical Action (2013).

Farmer Responses to Podcasts

An early finding in the pilot was that farmers exposed to podcasting consistently felt prompted to report and discuss their indigenous knowledge and methods for dealing with the issue at hand. Farmers spontaneously also often raised other relevant development topics, including human health.

Indigenous knowledge is highly valued in Zimbabwe farming, as it offers inputs that are locally available and does not require cash. In comparison, scientific solutions offered by development agents are likely to meet reluctance both on the grounds of affordability and perception of being "not done here." However, community animators discovered that this indigenous knowledge, while valued, often did not circulate widely. An effective indigenous technique was often known only in one village but not the next one, or was even restricted to a family group, often the dominant or most wealthy farmer.

A second stage of content production, therefore, involved revising the podcast content to reflect indigenous methods and knowledge. Following validation of the techniques by agricultural agents, and with the permission of the knowledge-holders to share the knowledge, additional indigenous knowledge was added into many podcasts as a revision or update. Topics updated in this way included treatment of animal wounds with local plants, methods for storing grains, and techniques for pest control.

Practical Action project leader for this pilot, Lawrence Gudza, commented:

> The processes around indigenous knowledge were an unexpected additional benefit from the podcasting method. Podcasting turned out to be a two-way information exchange. There were great techniques out there, which needed to be shared more widely. Because the process of writing and recording the knowledge products is simple and cheap, we were easily able to adapt the recordings and add new knowledge in. This increased their value and their acceptance. It also increased the engagement of the farmers enormously. At the end, we had some farmers making their own podcasts.

Impact Data

The project outcomes and impacts as reported by the project partners are:

- Twenty thousand people in Mbire obtained access to extension messages at times of their choosing using ICTward development meetings, EC Block Grant project workshops, Council meetings, and during individual or shared listening.
- The number of community members accessing knowledge content at podcasting sessions grew throughout the project, suggesting popularity and interest. From the first loudspeaker community sessions in November 2008, where the audience was typically 20–30 women and men, attendance rose within three months to an average of 50–70 women and men. The technology has reached about 75% of the local population. This compares to an estimated 50% reach for extension content delivered traditionally by agents face-to-face. Farmer-to-farmer knowledge exchange has also improved, with neighboring communities also benefiting from the information.
- Essential livestock treatment tasks in the pilot communities, such as castrating juvenile bullocks, dehorning, and deworming of both cattle and goats, are now successfully performed by knowledge-empowered villagers (Figure 20.6). (Treatment of livestock was previously done by veterinary officers employed by Department of Livestock Development.)
- A total of 604 cases of zoonotic and other infectious diseases were recorded by animators during the pilot period, and prompt measures were taken by the communities to save their animal lives. (Cases varied from trypanosomosis, dystockia, ophthalmia, lumpy skin, helminthiasis, and babesiosis and sweating sickness.)
- In the Mbire district, agricultural production indicators have responded positively in the wards which received podcast content. Milk production has risen from 0.5 liters to 2 liters per cow per day and livestock birth rates have increased by 18%. Observers report better management of livestock feed and an increase in new crop varieties and crop productivity. In most villages, livestock

Figure 20.6
Dehorning a Bullock

Source: Practical Action (2013).

loss in the rainy season has dropped from 10% of the cattle herd to zero.

- Podcast content has improved animators' and communities' knowledge in disease diagnosis and management generally.

- The fusing of indigenous development knowledge with scientific content has supported the administration of traditional methods of managing livestock health and crops when externally sourced medicines and treatments are not available or not affordable.

- The district administrator of Mbire, council chief executive officer and councilors have accepted podcasting in the district as an application that shall be promoted and supported by their policies. This is now on the district agenda, and other agencies beyond agricultural extension are asking to use the platform. The project framework has been adopted across other development themes in Zimbabwe such as water conservation and use.

- Project completion reports and concept papers have been circulated among funders and stakeholders in development including

USAID, World Bank, and FAO. Inside the funding and delivery partners Practical Action and HIVOS, the methodology of the pilot has been adopted and is part of the organizations knowledge base, and is deployed to other rural development projects

- The experience of the project also generated content for the NGO Practical Action to host on its Practical Answers portal, as well as project literature such as reports and impact assessment.

The validation method for this pilot involved the achievement of objective criteria which has been predicted before project commencement (e.g., reach of the service), the compilation of field reports, and external observation.

Discussion and Evaluation

Proof of Concept

The podcasting platform has been tested in two different dimensions: hardware and content.

As a hardware exercise, the podcasting pilot has shown that it is possible to disseminate development knowledge and information using ICT to an unlimited number of women and men in isolated rural communities, even without communications infrastructure or electricity. Podcasting has been proven as a workaround for environments that are ICT-poor, whether by policy deficiency (e.g., prohibitive policies on broadcasting) or by lack of hardware, skills, or access.

As a content exercise, the project has also proven a model where digital material enables the accessing of rural development knowledge and information on demand, as needed, in local voices and languages. It has also demonstrated the empowering of marginal farmers to undertake tasks they could not previously achieve independently, such as diagnosis and treatment of certain common livestock health problems. Finally, it has shown the use of diverse development pathways by evolving a fusion of indigenous knowledge with scientific content for the benefit of target communities

Need of Agricultural Extension Framework

The podcasting initiative in Mbire relied heavily on the participation of agricultural extension professionals and organizations. The model for achieving this, says project leader Lawrence Gudza, set out "to address directly the potential fear among extension workers and agencies, that a podcasting service might replace them and their jobs." The project's message to these stakeholders emphasized *extending* and *complementing* the agencies' work. By giving a central role to the community animators and local language speakers, the project demonstrated that dissemination with podcasting was still first and foremost a human process, albeit one with a standardized content and format.

The agricultural extension structures of Southern African states generally give significant roles to field officer networks, so Gudza is confident that the model for working with AE services could be replicated in similar territories. However, notes Gudza, it has not been tried in Bangladesh, Kenya, Sudan or Sri Lanka, where Practical Action is also an active NGO, because the same structures do not exist. On the other hand, it is under active development in Nepal and Peru, where it would also work supportively with the extension officer community.

Further Evolution and Applications

The immediate extension of the Mbire podcasting project upon closure in 2009 was to replicate it in Zimbabwe's Bindura district and also more extensively throughout Guruve district, using MP3 Devices. This second phase reached a further 50,000 smallholder farmers. A further extension to 100,000 smallholders of Mangwe and Bulilima in Matebeleland South Province on the Protracted Relief Programme was done and the project closed in November 2012, but the podcasts continue to be shared through the local lead farmer structures.

Underway now is the extension to 98,000 smallholders in the Gwanda district of Matabeleland South province of Zimbabwe and the Mwenezi district of Masvingo province. The two projects use the MP3 platform to focus on a different kind of content, water governance and the water, sanitation and health projects. The beneficiaries are at different community and social levels, as they include district sanitation water committee, schools, households, and local authorities. Podcasts being shared are equally at different levels according to beneficiaries.

Introduction of a Phone Platform

In these later phases of the project in Guruve and Bindura districts, and in the light of growing phone network penetration (60% of the Zimbabwe population at time of writing this report, February 2013), mobile phones are also being used to disseminate agricultural information. This is done by a bulk-SMS service targeting lead farmers who are equipped with mobile phones by the project. A series of messages focusing on crop and livestock production were developed and disseminated to 40 lead farmers in various wards. Each lead farmer is expected to reach out to at least 10 other farmers. Alongside the phone dimension, the later implementations of the podcasting format have also included knowledge nodes and multimedia knowledge resources.

The signal, and therefore the service, is only available at particular centers, but growth is rapid and Zimbabwe offers huge potential for mobile-based information services targeting rural communities. Practical Action and other partners are developing a short SMS messages for farmers in Zimbabwe, distributing information on market prices, local weather forecasts, farming practices for improved productivity, and the transfer of indigenous knowledge between communities.

Sustainability and Affordability

Good and best practice in the terms of INRULED's iERD case collection requires a project to be sustainable.

Many aspects of the podcasting format exhibit strong sustainability, including the factors of self-reliance, lack of dependence on third-party sources for electricity, network, etc., and the empowerment of local people. The expansion of the service from its initial pilot testifies to its longer term viability. The fact that, even after project closure, the MP3s and their content remained in location and were utilized by the village animators for several years, without the project support structure in place, also testifies to sustainability.

The economic and financial viability, from the point of view of project sponsors, can also be quantified, although this is not an exact science.

The project participants have compared costs for traditional extension and digital extension methods, in Table 20.2.

However, the nature of the service is that it must be centrally funded in order to be free to farmers to consume. To this extent, it is vulnerable to political will and this is a negative indicator for sustainability.

Podcast Cost Comparison

Assessing the impact of information provision on the holistic economic system of the activities is possible, and is attempted here as an approach to evaluating sustainability of the method. However, caution should be exercised when interpreting and reporting these figures, see note.

Table 20.2 is an attempt to compare the conventional extension system as it has always been conducted against the digital extension approach. While the two models can be compared, certain detail may not be apparent if one is not familiar with either of the extension systems, but of note is the following:

Table 20.2

Comparing the Cost of Conventional Extension System Versus the Cost of Digital Content Dissemination through MP3 Devices

Conventional Extension (One extensionist)	Item Description (Cost per annum, USD) (estimated by Practical Action)	Digital Extension (Podcasting) (7 Podcasting kits)
2,760	Annual Salary/Wages	0
1,572	Field Allowances	1,680
1,040	Motor cycle/bicycle	0
2,600	Transport: fuel	0
–	Content development and recording Quarterly visits by NGO	3,600
20,000.00	At least 20 sets of Brochures produced for 1 district	0
–	7 × Podcasting kit (MP3 Devices and speaker system)	1,050
27,972		6,330

Source: Practical Action (2013).

- A conventional extensionist is an employed person and therefore is on a monthly wage/salary while in digital extension, whereas the lead farmer is a village resident and is not on any wage/salary.
- Allowances. Lead farmers are not usually given any allowances. However, these have been listed in for purposes of this comparison as a cost of keeping the lead farmer enthused to continue with the practice after donor funding ends.
- While the conventional extensionist uses either a motor cycle or a bicycle, the lead farmer walks from village to village.
- Content development and recording shows a charge. In the Mbire podcasting project, the funders were not charged for content development or recording. The cost here is the NGO's cost for transport and accommodation over a period of one year, to cover the area a single extensionist would have covered.
- The conventional extension system generates a lot of brochures, posters, and technical briefs. The estimated cost of printing these over a period of one year can fluctuate around the figure shown.
- Figures include the cost of 7 × MP3 device kits including the spare batteries.

It is important to note that it is difficult to calculate how many people the conventional extension system records as contacted in a year. The challenges are those cited as the reasons for introducing the digital extension: impassable roads, flooded rivers, motor cycles and bicycles in states of disrepair, remoteness of areas making it unattractive for extensionists to live, demotivated extensionists, etc. The productivity of traditional extensionism is not only potentially low, but potentially measured with low accuracy.

Capability Enhancement

Another way of examining the sustainability of the podcasting project, and one that is proposed and preferred by the project sponsors and delivery teams, is Capability Approach Theory. This approach contends that the aim of development can be to expand peoples' capabilities, rather than achieving a change of their functionings. In this framework, functionings such as eating or treating a disease are contrasted to capabilities such as being part of a community, being confident, being able to use information.[1]

The prevailing approach to ICT in development and education is that the ICT platforms aim to stimulate behavior changes (such as different cropping techniques leading to higher yields) among a population which engages with the content at the level of executing its instructions. The Mbire podcasting experience shows an alternative approach which is, arguably, a valuable contribution to rural development practice.

From this perspective, one of the key successes of the project is its triggering of a local capability in information production and distribution. The outcome, whereby farmers came forward as empowered creators of content on an ICT platform, and contributed indigenous knowledge up to the point of recording their own content in 10 out of 32 of the knowledge products, constitutes an important element of the evaluation. Commitment to knowledge and information sharing among farmers is, in itself, a valuable development outcome. Insofar as this outcome emerged spontaneously, and continued, at no marginal cost, the capability enhancement dimension of the project does indeed look quite sustainable.

Bibliography

Oosterlaken, I., & van den Hoven, J. (eds). (2012). *The Capability Approach, Technology and Design, Philosophy of Engineering and Technology*. Dordrecht: Springer.

Practical Action. (2013). Podcasting in Zimbabwe. Retrieved from http://practicalaction.org/podcasting-in-zimbabwe-1 (accessed March 7, 2013).

UNICEF. (2013). Zimbabwe/UNICEF. Retrieved from http://www.unicef.org/zimbabwe/overview.html (accessed March 6, 2013).

---

[1] Functionings is a term proposed by the economist Amartya Sen, upon which the philosopher Martha Nussbaum has constructed the contrasting dialectic between human capability on the one hand and the realized domain of "beings and doings" on the other hand. The approach is expounded in the field of ICT and Development in

21

CocoaLink (Ghana)

Stephen Haggard

Methodology

This case study draws on meetings conducted with CocoaLink in Accra, Ghana, by the author in August 2012, further briefings with other similar or related organizations including CocoaLink technology supplier DreamOval, published documents, and field work in the Sefwi-Wiawso district in the Western Region of Ghana by Research Assistant I.A. Meriga in August 2012 under the author's supervision. The content has been additionally verified by CocoaLink staff for correctness.

Context

Ghana is one of Africa's stronger economies, with consistently high growth over recent years (Table 21.1), and a mobile telephone infrastructure that penetrates between 80% and 90% of the population by most estimates. The cocoa industry is a healthy sector and a major exporter worth USD 849 million in 2011, a bumper harvest year. The sector exhibits many kinds of production ranging from the predominant smallholder farms to large plantations employing labor.

Table 21.1
Ghana Key Indicators, 2011

Indicator	Units	
GDP per head	GNI in USD	1,820
GDP growth	Annual %	14
Population	Million	25
Life expectancy at birth	Years (2010 data)	64
Adult literacy rate	% (2009 data)	67

Source: World Bank.

Background: CocoaLink

CocoaLink is an SMS-based information service for cocoa farmers in Ghana that delivers cocoa-specific agricultural learning by mobile phone. This service aims to allow farmers to access important cocoa growing content to support increase in productivity and improvements in technique generally. The project is a collaboration between World Cocoa Foundation, World Education, and the Ghana Cocoa Board (COCOBOD) with funding from The Hershey Company.

As of summer 2012, the CocoaLink project was half way through a three-year pilot phase in 15 communities, having commenced in March 2011. The phone service had been operational for just over a year. The origins and inspirations of the project were diverse and included:

- University research by Ghanaian students in the period 2007–2008, highlighting the growing penetration of phones in cocoa-growing communities.
- Evaluation of the 2008–2010 cellphone-based literacy project Alphabetization a Base Cellulaire (ABC) in Niger, which demonstrated the value of this platform in delivering basic educational training in rural communities.[1]

---

[1] https://edutechdebate.org/meducation-initiatives/lets-get-informal-mobile-phones-for-adult-basic-education-in-west-africa/ (accessed May 19, 2013).

- Grameen Foundation (Uganda) basic work on ICT and village phone activities including use of phones to support village health-care services, which provided the base technology for CocoaLink's service architecture.
- A decline in the reach and quality of conventional agricultural extension services following dismantling of funding by the donor community in the 1990s—with a consequent search by Ghana's Ministry of Agriculture and Ghana's CoCoBo for ways to replace the lost services.
- Existing educational projects tackling children's education and adult literacy, including World Education's program ECHOES (Empowering Cocoa Households with Opportunities and Educational Solutions) and the World Cocoa Foundation (WCF) Cocoa Livelihoods program offering basic training.
- The collaboration of COCOBOD with the World Cocoa Foundation and The Hershey Company, to realize the CocoaLink proposal.

The project merits inclusion as an illustrative example of best practice in use of ICT for rural development and education because of:

- Its broad delivery model involving private sector, state organizations, education, business federations, and subcontractors.
- Its striking success in attracting significant numbers of participants to a mobile education/development service.
- Its stable funding has allowed a significant and sustained period of operation.

Agricultural Extension Services and More

The original concept (and still the core) of CocoaLink is as a supporting channel for the delivery of extension services as once offered by the ministry of agriculture and which are now handled through COCOBOD. Moreover, a lack of infrastructure and financial capacity in the available extension services, following their restructuring after World Bank scrutiny questioned COCOBOD's effectiveness (Anderson and Feder, 2004) more than 10 years ago, drew attention to farmers' need for information. During the years from 2000 onwards, innovative alternatives for agricultural information were at a premium.

The farmers targeted through the CocoaLink pilot were those already in receipt of extension services. The content for the service is offered by and in collaboration with the original COCOBOD extension agents. The content covers: farming practice, disease prevention, post-harvest production, and crop marketing, with additional focus on social issues including child labor and farm safety.

The CocoaLink project currently addresses a wider range of content than the technical remit of COCOBOD agricultural extension. Issues including business training, use of mobile technology, financial management, literacy, and health are also now addressed. For example, CocoaLink agents made the unexpected discovery that many farmers were unaware that their mobile had a "calculator" mode, and this could help them compute yields. Basic training in calculation technique on phones is now offered as part of CocoaLink, and it has proven to be appreciated, useful, and popular.

The CocoaLink staff emphasized in an interview show that basic training in mobile phone SMS features was often required. They found this to be true particularly for farmers in the 50–60 age range, which is the average in Sefwi-Wiawso, because they were less familiar with the technology. However, farmers frequently report anecdotally that they use children or grandchildren to administer their messages.

Scheduled content issued in bulk takes the form of seasonal or topical advice (Spray in XXX month with YYY product) and this includes non-farm content. The non-farm content includes social messaging to engage in literacy programs and special reminders about events, such as, farmer to farmer village meetings scheduled by extension services. Such add-ons further fulfill the original remit of supporting agricultural extension. The bulk messaging system delivers content either in the local language, Twi, or in English. A voice version for farmers with low literacy skills is being rolled out.

The farmers in the Sefwi-Wiawso district had not yet been exposed to the voice service but were expecting it and looking forward to it. Several reported problems with not being able to easily read text messages.

The User Journey

There are two modes of registration for service users: through short code and through in-person register.

In the short-code mode, users can text a short code (a dedicated code is provided by Network Operator Airtel), to register directly to the system. However, this does not capture information beyond their phone number. About a quarter of registrations happen this way.

In-person registration is conducted within the communities. This village registration process was observed in the field for this study, in the Sefwi-Wiawso district in the Western Region of Ghana.[2] Nokia C3 smartphone with a mobile version of the CocoaLink Mobile Application issued to conduct a questionnaire in English and the local Twi language. The application populates basic information: age, gender, community, language, farm size, estimates of recent production level, picture, and phone number.

During the village registration event, a total of 11 farmers gave their details to a World Education Coordinator, who was supported by a local facilitator, in a one-to-one exchange. This followed a group meeting at which the WCF coordinator presented the CocoaLink service and an open discussion about it with the farmers took place. The farmers had little or no formal education or technical knowledge. Their production volumes ranged from 20 to 200 bags per year. When these farmers were later questioned independently about their motivations for registering with CocoaLink, they mentioned that the CocoaLink service is attractive to them because they see it as modern and educative. The farmers expressed the view that the CocoaLink service was worth subscribing to because they had little or no direct access to agricultural extension officers.

Several of the farmers also expressed the belief that CocoaLink might be a route to financial assistance in the future, not for individuals but

---

[2] The event took place on August 27, 2012. Two CocoaLink personnel ran the operation: Richard, the WCF coordinator, and Peter, a local facilitator. The location was the village of Punikrom in an area of forest, where there is electricity but weak network coverage. The event was observed by Twi-speaking researcher I.A. Meriga who took field notes of farmers comments in English equivalent.

for their growers' association. (We understand that CocoaLink does not in fact have any such plans.) We noted the following words from one farmer:

> We strongly believe that CocoaLink might give a loan or incentives for us if our association becomes stronger. Because CocoaLink is helping us now with the mobile technology, it means there would be more help to come in the future.

This sentiment may in part be fueled by the fact that government-funded projects for free spraying, free seedlings, and free fertilizers are common.

Finally, the message content from CocoaLink most highly valued by the farmers we spoke to was content regarding fertilizer dosage regimes. One farmer we met offered testimony that his yearly pesticide dosage now, under CocoaLink advice, was about a fifth of what it had been before.

Interactions on the SMS Service

CocoaLink service content is designed as a two-way system for registered users. Farmers pay to send their messages to the CocoaLink server, at the standard rate. Messages received are free to farmers.

Messages and/or questions sent or phoned in by registered users most typically fall into technical categories such as: How much fertilizer should I use and what is the best price? Where can I get a certain type of hybrid seedling? These queries are answered by World Education CocoaLink officers who have agronomy backgrounds and answer using COCOBOD extension manual to ensure continuity between services. The extension manuals tied to the growing calendar is the standard reference text for extension officers. In this respect, CocoaLink functions as a version of the existing extension materials as a way to intensify messaging and learning that exists in other channels.

Users' queries are logged against the user profile before answers are issued. The library of previous answers provides a resource for faster response compilations. At present the demand for this query-response service is not strong but CocoaLink is optimistic that uptake will increase. Farmers questioned in the Sefwi-Wiawso district confirmed that the affordability of SMS messages was not an issue for them; they were content to pay this cost for obtaining information. However, some of them reported that they felt their SMS questions were occasionally misinterpreted.

It is recognized at CocoaLink that this method of responding to queries is intermediate and will evolve in due course, either towards more local and decentralized sources of response, and/or a rule-based expert system. One proposed scenario is that extension workers will be able to use the system to increase their response capacity, by receiving queries in the field, accessing the response system through a smartphone application, and responding to the query over the network either with a packet of relevant content or a personalized phone call [often preferred by users]. This response mode fulfills the original vision of the service, as a means to increase the capacity of extension services.

Connected Training Activity by World Education

A program of basic community education called "WCF ECHOES,"[3] emphasizing Information Communications Technology (ICT) and literacy, has been presented throughout the CocoaLink project. It is funded by The United States Agency for international development in partnership with World Cocoa Foundation and 16 of its members, programed by partner World Education (WorldEd), and delivered by local NGO CENCOSAD (Centre for Community Studies Action and Development). The community education projects in fact pre-date CocoaLink. Forty percent of the farmers who have registered on CocoaLink were already enrolled in the basic education services provided under WCF funding.

This foundation-level village community education activity aims to support farmers using the CocoaLink mobile phone service. CocoaLink estimates that some 40% of its registered farmers have taken up training or educational activity. Courses include literacy and numeracy, and the application of new technologies to increase crop yields, understand basic

---

[3] Empowering Cocoa households through opportunities and education.

Figure 21.1
World Education Trainers Interacting with Cocoa Farmers in Ghana

Source: World Education.

business concepts, and build networks for learning. These initiatives target both adults and children of school age.

In the Sefwi-Wiawso district, farmers expressed the view that the learning centers and associated educational interventions have contributed not only by supplementing basic education, but also serve as a clear symbol of community investment (Figure 21.1). Farmers explained that the centers are in nine surrounding community and equipped with computers, printers, and other equipment, exhibiting a high level of awareness about the WCF funded learning facilities.

The learning centers' mission to school age students addresses particularly those who have fallen by the wayside, aiming to proactively address literacy problems and educational failure.

Uptake of the Service

When CocoaLink was first launched, the target to reach farmers was 1500. As of September 2012, a year later, the total already stood at 4,650. Revised targets have been set as follows:

December 2012: 25,000
Project close 2014: 100,000

If this target is achieved, approximately 20% of Ghanaian cocoa farmers will have been brought into the CocoaLink system within three years. Experience in the pilot communities suggests this target is achievable. In the community of Sui, also in Sefwi-Wiawso, for example, numbering approximately 1,500 adults, 412 farmers have registered with CocoaLink in just a year, representing over 25% of the adult population.

The significance of the scale of registration so far, and the revised targets, is enormous. CocoaLink stands out for this. Comparable operations known to the author, using either mobile platforms in rural areas, or trying to impact rural development by other means in West Africa, including Esoko, Africa Rice, CIDR (Program: Access to Markets for Small Rural Rice Producers[4]) have not achieved anything like this pace of growth or critical mass in the producer communities they target. In an environment of many very small pilots, which seldom achieve scale or impact, CocoaLink's case shows that large numbers and significant proportions of farming communities will engage in development and education using mobile platforms. We cannot discount specific factors applying only to Ghana, to cocoa, or to the target communities as explanations. However, it is worth assessing the causes of the success in the hope that they can be generalized into best practice elsewhere and in other sectors.

Farmers in the project, when interviewed for this study, described the following factors for why they signed up willingly and used the service.

- The project personnel are local people. In the Sefwi-Wiawso district they noted that both the World Cocoa Foundation coordinator and the local facilitator, Mr Richard and Mr Peter, were local people.
- There is a suppressed demand for pest and disease control techniques, caused by the collapse of face to face agricultural extension services.

---

[4] http://www.cidr.org/Rapport-d-activites-2010,582.html?artpage=3-3#iii_evolution_des_programmes (accessed May 19, 2013).

- The existing farmers association and CocoaLink have worked together and this helped CocoaLink to be popular.
- Farmers have seen with their own eyes the increase of production among CocoaLink users. One farmer told us that since he started to use CocoaLink services, his yield from his 10 acre plot had risen from 30 to 40 bags.

An analysis at greater distance suggests the following two additional factors favoring take-up. The project:

- Capitalized on existing capacity and institutions with legacy influence.
- Did not have to sensitize farmers to a new idea or source of trusted content: to the extent that it simply extended existing F2F information transactions, the ICT solution did not involve scaling up new activities, rather substituting them.

Main constraints upon the uptake of the service, as seen by the CocoaLink staff, are as follows:

- *Literacy*. This includes technical literacy: using the phone to access messages. The roll-out of voice messaging, and the advent of a more technological and literate generation, are seen as reasons to hope that this constraint will eventually become less severe.
- *Network Operators*. The reluctance of network operators to offer short codes for easy sign-up, which took over a year to resolve, and to improve bad coverage in rural areas. This last factor was also cited as a major hindrance by the farmers. Again, CocoaLink implementing staff believes that these factors are headed eventually towards resolution.

Monitoring and Evaluation

The pilot stage of the project means that while monitoring and evaluation is underway, no formal reports are yet available. Therefore for the time being we can only describe its approach.

Metrics being collected from the original 1500 target pilot users include input and output of messages, results from associated CocoaLink trainings (mobile phone use, understanding of messages, etc.), productivity change from the baseline over the three years of the pilot and gender metrics. Field officers also collect data through routine monitoring, output tracking, and spotlight observations. An agricultural researcher from Kumasi's Kwami Nkrumah University of Science and Technology (KNUST) is also monitoring the project. The metrics will be compiled for presentation in 2013.

CocoaLink believes that because cocoa farmers tend to be diversified, the impacts will be seen beyond their cocoa-growing activity, in improved practice in other crops, and that a full evaluation might therefore need to look wider than cocoa production. Such an impact evaluation was due to begin at the end of 2012.

Sustainability of the Service and Future Plans

The sustainability of CocoaLink is an important discussion point. Financially, the current business model features one direct funder (The Hershey Company) accessing a generous Corporate Social Responsibility (CSR) budget stated by the company at USD 10 million across six years for its West African sustainability and responsible sourcing project. This includes the three-year CocoaLink project.[5] The CocoaLink project's other partners (WCF, World Ed., and COCOBOD) are not direct financial contributors to the core CocoaLink messaging platform and associated services.

After the period of building and launching the service, the cost profile of CocoaLink is set to decline, but this does not in itself resolve the issue of sustainability. Against this uncertainty should be set the fact that the Hershey Company's broader CSR engagement in Ghana gives a significant role to digital technologies, for example, satellite GPS farm mapping, and CocoaLink may eventually assume its place in this larger

---

[5] Hershey Press Release cited in EON businesswire http://eon.businesswire.com/news/eon/20120806005744/en (accessed May 21, 2013).

suite of technical solutions (Figure 21.2). Additionally, CocoaLink believes that other participants in the industry can be induced to step up as financial contributors. Ultimately, COCOBOD will be responsible for the managing and operation of CocoaLink.

Sustainable financing for the service is a top task on the CocoaLink agenda for year three (2014). Solutions under investigation include:

- Extending funding roles to other WCF members: 16 other cocoa purchasing companies are closely linked to the project and some may step up to funding partner level.
- Cost reduction: mobile phone companies may offer concessionary tariffs
- Income generation: an eventual audience of 100,000 specialized producers may be monetizable with paid content, e.g., from fertilizer manufacturers

Figure 21.2

Infographic About CocoaLink Published by The Hershey Company. The Project Features Strongly in Hershey's Public Affairs Portfolio

Source: http://www.hersheycocoasustainability.com/resources/pdf/ Hershey_Cocoa_Snapshot_v8.jpg

Expansion of CocoaLink services into other cocoa-producing territories in the West African region is in the stage of advanced planning, as are new service elements from other WCF programing in Ghana. For example, the Cocoa Livelihoods Program's (CLP) is piloting a farmer-produced video project. These videos are designed by farmers in consultation with a production company, and with input from extension officers. Once recorded, the WCF staff and consultants edit it. The videos will be used during farmer trainings to showcase good agricultural practices. The videos will also be broadcast in communities from PC computers using a micro-projector. CocoaLink messaging would have a role in promoting attendance by farmers at these broadcasts.

To see test videos, visit:

- http://www.youtube.com/watch?v=j3XvpglImEg
- http://www.youtube.com/watch?v=mlZKSyQ3pzg
- http://www.youtube.com/watch?v=TarrTvRA5-o

Technology Platform

The CocoaLink technology platform is provided by local IT developer DreamOval[6] on a commercial basis. The platform provides the Java framework and mobile application for registration and the MySQL database in a web browser. The SMS pull–push engine is an open source software from university developers. The platform appears stable and fit for purpose, and capable of scaling to meet new targets as well as running in separate instances for other territories if the service expands to other cocoa-producing nations.

The origins of DreamOval's capacity, which led to it providing the back end and technology platform for CocoaLink, were in the Grameen-funded maternal health mobile phone program (MOTECH), which disseminated SMS information to Ghanaian mothers during pregnancy and nursing. This architecture was redeveloped for CocoaLink and has also been used by DreamOval for other M-Agri initiatives.

---

[6] http://www.dreamoval.com/

DreamOval CEO, Derrydean Dadzie, was interviewed for this case study about the platform. Identifying two key factors behind the technical success of the platform in operation, he told us,

> The CocoaLink people had a clear idea about what they required in the feature-set, but they were willing to launch with just a few features and evolve gradually. Also, we were able to remove technical risk. The SMS pull–push technology on their platform is all second-hand. We had already put it into many settings, like banking, health, phone voting. CocoaLink got the benefit of working with something that had already been fully debugged, and this really helps on a technology project.

Dadzie pointed out that many features available in the platform had yet to be implemented, including modules for trading, payment gateway, and mobile banking. He forecasts that by 2015 (co-incidentally the end of the CocoaLink pilot period) around half of all payments in Ghana will be by mobile cash transfer in a service that integrates banks, cards, and networks. It is likely, Dadzie believes, that farmers on the CocoaLink platform would be receptive to extending their engagement with it to the use of e-cash.

Conclusion

The CocoaLink project occupies a prominent place among technology-based initiatives for rural development. The broad range of its interventions and partners, their successful coordination, and the strong success in user recruitment, make it exemplary in many respects. However, its scale and impact also make its repeatability and sustainability an issue. It has already set a benchmark of good practice for deployment of mobile technology, partnership working, and content provision. By 2015, we will know if it can also provide a yard stick for sustainability.

Bibliography

Anderson, J.R., & Feder, G, (Spring 2004). Agricultural Extension: Good Intentions, Hard Realities. *World Bank Research Observer*, 19(1): 41–60.

22

Farmerline (Ghana)

Stephen Haggard

Methodology

This case study is based on an extended set of meetings with Farmerline founders and their team at their offices in Kumasi and Ghana, conducted in English by the author, in August 2012. These meetings were followed by two days of further visits to meet Farmerline users and stakeholders in rural settings conducted by a local Twi-speaking researcher I.A. Meriga working under the author's supervision. Other types of sources include the published literature and comments from appropriately placed observers. Notes were made in these meetings and have been transcribed as indirect speech unless directly quoted. The text of this study has been submitted to Farmerline for verification of accuracy.

Context

Ghana's software technology industry is one of West Africa's healthiest, and the country has a number of IT contractors capable of meeting fairly sophisticated B to B and B to C service requirements including banking and money transfer.

Background: Farmerline

Farmerline[1] is a start-up company in the early stages of delivering a mobile-based service of agricultural information, training, and market data to farmers. Currently in its pilot phase (at the date of this case study, November 2012), it operated in the fish-farming sector around the Kumasi area for the time being. It aims in due course to operate at a large scale in a much wider area and across several agricultural sectors, pursuing its mission of impacting upon subsistence farmers at the bottom-of-the-pyramid.

In terms of exemplifying good or best practice, Farmerline as an early-stage company qualifies because of its practice in *service development* and not because of services it delivers. Farmerline is developing a commercial model for its agricultural development service. This is both topical and innovative.

Innovative because the vast majority of ICT services for education and development are marketed to NGO funders and are monetizable to the extent that they deliver to an NGO's development agenda (B to B model).[2] By contrast, Farmerline ICT services for education and rural

---

[1] The core Farmerline team is: AlloysiusAttah (Co-founder/CEO), Emmanuel OwusuAddai (Co-founder/Tech Lead), and Rebecca Peel (User Experience and Business Model Innovation).

[2] Laurence Allard, Reader at Université de Lille-III, argues in *Mythologie du Portable* (Cavalier Bleu, Paris 2010) and in *La Diplomatie du téléphone portable à la conquète des Pauvres* (Le Monde Diplomatique, May 2012) that the American information industry and its retired billionaire philanthropists are monetizing phone-based rural development and education services as a way of conquering emerging markets for IT. She says: "The mobile phone is to capitalist philanthropy what the chronometer is to Taylorism." Allard's argument is that the technology, pricing, and funding model for launching phone-based education and development services in low-income markets is dominated by the Bill and Melinda Gates Foundation, supported by Warren Buffet, and a few other wealthy donors such as the Clinton Global Initiative supported by the Omidyar Foundation (funded by the fortune of eBay founder Peter Omidyar). The interests of these players are not aligned to the needs of the world's rural poor, according to Allard. It is not the job of a case study like this to comment upon such a thesis. However, these arguments do show that ventures such as Farmerline create a new paradigm in ICT for rural education and development.

development are marketed to the end users and monetized by delivering a service they will pay for (B to C model).

Topical because of the current trend to establish ICT-based services of development or education through social entrepreneurship, often backed by investment funders looking for financial returns. This approach is controversial, with some commentators identifying a bubble phenomenon.[3] It is as yet unproven at scale as a sustainable and effective approach to ICT for development and education in rural areas. However, there is optimism and energy around this approach, and at Africa's two main technology hubs (Nairobi and Accra-Kumasi) it is being rapidly and widely copied, and is becoming a strong feature of the ICT Development scene.

Farmerline exemplifies a new benchmark in ICT practice in rural development in the following ways:

- entrepreneurship model rooted in the knowledge economy, featuring extreme speed and youth
- business orientation: the company seeks revenue from providing rural education services to paying end-users
- operates outside the normal funding and support systems of Government, NGO, sponsorship, etc.

The success or failure of Farmerline's operations will show the potential of non-traditional approaches, and new kinds of players such as universities, younger entrepreneurs, and commercial operators, to innovate in African education and development technology.

This company changes the technology, pricing, and funding model to one in which a rural population would pay its own cash to consume ICT services delivering content about health, education and development, whereas such services currently operate only to the extent that they serve the agendas set by an NGO or Government Agency, often driven by externally set policies.

[3] For example, Jonathan Kalan writing in ImpactIQ, September 30, 2012, http://impactiq.org/letter-from-nairobi-vanity-capital-and-vanity-companies/ (accessed June 5, 2013).

Origins: California-style Start-up Entrepreneurs Crossing Over from Academic to Commercial Worlds

Farmerline is the brainchild of its two founders, both graduates of Kwame Nkrumah University of Science and Technology (KNUST) in Kumasi. AlloysiusAttah studied fisheries and is an aquaculture graduate while Emmanuel Owusu Addai took an M.Sc. in Geodetics at the College of Engineering. Even while students, these two took an entrepreneurial path that typifies California start-upsand is unusual in Africa.

As final-year students rehearsing in the University Choir of KNUST in December 2011, Alloysius and Emmanuel brainstormed their ideas for Farmerline, developed a business plan alongside their academic work, and formed the company in February 2012. Astute self-publicists, they won cash prizes in competitions such as Apps4Africa 2011 and Mobile Web Ghana. To this cash they added valuable in kind support from Engineers Without Borders (EWB) Canada, including user experience expertise from Rebecca Peel who has since become a business partner. The support of EWB, a development NGO, has provided three successive deployments of professional or trainee engineers on two- and four-month fellowships to Kumasi. The Canadian personnel works inside Farmerline, providing additional brainpower, capacity, advice, and mentorship.

The founders bring prior experience as entrepreneurs, having earlier launched a successful company undertaking bulk SMS delivery. This business, called TXTUnlimited, launched when the University's Student Representative Council (of which both founders were members) was looking for a bulk message delivery solution for communicating with KNUST students. Alloysius and Emmanuel formed the vehicle to provide it, working in between lectures to set up the system. The University Community then became the next client, seeing the advantages of interfacing with students on mobile. Banks, churches, and national content publishers are now on their client list. The bulk SMS delivery company is busy and cash-generative and provides enough earnings for its founders to work unpaid at Farmerline while they nurture its growth.

The founders have recruited a KNUST lecturer and fisheries expert, Dr PokuGyinaye, as an advisor. As a leading member of Ghana's National Aquaculture Development Plan Advisory Group, a research and industry body supported by the World Bank, Gyinaye is already deeply involved in creating the liaison between fish farmers and the government. Interestingly, and typical of the Farmerline approach of mixing commerce, networks, and knowledge, Dr Gyinaye is also the owner of a large private fish farming company and thus qualified to understand commercial perspectives. Members of several regional Fish Farming Associations also sit on the Acquaculture Advisory Group alongside Gyinaye, which offers a further route for influence in the sector.

Technical Details of a Service Platform

In technical terms, Farmerline platform is the simple push–pull phone messaging system which the founders have cloned from their TXTUnlimited technology. It merely delivers SMS and voice traffic to mobiles. It sits on top of MySQL databases and an HTML interface which manages the subscribers and programs the message content from agricultural content sources. It is cloud hosted. It has been launched and debugged in a range of settings from education to banking, ironed out in commercial use, and contains no technical innovations.

Service Need

The fish farming vertical has been chosen by Farmerline for tactical reasons, as a test bed in which to launch their service approach and business model. Both founders had discovered, from practical experience in snail-farming and fish-farming, that well-informed advice for these sectors was hard to obtain. Fish farming exhibits several characteristics which make it potentially suitable for a paid information delivery service.

- Farmers must be consistently on site at their farms to monitor the product hour by hour.

- Farmers have already shown willingness to risk their cash in equipment and feed supplies so the step to invest in information is relatively small.
- Fish farmers are literate, numerate, and able to afford smartphone hardware and phone subscription packages with sufficient bandwidth for data.
- Farmers in the sector always have available cash to purchase inputs and are therefore used to budgeting for regular cash outflows.
- The cost to farmers of information failure would be very high (unsellable product goes rotten in a few days) so information of good quality has a premium value
- Timeliness of information is also at a premium (risk of lost harvest after just an hour of mismanaged water quality) so the users will value fast-responding service channels
- The market for farmed fish is strong (Ghana's imports USD 200 million of Tilapia annually—to be potentially substituted by local production), and the sector has some large sophisticated players as well as smaller farms and ponds.

The Farmerline proposition to fish farmers exploits these characteristics by offering a package which aims to improve yield, increase profit, and create access to markets. The service is avowedly commercial in concept and although not yet monetized. Farmerline is strongly focused on how to extract revenue and profit from operating the information service. The company believes that in addition to subscription revenue, it will be able to tap income from leveraging Farmerlines mobile databases for advertising sales to agribusinesses, input dealers, and market supply chain actors. Package details are given elsewhere in this study.

Lack of Alternative Sources of Extension Content

Ghana's official channel for agricultural extension support to fish farmers is diagnosed as deficient by all the observers spoken to for this case study. While expertise is, in theory, at hand through the Fisheries Commission of the Government, in practice it is an unrealistic proposition for farmers.

Anecdotal reports, of which the Farmerline founders were well aware, revealed that extension officers in the fish farming sector were often unavailable to fulfill farmers' requests to make site visits and deliver specific expertise.

Pilot Phase September 2012–March 2013: First Iteration

Farmerline's first planned pilot phase aimed to last six months and to serve just 15 farmers. The objective was to study the farmers very closely, to measure the demand for various kinds of services, launch trial services, and refine them. The activities during this pilot phase consisted of:

- Fish-farmer workshops consisting of service demonstrations, opinion gathering, market research, and analyzing farmer reaction and some incidental registering of farmers. (A workshop extends to many more farmers than the 15 in the pilot.)
- Weekly contact with the trial group of farmers to monitor their information demand and consumption,
- Training of technical coordinators.
- Ongoing technical platform development.
- Incidental farmer recruitment. This is about recruiting a larger body of fish farmers, who would be potential subscribers beyond the trial period. It is not a priority at this stage.
- Creation of a fish farmer database with capacity, input and production records (The Ghana Fisheries Commission keeps no farmer records of any value).

During this first pilot phase, Farmerline has had a Fisheries Commission Agricultural Extension agent on its team to assist in providing the expert technical content. It has also demonstrated the platform regularly to agricultural extension officers. Familiarity with the agricultural extension content offered in government channels enables Farmerline to develop its own content strategy. Agricultural content expertise also comes from KNUST campus, and academic staff is involved in content quality assurance.

Ongoing technical platform development is carried out by Farmerline using an extended network of systems and software engineers.

User Recruitment and Registration

Farmerline, in its first pilot phase, resisted the temptation to go for the growth of its user base. Rather, they sought to work initially with a very small sample of farmers, but understand in great detail the impact of an SMS service upon them. A wider range of farmers beyond the core pilot sample of 15 farmers has subscribed to the service, but the focus at the outset was entirely on engaging in depth with the core pilot group.

Farmerline has identified, from this initial pilot experience, relevant formats for recruitment and registration in the future. They include, for the time being, introductions through Farmer Associations, advertising, use of local representatives to recruit users, and viral effects. However, none of these methods is being developed or optimized at present.

Subscription package models are not yet ready to be firmly established. However, Farmerline's expectation is to offer a tiered pricing structure with a baseline subscription at GHC10/month (USD 5 equiv) rising to GHC 20/month (USD 10 equiv) and also including bespoke services individually priced. Packages will include:

- *New Farmer*. A service offering land assessment, permit, and technical information updates
- *Existing Farmer*. A service offering technical advice, data collection, and commercial/business advice
- *Expert Farmer*. A service including research, study, and support in implementing advanced techniques.

By way of price comparison, membership dues for Fish Farmer Association membership are currently GHC5/month (USD 2.50 equiv)

Approach to Service Development

The service design approach chosen during the first Pilot phase is inspired by a mixture of "Human Centered Design Approach," with elements of a global design company IDEO[4] methodology. Farmerline commented that they define these methodologies, in their case, as "a rigorous focus on the needs of all service users and stakeholders". This means not just farmers but also extension officers, who will need to feel the service is designed for them, and that Farmerline assists rather than threatens their livelihood (Figure 22.1). One of the co-founders offered the candid observation, "The Extension Officers are inside our team for two reasons. They have a lot of the content. But also, we have to work with them because if we excluded them, they would be able to ensure that Farmerline fails."

An illustration of this approach concerns message content and format. In a workshop on the subject of feed quantities, farmers were shown a range of example SMS messages about the level of feed to give for certain oxygen levels in the ponds. Feedback showed which of the optional wordings were sufficiently specific to consistently trigger the right farmer interpretation of the message. It was discovered, for example, that use of percentages in calculations will mislead some users.

Digital Record-Keeping Opportunity

The early Pilot Phase has also revealed that record-keeping is a service that is both in demand from farmers (who reportedly do it badly, know they do it badly, and dislike doing it), and is essential to getting best practice outcomes in the sector. Further research in the early Pilot Phase has also shown that fish farmers will pay Farmerline to undertake their record keeping in the Cloud. Co-founder Alloysius Attah said,

> We discovered at the start of the Pilot that being each farmer's record keeper could be a key part of our service business. This was a surprise. But it shows that our Human Centred Design Approach can be fruitful. And it has brought a new area of business into our portfolio.

How this discovery of a business in virtual record-keeping is turned into a scalable profitable and technologically viable activity is yet to

---

[4] http://www.ideo.com/about/

Figure 22.1
Farmerline Demonstrations and Trainings with Agricultural Extension Officers, Kumasi, April 2012

Source: Farmerline (http://farmerline.org/ [accessed March 7, 2013]).

be answered. The company is now developing technical models for automated data submission by SMS, voice, and potentially by native mobile apps.

Record-keeping will, in principle, integrates well into the main business of technical advice. Extension officers are already able to improve the quality of advice, by referring to video and picture of ponds captured and sent by farmers using smartphones. The power to impose consistent categories and standards when managing records with will also enable Farmerline to automate its service faster and more efficiently.

Revisions to the Pilot Phase

The initial 15-farmer focused user and technology pilot had a relatively short life. In October 2012, after a month in operation, the pilot was paused and is now being redesigned at a larger scale. Several factors contributed to this change. An investment from Indigo Trust made a larger iteration of the pilot possible, financially. An award from a digital entrepreneur competition in Canada created further possibilities.

The participation by Farmerline in Social Capital Markets, a San Francisco USA meeting of social entrepreneurs[5], highlighted that commercial investors and venture funding partners would require a larger pilot in order to prove, to their criteria, the scalability of the Farmerline service. The SOCAP12 meeting, attended by Alloysius Attah, highlighted for Farmerline that they risked falling into a so-called "financing gap". This is the gap between the small-scale funding that is affordable at early stages to achieve research and understanding and the larger scale funding that enables socially innovative services to grow and operate at a significant scale. Farmerline was caught in-between. With the financial possibility now existing to run a larger scale pilot, the organization has decided to move immediately to a second iteration of its plans for piloting, which aims at a pilot of 500 farmers. This pilot stage is in design at time of writing this case study (November 2012) and will probably be undertaken in partnership with an organization with specialist capabilities in designing pilots.

[5] http://socap12.pathable.com/#

The approach of rapid prototyping, abandoning pilots quickly in order to reiterate the project, and responding to investor opinion, is again the characteristic of best practice in commercial entrepreneurship and shows Farmerline operating in a distinctive pattern, and one which has not been widely observed in other ICT ventures in the education and development sector.

Data Security

Farmerline reports that privacy and security of data is an issue that has emerged from its work with farmers. Alloysius Attah says, "Farmers have been resistant to giving us information in the pilot phase. They are concerned about information around profit in particular. We have a challenge to convince them that their information is secure".

Field Reports

For this case study, two field visits were carried out on two separate days to make further observations:

In the first field visit, we met with Poku Gyinaye, who is an advisor/mentor to Farmerline, a fish farming tutor at KNUST, Chairman of the Ghana National Aquaculture Development Plan Advisory Group, Chair of the Fish Farming Association and owner of a large farm, Bosomtwe Integrated Aqua Life Village (BIAV) in the Ashanti region of Ghana. With 17 tanks, 6 nursery ponds, 3 food silos and two permanent staff, the BIAV farm represents the top end of the potential market for Farmerline information services.

Gyinaye himself, as an accomplished technical expert, who keeps thorough records, will not be a likely paying subscriber for information or book-keeping services. However, during our visit we solicited his views. Through Gyinaye's extensive contact with lower-level fish farmers who are members of the Fish Farming Association, he regularly samples typical farmers' needs for information, and reports these back to Farmerline. He described how at a typical monthly meeting of the Fish Farming Association, which he chairs, he will meet with around

25 of the Association's 170 members, and find out where they are deficient in information. He also reports the frustrations, for Fish Farmers, of the current model for working with extension officer experts from the Government's Fisheries Commission. The Association members state to Gyinaye that they sometimes have to pay GHC100 to obtain a visit from the government extension officer (who has no access to car or petrol, and who can only therefore visit a farmer at the farmer's expense).

Gyinaye is an expert and businessman who has seen the potential for supplying support to his sector on a different model. His central role in Farmerline testifies to the way the company stays close to the commercial realities of its market.

In the second field visit, we met Mr Yaw, a fish farmer on an 8-ha farm, with a 3.5-ha pond. Working on a slightly smaller scale than the BIAV farm, Yaw typifies the commercial approach of the mid-range of the sector, hiring in machinery as needed rather than owning it. Yaw is technically sophisticated, owns a smartphone, has studied Agriculture at a high level, and calculates his own levels of alkalinity, feed, oxygen concentration, etc. His engagement with Farmerline is an unpaid evaluator of the platform, who helps to identify improvements, recruit suitable farmers for the pilot phase, and may eventually provide a marketing channel for the platform.

Yaw said his main motivation for subscribing to Farmerline would be that the Government Extension Office services did not give him high enough information quality on specific technical issues where he needed advice. Provided that the quality of information and advice on Farmerline was high enough, and specific enough, Yaw stated that despite already possessing good technical knowledge, he personally would subscribe to Farmerline at GHC 10 a month. However, he defined himself as not the ideal target subscriber, since he is already quite well informed. He described farmers with lower levels of knowledge, mostly new entrants to the industry, who lacked basic knowledge, and for whom the Farmerline package would be an essential and effective investment.

Yaw also described how (acting as a publicist for Farmerline among Fish Farmers) he had shown the product to other farmers at a Fish Farming Association meeting, as part of the process of recruiting potential members for the pilot study. He reported an enthusiastic reaction, and that the farmers wanted to subscribe immediately, and had not worried about the proposed GHC 10/month cost.

Discussion: Commercial Sustainability of Phone-based Extension Support

The key issue raised by the Farmerline case is the possibility and sustainability of delivering extension services to farmers using ICT on a commercial model monetized by the recipients of the service. Farmerline itself is not at a stage where it can offer hard data on this point. However, the published literature on this topic highlights the relevant arguments.

Extension services do unquestionably create income for their recipients. Farmer Field Schools have been shown to increase farm incomes by 60% to 100% (the only reliable and thorough studies are from East Africa[6]). The idea that some portion of this increased income could be spent by the recipients, to cover the costs of obtaining the services, is not unreasonable.

Whether for such services ICT is an efficient channel has yet to be proven. One survey of 280 different projects in the use of ICT in development applications found that over half were demonstrably unsustainable from the start, while the remainder had yet to prove their sustainability. The same study found that around half were entirely reliant on donor funding.[7]

Non-ICT based methods of delivering extension information may have their own economic advantages. The East Africa Dairy Development project [EADD], for example, currently in validation under randomized trials funded by 3ie,[8] suggests that "the use of farmer trainers is an effec-

---

[6] http://www.ifpri.org/sites/default/files/publications/ifpridp00992.pdf (accessed June 7, 2013).

[7] Leveraging Information and Communication Technology (ICT) for the Base of the Pyramid (BoP)Hystra Partners for Orange and others, 2011, at http://www.hystra.com/opensource/Rapport_ICT_Executive_summary.pdf (accessed June 15, 2013).

[8] http://www.3ieimpact.org/en/evidence/impact-evaluations/details/736/ (accessed June 20, 2013).

tive approach of passing on new farming technologies to many farmers in a relatively short time and in a cost effective manner." The EADD project simply encourages lead farmers to assume additional roles in training and dissemination of techniques.[9]

A phone-based paid agricultural query and information service in India, Farmer Helpline, has been analyzed for financial sustainability by the World Wide Web Foundation. The findings show that for that service where queries are handled manually by knowledge workers, a crisis in affordability arrives when the service expands to cover more than a handful of villages (Figure 22.2).

An automated model of response delivery, from a database of answers selected by keywords (since 85% of queries have been asked before) offers a different set of cost curves, in which service expansion brings long-run reduction of costs if the service can achieve wide reach (Figure 22.3).

Figure 22.2

Costs of an Agricultural Query Service Staffed by Knowledge Workers

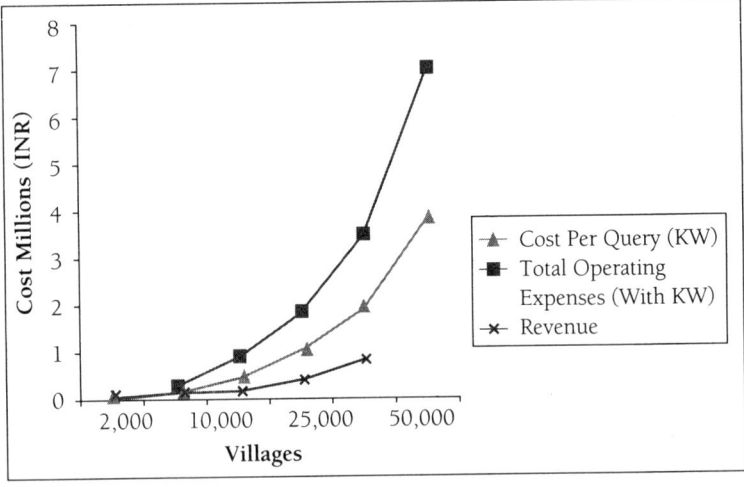

Source: Boyer (2011).

[9] http://www.gatesfoundation.org/learning/Pages/east-africa-dairy-project-training-farmers-heifer-newsletter.aspx (accessed June 23, 2013).

Figure 22.3

*Cost Curve for a Query Service Delivered by Automated
Response Rather Than Knowledge Workers (KWs)*

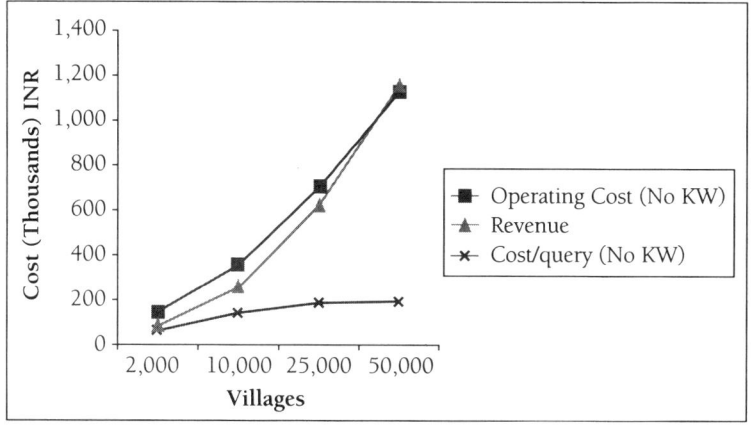

Source: Boyer (2011).

As Farmerline has not yet approached the issue of automating its query responses (either in technical terms, or acceptability to users), the company has yet to prove, even on a theoretical basis, that its commercial model could be successfully applied. On the other hand, this lack of proof simply reflects the early stage of the business, and does not imply any fundamental problem with its approach.

Summary and Conclusion

Farmerline's careful approach so far to understanding user demand and user willingness to pay, mean that this company could, potentially, pioneer a new model for funding ICT-based extension services. Demonstrably, this is an approach that embeds self-determination, responsibility, and localism. By its use of piloting and available technology to reduce risk and cost, it creates new possibilities for rural education and development. However, its good progress to date does not make future success certain.

If it succeeds, Farmerline will occupy a pioneer position in the annals of best practice in use of ICT for rural education and development. A next frontier of commercially funded services for farmers in less-prosperous verticals would open. If it fails financially or organizationally, the social entrepreneurship model of commercially viable ICT-based rural education will take a dent. However, this would be in keeping with the laws of the market: individual failures are a necessary condition for overall progress. One can be confident that the social and intellectual capital of its founders would be reinvested in a new iteration of ICT-based approaches to development, meaning that much of its achievement would be preserved.

Bibliography

Boyer, Stephane. (October 2011). Report on mobile for agriculture [Review of Vodafone/Accenture]. World Wide Web Foundation blog. Retrieved from http://www.webfoundation.org/2011/10/review-of-the-new-vodafoneoxfamaccenture-report-on-mobile-for-agriculture/

23

Womens' Action Network (Burkina Faso)

Stephen Haggard

Methodology

This case study draws on meetings in Burkina Faso conducted by the author in August 2012, and further briefings with other similar or related organizations published documents. The content has additionally been submitted to Reseau Femmes en Action for verification.

Background: Reseau Femmes en Action: The Key Points

Reseau Femmes en Action (RFA) is an NGO founded in 2003 with a mission focused on the base level needs of agricultural communities and working exclusively with Burkina Faso's rural women on the special problems of womens' rural development.

At first, RFA had no remit or concern with ICT. However, ICT is now probably its most important axis. The organization's assets consist of around 20 field-focused personnel, an administrative team, permanent "cybercafé" venues in three major agricultural centers, and some networks of content carried in ICT channels.

The organization is typical of the smaller nationally focused NGO in Africa, surviving with a low level of funding from a variety of local and international sources including charity and official donors, facing its own internal capacity and delivery issues alongside those of the groups it serves, and coming relatively late in its own life to the use of ICT.

RFA is worth noting as an example of good practice in terms of ICT and rural development on account of:

- Deploying ICT for a targeted user group in one of the world's most challenging environments for education and development
- The multiple dimensions of ICT in which it is active
- Innovative use of available mobile technology solutions

Setting and Context

The aspects of Burkina Faso's physical and sociopolitical infrastructure are of notably higher quality than similar and neighboring nations, due to the country's relative recent stability, low prevalence of corruption, and latterly its healthy economic growth. Burkina Faso remains however on a general analysis one of the world's least developed nations, with strikingly low literacy rates, an overwhelmingly rural population (80%), and extremely low income per head (Table 23.1).

Table 23.1
Burkina Faso Key Data, 2010

Population, total (millions)	16.5
Population growth (annual %)	3.0
GDP (current USD) (billions)	8.8
GDP per capita (current USD)	536
GDP growth (annual %)	7.9
Life expectancy at birth, total (years)	54.9
Literacy rate, youth female (% of females ages 15–24)	33.1

Source: World Bank Development Indicators.

Rural women face hardships ranging from low empowerment, status, low literacy and education, female genital mutilation (FGM), abuse, and lack of access to land and information.

Addressing these issues in Burkina Faso is a large state and NGO sector. However, its effectiveness is hampered by funding constraints, capacity problems, and inertia. For example, state and NGO agricultural extension workers (reported anecdotally but consistently by independent observers) frequently lack petrol or vehicles or sufficient incentives to visit rural areas. They therefore often have little meaningful contact with farmers. These bureaucracies practice no effective record keeping about rural conditions.

An important factor in all Burkina Faso initiatives of development and education is the 2006 Law of Communalization which requires any actions concerning education and development (among others) to be sponsored, budgeted, approved, and supervised at the level of the local community. In this distinctive balance between local responsiveness and coherence at national scale, the capacity of village administrators to understand issues of IT, gender, and agricultural improvement techniques is often challenged.

Reseau Femmes en Action: What It Does

The mission of RFA is to support base level communities and associations in Burkina Faso of any kind (whether or not formally constituted) with capacity building and developing action plans and tools that will improve the economic and social conditions of the poorest women.

The major themes of actions are

- advocacy, including campaigning, especially over access to land, eviction, and women's rights,
- improving access to information on topics touching farming, and generally improving the circulation of information among rural women, and
- supporting commercial and income-generating actions by rural women.

A geographical focus for RFA is the "Pole de Croissance" (Growth Zone) initiative at the Bagrébarrage (Figure 23.1) which is a USD 115 million World Bank funded development initiative exploiting that damming of the Nakambé river (Province: Boulgou) in 2002. The original Bagrédamming scheme after creating many upheavals for local communities has since spawned an official hub for agricultural production[1] which was formally opened in April 2012 (Figures 23.2 and 23.3). The growth zone includes 3000 ha of irrigated rice paddy, and commercial farming investment is encouraged.

Figure 23.1
Bagré Barrage

Source: RFA.

---

[1] The impacts of Bagré are covered in a study by ICI consultancy for International Institute for Environment and Development 2010. See http://cmsdata.iucn.org/downloads/etat_des_lieux_autour_du_barrage_de_bagre_au_burkina_faso.pdf (accessed July 5, 2013).

Figure 23.2
Bagré Growth Zone Official Launch Poster, April 2012

Source: RFA.

Figure 23.3
Rice Processing Infrastructure in Bagré—an Official Opening Ceremony. Note the Predominance of Women

Source: RFI/SayoubaTraoré.

In this zone as elsewhere RFA targets poorer women farmers of two traditional products (local rain-fed rice and sumbala) by delivering technical information and training along with a sales point.

Concerning rice, the local rice variety from rain-fed agriculture, although it cannot compete for price with imported Asian rice, has better nutritive qualities. By addressing quality, productivity, and marketing, RFA helps women to enhance their rice product and find markets for it, and thus increase their incomes (Figure 23.4). Sales points, training, and marketing networks have been deployed.

This and other projects by RFA revealed the underlying problem of a severe lack of information around the agricultural and post-harvest techniques. With support and inspiration from The Technical Centre for Agricultural and Rural Cooperation (CTA) at Wegenigen University in Netherlands, RFA has set about obtaining and disseminating information using ICT.

Figure 23.4
Small-Scale Rice Production in Burkina Faso Is by Family Units

Source: RFA.

ICT Formats

The forms in which RFA now uses ICT to pursue its themes are

- digital content accessed in the cybercafés,
- radio broadcasting of content it commissions or produces, and
- mobile phone-based information networks.

Each of these forms offers advantages and challenges, which are explored below.

Project: Digital Content in the Cybercafés

The three cybercafés of RFA are known as its Espaces Communautaires d'Informationet de Promotion (ECIP) (Community spaces for information and advancement) where women farmers come for any of the organization's purposes (Figure 23.5). With an open door and a range

Figure 23.5
Community Space

Source: RFA.

of facilities, including three permanent advisors in each center, PCs, brochures, and general support, these locations are designed to offer a kind of welcome appealing to women farmers.

The ECIP centers feature a small number of Internet-connected PCs. However, in practice, connections are unstable, unreliable, and slow. Content loaded onto PC memory or on CD is the only viable mode of use for the PCs. They therefore function only as stand-alone information points.

The digital content served on PCs in the ECIPs is provided by Third Parties. A CD created by FAO agency Africa Rice, on post-harvest processing techniques for rice, which is versioned in the local Mòoré language (among others) is a popular and high-quality piece of electronic content. Its significance and distribution has been enhanced in the CTA setting as journalists including radio journalists visiting the cybercafé have picked up on the CD's content, and used it for articles and broadcasts.

In general, however, content is a challenge for the cybercafé format. Web content is essentially unavailable. CD or downloadable content is scarce and seldom appropriate. RFA Director Francoise Yoda says that content scarcity is the organization's greatest constraint. Supply of electricity and IT equipment will eventually be within the range of satisfactory solutions, she says, but until the content is appropriate and available, it is necessary for RFA to make content itself, which presents issues of cost, sustainability, and scale.

Project: Radio Broadcasting

In response to the challenges of locating a suitable content, RFA has developed a standard format for producing content: recorded demonstration/discussion events (*causeries* in French) on technical farming issues, which are later broadcast on national and local radio. Topics covered are:

- Production factors: land access, knowledge, post-harvest techniques
- Commercialization of the products
- Visibility and publicity for local rice varieties

The participants at these events will include: experienced farmers with high competencies, agricultural advisers, and journalists. The participants are all or predominantly female. The brief is to discuss the positive and the negative points of the issue. Questions during the shows are possible: in person or phoned in. Publicity is by word of mouth among women's networks: each contact of RFA is tasked to recruit 10 women acquaintances to listen to the broadcast.

RFA paid RTB the national broadcaster the sum of CFA 450,000 (USD 900) to produce and record three of these events, and a further CFA 250,000 (USD 500) to make 10 broadcasts of the recordings in the 80-km radius around the Bagré Pole de Croissance.

By way of evaluation, radio is a popular channel for women in Burkina Faso. It is compatible with womens' other domestic and farming activities, and is also seen by men as appropriate activity for wives. In the context of a country where rural information is consumed and discussed by men at all-male village gatherings under the central tree of the community, at which women do not participate, the radio format allows women to break this male monopoly and engage in public debate, information exchange, and discussion.

Project: Mobile Phone Information Networks for Commercial Support

RFA has delivered a pilot mobile phone calling-group for women farmers. RFA's aim for this exercise was to use mobile phones to empower the women to address commercial challenges better. Within the Bagré area, a group of 30 women engaged in rice and sumbala farming have each paid CFA 1000 (USD 2) to create and join a calling-group in which they have unlimited free calls between each other. The calling-group facility costs CFA 60,000 per year (USD 120) and RFA has sponsored half the cost with the women paying the rest. RFA uses the calling-group facility as a channel on which it can push its content of education, information, and advice.

Microcredit

One action RFA conducts through this channel is the distribution of advice. In one initiative, women were encouraged to use microcredit in periods of seasonal glut of key products such as sesame, meal, and oil, to buy at low prices and resell when prices rose. The channel enabled the Bagré women in the group to obtain the credit as a collective group and undertake this trading action.

Price Stability

Probably the most striking action on this network was on price fixing. The women had often experienced that at market, they came under pressure to lower their prices. The buyers are men, holding cash, with lorries at hand to transport the goods, and they assert that they can buy at lower prices elsewhere. The prices the women obtained for their hulled polished rice in 2010 were often as low as CFA 250/kg against a standard floor price in the market of CFA 400/kg. As a result, they were incurring debt, or requiring their children to process the grains: bad both for their production activities and bad for their children.

RFA encouraged the women to use the calling-group to fix a high price among all 30 members, and to support each other at market by telephone, to ensure that they all stuck to the same price and did not bow to traders' pressure. With no downward flexibility on price, the women were also able to compete on quality.

The result was a 2011 average price obtained of CFA 500/kg for the women in the calling-group. (NB 2011's low rains also raised prices generally so not all this increase can be attributed to the operation of the calling-group). The 2011 revenues have wiped out the 2010 losses.

The women in the calling group reckon the benefit to them of the calling-group and the programes of trading and price fixing distributed through the mobile channel has worked out at average CFA 90,000 (USD 180) for the year per participant. To this extent, assuming an investment in the phone technology per participant of USD 12 (phone plus calling-group membership) the ROI to the farmer from the technology and application is in the order of 1040%.

Other benefits from running the calling-group are cited by RFA as follows:

- Avoids information failures caused by lack of credit or lack of own phone
- Spreads awareness of value of private phone ownership by women
- Enabled other benefits from communication: especially

  o Ability to maintain family contact if menfolk absent on migrant labor elsewhere (a common pattern in farming areas)
  o Reduced isolation for women in rural areas who had previously only had reliable contact on market days

- Increased women's confidence in use of technology

The pilot calling-group continued to operate autonomously in 2012 and there are no further significant inputs required from RFA.

Comparison: Other Rice Initiatives

To appreciate the significance of RFA's entirely ICT-based approach to education and development in the rice growing communities, for this study we have also looked at two comparable initiatives in Burkina Faso's Bagré Growth Zone. These comparison projects use other mechanisms, not ICT. They are: Women's Union and RizDelice.

Womens Union: Rice Processing

Organizations in the Bagré area are also addressing the rice economy in more conventional ways. These are worth mentioning for comparison with the ICT approach. The Womens' Union in Bagré, for example, demonstrates a project run by 15 women who in 2012 using a commercial loan have built a collectively owned physical infrastructure for part of the post-harvest rice processing (see Figure 23.3). Using the physical structure of the buildings and equipment, and taking the rice processing into their own hands, exposes them to additional profit higher up the post-harvest value chain. Explaining the benefits for her members, Union leader Nana Mariam said:

> The women can now have motorbikes. This allows them to be more productive. They can take their children to school, and then get to the fields to work with their husbands. A woman can also now in the same day get home to cook the meal so her husband can eat well.[2]

The perception that a motorbike delivers the same kind of benefits as a phone, including educational access (for children) captures the current phase of technology transition.

RizDelice Collectives

Another Burkina Faso project in rice aiming at education and development is CIDR's (Centre International de Developpement et Recherche [International Centre for Research and Development]) "RizDelice" (Delicious Rice) initiative. CIDR, a French NGO, has successfully operated this project in other West African territories (Togo, Benin) since 2007and is transferring the model to Burkina Faso. For this case study, we interviewed Regional Director Olivier Legros during a visit to Ouagadougou.

Using a specially bred rice strain (IR841) marketed as RizDelice, this project supplies seeds (on credit) and a package of information and training to allow local collectives of approximately 500 small farmers to grow a premium project that can command higher market prices in local markets. RizDelice has the traits of Asian rice, which is most demanded by the West African market. The innovation here is not technology but financing: the harvest value is advanced to the farmers by the project, based on a fixed value set in advance. These deals are possible because the produce of many small farmers is aggregated by the project into a collective production. This cash flow model allows farmers to make capital purchases and raise productivity. Typically, these will be farm equipment or an animal. Education is at the core of the project as most of the inputs that create premium quality rice take place during the growing phase where the farmers have to control the conditions in great detail. The profits also pay for a technical officer, effectively delivering

---

[2] Interview collected by SayoubaTraore.

what a Government Extension Officer would have supplied, on a private commercial basis.

Project Director Olivier Legros, interviewed for this case study, said that ICT had not been important to date in delivering training for the RizDelice project. The model of a locally based face-to-face dedicated training officer had been sustainable, because the increase of yield from the training was so high. It had also been feasible because the farmers were all physically close. Finally, face-to-face interventions were, Legros argued, often the most effective. He cited CIDR's experience of training farmers in building contour-mapped dykes and gravity-fed drainage channels for their rice fields. This training has to be delivered on the ground in the farmer's fields. It adds 5 Tonnes/ha to the yield, which is the same increase as the farmer can obtain by purchasing fertilizer, but achieved at less cost and, arguably, more sustainably. Although a fertilizer-based yield improvement program could in theory be supported by mobile phone, the contour-mapped farming training could not.

CIDR is however, considering the case for deploying an ICT solution in the future for RizDelice. Olivier Legros stated in interview:

> The aim would be to link up all our technical officers. There are about 100 of them delivering training and education to farmers across West Africa. They are in the field and don't get opportunities to share their own practice and learning. That requires an IT response. Mobile might be the way we go forward for this.

The comparison of the Women's Union and RizDelice initiatives, with no ICT element, and the RFA project, based on ICT, is instructive. ICT appears not to be an essential ingredient for addressing Burkina Faso rice farmers' education and development at the moment. However, it does offer advantages of agility, requiring only very lightweight organization and infrastructure, in order to deliver the same benefits as other models with larger fixed costs and timescales.

Reseau Femmes en Action: Scale and Expansion Challenge

The scaling and extension of the mobile calling-group format is a challenge that RFA has not yet tackled successfully. The organization reports that the original nucleus of 30 women in the Bagré area were asked in its early days to recruit new members to the calling-group, and did not manage to do so. The factors may be that joining the established group was not attractive to outsiders; or that the justifications for joining it were not well communicated. Whatever the reasons, there is not yet a model for expanding groups or replicating them with little effort. A further challenge for replicating and sustaining this format is the administrative policy environment in Burkina Faso.

Launching Rural ICT Services in Devolved Administrations: A New Challenge

Burkina Faso's 2006 Communalization Law[3] created a sharp and significant decentralization of government capability regarding education, training, and development to the level of elected local community institutions. The move had the backing of the major international and regional Development institutions. It now represents the main strand of Burkina Faso's political and economic development.

Educating the Officials about ICT

Since 2006, the statutory gatekeepers for any projects like those RFA delivers are a body of some 11,500 elected councillors at a village level, of whom over half are women. While the devolution of powers may have helped to give a voice to women, as far as the use of ICT is concerned, the policy has had a negative impact (at least in the experience of RFA) because:

- ICT projects require scale but the effort and risk of securing support across several communes is high.

---

[3] For text see http://www.droitafrique.com/images/textes/Burkina/Burkina%20%20Ressources%20collectivites%20territoriales.pdf (accessed July 8, 2013) and especially Article 20 regarding responsibility of the Commune regarding matters of development.

- Village mayors and administrators are unlikely to understand or support the role of ICT (initiatives such as classrooms top the education agenda, and electricity gets the technology vote).

RFA has recently found its energies consumed by the process of educating mayors and councilors (rather than the women it targets) about the benefits of ICT-based projects.

Optimism

RFA expresses optimism that this situation will improve (a new crop of younger councilors with awareness of technology will come into service in the upcoming elections). Using its three community spaces (see above) and in three other locations, RFA is now engaged in a new program of sensitizing local officials to the benefits of economic development for women farmers using ICT.

The Ministere de L'Economie (*Ministry of the Economy*) has pledged for its 2012–2017 program to transfer all competencies including IT to local communities. With this (RFA hopes), and the associated budget for IT initiatives, will come the opportunity for RFA to deploy its models for ICT-based education and development in rural areas. When this happens, RFA would be acting as a service delivery partner, commissioned and funded by the state, at local level, to deliver its programs.

The organization expects to evolve in two different directions: a new role as provider of rural education and development services selling its technical competence to government on a commercial basis; and its original role of a research, advocacy, and project managing campaigning organization for poorer Burkinabe women in farming.

For its new role in executing capacity building on behalf of government, the RFA created a new organization Centre de Ressources et d'Appui au Developpement Local (Centre for Resources and Action for Local Development) (CERADEL) in 2011. The delivery platforms are nearly all ICT based. It is too early at time of collecting this case study to report on the outcomes of the CERADEL wing of the network. However, its creation does demonstrate that a vision for social and economic development can be entirely centerd around ICT.

About the Editors and Contributors

Editors

Zeng Haijun is currently working as Program Coordinator at UNESCO International Research and Training Centre for Rural Education (INRULED) and C&B Manager in Human Resources Department of Beijing Normal University (BNU). He started his research on ICT in education when he was working in Research Centre of Knowledge Engineering and Laboratory of e-Learning in BNU in 2001. He worked in the Division of Distance and Continuing Education of Department of Higher Education, China Ministry of Education from 2005 to 2010. He edited a book named *What Happened in e-Learning in Chinese Universities* (in Chinese), which was published in 2009. His doctoral thesis, *Study on Public Support Service System of E-learning* (in Chinese), as a monograph was published in 2012. His research book *e-Learning in China* (in English) was published by SAGE in 2014. He has set up a special column in the *Journal of China Distance Education* and invites many international experts to share their findings. He also works as the reviewer for *International Review of Research in Open and Distance Learning* and *Journal of Open Education Research*.

Xia Weifeng is Executive Editor-in-Chief of the *Journal of Distance Education in China*, founder of Learning Habour and the website E-learning World. He has established comprehensive and innovative media service mode of distance education in 10 years which combined print media, online media, enrollment service, industrial organization, annual conference, professional seminar, and social platform.

Wang Jinghua is CEO of Beijing TianDiShang Science and Technology Co., Ltd and LiuQi Group, and Executive Vice Chairman of Information Security Branch of China Communications Industry Association. He has worked on government informatization and education informatization for years and laid emphasis on solution to e-learning, vocational education, and smart city.

Wang Rong is Program Assistant at UNESCO International Research and Training Centre for Rural Education. She joined the project team after completing her master's from Beijing Normal University in 2012 and paid special attention to international organization's program on ICT in education.

Contributors

Diao Qingjun is associated with School Continuing Education at Tsinghua University.

Eilean von Lautz-Cauzanet is Program Assistant at UNESCO.

Ge Yi is Program Assistant at UNESCO-INRULED.

Hao Yingping is Program Specialist at Tsinghua University Poverty Alleviation Office.

Huang Ronghuai is Professor at Beijing Normal University.

Jiao Yiju is Program Specialist at Tsinghua University Poverty Alleviation Office.

Li Dan is Program Assistant at teacher.com.cn.

Liang Shuhua is Dean of E-learning College of China Agricultural University.

Liu Weibin is Research Director of E-learning College of China Agricultural University.

Long Youhua is Program Coordinator at teacher.com.cn.

Stephen Haggard is Consultant at E-learning Media & Tech.

Wang Hai is Program Coordinator at E-learning College of China Agricultural University.

Wang Yanchang is Program Coordinator at School of Distance Education, Shaanxi Normal University.

Wang Ying is Professor at The Open University of China.

Wang Zhuzhu is Director of National Center for Educational Technology.

Wei Tao is Program Coordinator at Tsinghua University Poverty Alleviation Office.

Xu Dian is Associate Professor at The Open University of China.

Xu Xiaoyi is Dean of School of Distance Learning of South China Normal University.

Yu Shengquan is Professor at Beijing Normal University.

Zhang Jinbao is Associate Professor at Beijing Normal University.

Zhang Jufan is Dean of School of Distance Education, Shaanxi Normal University.

Zhang Zhijun is Associate Professor and Program Coordinator at The Open University of China.

Zhao Yuchi is Program Coordinator at UNESCO-INRULED.

Zheng Lanqin is a lecturer at Beijing Normal University.

Index